WORDSWORTH LITERARY LIVES

SIR ARTHUR
CONAN DOYLE

Memories and Adventures

Sir Arthur Conan Doyle

Memories and Adventures

AN AUTOBIOGRAPHY

Introduction by
DAVID STUART DAVIES

WORDSWORTH EDITIONS

In loving memory of
MICHAEL TRAYLER
the founder of Wordsworth Editions

I

Readers who are interested in other titles from
Wordsworth Editions are invited to visit our website at
www.wordsworth-editions.com

For our latest list and a full mail-order service, contact
Bibliophile Books, 5 Thomas Road, London E14 7BN
TEL: +44 (0)20 7515 9222 FAX: +44 (0)20 7538 4115
E-MAIL: orders@bibliophilebooks.com

First published in 2007 by Wordsworth Editions Limited
8B East Street, Ware, Hertfordshire SG12 9HJ

ISBN 978 1 84022 570 9

Typeset in Great Britain by Antony Gray
Printed and bound by Clays Ltd, St Ives plc

Contents

Introduction

Anyone who writes their autobiography is concerned with presenting to the world a version of their life and personality as they see it or as they wish it to be seen. They will edit events and characteristics to suit their purpose. Even the most honest of autobiographies is bound to have its blind spots. This is certainly the case with Arthur Conan Doyle, who in his days of success was the most public of figures and led a great deal of his life in the spotlight. However, he had a perception of himself as a bluff, honest and uncomplicated character, a persona which he was keen to portray in his autobiography. There is little introspection or personal musing in these memoirs. Nevertheless, it is true to say that Conan Doyle was too decent and honest to attempt to mislead the reader by deliberately altering facts or bending the truth, but he did commit the sin of omission. He was a far more complex individual than he was prepared to confess in print. His father's illness and hospital-isation in a mental institution and the reason for his first marriage to Louise Hawkins and the courtship of his second wife are incidents that had a great impact on his life and his mental state but these are not alluded to at all in this volume.

It is appropriate that his autobiography is called *Memories and Adventures*. The *Adventures* part is apt for Conan Doyle had many: his life was filled with incident. The *Memories* part perhaps suggests that he is looking back on the past and patching together what he can remember: an activity that allows one with justification to be selective.

It is nearly eighty years since Doyle died and over that time his reputation, particularly as the creator of the great detective Sherlock Holmes, has grown. Time has also furnished us with more information about the man and his life. Before you embark of his version of events, it might be appropriate, as Holmes himself might say, to consider the evidence.

Let us begin at the beginning.

Arthur Ignatius Conan Doyle was born in Edinburgh on 22 May

1859. He was one of ten children, three of whom died before reaching maturity. His father was Charles Altamont Doyle, who at the time of Arthur's birth was a civil servant in the Office of Works. He was also an artist and a gentle, weak-willed alcoholic whose condition worsened, making the home life of the Doyles intolerable. Arthur's mother, Mary, was an indomitable woman who against all the odds kept house and family together. She also instilled the sense of chivalrous romanticism which developed within young Arthur's breast. Even in old age, Conan Doyle remembered the stories his mother had told him – stories of knights and adventurers, exciting narratives of heroes and villains. However, in his autobiography Doyle says little of his formative years at home; while of his father, he merely observes: 'My father, I fear, was of little help . . . for his thoughts were always in the clouds.'

By the age of ten, young Arthur was sent away to school – to Stonyhurst, a strict Jesuit establishment in the wilds of Lancashire. His mother was determined that her bright boy should be taken away from the stresses of home life and the distress caused by the deterioration of his father. It is possible that there was another reason why Mary Doyle wanted her son away from home: her growing friendship with their lodger and the family's benefactor, Dr Bryan Waller. There is no evidence that there was anything more than a deep friendship between Mrs Doyle and Waller but their closeness must have been distressing to Charles Doyle and unsettling for Arthur. Eventually, when Charles Doyle was institutionalised, Mary Doyle left Edinburgh to take up residence at Masongill Cottage in Yorkshire, on an estate belonging to Waller. He charged her no rent and often took his meals with her. It is remarkable therefore that Conan Doyle fails to mention Waller in his autobiography – the man who had coached him in his exams and encouraged him in his work and who had shared the same house for several years.

Effectively, the strict and often cruel regime at Stonyhurst beat religion out of the young Arthur Conan Doyle and set him on the questing path to find a belief to which he could adhere. The cloistered existence at the college gave Conan Doyle an appetite for life, the dangers and the thrills of it. When he was only twenty-one, he did escape from the mundanity of existence by interrupting his medical studies and signing on as a surgeon on a whaling ship, the *Hope*, which sailed from Peterhead to the Arctic Ocean. Family and friends advised against this rash decision, but Doyle saw that seven months of isolation and adventure at sea was the ideal escape from the reality of his father's breakdown and hospitalisation.

It was while he was training to be a doctor at Edinburgh University that Conan Doyle met Joseph Bell, one of the models for Sherlock Holmes. Because this aspect of his life is very much in the public domain, Doyle deals with it in detail in the autobiography and is fulsome in his praise of and gratitude to Bell. However, as with all of his intimates, he fails to provide a detailed portrait of the professor.

Strangely, the same attention to detail given to Bell's influence on his thoughts and writings is not paid to his courtship and marriage to his first wife, Louise. This warrants barely a page in these memoirs. And in this instance, he doesn't even mention the girl's name. Why is this? Conan Doyle first met his future wife when he agreed to look after her brother who was suffering from cerebral meningitis. At the suggestion of another doctor, he accepted the boy as a resident patient. This brought him into close contact with his mother and sister. However, the boy died a short while after Conan Doyle had begun his ministrations. Whether he felt any guilt about the situation we do not know, but the upshot of the matter was that Conan Doyle and Louise Hawkins became engaged and were married shortly afterwards, in 1885. It is clear that this was not a marriage of passion and one can only surmise that Conan Doyle may have felt a certain duty or responsibility towards the young girl. One of Conan Doyle's many biographers, Michael Coren, made the following suggestion concerning the marriage:

It was not so much a love affair as a friendship that was intensely enjoyable for both of them. They appeared to agree about everything, or at least Louise did not disagree with her young man. Mary Doyle did not like Louise and thought her a bad choice for her son.

It is obvious from Conan Doyle's writings – but much less so from his autobiography – that he was a passionate and romantic soul. So much so that it is clear that no platonic marriage scenario would have met his emotional needs. He married young, as many do, without perhaps realising the ramifications of such an act. He found himself shackled – and I use that word in its full emotional sense – to a woman he cared about deeply but with whom he was not actually in love. Louise was diagnosed with tuberculosis and remained an invalid for the last fifteen years or so of her life. It was not until he met Jean Leckie that he experienced the true passionate fervour of romantic love. He met this attractive Scotswoman – fourteen years his junior – at a party in March 1897 and fell head over heels in love with her. He confessed to his mother how he felt about Jean. He told close friends, too, who were divided on the subject. His brother-in-law, E. W. Hornung, the writer of the Raffles stories, was furious at what he conceived as Conan Doyle's infidelity. But he was not physically unfaithful to Louise, his wife. His strong personal code of chivalry forbade him to take his affair with Jean Leckie into the realms of sexual congress. Nevertheless, the strain must have placed Conan Doyle upon the psychological rack. His fondness and duty to Louise, his invalid wife, kept him by her side, while his passion for Jean Leckie tormented his heart and mind. To add to his mental anguish must have been the thought that Jean would not wait for ever. She was a young vibrant woman who could easily find herself another man – and one with less complicated baggage. Inevitably, at times Conan Doyle must have struggled with thoughts concerning Louise's illness, wondering how long she would linger in this life. As he records, briefly, in *Memories and Adventures*: 'In 1906 my wife passed away after a long illness which she had borne with exemplary patience.'

Louise's passing merits just one brief paragraph before he takes the reader back into the public arena and discusses his crusading efforts in the Edalji Case. However, within the same chapter, The Years between the Wars, he makes a fleeting reference to his marriage to Jean: 'On September 18, 1907, I married Miss Jean Leckie, the younger daughter of a Blackheath family whom I had known for years, and who was a dear friend of my mother and sister.'

Conan Doyle makes the marriage appear as though it was one of convenience – two old friends drifting into a comfortable union. There is no sense of the passion and desire that really existed between the two, although the brief gap between Louise's death and his remarriage speaks volumes.

This very complex man was determined that his autobiography was to be the presentation of his public face. His personal and private worlds would remain so; the inner man would not be revealed. And so you will find within these pages much to interest you concerning the public aspect of his life. On the public stage he was a remarkable man: a Victorian with a twentieth-century outlook which led him to follow many pathways. He ran for Parliament (unsuccessfully); he played cricket for the MCC; he enlisted at the age of forty to serve in the Boer

War; he evolved a method for turning a rifle into 'a sort of portable howitzer'; he took up causes of individuals whom he considered had been unjustly treated by the law, most notably Sir Roger Casement, George Edalji and Oscar Slater; he conceived the practice of cross-country skiing; and in later life he devoted much of his time, money and energy to the study and promotion of Spiritualism. But what actually made the man tick and what his real thoughts were are not recorded here. To discover those we have to play detective and make deductions (and indeed, assumptions), assemble the clues and reach our own conclusions . . . rather like Sherlock Holmes.

Ah, Sherlock Holmes.

It is true to say that Arthur Conan Doyle is famous today primarily if not exclusively as the creator of Sherlock Holmes, the most celebrated detective in the world. If Conan Doyle could return to us now and see how incredibly popular and revered his detective remains, he would be amazed. During his lifetime, I do not believe he was fully aware what a potent and charismatic character he had created in Holmes. He had the mistaken view, which he expresses in these memoirs, that ' . . . if I had never touched Holmes, who has tended to obscure my higher work, my position in literature would . . . be a more commanding one'. Indeed Doyle very quickly grew tired of his creation. But the reading public knew better.

Edgar Allan Poe (1809–1849) is generally regarded as the father of the detective story. This view is based on his creation of the ascetic reasoner Auguste Dupin, who solves a series of baffling crimes in five of Poe's short stories, the most famous being *The Murders in the Rue Morgue* (1841), in which the murderer turns out to be an orang-utan. There is no doubt that in the Dupin tales Poe created the basic template for the detective stories of the future but it is equally true to say that they lack real drama, tension and rich characterisation. Dupin is a mere cipher, not a fully rounded character, and his companion, the unnamed narrator, is featureless. While the puzzles in these tales intrigue the mind they do not engage the emotions or generate strong enthusiasms; certainly not in the way the Sherlock Holmes stories were destined to do. In essence it is the author of these detective yarns, Arthur Conan Doyle, who is the real begetter of the detective fiction genre as we know it. From boyhood Poe's Dupin had been one of his heroes. He had also admired 'the neat dovetailing' of the plots in Gaboriau's crime novels. And then there was Professor Joseph Bell at Edinburgh University, who had the most remarkable powers of observation. These influences mixed with Conan Doyle's own bright imagination brought about the birth of Sherlock Holmes. Apart from details concerning Holmes's genesis and the first novel, *A Study in Scarlet* (1887), and a chapter focusing on incidentals about the character, there is little detail about Sherlock in Doyle's autobiography. Surprisingly there is no reference to the creation of *The Hound of the Baskervilles* (1901), in which Doyle brought the detective back after killing him off at the Reichenbach Falls in what was intended to be the last Holmes story, 'The Final Problem' (1891). In avoiding dealing with the creation of the *Hound* novel, once again Conan Doyle is covering his tracks and avoiding a controversial issue.

The idea for *The Hound of the Baskervilles* was conceived on a holiday in Norfolk. In March 1901, Conan Doyle had taken a golfing break with his friend, journalist Bertram Fletcher Robinson. Staying at the Royal Links Hotel near Cromer, they spent time between rounds of golf discussing various topics, including folklore. The story goes that one night in the hotel Robinson recounted the legend of the spectral hound that supposedly haunted Dartmoor, close to his home. This was most likely the tale of Richard Cabell, the wicked lord of Brook Manor in the parish of Buckfastleigh, who was rumoured to have been chased to death in 1672 by a pack of demonic 'whist' hounds. Conan Doyle was greatly taken with this account and it sparked his imagination. He realised that a ghostly hound threatening a noble family could form the basis of a very exciting novel. So inspired was he that he began working out a plot then and there with Robinson. While still at Cromer, Conan Doyle wrote a breathless note to his mother: 'Fletcher Robinson came here with me and we are going to do a book together, *The Hound of the Baskervilles*.' This note clearly indicates that at this early stage Conan Doyle saw Robinson as his collaborator and co-author.

However, it is not clear when Robinson's role in the venture became reduced or whether it was a mutual decision, but in plotting the novel Conan Doyle realised that he needed a central character to unravel the mystery, a catalyst figure who would bring together the various strands of the plot – in other words, a brilliant detective. Reluctantly Conan Doyle decided to bring back Sherlock Holmes for one last case; although he was adamant that this investigation took place before the detective's disappearance at the Reichenbach Falls. Of course the publishers and the reading public were ecstatic.

When the *The Hound* came out in book form in 1902, it had a small note printed prior to the contents page which read:

MY DEAR ROBINSON – It was to your account of a West Country legend that this tale owed its inception. For this and help in the details all thanks.
Yours most truly,

A. CONAN DOYLE

Fletcher Robinson was no longer a collaborator nor a co-author, just a helper 'in the details'. This was the first salvo in downscaling Fletcher Robinson's involvement in the project. By the time *Sherlock Holmes: The Complete Long Stories* was published in 1929, when Fletcher Robinson was dead, Doyle asserted in his Introduction that: '[*The Hound of the Baskervilles*] arose from a remark by that fine fellow . . . Fletcher Robinson, that there was a spectral dog near his home on Dartmoor. That remark was the inception of the book, but I should add that the plot and every word of the narrative were my own.'

This effectively slams the door shut on Fletcher Robinson, leaving him totally out in the cold. There has been a tremendous shift from the note Conan Doyle sent to his mother in the spring of 1901, in which he stated that he and Robinson were 'going to do a book together', and to the inscription in the first edition, which refers to Robinson's 'account' of the phantom hound and 'help in the details', to this final marginalising reference to a mere 'remark' Robinson made. Also the fact that Conan Doyle feels it necessary to stress, after nearly thirty years, that 'the plot and every word of the narrative' were his own creates the impression that the author 'doth protest too much'. The truth of the matter is a mystery and is likely to remain so. It is all the more fascinating therefore that Conan Doyle makes no reference to the book, its creation or his involvement with Fletcher Robinson in his autobiography.

As he grew older, Conan Doyle's enthusiasm for writing fiction dwindled somewhat. He had a new passion in his life – his interest in Spiritualism. In a rare moment in these memoirs Conan Doyle admits:

[The promotion of Spiritualism] is the thing for which every pre-ceding phase – my gradual religious development, my books, which gave me an introduction to the public, my modest fortune, which enables me to devote myself to unlucrative work, my platform work, which helps to convey the message, and my physical strength, which is still sufficient to stand arduous tours and to fill the largest halls for an hour and a half with my voice – have each and all been an unconscious preparation.

For Conan Doyle, his long search for the meaning of life and the pain of death had ended with his acceptance of the spirit world. As he stated in his book on the subject, *The New Revelation* (1918), all the wartime deaths, including, tragically, those of his own son Kingsley and his younger brother Innes, had convinced him that those we love must continue to exist after death. Publicly, at least, he never conceded that this notion might have more to do with emotional wish fulfilment than rational thought. Not only did Conan Doyle become a convert to Spiritualism but he also became an enthusiastic evangelist of the cause. Consequently he had little time for – or, indeed, interest in – writing fiction, and when he put pen to paper it was only as a means to securing funds to finance the crusade which took him to many parts of the world.

From 1920 to 1927, apart from a terribly weak Professor Challenger novella *The Land of Mist*, the only fiction that Conan Doyle produced was a further series of Sherlock Holmes stories. He turned to his old character not out of fondness but with a calculating eye, aware that the Holmes tales would generate the largest fees. They were money spinners. The stories were collected in book form in 1927 and called *The Casebook of Sherlock Holmes*. It is generally regarded as the weakest of the Holmes short-story collections. And no wonder, for the author's heart was not in it and his mind was elsewhere.

In this autobiography, the chapter called The Psychic Quest details Conan Doyle's gradual acceptance of Spiritualism and his personal experiences in communicating with the dead, and we can feel for the first time in the whole book something of the passion and fervour of the man and his beliefs. No longer is he coolly and carefully recollecting his public life, but he is, metaphorically, up there on the stage, draining himself emotionally on behalf of the cause.

However, yet again, even on the subject of Spiritualism, he commits the sin of omission by making no reference to what Dr Watson might have entitled 'The Case of the Cottingley Fairies'. Two young girls in Yorkshire claimed to have seen fairies flitting around a stream near to where they lived. They had proof in the form of photographs taken with their father's camera. Conan Doyle, along with a number of other misguided spiritualists, believed the photographs were genuine. He closed his ears to all arguments to the contrary and was naïve enough to believe that two young girls could not be so devious as to fake the photographs. His own children would never lie so why should they? He even dismissed his own doubts, aware that the fairies in the photographs seemed to be dressed in the latest fashions. As Conan Doyle's biographer, Martin Booth observed, 'The truth is, he wanted to believe in them, so he did. If he stated that fairies lived in dells by the streams of Yorkshire then he was right and there was no argument to be countenanced about it. Once his mind was set, his opinion was, infallibly, correct.'

Conan Doyle professed his belief in the fairies in an article in *The Strand Magazine*. His foolish adherence to the notion that the fairies were genuine dented his reputation greatly. Soon he became the butt of jokes, the most memorable one claiming that he was the first member of the audience to clap his hands on request to revive Tinkerbell, the fairy in J. M. Barrie's play *Peter Pan*.

One strange and again unexplained aspect of this affair is the fact that Conan Doyle's father and his uncle, Richard, were both believers in fairies. It has been suggested by some commentators that the author was desperate to prove that fairies existed in order to show that his father was not mad and therefore he himself was not likely to go insane and be locked away in an asylum. This may well be fanciful but as Conan Doyle makes no reference to fairies or the Cottingley incident in his memoirs we are left to form our own theories.

The Spiritualist tours were arduous and physically draining and Conan Doyle's health suffered as a result. He was now in his late sixties but it appeared he was making no allowances for his advancing age. In 1929 Conan Doyle suffered severe pains in his chest. He was diagnosed with angina and the doctors advised that he cancel all his Spiritualist lectures, but the author was adamant that he would not let the public down by failing to honour his engagements. On his way to the Albert Hall one evening he suffered a violent attack and from then on all physical exertion was forbidden.

Throughout the early months of 1930, he experienced brief periods of improved health, but he was a shadow of his former self. On 1 July he roused himself once more and for the last time. For some months he had been lobbying against the Witchcraft Act, an ancient piece of legislation which had been revived as a means of prosecuting mediums.

Conan Doyle saw this as a great injustice to those special individuals who were able to act as a channel between this world and the next. His copious correspondence on the matter had brought about an invitation to a meeting with the Home Secretary, J. R. Clynes. In a feeble and debilitated condition, Conan Doyle travelled to the Home Office to read his prepared statement, which he recited with as much gusto as he could muster. The whole event sapped the last of the energy from his fragile frame. He returned home in a greatly weakened state. Some little time later he was discovered lying prone in the hallway at his home clutching a single white snowdrop in his hand. He had seen the flowers through his window and had struggled from his sickbed to take one of the blooms.

By now Conan Doyle knew he was dying and he told the family that he did not wish to pass away in bed. They helped him to a chair where he could look through the window at the Sussex countryside beyond. He died there surrounded by his family on the morning of Monday, 7 July 1930. His last words were to his beloved Jean: 'You are wonderful,' he said.

Aware that time was running out, he had written a few days earlier, 'The reader will judge that I have had many adventures. The greatest and most glorious awaits me now.'

Arthur Conan Doyle was a brilliant, fascinating and remarkable man. In many ways he was unique and far from the bluff straightforward fellow he would have had us believe him to be. Take with you the information I have laid before you in this Introduction and bear it in mind as you read about the life of one of the most important popular British writers of all time.

DAVID STUART DAVIES

Author's Preface

I have had a life which, for variety and romance, could, I think, hardly be exceeded. I have known what it was to be a poor man and I have known what it was to be fairly affluent. I have sampled every kind of human experience. I have known many of the most remarkable men of my time. I have had a long literary career after a medical training which gave me the MD of Edinburgh. I have tried my hand at very many sports, including boxing, cricket, billiards, motoring, football, aeronautics and skiing, having been the first to introduce the latter for long journeys into Switzerland. I have travelled as doctor to a whaler for seven months in the Arctic and afterwards in the West Coast of Africa. I have seen something of three wars, the Sudanese, the South African and the German. My life has been dotted with adventures of all kinds. Finally I have been constrained to devote my latter years to telling the world the final result of thirty-six years' study of the occult, and in endeavouring to make it realise the overwhelming importance of the question. In this mission I have already travelled more than fifty thousand miles and addressed three hundred thousand people, besides writing seven books upon the subject. Such is the life which I have told in some detail in my *Memories and Adventures*.

ARTHUR CONAN DOYLE
Crowborough
June 1924

I

Early Recollections

Extraction – 'H. B.' – Four Remarkable Brothers – My Mother's
Family Tree – An Unrecognised Genius – My First Knockout –
Thackeray – The Fenians – Early Reading – My First Story

I was born on May 22, 1859, at Picardy Place, Edinburgh, so named because in old days a colony of French Huguenots had settled there. At the time of their coming it was a village outside the city walls, but now it is at the end of Queen Street, abutting upon Leith Walk. When last I visited it, it seemed to have degenerated, but at that time the flats were of good repute.

My father was the youngest son of John Doyle, who under the *nom de crayon* of 'H. B.' made a great reputation in London from about 1825 to 1850. He came from Dublin about the year 1815 and may be said to be the father of polite caricature, for in the old days satire took the brutal shape of making the object grotesque in features and figure. Gilray and Rowlandson had no other idea. My grandfather was a gentleman, drawing gentlemen for gentlemen, and the satire lay in the wit of the picture and not in the misdrawing of faces. This was a new idea, but it has been followed by most caricaturists since and so has become familiar. There were no comic papers in those days, and the weekly cartoon of 'H. B.' was lithographed and distributed. He exerted, I am told, quite an influence upon politics, and was on terms of intimacy with many of the leading men of the day. I can remember him in his old age, a very handsome and dignified man with features of the strong Anglo-Irish, Duke of Wellington stamp. He died in 1868.

My grandfather was left a widower with a numerous family, of which four boys and one girl survived. Each of the boys made a name for himself, for all inherited the artistic powers of their father. The elder, James Doyle, wrote *The Chronicles of England*, illustrated with coloured pictures by himself – examples of colour printing which beat any subsequent work that I have ever seen. He also spent thirteen years in doing

The Official Baronage of England, a wonderful monument of industry and learning. Another brother was Henry Doyle, a great judge of old paintings, and in later years the manager of the National Gallery in Dublin, where he earned his CB. The third son was Richard Doyle, whose whimsical humour made him famous in *Punch*, the cover of which with its dancing elves is still so familiar an object. Finally came Charles Doyle, my father.

The Doyle family seem to have been fairly well-to-do, thanks to my grandfather's talents. They lived in London in Cambridge Terrace. A sketch of their family life is given in 'Dicky Doyle's Diary'. They lived up to their income, however, and it became necessary to find places for the boys. When my father was only nineteen a seat was offered him in the Government Office of Works in Edinburgh, whither he went. There he spent his working life, and thus it came about that I, an Irishman by extraction, was born in the Scottish capital.

The Doyles, Anglo-Norman in origin, were strong Roman Catholics. The original Doyle, or D'Oil, was a cadet-branch of the Staffordshire Doyles, which has produced Sir Francis Hastings Doyle and many other distinguished men. This cadet shared in the invasion of Ireland and was granted estates in County Wexford, where a great clan rose of dependants, illegitimate children and others, all taking the feudal lord's name, just as the de Burghs founded the clan of Burke. We can only claim to be the main stem by virtue of community of character and appearance with the English Doyles and the unbroken use of the same crest and coat-of-arms.

My forbears, like most old Irish families in the south, kept to the old faith at the Reformation and fell victims to the penal laws in consequence. These became so crushing upon landed gentry that my great-grandfather was driven from his estate and became a silk mercer in Dublin, where 'H. B.' was born. This family record was curiously confirmed by Monsignor Barry Doyle, destined, I think, for the highest honours of the Roman Church, who traces back to the younger brother of my great-grandfather.

I trust the reader will indulge me in my excursion into these family matters, which are of vital interest to the family but must be tedious to the outsider. As I am on the subject, I wish to say a word upon my mother's family, the more so as she was great on archaeology, and had, with the help of Sir Arthur Vicars, Ulster King of Arms, and himself a relative, worked out her descent for more than five hundred years, and so composed a family tree which lies before me as I write and on which many of the great ones of the earth have roosted.

Her father was a young doctor of Trinity College, William Foley, who died young and left his family in comparative poverty. He had married one Katherine Pack, whose deathbed – or rather the white waxen thing which lay upon that bed – is the very earliest recollection of my life. Her near relative – uncle, I think – was Sir Denis Pack, who led the Scottish brigade at Waterloo. The Packs were a fighting family, as was but right since they were descended in a straight line from a major in Cromwell's army who settled in Ireland. One of them, Anthony Pack, had part of his head carried off at the same battle, so I fear it is part of our family tradition that we lose our heads in action. His brain was covered over by a silver plate and he lived for many years, subject only to very bad fits of temper, which some of us have had with less excuse.

But the real romance of the family lies in the fact that about the middle of the seventeenth century the Reverend Richard Pack, who was head of Kilkenny College, married Mary Percy, who was heir to the Irish branch of the Percys of Northumberland. By this alliance we all connect up (and I have every generation by name, as marked out by my dear mother) with that illustrious line up to three separate marriages with the Plantagenets. One has, therefore, some strange strains in one's blood which are noble in origin and, one can but hope, are noble in tendency.

But all this romance of ancestry did not interfere with the fact that when Katherine Pack, the Irish gentlewoman, came in her widowhood to Edinburgh, she was very poor. I have never been clear why it was Edinburgh for which she made. Having taken a flat she let it be known that a paying-guest would be welcome. Just at this time, 1850 or thereabouts, Charles Doyle was sent from London with a recommendation to the priests that they should guard his young morals and budding faith. How could they do this better than by finding him quarters with a well-born and orthodox widow? Thus it came about that two separate lines of Irish wanderers came together under one roof.

I have a little bundle of my father's letters written in those days, full of appreciation of the kindness which he met with and full, also, of interesting observations on that Scottish society, rough, hard-drinking and kindly, into which he had been precipitated at a dangerously early age, especially for one with his artistic temperament. He had some fine religious instincts, but his environment was a difficult one. In the household was a bright-eyed, very intelligent younger daughter, Mary, who presently went off to France and returned as a very cultivated young woman. The romance is easily understood, and so Charles Doyle in the year 1855 married Mary Foley, my mother, the young couple still residing with my grandmother.

Their means were limited, for his salary as a civil servant was only about two hundred and forty pounds. This he supplemented by his drawings. Thus matters remained for practically all his life, for he was quite unambitious and no great promotion ever came his way. His painting was done spasmodically and the family did not always reap the benefit, for Edinburgh is full of watercolours which he had given away. It is one of my unfulfilled schemes to collect as many as possible and to have a Charles Doyle exhibition in London, for the critics would be surprised to find what a great and original artist he was – far the greatest, in my opinion, of the family. His brush was concerned not only with fairies and delicate themes of the kind, but with wild and fearsome subjects, so that his work had a very peculiar style of its own, mitigated by great natural humour. He was more terrible than Blake and less morbid than Wiertz. His originality is best shown by the fact that one hardly knows with whom to compare him. In prosaic Scotland, however, he excited wonder rather than admiration, and he was only known in the larger world of London by pen-and-ink book-illustrations which were not his best mode of expression. The prosaic outcome was that including all his earnings my mother could never have averaged more than three hundred pounds a year on which to educate a large family. We lived in the hardy and bracing atmosphere of poverty and we each in turn did our best to help those who were younger than ourselves. My noble sister Annette, who died just as the sunshine of better days came into our lives, went out at a very early age as a governess to Portugal and sent all her salary home. My younger sisters, Lottie and Connie, both did the same thing; and I helped as I could. But it was still my dear mother who bore the long, sordid strain. Often I said to her, 'When you are old, mammie, you shall have a velvet dress and gold glasses and sit in comfort by the fire.' Thank God, it so came to pass. My father, I fear, was of little help to her, for his thoughts were always in the clouds and he had no appreciation of the realities of life. The world, not the family, gets the fruits of genius.

Of my boyhood I need say little, save that it was Spartan at home and more Spartan at the Edinburgh school where a tawse-brandishing schoolmaster of the old type made our young lives miserable. From the age of seven to nine I suffered under this pockmarked, one-eyed rascal who might have stepped from the pages of Dickens. In the evenings, home and books were my sole consolation, save for weekend holidays. My comrades were rough boys and I became a rough boy, too. If there is any truth in the idea of reincarnation – a point on which my mind is still open – I think some earlier experience of mine must have been as a stark fighter, for it came out strongly in youth, when I rejoiced in battle. We lived for some time in a *cul de sac* street with a very vivid life of its own and a fierce feud between the small boys who dwelt on either side of it. Finally it was fought out between two champions, I representing the poorer boys who lived in flats and my opponent the richer boys who lived in the opposite villas. We fought in the garden of one of the said villas and had an excellent contest of many rounds, not being strong enough to weaken each other. When I got home after the battle, my mother cried, 'Oh, Arthur, what a dreadful eye you have got!' To which I replied, 'You just go across and look at Eddie Tulloch's eye!'

I met a well-deserved setback on one occasion when I stood forward to fight a bootmaker's boy, who had come into our preserve upon an errand. He had a green baize bag in his hand which contained a heavy boot, and this he swung against my skull with a force which knocked me pretty well senseless. It was a useful lesson. I will say for myself, however, that though I was pugnacious I was never so to those weaker than myself and that some of my escapades were in the defence of such. As I will show in my chapter on sport, I carried on my tastes into a later period of my life.

One or two little pictures stand out which may be worth recording. When my grandfather's grand London friends passed through Edinburgh they used, to our occasional embarrassment, to call at the little flat 'to see how Charles is getting on'. In my earliest childhood such a one came, tall, white-haired and affable. I was so young that it seems like a faint dream, and yet it pleases me to think that I have sat on Thackeray's knee. He greatly admired my dear little mother with her grey Irish eyes and her vivacious Celtic ways – indeed, no one met her without being captivated by her.

Once, too, I got a glimpse of history. It was in 1866, if my dates are right, that some well-to-do Irish relatives asked us over for a few weeks, and we passed that time in a great house in King's County. I spent much of it with the horses and dogs, and became friendly with the young groom. The stables opened on to a country road by an arched gate with a loft over it. One morning, being in the yard, I saw the young groom rush into the yard with every sign of fear and hastily shut and bar the doors. He then climbed into the loft, beckoning to me to come with him. From the loft window we saw a gang of rough men, twenty or so, slouching along the road. When they came opposite to the gate they stopped and looking up shook their fists and cursed at us. The groom answered back most volubly. Afterwards I understood that these men were a party of Fenians, and that I had had a glimpse of one of the periodical troubles which poor old Ireland has endured. Perhaps now, at last, they may be drawing to an end.

During these first ten years I was a rapid reader, so rapid that some small library with which we dealt gave my mother notice that books would not be changed more than twice a day. My tastes were boylike enough, for Mayne Reid was my favourite author, and his *Scalp Hunters* my favourite book. I wrote a little book and illustrated it myself in early days. There was a man in it and there was a tiger who amalgamated shortly after they met. I remarked to my mother with precocious wisdom that it was easy to get people into scrapes, but not so easy to get them out again, which is surely the experience of every writer of adventures.

2

Under the Jesuits

The Preparatory School – The Mistakes of Education – Spartan
Schooling – Corporal Punishment – Well-known Schoolfellows –
Gloomy Forecasts – Poetry – London Matriculation – German
School – A Happy Year – The Jesuits – Strange Arrival in Paris

I was in my tenth year when I was sent to Hodder, which is the preparatory school for Stonyhurst, the big Roman Catholic public school in
Lancashire. It was a long journey for a little boy who had never been
away from home before, and I felt very lonesome and wept bitterly
upon the way, but in due time I arrived safely at Preston, which was
then the nearest station, and with many other small boys and our black-
robed Jesuit guardians we drove some twelve miles to the school.
Hodder is about a mile from Stonyhurst, and as all the boys there are
youngsters under twelve, it forms a very useful institution, breaking a
lad into school ways before he mixes with the big fellows.

I had two years at Hodder. The year was not broken up by the
frequent holidays which illuminate the present educational period. Save
for six weeks each summer, one never left the school. On the whole,
those first two years were happy years. I could hold my own both in
brain and in strength with my comrades. I was fortunate enough to get
under the care of a kindly principal, one Father Cassidy, who was more
human than Jesuits usually are. I have always kept a warm remembrance of this man and of his gentle ways to the little boys – young
rascals many of us – who were committed to his care. I remember the
Franco-German War breaking out at this period, and how it made a
ripple even in our secluded backwater.

From Hodder I passed on to Stonyhurst, that grand mediaeval
dwelling-house which was left some hundred and fifty years ago to the
Jesuits, who brought over their whole teaching staff from some college
in Holland in order to carry it on as a public school. The general
curriculum, like the building, was mediaeval but sound. I understand it
has been modernised since. There were seven classes – elements,

figures, rudiments, grammar, syntax, poetry and rhetoric – and you were allotted a year for each, or seven in all – a course with which I faithfully complied, two having already been completed at Hodder. It was the usual public-school routine of Euclid, algebra and the classics, taught in the usual way, which is calculated to leave a lasting abhorrence of these subjects. To give boys a little slab of Virgil or Homer with no general idea as to what it is all about or what the classical age was like, is surely an absurd way of treating the subject. I am sure that an intelligent boy could learn more by reading a good translation of Homer for a week than by a year's study of the original as it is usually carried out. It was no worse at Stonyhurst than at any other school, and it can only be excused on the plea that any exercise, however stupid in itself, forms a sort of mental dumb-bell by which one can improve one's mind. It is, I think, a thoroughly false theory. I can say with truth that my Latin and Greek, which cost me so many weary hours, have been little use to me in life, and that my mathematics have been no use at all. On the other hand, some things which I picked up almost by accident, the art of reading aloud, learned when my mother was knitting, or the reading of French books, learned by spelling out the captions of the Jules Verne illustrations, have been of the greatest possible service. My classical education left me with a horror of the classics, and I was astonished to find how fascinating they were when I read them in a reasonable manner in later years.

Year by year, then, I see myself climbing those seven weary steps and passing through as many stages of my boyhood. I do not know if the Jesuit system of education is good or not; I would need to have tried another system as well before I could answer that. On the whole it was justified by results, for I think it turned out as decent a set of young fellows as any other school would do. In spite of a large infusion of foreigners and some disaffected Irish, we were a patriotic crowd, and our little pulse beat time with the heart of the nation. I am told that the average of VCs and DSOs now held by old Stonyhurst boys is very high as compared with other schools. The Jesuit teachers have no trust in human nature, and perhaps they are justified. We were never allowed for an instant to be alone with each other, and I think that the immorality which is rife in public schools was at a minimum in consequence. In our games and our walks the priests always took part, and a master perambulated the dormitories at night. Such a system may weaken self-respect and self-help, but it at least minimises temptation and scandal.

The life was Spartan, and yet we had all that was needed. Dry bread and hot well-watered milk was our frugal breakfast. There was a 'joint' and twice a week a pudding for dinner. Then there was an odd snack called 'bread and beer' in the afternoon, a bit of dry bread and the most extraordinary drink, which was brown but had no other characteristic of beer. Finally, there was hot milk again, bread, butter, and often potatoes for supper. We were all very healthy on this regime, with fish, on Fridays. Everything in every way was plain to the verge of austerity, save that we dwelt in a beautiful building, dined in a marble-floored hall with minstrels' gallery, prayed in a lovely church, and generally lived in very choice surroundings so far as vision and not comfort was concerned.

Corporal punishment was severe, and I can speak with feeling as I think few, if any, boys of my time endured more of it. It was of a peculiar nature, imported also, I fancy, from Holland. The instrument was a piece of india-rubber of the size and shape of a thick boot sole. This was called a 'tolley' – why, no one has explained, unless it is a Latin pun on what we had to bear. One blow of this instrument, delivered with intent, would cause the palm of the hand to swell up and change colour. When I say that the usual punishment of the larger boys was nine on each hand, and that nine on one hand was the absolute minimum, it will be understood that it was a severe ordeal, and that the sufferer could not, as a rule, turn the handle of the door to get out of the room in which he had suffered. To take twice nine upon a cold day was about the extremity of human endurance. I think, however, that it was good for us in the end, for it was a point of honour with many of us not to show that we were hurt, and that is one of the best trainings for a hard life. If I was more beaten than others it was not that I was in any way vicious, but it was that I had a nature which responded eagerly to affectionate kindness (which I never received), but which rebelled against threats and took a perverted pride in showing that it would not be cowed by violence. I went out of my way to do really mischievous and outrageous things simply to show that my spirit was unbroken. An appeal to my better nature and not to my fears would have found an answer at once. I deserved all I got for what I did, but I did it because I was mishandled.

I do not remember anyone who attained particular distinction among my schoolfellows, save Bernard Partridge of *Punch*, whom I recollect as a very quiet, gentle boy. Father Thurston, who was destined to be one of my opponents in psychic matters so many years later, was in the class above me. There was a young novice, too, with whom I hardly came in contact, but whose handsome and spiritual appearance I well remember. He was Bernard Vaughan, afterwards the famous preacher. Save for one schoolfellow, James Ryan – a remarkable boy who grew into a remarkable man – I carried away no lasting friendship from Stonyhurst.

It was only in the latest stage of my Stonyhurst development that I realised that I had some literary streak in me which was not common to all. It came to me as quite a surprise, and even more perhaps to my masters, who had taken a rather hopeless view of my future prospects. One master, when I told him that I thought of being a civil engineer, remarked, 'Well, Doyle, you may be an engineer, but I don't think you will ever be a civil one.' Another assured me that I would never do any good in the world, and perhaps from his point of view his prophecy has been justified. The particular incident, however, which brought my latent powers to the surface depended upon the fact that in the second highest class, which I reached in 1874, it was incumbent to write poetry (so called) on any theme given. This was done as a dreary unnatural task by most boys. Very comical their wooings of the muses used to be. For one saturated as I really was with affection for verse, it was a labour of love, and I produced verses which were poor enough in themselves but seemed miracles to those who had no urge in that direction. The particular theme was the crossing of the Red Sea by the Israelites and my effort from –

> Like pallid daisies in a grassy wood,
> So round the sward the tents of Israel stood;

through –

> There was no time for thought and none for fear,
> For Egypt's horse already pressed their rear;

down to the climax –

> One horrid cry! The tragedy was o'er,
> And Pharaoh with his army seen no more –

was workmanlike though wooden and conventional. Anyhow, it marked what Mr Stead used to call a signpost, and I realised myself a little. In the last year I edited the college magazine and wrote a good deal of indifferent verse. I also went up for the matriculation examination of London University, a good all-round test which winds up the

Stonyhurst curriculum, and I surprised everyone by taking honours, so after all I emerged from Stonyhurst at the age of sixteen with more credit than seemed probable from my rather questionable record.

Early in my career there, an offer had been made to my mother that my school fees would be remitted if I were dedicated to the Church. She refused this, so both the Church and I had an escape. When I think, however, of her small income and great struggle to keep up appearances and make both ends meet, it was a fine example of her independence of character, for it meant paying out some fifty pounds a year which might have been avoided by a word of assent.

I had yet another year with the Jesuits, for it was determined that I was still too young to begin any professional studies, and that I should go to Germany and learn German. I was despatched, therefore, to Feldkirch, which is a Jesuit school in the Vorarlberg province of Austria, to which many better-class German boys are sent. Here the conditions were much more humane and I met with far more human kindness than at Stonyhurst, with the immediate result that I ceased to be a resentful young rebel and became a pillar of law and order.

I began badly, however, for on the first night of my arrival I was kept awake by a boy snoring loudly in the dormitory. I stood it as long as I could, but at last I was driven to action. Curious wooden compasses called *bett-scheere*, or 'bed-scissors', were stuck into each side of the narrow beds. One of these I plucked out, walked down the dormitory, and, having spotted the offender, proceeded to poke him with my stick. He awoke and was considerably amazed to see in the dim light a large youth whom he had never seen before – I arrived after hours – assaulting him with a club. I was still engaged in stirring him up when I felt a touch on my shoulder and was confronted by the master, who ordered me back to bed. Next morning I got a lecture on free-and-easy English ways, and taking the law into my own hands. But this start was really my worst lapse and I did well in the future.

It was a happy year on the whole. I made less progress with German than I should, for there were about twenty English and Irish boys who naturally baulked the wishes of their parents by herding together. There was no cricket, but there was tobogganing and fair football, and a weird game – football on stilts. Then there were the lovely mountains round us, with an occasional walk among them. The food was better than at Stonyhurst and we had the pleasant German light beer instead of the horrible swipes of Stonyhurst. One unlooked-for accomplishment I acquired, for the boy who played the big brass bass instrument in the fine school band had not returned, and, as a well-grown lad was needed, I was at once enlisted in the service. I played in public – good music, too, *Lohengrin* and *Tannhäuser* – within a week or two of my first lesson, but they pressed me on for the occasion and the Bombardon, as it was called, only comes in on a measured rhythm with an occasional run, which sounds like a hippopotamus doing a step-dance. So big was the instrument that I remember the other bandsmen putting my sheets and blankets inside it and my surprise when I could not get out a note. It was in the summer of 1876 that I left Feldkirch, and I have always had a pleasant memory of the Austrian Jesuits and of the old school.

Indeed I have a kindly feeling towards all Jesuits, far as I have strayed from their paths. I see now both their limitations and their virtues. They have been slandered in some things, for during eight years of constant contact I cannot remember that they were less truthful than their fellows, or more casuistical than their neighbours. They were keen, clean-minded, earnest men, so far as I knew them, with a few black sheep among them, but not many, for the process of selection was careful and long. In all ways, save in their theology, they were admirable, though this same theology made them hard and inhuman upon the surface, which is indeed the general effect of Catholicism in its more extreme forms. The convert is lost to the family. Their hard, narrow outlook gives the Jesuits driving power, as is noticeable in the Puritans and all hard, narrow creeds. They are devoted and fearless and have again and again, in Canada, in South America and in China, been the vanguard of civilisation to their own grievous hurt. They are the old guard of the Roman Church. But the tragedy is that they, who would gladly give their lives for the old faith, have in effect helped to ruin it, for it is they, according to Father Tyrrell and the modernists, who have been at the back of all those extreme doctrines of papal infallibility and immaculate conception, with a general all-round tightening of dogma, which have made it so difficult for the man with a scientific desire for truth or with intellectual self-respect to keep within the Church. For some years Sir Charles Mivart, the last of Catholic scientists, tried to do the impossible, and then he also had to leave go his hold, so that there is not, so far as I know, one single man of outstanding fame in science or in general thought who is a practising Catholic. This is the work of the extremists and is deplored by many of the moderates and fiercely condemned by the modernists. It depends also upon the inner Italian

directorate who give the orders. Nothing can exceed the uncom-
promising bigotry of the Jesuit theology, or their apparent ignorance of
how it shocks the modern conscience. I remember that when, as a
grown lad, I heard Father Murphy, a great fierce Irish priest, declare
that there was sure damnation for everyone outside the Church, I
looked upon him with horror, and to that moment I trace the first rift
which has grown into such a chasm between me and those who were
my guides.

On my way back to England I stopped at Paris. Through all my life
up to this point there had been an unseen grand-uncle, named Michael
Conan, to whom I must now devote a paragraph. He came into the
family from the fact that my father's father ('H. B.') had married a Miss
Conan. Michael Conan, her brother, had been editor of the *Art Journal*
and was a man of distinction, an intellectual Irishman of the type
which originally founded the Sinn Fein movement. He was as keen on
heraldry and genealogy as my mother, and he traced his descent in
some circuitous way from the Dukes of Brittany, who were all Conans;
indeed Arthur Conan was the ill-fated young duke whose eyes were put
out, according to Shakespeare, by King John. This uncle was my
godfather, and hence my name Arthur Conan.

He lived in Paris and had expressed a wish that his grandnephew and
godson, with whom he had corresponded, should call *en passant*. I ran
my money affairs so closely, after a rather lively supper at Strasburg,
that when I reached Paris I had just twopence in my pocket. As I could
not well drive up and ask my uncle to pay the cab I left my trunk at the
station and set forth on foot. I reached the river, walked along it, came
to the foot of the Champs Elysées, saw the Arc de Triomphe in the
distance, and then, knowing that the Avenue Wagram, where my uncle
lived, was near there, I tramped it on a hot August day and finally found
him. I remember that I was exhausted with the heat and the walking,
and that when at the last gasp I saw a man buy a drink of what seemed
to be porter by handing a penny to a man who had a long tin on his
back, I therefore halted the man and spent one of my pennies on a
duplicate drink. It proved to be liquorice and water, but it revived me
when I badly needed it, and it could not be said that I arrived penniless
at my uncle's, for I actually had a penny.

So, for some penurious weeks, I was in Paris with this dear old
volcanic Irishman, who spent the summer days in his shirt-sleeves, with
a little dicky-bird of a wife waiting upon him. I am built rather on his

lines of body and mind than on any of the Doyles. We made a true friendship, and then I returned to my home conscious that real life was about to begin.

3

Recollections of a Student

Edinburgh University – A Sad Disappointment – Original of
Professor Challenger – Of Sherlock Holmes – Deductions –
Sheffield – Ruyton – Birmingham – Literary Aspirations – First
Accepted Story – My Father's Death – Mental Position –
Spiritual Yearnings – An Awkward Business

When I returned to Edinburgh, with little to show, either mental or
spiritual, for my pleasant school year in Germany, I found that the
family affairs were still as straitened as ever. No promotion had come to
my father, and two younger children, Innes, my only brother, and Ida,
had arrived to add to the calls upon my mother. Another sister, Julia,
followed shortly afterwards. But Annette, the eldest sister, had already
gone out to Portugal to earn and send home a fair salary, while Lottie
and Connie were about to do the same. My mother had adopted the
device of sharing a large house, which may have eased her in some
ways, but was disastrous in others.

Perhaps it was good for me that the times were hard, for I was wild,
full-blooded and a trifle reckless, but the situation called for energy and
application, so that one was bound to try to meet it. My mother had
been so splendid that we could not fail her. It had been determined that
I should be a doctor – chiefly, I think, because Edinburgh was so famous
a centre for medical learning. It meant another long effort for my
mother, but she was very brave and ambitious where her children were
concerned, and I was not only to have a medical education, but to take
the university degree, which was a larger matter than a mere licence to
practise. When I returned from Germany I found that there was a long
list of bursaries and scholarships open for competition. I had a month in
which to brush up my classics and then I went in for these, and was
informed a week later that I had won the Grierson bursary of forty
pounds for two years. Great were the rejoicings and all shadows seemed
to be lifting. But on calling to get the money I was informed that there
had been a clerical error, and that this particular bursary was only open

to arts students. As there was a long list of prizes I naturally supposed that I would get the next highest, which was available for medicals. The official pulled a long face and said: 'Unfortunately the candidate to whom it was allotted has already drawn the money.' It was manifest robbery, and yet I, who had won the prize and needed it so badly, never received it, and was eventually put off with a solatium of seven pounds, which had accumulated from some fund. It was a bitter disappointment and, of course, I had a legal case, but what can a penniless student do, and what sort of college career would he have if he began it by suing his university for money? I was advised to accept the situation, and there seemed no prospect of accepting anything else.

So now behold me, a tall strongly-framed but half-formed young man, fairly entered upon my five years' course of medical study. It can be done with diligence in four years, but there came, as I shall show, a glorious interruption which held me back for one year. I entered as a student in October 1876, and I emerged as a bachelor of medicine in August 1881. Between these two points lies one long weary grind at botany, chemistry, anatomy, physiology, and a whole list of compulsory subjects, many of which have a very indirect bearing upon the art of curing. The whole system of teaching, as I look back upon it, seems far too oblique and not nearly practical enough for the purpose in view. And yet Edinburgh is, I believe, more practical than most other colleges. It is practical, too, in its preparation for life, since there is none of the atmosphere of an enlarged public school, as is the case in English universities, but the student lives a free man in his own rooms with no restrictions of any sort. It ruins some and makes strong men of many. In my own case, of course, this did not apply, since my family lived in the town, and I worked from my own home.

There was no attempt at friendship, or even acquaintance, between professors and students at Edinburgh. It was a strictly business arrangement by which you paid, for example, four guineas for anatomy lectures and received the winter course in exchange, never seeing your professor save behind his desk and never under any circumstances exchanging a word with him. They were remarkable men, however, some of these professors, and we managed to know them pretty well without any personal acquaintance. There was kindly Crum Brown, the chemist, who sheltered himself carefully before exploding some mixture, which usually failed to ignite, so that the loud 'Boom!' uttered by the class was the only resulting sound. Brown would emerge from his retreat with a

'Really, gentlemen!' of remonstrance, and go on without allusion to the abortive experiment. There was Wyville Thomson, the zoologist, fresh from his *Challenger* expedition, and Balfour, with the face and manner of John Knox, a hard, rugged old man, who harried the students in their exams, and was in consequence harried by them for the rest of the year. There was Turner, a fine anatomist, but a self-educated man, as was betrayed when he used to 'take and put this structure on the handle of this scalpel'. The most human trait that I can recall of Turner was that upon one occasion the sacred quadrangle was invaded by snowballing roughs. His class, of whom I was one, heard the sounds of battle and fidgeted in their seats, on which the professor said: 'I think, gentlemen, your presence may be more useful outside than here,' on which we flocked out with a whoop, and soon had the quadrangle clear. Most vividly of all, however, there stands out in my memory the squat figure of Professor Rutherford with his Assyrian beard, his prodigious voice, his enormous chest and his singular manner. He fascinated and awed us. I have endeavoured to reproduce some of his peculiarities in the fictitious character of Professor Challenger. He would sometimes start his lecture before he reached the classroom, so that we would hear a booming voice saying: 'There are valves in the veins,' or some other information, when the desk was still empty. He was, I fear, a rather ruthless vivisector, and though I have always recognised that a minimum of painless vivisection is necessary, and far more justifiable than the eating of meat as a food, I am glad that the law was made more stringent so as to restrain such men as he. 'Ach, these Jarman frags!' he would exclaim in his curious accent, as he tore some poor amphibian to pieces. I wrote a students' song which is still sung, I understand, in which a curious article is picked up on the Portobello beach and each professor in turn claims it for his department. Rutherford's verse ran:

> Said Rutherford with a smile,
> 'It's a mass of solid bile,
>   And I myself obtained it, what is more,
> By a stringent cholagogue
> From a vivisected dog,
>   And I lost it on the Portobello shore.'

If the song is indeed still sung it may be of interest to the present generation to know that I was the author.

But the most notable of the characters whom I met was one Joseph

Bell, surgeon at the Edinburgh Infirmary. Bell was a very remarkable man in body and mind. He was thin, wiry, dark, with a high-nosed acute face, penetrating grey eyes, angular shoulders and a jerky way of walking. His voice was high and discordant. He was a very skilful surgeon, but his strong point was diagnosis, not only of disease, but of occupation and character. For some reason which I have never under-stood he singled me out from the drove of students who frequented his wards and made me his outpatient clerk, which meant that I had to array his outpatients, make simple notes of their cases, and then show them in, one by one, to the large room in which Bell sat in state surrounded by his dressers and students. Then I had ample chance of studying his methods and of noticing that he often learned more of the patient by a few quick glances than I had done by my questions. Occasionally the results were very dramatic, though there were times when he blundered. In one of his best cases he said to a civilian patient: 'Well, my man, you've served in the army.'

'Aye, sir.'

'Not long discharged?'

'No, sir.'

'A Highland regiment?'

'Aye, sir.'

'A non-com. officer?'

'Aye, sir.'

'Stationed at Barbados?'

'Aye, sir.'

'You see, gentlemen,' he would explain, 'the man was a respectful man but did not remove his hat. They do not in the army, but he would have learned civilian ways had he been long discharged. He has an air of authority and he is obviously Scottish. As to Barbados, his complaint is elephantiasis, which is West Indian and not British.' To his audience of Watsons it all seemed very miraculous until it was explained, and then it became simple enough. It is no wonder that after the study of such a character I used and amplified his methods when in later life I tried to build up a scientific detective who solved cases on his own merits and not through the folly of the criminal. Bell took a keen interest in these detective tales and even made suggestions which were not, I am bound to say, very practical. I kept in touch with him for many years and he used to come upon my platform to support me when I contested Edinburgh in 1901.

When I took over his out-patient work he warned me that a knowledge of Scottish idioms was necessary, and I, with the confidence of youth, declared that I had got it. The sequel was amusing. On one of the first days an old man came who, in response to my question, declared that he had a 'bealin' in his oxter'. This fairly beat me, much to Bell's amusement. It seems that the words really mean an abscess in the armpit.

Speaking generally of my university career I may say that though I took my fences in my stride and balked at none of them, still I won no distinction in the race. I was always one of the ruck, neither lingering nor gaining – a sixty-per-cent man at examinations. There were, however, some reasons for this which I will now state.

It was clearly very needful that I should help financially as quickly as possible, even if my help only took the humble form of providing for my own keep. Therefore I endeavoured almost from the first to compress the classes for a year into half a year, and so to have some months in which to earn a little money as a medical assistant, who would dispense and do odd jobs for a doctor. When I first set forth to do this my services were so obviously worth nothing that I had to put that valuation upon them. Even then it might have been a hard bargain for the doctor, for I might have proved like the youth in *Pickwick* who had a rooted idea that oxalic acid was Epsom salts. However, I had horse sense enough to save myself and my employer from any absolute catastrophe. My first venture, in the early summer of 1878, was with a Dr Richardson, running a low-class practice in the poorer quarters of Sheffield. I did my best, and I dare say he was patient, but at the end of three weeks we parted by mutual consent. I went on to London, where I renewed my advertisements in the medical papers, and found a refuge for some weeks with my Doyle relatives, then living at Clifton Gardens, Maida Vale. I fear that I was too Bohemian for them and they too conventional for me. However, they were kind to me, and I roamed about London for some time with pockets so empty that there was little chance of idleness breeding its usual mischief. I remember that there were signs of trouble in the East and that the recruiting sergeants, who were very busy in Trafalgar Square, took my measure in a moment and were very insistent that I should take the shilling. There was a time when I was quite disposed to do so, but my mother's plans held me back. I may say that late in the same year I did volunteer as a dresser for the English ambulances sent to Turkey for the Russian War, and was on the Red Cross list, but the collapse of the Turks prevented my going out.

Soon, however, there came an answer to my advertisement: 'Third year's student, desiring experience rather than remuneration, offers his services, &c., &c.' It was from a Dr Elliot living in a townlet in Shropshire which rejoiced in the extraordinary name of 'Ruyton-of-the-Eleven-Towns'. It was not big enough to make one town, far less eleven. There for four months I helped in a country practice. It was a very quiet existence and I had a good deal of time to myself under very pleasant circumstances, so that I really trace some little mental progress to that period, for I read and thought without interruption. My medical duties were of a routine nature save on a few occasions. One of them still stands out in my memory, for it was the first time in my life that I ever had to test my own nerve in a great sudden emergency. The doctor was out when there came a half-crazed messenger to say that in some rejoicings at a neighbouring great house they had exploded an old cannon which had promptly burst and grievously injured one of the bystanders. No doctor was available, so I was the last resource. On arriving there I found a man in bed with a lump of iron sticking out of the side of his head. I tried not to show the alarm which I felt, and I did the obvious thing by pulling out the iron. I could see the clean white bone, so I could assure them that the brain had not been injured. I then pulled the gash together, staunched the bleeding, and finally bound it up, so that when the doctor did at last arrive he had little to add. This incident gave me confidence and, what is more important still, gave others confidence. On the whole I had a happy time at Ruyton, and have a pleasing memory of Dr Elliot and his wife.

After a winter's work at the university my next assistantship was a real money-making proposition to the extent of some two pounds a month. This was with Dr Hoare, a well-known Birmingham doctor, who had a five-horse city practice, and every working doctor, before the days of motors, would realise that this meant going from morning to night. He earned some three thousand a year, which takes some doing when it is collected from 3s. 6d. visits and 1s. 6d. bottles of medicine among the very poorest classes of Aston. Hoare was a fine fellow, stout, square, red-faced, bushy-whiskered and dark-eyed. His wife was also a very kindly and gifted woman, and my position in the house was soon rather that of a son than of an assistant. The work, however, was hard and incessant, and the pay very small. I had long lists of prescriptions to make up every day, for we dispensed our own medicine, and one hundred bottles of an evening were not unknown. On the whole I made few mistakes, though I have been known to send out ointment and pill boxes with elaborate directions on the lid and nothing inside. I had my own visiting list, also, the poorest or the most convalescent, and I saw a great deal, for better or worse, of very low life. Twice I returned to this Birmingham practice and always my relations with the family became closer. At my second visit my knowledge had greatly extended and I did midwifery cases, and the more severe cases in general practice as well as all the dispensing. I had no time to spend any money and it was as well, for every shilling was needed at home.

It was in this year that I first learned that shillings might be earned in other ways than by filling phials. Some friend remarked to me that my letters were very vivid and surely I could write some things to sell. I may say that the general aspiration towards literature was tremendously strong upon me, and that my mind was reaching out in what seemed an aimless way in all sorts of directions. I used to be allowed twopence for my lunch, that being the price of a mutton pie, but near the pie shop was a second-hand book shop with a barrel full of old books and the legend 'Your choice for 2d.' stuck above it. Often the price of my luncheon used to be spent on some sample out of this barrel, and I have within reach of my arm as I write these lines copies of Gordon's *Tacitus*, Temple's works, Pope's Homer, Addison's *Spectator* and Swift's works, which all came out of the twopenny box. Anyone observing my actions and tastes would have said that so strong a spring would certainly overflow, but for my own part I never dreamed I could myself produce decent prose, and the remark of my friend, who was by no means given to flattery, took me greatly by surprise. I sat down, however, and wrote a little adventure story which I called 'The Mystery of the Sassassa Valley'. To my great joy and surprise it was accepted by *Chambers' Journal*, and I received three guineas. It mattered not that other attempts failed. I had done it once and I cheered myself by the thought that I could do it again. It was years before I touched *Chambers* again, but in 1879 I had a story, 'The American's Tale', in *London Society*, for which also I got a small cheque. But the idea of real success was still far from my mind.

During all this time our family affairs had taken no turn for the better, and had it not been for my excursions and for the work of my sisters we could hardly have carried on. My father's health had utterly broken, he had to retire to that convalescent home in which the last years of his life were spent, and I, aged twenty, found myself practically the head of a large and struggling family. My father's life was full of the tragedy of unfulfilled powers and of undeveloped gifts. He had his weaknesses, as all of us have ours, but he had also some very remarkable and outstanding virtues. A tall man, long-bearded, and elegant, he had a charm of manner and a courtesy of bearing which I have seldom seen equalled. His wit was quick and playful. He possessed, also, a remarkable delicacy of mind which would give him moral courage enough to rise and leave any company which talked in a manner which was coarse. When he passed away a few years later I am sure that Charles Doyle had no enemy in the world, and that those who knew him best sympathised most with the hard fate which had thrown him, a man of sensitive genius, into an environment which neither his age nor his nature was fitted to face. He was unworldly and unpractical and his family suffered for it, but even his faults were in some ways the result of his developed spirituality. He lived and died a fervent son of the Roman Catholic faith. My mother, however, who had never been a very devoted daughter of that great institution, became less so as life progressed, and finally found her chief consolation in the Anglican fold.

This brings me to my own spiritual unfolding, if such it may be called, during those years of constant struggle. I have already in my account of the Jesuits shown how, even as a boy, all that was sanest and most generous in my nature rose up against a narrow theology and an uncharitable outlook upon the other great religions of the world. In the Catholic Church to doubt anything is to doubt everything, for since it is a vital axiom that doubt is a mortal sin when once it has, unbidden and unappeasable, come upon you, everything is loosened and you look upon the whole wonderful interdependent scheme with other and more critical eyes. Thus viewed there was much to attract – its traditions, its unbroken and solemn ritual, the beauty and truth of many of its observances, its poetical appeal to the emotions, the sensual charm of music, light and incense, its power as an instrument of law and order. For the guidance of an unthinking and uneducated world it could in many ways hardly be surpassed, as has been shown in Paraguay, and in the former Ireland where, outside agrarian trouble, crime was hardly known. All this I could clearly see, but if I may claim any outstanding characteristic in my life, it is that I have never paltered or compromised with religious matters, that I have always weighed them very seriously, and that there was something in me which made it absolutely impossible, even when my most immediate interests were concerned, to say anything about them save that which I, in the depth of my being, really believed to be true. Judging it thus by all the new knowledge which came to me both from my reading and from my studies, I found that the foundations not only of Roman Catholicism but of the whole Christian faith, as presented to me in nineteenth-century theology, were so weak that my mind could not build upon them. It is to be remembered that these were the years when Huxley, Tyndall, Darwin, Herbert Spencer and John Stuart Mill were our chief philosophers, and that even the man in the street felt the strong sweeping current of their thought, while to the young student, eager and impressionable, it was overwhelming. I know now that their negative attitude was even more mistaken, and very much more dangerous, than the positive positions which they attacked with such destructive criticism. A gap had opened between our fathers and ourselves so suddenly and completely that when a Gladstone wrote to uphold the Gadarene swine, or the six days of Creation, the youngest student rightly tittered over his arguments, and it did not need a Huxley to demolish them. I can see now very clearly how deplorable it is that manifest absurdities should be allowed to continue without even a footnote to soften them in the sacred text, because it has the effect that what is indeed sacred becomes overlaid, and one can easily be persuaded that what is false in parts can have no solid binding force. There are no worse enemies of true religion than those who clamour against all revision or modification of that strange mass of superbly good and questionable matter which we lump all together into a single volume as if there were the same value to all of it. It is not solid gold, but gold in clay, and if this be understood the earnest seeker will not cast it aside when he comes upon the clay, but will value the gold the more in that he has himself separated it.

It was, then, all Christianity, and not Roman Catholicism alone, which had alienated my mind and driven me to an agnosticism, which never for an instant degenerated into atheism, for I had a very keen perception of the wonderful poise of the universe and the tremendous power of conception and sustenance which it implied. I was reverent in all my doubts and never ceased to think upon the matter, but the more I thought the more confirmed became my nonconformity. In a broad sense I was a Unitarian, save that I regarded the Bible with more criticism than Unitarians usually show. This negative position was so firm that it seemed to me to be a terminus; whereas it proved only a junction on the road of life where I was destined to change from the old well-worn line on to a new one. Every materialist, as I can now clearly see, is a case of arrested development. He has cleared his ruins, but has not begun to build that which would shelter him. As to psychic knowledge, I knew it only by the account of exposures in the police courts and the usual wild and malicious statements in the public press. Years were to pass before I understood that in that direction might be found the positive proofs which I constantly asserted were the only conditions upon which I could resume any sort of allegiance to the unseen. I must have definite demonstration, for if it were to be a matter of faith then I might as well go back to the faith of my fathers. 'Never will I accept anything which cannot be proved to me. The evils of religion have all come from accepting things which cannot be proved.' So I said at the time and I have been true to my resolve.

I would not give the impression that my life was gloomy or morbidly thoughtful because it chanced that I had some extra cares and some worrying thoughts. I had an eager nature which missed nothing in the way of fun which could be gathered, and I had a great capacity for enjoyment. I read much. I played games all I could. I danced, and I sampled the drama whenever I had a sixpence to carry me to the gallery. On one occasion I got into a row which might have been serious. I was waiting on the gallery steps with a great line of people, the shut door still facing us. There were half a dozen soldiers in the crowd and one of these squeezed a girl up against the wall in such a way that she began to scream. As I was near them I asked the man to be more gentle, on which he dug his elbow with all his force into my ribs. He turned on me as he did so, and I hit him with both hands in the face. He bored into me and pushed me up into the angle of the door, but I had a grip of him and he could not hit me, though he tried to kick me in cowardly fashion with his knee. Several of his comrades threatened me, and one hit me on the head with his cane, cracking my hat. At this moment luckily the door opened and the rush of the crowd carried the soldiers on, one sympathetic corporal saying, 'Take your breath, sir! Take your breath!' I threw my man through the open door and came home, for it was clearly asking for trouble if I remained. It was a good escape from an awkward business.

And now I come to the first real outstanding adventure in my life, which is worthy of a fresh chapter and of a more elaborate treatment.

4

Whaling in the Arctic Ocean

It was in the *Hope*, under the command of the well-known whaler John Gray, that I paid a seven months' visit to the Arctic Seas in the year 1880. I went in the capacity of surgeon, but as I was only twenty years of age when I started, and as my knowledge of medicine was that of an average third year's student, I have often thought that it was as well that there was no very serious call upon my services.

It came about in this way. One raw afternoon in Edinburgh, whilst I was sitting reading hard for one of those examinations which blight the life of a medical student, there entered to me one Currie, a fellow-student with whom I had some slight acquaintance. The monstrous question which he asked drove all thought of my studies out of my head.

'Would you care,' said he, 'to start next week for a whaling cruise? You'll be surgeon, two pound ten a month and three shillings a ton oil money.'

'How do you know I'll get the berth?' was my natural question.

'Because I have it myself. I find at this last moment that I can't go, and I want to get a man to take my place.'

'How about an Arctic kit?'

'You can have mine.'

In an instant the thing was settled, and within a few minutes the current of my life had been deflected into a new channel.

In little more than a week I was in Peterhead, and busily engaged, with the help of the steward, in packing away my scanty belongings in the locker beneath my bunk on the good ship *Hope*.

I speedily found that the chief duty of the surgeon was to be the companion of the captain, who is cut off by the etiquette of the trade from anything but very brief and technical talks with his other officers. I should have found it intolerable if the captain had been a bad fellow, but John Gray of the *Hope* was a really splendid man, a grand seaman and a serious-minded Scot, so that he and I formed a comradeship which was never marred during our long tête-à-tête. I see him now, his ruddy face, his grizzled hair and beard, his very light blue eyes always looking into far spaces, and his erect muscular figure. Taciturn, sardonic, stern on occasion, but always a good just man at bottom.

There was one curious thing about the manning of the *Hope*. The man who signed on as first mate was a little, decrepit, broken fellow, absolutely incapable of performing the duties. The cook's assistant, on the other hand, was a giant of a man, red-bearded, bronzed, with huge limbs and a voice of thunder. But the moment that the ship cleared the harbour the little, decrepit mate disappeared into the cook's galley, and acted as scullery-boy for the voyage, while the mighty scullery-boy walked aft and became chief mate. The fact was, that the one had the certificate, but was past sailoring, while the other could neither read nor write, but was as fine a seaman as ever lived; so, by an agreement to which everybody concerned was party, they swapped their berths when they were at sea.

Colin McLean, with his six foot of stature, his erect, stalwart figure, and his fierce, red beard, pouring out from between the flaps of his sealing-cap, was an officer by natural selection, which is a higher title than that of a Board of Trade certificate. His only fault was that he was a very hot-blooded man, and that a little would excite him to a frenzy. I have a vivid recollection of an evening which I spent in dragging him off the steward, who had imprudently made some criticism upon his way of attacking a whale which had escaped. Both men had had some rum, which had made the one argumentative and the other violent, and as we were all three seated in a space of about seven by four, it took some hard work to prevent bloodshed. Every now and then, just as I thought all danger was past, the steward would begin again with his fatuous, 'No offence, Colin, but all I says is that if you had been a bit quicker on the fush – ' I don't know how often this sentence was begun, but never once was it ended; for at the word 'fush' Colin always seized him by the throat, and I Colin round the waist, and we struggled until we were all panting and exhausted. Then when the steward had recovered a little breath he would start that miserable sentence once more, and the 'fush' would be the signal for another encounter. I really believe that if I had not been there the mate would have hurt him, for he was quite the angriest man that I have ever seen.

There were fifty men upon our whaler, of whom half were Scotchmen and half Shetlanders, whom we picked up at Lerwick as we passed. The Shetlanders were the steadier and more tractable, quiet, decent and soft-spoken; while the Scotch seamen were more likely to give trouble, but also more virile and of stronger character. The officers and harpooners were all Scotch, but as ordinary seamen, and especially as boatmen, the Shetlanders were as good as could be wished.

There was only one man on board who belonged neither to Scotland nor to Shetland, and he was the mystery of the ship. He was a tall, swarthy, dark-eyed man, with blue-black hair and beard, singularly handsome features, and a curious, reckless sling of his shoulders when he walked. It was rumoured that he came from the south of England, and that he had fled thence to avoid the law. He made friends with no one, and spoke very seldom, but he was one of the smartest seamen in the ship. I could believe from his appearance that his temper was Satanic, and that the crime for which he was hiding may have been a bloody one. Only once he gave us a glimpse of his hidden fires. The cook – a very burly, powerful man – the little mate was only assistant – had a private store of rum, and treated himself so liberally to it that for three successive days the dinner of the crew was ruined. On the third day our silent outlaw approached the cook with a brass saucepan in his hand. He said nothing, but he struck the man such a frightful blow that his head flew through the bottom and the sides of the pan were left dangling round his neck. The half-drunken, half-stunned cook talked of fighting, but he was soon made to feel that the sympathy of the ship was against him, so he reeled back, grumbling, to his duties, while the avenger relapsed into his usual moody indifference. We heard no further complaints of the cooking.

I have spoken of the steward, and as I look back at that long voyage, during which for seven months we never set foot on land, the kindly open face of Jack Lamb comes back to me. He had a beautiful and sympathetic tenor voice, and many an hour have I listened to it with its accompaniment of rattling plates and jingling knives, as he cleaned up the dishes in his pantry. He had a great memory for pathetic and sentimental songs, and it is only when you have not seen a woman's face for six months that you realise what sentiment means. When Jack trilled out 'Her bright smile haunts me still', or 'Wait for me at Heaven's Gate, sweet Belle Mahone', he filled us all with a vague sweet discontent which comes back to me now as I think of it. To appreciate a woman one has to be out of sight of one for six months. I can well remember that as we rounded the north of Scotland on our return we dipped our flag to the lighthouse, being only some hundreds of yards from the shore. A figure emerged to answer our salute, and the excited whisper ran through the ship, 'It's a wumman!' The captain was on the bridge with his telescope. I had the binoculars in the bows. Everyone was staring. She was well over fifty, short skirts and sea boots – but she was a 'wumman'. 'Anything in a mutch!' the sailors used to say, and I was of the same way of thinking.

However, all this has come before its time. It was, I find by my log, on February 28 at 2 p.m. that we sailed from Peterhead, amid a great crowd and uproar. The decks were as clean as a yacht, and it was very unlike my idea of a whaler. We ran straight into bad weather and the glass went down at one time to 28.375, which is the lowest reading I can remember in all my ocean wanderings. We just got into Lerwick Harbour before the full force of the hurricane broke, which was so great that lying at anchor with bare poles and partly screened we were blown over to an acute angle. If it had taken us a few hours earlier we should certainly have lost our boats – and the boats are the life of a whaler. It was March 11 before the weather moderated enough to let us get on, and by that time there were twenty whalers in the bay, so that our setting forth was quite an occasion. That night and for a day longer the *Hope* had to take refuge in the lee of one of the outlying islands. I got ashore and wandered among peat bogs, meeting strange, barbarous, kindly people who knew nothing of the world. I was led back to the ship by a wild, long-haired girl holding a torch, for the peat holes make it dangerous at night – I can see her now, her tangled black hair, her bare legs, madder-stained petticoat, and wild features under the glare of the torch. I spoke to one old man there who asked me the news. I said, 'The Tay Bridge is down,' which was then a fairly stale item. He said, 'Eh, have they built a brig over the Tay?' After that I felt inclined to tell him about the Indian Mutiny.

What surprised me most in the Arctic regions was the rapidity with which you reach them. I had never realised that they lie at our very doors. I think that we were only four days out from Shetland when we were among the drift ice. I awoke one morning to hear the bump, bump of the floating pieces against the side of the ship, and I went on deck to see the whole sea covered with them to the horizon. They were none of them large, but they lay so thick that a man might travel far by springing from one to the other. Their dazzling whiteness made the sea seem bluer by contrast, and with a blue sky above, and that glorious Arctic air in one's nostrils, it was a morning to remember. Once on one of the swaying, rocking pieces we saw a huge seal, sleek, sleepy and imperturbable, looking up with the utmost assurance at the ship, as if it knew that the close time had still three weeks to run. Farther on we saw on the ice the long human-like prints of a bear. All this with the snowdrops of Scotland still fresh in our glasses in the cabin.

I have spoken about the close time, and I may explain that, by an agreement between the Norwegian and British Governments, the subjects of both nations are forbidden to kill a seal before April 3. The reason for this is that the breeding season is in March, and if the mothers should be killed before the young are able to take care of themselves, the race would soon become extinct. For breeding purposes the seals all come together at a variable spot, which is evidently prearranged among them, and as this place can be anywhere within many hundreds of square miles of floating ice, it is no easy matter for the fisher to find it. The means by which he sets about it are simple but ingenious. As the ship makes its way through the loose ice-streams, a school of seals is observed travelling through the water. Their direction is carefully taken by compass and marked upon the chart. An hour afterwards perhaps another school is seen. This is also marked. When these bearings have been taken several times, the various lines upon the chart are prolonged until they intersect. At this point, or near it, it is likely that the main pack of the seals will be found.

When you do come upon it, it is a wonderful sight. I suppose it is the largest assembly of creatures upon the face of the world – and this upon the open icefields hundreds of miles from the Greenland coast. Somewhere between 71° and 75° is the rendezvous, and the longitude is even vaguer; but the seals have no difficulty in finding the address. From the crow's nest at the top of the main-mast, one can see no end of them. On the farthest visible ice one can still see that sprinkling of pepper grains. And the young lie everywhere also, snow-white slugs, with a little black nose and large dark eyes. Their half-human cries fill the air; and when you are sitting in the cabin of a ship which is in the heart of the seal-pack, you would think you were next door to a monstrous nursery.

The *Hope* was one of the first to find the seal-pack that year, but before the day came when hunting was allowed, we had a succession of strong gales, followed by a severe roll, which tilted the floating ice and launched the young seals prematurely into the water. And so, when the law at last allowed us to begin work, Nature had left us with very little work to do. However, at dawn upon April 3, the ship's company took to the ice, and began to gather in its murderous harvest. It is brutal work, though not more brutal than that which goes on to supply every dinner-table in the country. And yet those glaring crimson pools upon the dazzling white of the icefields, under the peaceful silence of a blue Arctic sky, did seem a horrible intrusion. But an inexorable demand creates an inexorable supply, and the seals, by their death, help to give a living to the long line of seamen, dockers, tanners, curers, triers, chandlers, leather merchants and oil-sellers who stand between this annual butchery on the one hand, and the exquisite, with his soft leather boots, or the savant, using a delicate oil for his philosophical instruments, upon the other.

I have cause to remember that first day of sealing on account of the adventures which befell me. I have said that a strong swell had arisen, and as this was dashing the floating ice together the captain thought it dangerous for an inexperienced man to venture upon it. And so, just as I was clambering over the bulwarks with the rest, he ordered me back and told me to remain on board. My remonstrances were useless, and at last, in the blackest of tempers, I seated myself upon the top of the bulwarks, with my feet dangling over the outer side, and there I nursed my wrath, swinging up and down with the roll of the ship. It chanced, however, that I was really seated upon a thin sheet of ice which had formed upon the wood, and so when the swell threw her over to a particularly acute angle, I shot off and vanished into the sea between two ice-blocks. As I rose, I clawed on to one of these, and soon scrambled on board again. The accident brought about what I wished, however, for the captain remarked that as I was bound to fall into the ocean in any case, I might just as well be on the ice as on the ship. I justified his original caution by falling in twice again during the day, and I finished it ignominiously by having to take to my bed while all my clothes were drying in the engine-room. I was consoled for my misfortunes by finding that they amused the captain to such an extent that they drove the ill-success of our sealing out of his head, and I had to answer to the name of 'the great northern diver' for a long time thereafter. I had a narrow escape once through stepping backwards over the edge of a piece of floating ice while I was engaged in skinning a seal. I had wandered away from the others, and no one saw my misfortune. The face of the ice was so even that I had no purchase by which to pull myself up, and my body was rapidly becoming numb in the freezing water. At last, however, I caught hold of the hind flipper of the dead seal, and there was a kind of nightmare tug-of-war, the question being whether I should pull the seal off or pull myself on. At last, however, I got my knee over the edge and rolled on to it. I remember that my clothes were as hard as a suit of armour by the time I reached the ship, and that I had to thaw my crackling garments before I could change them.

This April sealing is directed against the mothers and young. Then, in May, the sealer goes farther north, and about latitude 77° or 78° he comes upon the old male seals, who are by no means such easy victims. They are wary creatures, and it takes good long-range shooting to bag them. Then, in June, the sealing is over, and the ship bears away farther north still, until in the 79th or 80th degree she is in the best Greenland whaling latitudes. There we stayed for three months or so, with very varying fortunes, for though we pursued many whales, only four were slain.

There are eight boats on board a whaler, but it is usual to send out only seven, for it takes six men to man each, so that when seven are out no one is left on board save the so-called 'idlers' who have not signed to do seaman's work at all. It happened, however, that aboard the *Hope* the idlers were rather a hefty crowd, so we volunteered to man the odd boat, and we made it, in our own estimation at least, one of the most efficient, both in sealing and in whaling. The steward, the second engineer, the donkey-engine man, and I were the oars, with a red-headed Highlander for harpooner and the handsome outlaw to steer. Our tally of seals was high, and in whaling we were once the lancing and once the harpooning boat, so our record was good. So congenial was the work to me that Captain Gray was good enough to offer to make me harpooner as well as surgeon, with the double pay, if I would come with him on a second voyage. It is well that I refused, for the life is dangerously fascinating.

It is exciting work pulling on to a whale. Your own back is turned to him, and all you know about him is what you read upon the face of the boat-steerer. He is staring out over your head, watching the creature as it swims slowly through the water, raising his hand now and again as a signal to stop rowing when he sees that the eye is coming round, and then resuming the stealthy approach when the whale is end on. There are so many floating pieces of ice, that as long as the oars are quiet the boat alone will not cause the creature to dive. So you creep slowly up, and at last you are so near that the boat-steerer knows that you can get there before the creature has time to dive – for it takes some little time to get that huge body into motion. You see a sudden gleam in his eyes, and a flush in his cheeks, and it's, 'Give way, boys! Give way, all! Hard!' Click goes the trigger of the big harpoon gun, and the foam flies from your oars. Six strokes, perhaps, and then with a dull greasy squelch the bows run upon something soft, and you and your oars are sent flying in every direction. But little you care for that, for as you touched the whale you have heard the crash of the gun, and know that the harpoon has been fired point-blank into the huge, lead-coloured curve of its side. The creature sinks like a stone, the bows of the boat splash down into the water again, but there is the little red Jack flying from the centre thwart to show that you are fast, and there is the line whizzing swiftly under the seats and over the bows between your outstretched feet.

And this is the great element of danger – for it is rarely indeed that the whale has spirit enough to turn upon its enemies. The line is very carefully coiled by a special man named the line-coiler, and it is warranted not to kink. If it should happen to do so, however, and if the loop catches the limbs of any one of the boat's crew, that man goes to his death so rapidly that his comrades hardly know that he has gone. It is a waste of fish to cut the line, for the victim is already hundreds of fathoms deep.

'Haud your hand, mon,' cried the harpooner, as a seaman raised his knife on such an occasion. 'The fush will be a fine thing for the widdey.' It sounds callous, but there was philosophy at the base of it.

This is the harpooning, and that boat has no more to do. But the lancing, when the weary fish is killed with the cold steel, is a more exciting because it is a more prolonged experience. You may be for half an hour so near to the creature that you can lay your hand upon its slimy side. The whale appears to have but little sensibility to pain, for it never winces when the long lances are passed through its body. But its instinct urges it to get its tail to work on the boats, and yours urges you to keep poling and boat-hooking along its side, so as to retain your safe position near its shoulder. Even there, however, we found on one occasion that we were not quite out of danger's way, for the creature in its flurry raised its huge side-flapper and poised it over the boat. One flap would have sent us to the bottom of the sea, and I can never forget how, as we pushed our way from under, each of us held one hand up to stave off that great, threatening fin – as if any strength of ours could have availed if the whale had meant it to descend. But it was spent with loss of blood, and instead of coming down the fin rolled over the other way, and we knew that it was dead. Who would swap that moment for any other triumph that sport can give?

The peculiar other-world feeling of the Arctic regions – a feeling so singular that if you have once been there the thought of it haunts you all your life – is due largely to the perpetual daylight. Night seems more orange-tinted and subdued than day, but there is no great difference. Some captains have been known to turn their hours right round out of caprice, with breakfast at night and supper at ten in the morning. There are your twenty-four hours, and you may carve them as you like. After a month or two the eyes grow weary of the eternal light, and you appreciate what a soothing thing our darkness is. I can remember as we came abreast of Iceland, on our return, catching our first glimpse of a star, and being unable to take my eyes from it, it seemed such a dainty little twinkling thing. Half the beauties of nature are lost through over-familiarity.

Your sense of loneliness also heightens the effect of the Arctic seas. When we were in whaling latitudes it is probable that, with the exception of our consort, there was no vessel within eight hundred miles of us. For seven long months no letter and no news came to us from the southern world. We had left in exciting times. The Afghan campaign had been undertaken, and war seemed imminent with Russia. We returned opposite the mouth of the Baltic without any means of knowing whether some cruiser might not treat us as we had treated the whales. When we met a fishing-boat at the north of Shetland our first enquiry was as to peace or war. Great events had happened during those seven months: the defeat of Maiwand and the famous march of Roberts from Kabul to Kandahar. But it was all haze to us; and, to this day, I have never been able to get that particular bit of military history straightened out in my own mind.

The perpetual light, the glare of the white ice, the deep blue of the water, these are the things which one remembers most clearly, and the dry, crisp, exhilarating air, which makes mere life the keenest of pleasures. And then there are the innumerable sea-birds, whose call is forever ringing in your ears – the gulls, the fulmars, the snow-birds, the burgomasters, the looms and the rotjes. These fill the air and, below, the waters are forever giving you a peep of some strange new creature. The commercial whale may not often come your way, but his less valuable brethren abound on every side. The finner shows his ninety feet of worthless tallow, with the absolute conviction that no whaler would condescend to lower a boat for him. The misshapen hunchback whale, the ghostlike white whale, the narwhal, with his unicorn horn, the queer-looking bottle-nose, the huge, sluggish, Greenland shark, and the terrible killing grampus, the most formidable of all the monsters of the deep – these are the creatures who own those unsailed seas. On the ice are the seals, the saddlebacks, the ground seals and the huge bladder-noses, twelve feet from nose to tail, with the power of blowing up a great blood-red football upon their noses when they are angry, which they usually are. Occasionally one sees a white Arctic fox upon the ice, and everywhere are the bears. The floes in the neighbourhood of the sealing-ground are all crisscrossed with their tracks – poor harmless creatures, with the lurch and roll of a deep-sea mariner. It is for the sake of the seals that they come out over those hundreds of miles of ice; and they have a very ingenious method of catching them, for they will choose a big icefield with just one blow-hole for seals in the middle of it. Here the bear will squat, with its powerful forearms crooked round the hole. Then, when the seal's head pops up, the great paws snap together, and Bruin has got his luncheon. We used occasionally to burn some of the cook's refuse in the engine-room fires, and the smell would, in a few hours, bring up every bear for many miles to leeward of us.

Though twenty or thirty whales have been taken in a single year in the Greenland seas, it is probable that the great slaughter of last century has diminished their number until there are not more than a few hundred in existence. I mean, of course, of the right whale, for the others, as I have said, abound. It is difficult to compute the numbers of a species which comes and goes over great tracts of water and among huge icefields, but the fact that the same whale is often pursued by the same whaler upon successive trips shows how limited their number must be. There was one, I remember, which was conspicuous through having a huge wart, the size and shape of a beehive, upon one of the flukes of its tail. 'I've been after that fellow three times,' said the captain, as we dropped our boats. 'He got away in 1871. In '74 we had him fast, but the harpoon drew. In '76 a fog saved him. It's odds that we have him now!' I fancied that the betting lay rather the other way myself, and so it proved, for that warty tail is still thrashing the Arctic seas for all that I know to the contrary.

I shall never forget my own first sight of a right whale. It had been seen by the look-out on the other side of a small icefield, but had sunk as we all rushed on deck. For ten minutes we awaited its reappearance, and I had taken my eyes from the place, when a general gasp of astonishment made me glance up, and there was the whale *in the air*. Its tail was curved just as a trout's is in jumping, and every bit of its glistening lead-coloured body was clear of the water. It was little wonder that I should be astonished, for the captain, after thirty voyages, had never seen such a sight. On catching it we discovered that it was very thickly covered with a red, crab-like parasite, about the size of a shilling, and we conjectured that it was the irritation of these creatures which had driven it wild. If a man had short, nailless flippers, and a prosperous family of fleas upon his back, he would appreciate the situation.

Apart from sport, there is a glamour about those circum-polar regions which must affect everyone who has penetrated to them. My heart goes out to that old, grey-headed whaling captain who, having been left for an instant when at death's door, staggered off in his night gear, and was found by nurses far from his house and still, as he mumbled, 'pushing to the norrard'. So an Arctic fox, which a friend of mine endeavoured to tame, escaped, and was caught many months afterwards in a gamekeeper's trap in Caithness. It was also pushing norrard, though who can say by what strange compass it took its bearings? It is a region of purity, of white ice and of blue water, with no human dwelling within a thousand miles to sully the freshness of the breeze which blows across the icefields. And then it is a region of romance also. You stand on the very brink of the unknown, and every duck that you shoot bears pebbles in its gizzard which come from a land which the maps know not. It was a strange and fascinating chapter of my life.

I went on board the whaler a big, straggling youth, I came off it a powerful, well-grown man. I have no doubt that my physical health during my whole life has been affected by that splendid air, and that the inexhaustible store of energy which I have enjoyed is to some extent drawn from the same source. It was mental and spiritual stagnation, or even worse, for there is a coarsening effect in so circumscribed a life with comrades who were fine, brave fellows, but naturally rough and wild. However I had my health to show for it, and also more money than I had ever possessed before. I was still boyish in many ways, and I remember that I concealed gold pieces in every pocket of every garment, that my mother might have the excitement of hunting for them. It added some fifty pounds to her small exchequer.

Now I had a straight run in to my final examination, which I passed with fair but not notable distinction at the end of the winter session of 1881. I was now a Bachelor of Medicine and a Master of Surgery, fairly launched upon my professional career.

5

The Voyage to West Africa

It had always been my intention to take a voyage as ship's surgeon when I had taken my degree, as I could in this way see something of the world, and at the same time earn a little of the money which I so badly needed if I were ever to start in practice for myself. When a man is in the very early twenties he will not be taken seriously as a practitioner, and though I looked old for my age, it was clear that I had to fill in my time in some other way. My plans were all exceedingly fluid, and I was ready to join the army, navy, Indian Service or anything which offered an opening. I had no reason to think that I would find a billet upon a passenger ship and had nearly forgotten that I had my name down when I suddenly received a telegram telling me to come to Liverpool and to take medical charge of the African Steam Navigation Company's *Mayumba*, bound for the West Coast. In a week I was there, and on October 22, 1881, we started on our voyage.

The *Mayumba* was a trim little steamer of about 4,000 tons – a giant after my experience in the 200-ton whaler. She was built for commerce, carrying mixed cargoes to the coast and coming back with palm oil in puncheons, palm nuts in bulk, ivory and other tropical products. What with whale oil and palm oil there certainly seemed to be something greasy about my horoscope. There was room for twenty or thirty passengers, and it was for their behoof that I was paid some twelve pounds a month.

It was well that we were seaworthy, for we put out in a violent gale which became so bad as we emerged from the Mersey that we were forced into Holyhead for the night. Next day, in vile and thick weather, with a strong sea running, we made our way down the Irish Sea. I shall always believe that I may have saved the ship from disaster, for as I was standing near the officer of the watch I suddenly caught sight of a lighthouse standing out in a rift in the fog. It was on the port side and I could not imagine how any lighthouse could be on the port side of a ship which was, as I knew, well down on the Irish coast. I hate to be an alarmist, so I simply touched the mate's sleeve, pointed to the dim outline of the lighthouse, and said: 'Is that all right?' He fairly jumped as his eye lit upon it and he gave a yell to the men at the wheel and rang a violent signal to the engine-room. The lighthouse, if I remember right, was the Tuskar, and we were heading right into a rocky promontory which was concealed by the rain and fog.

I have been lucky in my captains, for Captain Gordon Wallace was one of the best, and we have kept in touch during the later years. Our passengers were mostly for Madeira, but there were some pleasant ladies bound for the Coast, and some unpleasant negro traders whose manners and bearing were objectionable, but who were patrons of the line and must, therefore, be tolerated. Some of these palm oil chiefs and traders have incomes of many thousands a year, but as they have no cultivated tastes they can only spend their money on drink, debauchery and senseless extravagance. One of them, I remember, had a choice selection of the *demi-monde* of Liverpool to see him off.

The storms followed us all the way down the Channel and across the Bay, which is normal, I suppose, at such a time of year. Everyone was seasick, so as doctor I had some work to do. However, before we reached Madeira we ran into fine weather and all our troubles were soon forgotten. One never realises the comfort of a dry deck until one has been ankle-deep for a week. I missed the sea-boots and rough-and-ready dress of the whaler, for when one is in blue serge and gilt buttons one does not care to take a ducking. Just as we thought, however, that we were all right a worse gale than ever broke over us, the wind luckily being behind us, so that it helped us on our way. With jib, trysail and main staysail, which was as much as we could stand, we lurched and staggered, swept every now and then by the big Atlantic combers, which were phosphorescent at night, so that flames of liquid fire came coursing down the decks. Very glad we were when after a week of storm we saw the rugged peaks of Porto Sancto, an outlier of Madeira, and finally came to anchor in Funchal Bay. It was dark when we reached our moorings and it was good to see the lights of the town, and the great dark loom of the hills behind it. A lunar rainbow spanned the whole scene, a rare phenomenon which I have never seen before or since.

Tenerife was our next stopping-place, Santa Cruz being the port of call. In those days it did a great trade in cochineal, which was derived from an insect cultivated on the cacti. When dried they furnished the dye, and a packet of the creatures averaged £350 at that time, but now I suppose that the German aniline dyes have killed the trade as completely as whaling has been killed by the mineral. A day later we were at Las Palmas, capital of Grand Canary, whence, looking back, we had a fine view of the famous Tenerife Peak some sixty miles away. Leaving Las Palmas we were in the delightful region of the north-east trade-winds, the most glorious part of the ocean, seldom rough, yet always lively, with foam-capped seas and a clear sky. Day by day it grew hotter, however, and when we lost the trades, and sighted the Isle de Los off the Sierra Leone coast, I began to realise what the Tropics meant. When you feel your napkin at meals to be an intolerable thing, and when you find that it leaves a wet weal across your white duck trousers, then you know that you really have arrived.

On November 9 we reached Freetown, the capital of Sierra Leone, our first port of call upon the African main – a lovely spot but a place of death. Here our ladies left us, and indeed it was sad to see them go, for female lives are even shorter than male upon the coast. I speak of the days of malaria and blackwater fever, before Ronald Ross and others had done their great work of healing and prevention. It was a truly dreadful place in the early 1880s, and the despair which reigned in the hearts of the white people made them take liberties with alcohol which they would not have dared to take in a healthier place. A year's residence seemed to be about the limit of human endurance. I remember meeting one healthy-looking resident who told me that he had been there three years. When I congratulated him he shook his head. 'I am a doomed man. I have advanced Bright's disease,' said he. One wondered whether the colonies were really worth the price we had to pay.

From Sierra Leone we steamed to Monrovia, which is the capital of the negro republic of Liberia, which, as the name implies, was founded mainly by escaped slaves. So far as I could see it was orderly enough, though all small communities which take themselves seriously have a comic aspect. Thus at the time of the Franco-German War, Liberia is said to have sent out its single customs boat, which represented its official navy, and stopped the British mail-ship in order to send word to Europe that it did not intend to interfere in the matter.

It is a very monotonous view, for whether it is the Ivory Coast or the Gold Coast or the Liberian shore, it always presents the same features – burning sunshine, a long swell breaking into a white line of surf, a margin of golden sand, and then the low green bush, with an occasional palm tree rising above it. If you have seen a mile, you have seen a thousand. As I write now, these ports at which we stopped, Grand Bassam, Cape Palmas, Accra, Cape Coast Castle, all form the same picture in my mind. One incident only I can remember. At some small village, the name of which I have forgotten, there came off a tall young Welshman in a state of furious excitement; his niggers had mutinied and he was in fear of his life. 'There they are waiting for me!' he cried, and pointed to a dusky group upon the distant beach. We offered to take him on, but he could not leave his property, so all we could do was to promise to send a gunboat up from Cape Coast Castle. I have often wondered how such people got on after the German menace compelled us to draw in all our outlying fleets.

This coast is dotted at night with native fires, some of them of great extent, arising no doubt from their habit of burning the grass. It is interesting that in Hanno's account of his journey down the coast – the only piece of Carthaginian literature which has reached us – he talks also of the fires which he saw at night. As he speaks of gorillas it is probable that he got as far as the Gabon, or south of the Line. He saw great volcanic activity, and the remains of it is still visible at Fernando Po, which is almost all volcanic. In Hanno's time, however, the hills were actually spouting fire and the country was a sea of flame, so that he dare not set foot on shore. I have wondered sometimes whether the last cataclysm at Atlantis may not have been much later than we think. The account of Plato puts it at about 9000 BC, but it may well have been a gradual thing and the last spasm have been that of which Hanno saw the traces. All this activity which he described is exactly opposite the spot where the old continent was supposed to have been.

Our ships have rough-and-ready ways as they jog down the coast. Once we moved on while a hundred native visitors were still on board. It was funny to see them dive off and make for their canoes. One of them had a tall hat, an umbrella, and a large coloured picture of the Saviour – all of which he had bought at the trading booths which the men rig up in the forecastle. These impedimenta did not prevent him from swimming to his boat. At another minor port, since we were pressed for time, we simply threw our consignment of barrel staves overboard, knowing that soon or late they would wash up on the beach, though how the real owner could make good his claim to them I do not know. Occasionally the native scores in this game. Some years ago, before Dahomey was annexed by the French, the captain took the oil casks on board at Whydah by means of a long rope and a donkey engine, an ingenious way of avoiding the surf which came to a sudden stop when a company of the famous Amazons appeared and threatened to fire upon the ship if they did not pay their dues to the surf boats in the ordinary fashion.

I had myself to pay my dues to the climate, for on November 18 I find an eloquent gap in my diary. We had reached Lagos, and there, rolling in a greasy swell off that huge lagoon, the germ or the mosquito or whatever it was reached me and I was down with a very sharp fever. I remember staggering to my bunk and then all was blotted out. As I was myself doctor there was no one to look after me and I lay for several days fighting it out with Death in a very small ring and without a second. It speaks well for my constitution that I came out the victor. I remember no psychic experience, no vision, no fears, nothing save a nightmare fog from which I emerged as weak as a child. It must have been a close call, and I had scarcely sat up before I heard that another victim who got it at the same time was dead.

A week later found me, convalescent and full of energy once more, up the Bonny River, which certainly never got its name from the Scotch adjective, for it is in all ways hateful with its brown smelling stream and its mango swamps. The natives were all absolute savages, offering up human sacrifices to sharks and crocodiles. The captain had heard the screams of the victims and seen them dragged down to the water's edge, while on another occasion he had seen the protruding skull of a man who had been buried in an ant-heap. It is all very well to make game of the missionaries, but how could such people ever be improved if it were not for the labours of devoted men?

We called at Fernando Po, and later at Victoria, a lovely little settlement upon the main, with the huge peak of the Cameroons rising behind it. A dear homely Scotch lassie was playing the part of missionary there, and if she did not evangelise she at least civilised, which is more important. It lies in a beautiful bay studded with islands and well wooded all round. For some reason the whole style of the scenery changes completely here, and it is the more welcome after the thousand miles of monotony to the north. All this land went, for some reason, to Germany later, and has now reverted to the French, who are not, as a rule, good colonial neighbours. I went ashore at Victoria, and I cannot forget my thrill when what I thought was a good-sized blue bird passed me and I found that it was a butterfly.

To reach Old Calabar we had to steam for sixty miles up the Old Calabar River, the channel lying so near the shore that we brushed the trees on one side. I lay in wait with my rifle, but though I saw the swirl of several alligators none emerged. Old Calabar seemed the largest and most prosperous place we had visited, but here also the hand of death was over all, and it was 'eat, drink, and be merry' for the old and unsatisfactory reason. Here again we met one of these young lady pioneers of civilisation. Civilisation is the better, but it is a stern and dreadful call which summons a woman to such a work.

Getting a canoe, I ascended the river for several miles to a place called Creektown. Dark and terrible mangrove swamps lay on either side with gloomy shades where nothing that is not horrible could exist. It is indeed a foul place. Once in an isolated tree, standing in a flood, I saw an evil-looking snake, worm-coloured and about three feet long. I shot him and saw him drift downstream. I learned later in life to give up killing animals, but I confess that I have no particular compunction about that one. Creektown is in native territory, and the king sent down a peremptory order that we should report ourselves to him, but as it sounded ominous and might mean a long delay we got our paddles out and were soon back in British waters.

I had a curious experience one morning. A large ribbon-shaped fish, about three or four feet long, came up and swam upon the surface near the ship. Having my gun handy, I shot it. I don't think five seconds could have elapsed before another larger and thicker fish – a big catfish, I should say – darted up from the depths, seized the wounded fish by the middle, and dragged it down. So murderous is the food-search, and so keen the watch in nature! I saw something similar in the mixed tank of an aquarium once, where a fish stunned himself by swimming against the glass front, and was instantly seized and devoured by his neighbour. A strange fish to which I was introduced at Calabar was the electrical torpedo fish. It is handed to you in an earthenware saucer – a quiet little drab creature about five inches long – and you are asked to tickle its back. Then you learn exactly how high you can jump.

The deathlike impression of Africa grew upon me. One felt that the white man with his present diet and habits was an intruder who was never meant to be there, and that the great sullen brown continent killed him as one crushes nits. I find in my diary:

> Oh Africa, where are the charms
> That sages have seen in thy face?
> Better dwell in Old England on alms
> Than be rich in that terrible place.

The life aboard ship, however, was an easy and, in some ways, a luxurious one – too luxurious for a young man who had his way to make in the world. Premature comfort is a deadly enervating thing. I remember considering my own future – I stood upon the poop with a raging thunderstorm around me – and seeing very clearly that one or two more such voyages would sap my simple habits and make me unfit for the hard struggle which any sort of success would need. The idea of success in literature had never crossed my mind. It was still of medicine only that I thought, but I knew by my Birmingham experience how long and rough a path it was for those who had no influence and could not afford to buy. Then and there I vowed that I would wander no more, and that was surely one of the turning-points of my life. A 'Wander-Jahr' is good, but two 'Wander-Jahre' may mean damnation – and it is hard to stop. I find that on the same day of fruitful meditation I swore off alcohol for the rest of the voyage. I drank quite freely at this period of my life, having a head and a constitution which made me fairly immune, but my reason told me that the unbounded cocktails of West Africa were a danger, and with an effort I cut them out. There is a certain subtle pleasure in abstinence, and it is only socially that it is difficult. If we were all abstainers as a matter of course, like the real Mahomedans, none of us would ever miss it.

I did a mad thing at Cape Coast Castle, for, in a spirit either of bravado or pure folly, I swam round the ship – or at least for some length along her and back again. I suppose it was the consideration that black folk go freely into the water which induced me to do it. For some reason white folk do not share the same immunity. As I was drying myself on deck I saw the triangular back fin of a shark rise to the surface. Several times in my life I have done utterly reckless things with so little motive that I have found it difficult to explain them to myself afterwards. This was one of them.

The most intelligent and well-read man whom I met on the Coast was a negro, the American consul at Monrovia. He came on with us as a passenger. My starved literary side was eager for good talk, and it was wonderful to sit on deck discussing Bancroft and Motley, and then suddenly realise that you were talking to one who had possibly been a slave himself, and was certainly the son of slaves. He had thought a good deal about African travel. 'The only way to explore Africa is to go without arms and with few servants. You would not like it in England if a body of men came armed to the teeth and marched through your land. The Africans are quite as sensitive.' It was the method of Livingstone as against the method of Stanley. The former takes the braver and better man.

This negro gentleman did me good, for a man's brain is an organ for the formation of his own thoughts and also for the digestion of other people's, and it needs fresh fodder. We had, of course, books aboard the ship, but neither many nor good. I cannot trace that I made any mental or spiritual advancement during the voyage, but I added one more experience to my chaplet, and I suppose it all goes to some ultimate result in character or personality. I was a strong full-blooded young man, full of the joy of life, with nothing of what Oliver Wendell Holmes calls 'pathological piety and tuberculous virtues'. I was a man among men. I walked ever among pitfalls and I thank all ministering angels that I came through, while I have a softened heart for those who did not.

Our voyage home – oil-gathering from port to port on the same but reversed route – was uneventful until the very last stride, when just as we were past Madeira the ship took fire. Whether it was the combustion of coal dust has never been determined, but certainly the fire broke out in the bunkers, and as there was only a wooden partition between these bunkers and a cargo of oil, we were in deadly danger. For the first day we took it lightly, as a mere smoulder, and for a second and third day we were content to seal the gratings as far as possible, to play down on it with the hose and to shift the coal away from the oil. On the fourth morning, however, things took a sudden turn for the worse. I copy from my log book:

JANUARY 9   I was awakened early in the morning by the purser, Tom King, poking his head in at my door and informing me that the ship was in a blaze, and that all hands had been called and were working down below. I got my clothes on, but when I came on deck nothing was to be seen of it save thick volumes of smoke from the bunker ventilators, and a lurid glow down below. I offered to go down, but there seemed to be as many working as could be fitted in. I was then asked to call the passengers. I waked each in turn, and they all faced the situation very bravely and coolly. One, a Swiss, sat up in his bunk, rubbed his eyes, and in answer to my remark: 'The ship is on fire!' said: 'I have often been on ships that were on fire.' *Splendide mendax* – but a good spirit! All day we fought the flames, and the iron side of the ship was red-hot at one point. Boats were prepared and provisioned and no doubt at the worst we could row or sail them to Lisbon, where my dear sisters would be considerably surprised if their big brother walked in. However, we are getting the better of it, and by evening those ominous pillars of smoke were down to mere wisps. So ends an ugly business!

On January 14 we were in Liverpool once more, and West Africa was but one more of the cinema reels of memory. It is, I am told, very much improved now in all things. My old friend and cricket companion Sir Fred Guggisberg is governor at Accra and has asked me to see the old ground under very different auspices. I wish I could, but the sands still run and there is much to be done.

6

My First Experiences in Practice

A Strange Character – His Honeymoon – His Bristol Practice –
Telegram from Plymouth – Six Amusing Weeks – A Deep Plot –
My Southsea Venture – Furnishing on the Cheap – The Plot
Explodes

I have now come to the temporary end of my voyages, which were to be renewed in years to come, and I have reached the time when, under very curious circumstances, I endeavoured to establish myself in medical practice. In a book written some years afterwards called *The Stark Munro Letter*s, I drew in very close detail the events of the next few years, and there the curious reader will find them more clearly and fully set out than would be to scale in these pages. I would only remark, should any reader reconstruct me or my career from that book, that there are some few incidents there which are imaginary, and that, especially, the whole incident of the case of a lunatic and of Lord Saltire in Chapter 4 occurred to a friend and not to myself. Otherwise the whole history of my association with the man whom I called Cullingworth, his extraordinary character, our parting and the way in which I was left to what seemed certain ruin, were all as depicted. I will here simply give the essentials of the story, and retain the fictitious name.

In my last year of study at Edinburgh I formed a friendship with this remarkable student. He came of a famous medical family, his father having been a great authority upon zymotic disease. He came also of famous athletic stock, and was a great Rugby forward himself, though rather handicapped by the berserk fury with which he would play. He was up to international form, and his younger brother was reckoned by good judges to be about the best forward who ever donned the rose-embroidered jersey of England.

Cullingworth was as strong mentally as physically. In person he was about 5 ft 9 in. in height, perfectly built, with a bulldog jaw, bloodshot deep-set eyes, overhanging brows and yellowish hair as stiff as wire, which spurted up above his brows. He was a man born for trouble and adventure, unconventional in his designs and formidable in his powers of execution – a man of action with a big but incalculable brain guiding the action. He died in early middle age, and I understand that an autopsy revealed some cerebral abnormality, so that there was no doubt a pathological element in his strange explosive character. For some reason he took a fancy to me, and appeared to attach an undue importance to my advice.

When I met him first he had just indulged in one of his wild escapades, which ended usually in a fight or in a transitory appearance in a police court, but on this occasion was more serious and permanent. He had run off with a charming young lady and married her, she being a ward in Chancery and under age. However, the deed was done and all the lawyers in the world could not undo it, though they might punish the culprit. He told me how he and the lady had gone over a *Bradshaw* with the intention that when they came on a station of which neither of them had ever heard, they would make for that place and spend their honeymoon there. They came therefore upon some awful name, Clod-pole-in-the-Marsh or something of the kind, and there they sojourned in the village inn. Cullingworth stained his yellow hair black, but the stain took in some places and not in others, so that he looked as if he had escaped from Barnum's show. What Clodpole-in-the-Marsh could have thought of such an extraordinary couple I cannot imagine, and it is probably the one occasion on which it ever buzzed. I cannot think of any surer way of getting publicity than that which Cullingworth took to avoid detection. In London they would have been perfectly un-observed. I remember that for years Cullingworth's hair presented curious iridescent tints which were the remains of his disguise.

He brought his bride safely to Edinburgh, where they hired a flat and lived in it without furnishing it save for the absolutely needful. I have dined with them there on an apple dumpling, seated on a pile of thick volumes as there was no chair. We introduced them to a few friends, did what we could for the lonely lady, and finally they drifted off, and for a time we heard no more.

Just before I started for Africa I got a long telegram from Culling-worth imploring me to go to Bristol as he needed my advice. I was in Birmingham and I set forth at once. When I reached Bristol he conducted me to a fine mansion, and there poured out his tale of woe. He had started in great style, hoping to rally the remains of his father's patients, but his money had run out, he was dunned by his tradespeople, there were no patients, and what was he to do? We had a joyous riotous time for two days, for there was an exuberant atmosphere about the man which rose above all trouble. The only advice I could give was that he should make a composition with his creditors. I heard afterwards that he assembled them, addressed them in a long and emotional speech, reduced them almost to tears with his picture of the struggles of a deserving young man, and finally got a unanimous vote of confidence from them with full consent that he should pay at his own leisure. It was the sort of thing that he would do, and tell the story afterwards with a bull's roar of laughter which could be heard down the street.

When I had been back a couple of months from Africa, I received another telegram – he always telegraphed and never wrote – which ran in some such way as this: 'Started here last June. Colossal success. Come down by next train if possible. Plenty of room for you. Splendid opening.' The telegram was stamped Plymouth. A second even more explosive telegram upbraided me for delay and guaranteed me three hundred pounds the first year. This looked like business, so off I went.

The events of the next six weeks, in the late spring and early summer of 1882, were more fitted for some rollicking novel than for the sober pages of a veracious chronicle. The conditions which I found at Plymouth were incredible. In a short time this man, half genius and half quack, had founded a practice worth several thousand pounds of ready money in the year. 'Free consultations but pay for your medicine', was his slogan, and as he charged a good price for the latter it worked out all the same in the end. The mere words 'Free Consultations' attracted crowds. He used drugs in a heroic and indiscriminate manner which produced dramatic results but at an unjustifiable risk. I remember one instance where dropsy had disappeared before a severe dose of croton oil in a way that set all the gossips talking. People flocked into the town from twenty and thirty miles round, and not only his waiting-rooms, but his stairs and his passages, were crammed. His behaviour to them was extraordinary. He roared and shouted, scolded them, joked them, pushed them about and pursued them sometimes into the street or addressed them collectively from the landing. A morning with him when the practice was in full blast was as funny as any pantomime and I was exhausted with laughter. He had a well-worn volume on medical jurisprudence which he pretended was the Bible, and he swore old women on it that they would drink no more tea. I have no doubt he did a great deal of good, for there was reason and knowledge behind all that he did, but his manner of doing it was unorthodox in the extreme. His wife made up the prescriptions at a pigeonhole at the end of a passage, and received the price which was marked on the label carried down by the patient. Every evening Cullingworth walked back to his great residential house upon the Hoe, bearing his bag of silver, his coat flying, his hat on the back of his head, and his great fangs grinning up at every doctor whose disgusted face showed at a window.

Cullingworth had rigged me up a room, furnished with one table and two chairs, in which I could take surgical or other cases which he did not care to handle. I fear that my professional manners were very unexciting after his more flamboyant efforts, which I could not imitate even if I would. I had, however, a steady dribble of patients, and it looked as if I might build something up. I went up country once, and operated upon an old fellow's nose which had contracted cancer through his holding the bowl of a short clay pipe immediately beneath it. I left him with an aristocratic not to say supercilious organ, which was the wonder of the village and might have been the foundation of my fame.

But there were other influences at work, and the threads of fate were shooting out at strange unexpected angles. My mother had greatly resented my association with Cullingworth. Her family pride had been aroused, and justly as I can now see, though my wanderings had left me rather too Bohemian and careless upon points of etiquette. But I liked Cullingworth and even now I can't help liking him – and I admired his strong qualities and enjoyed his company and the extraordinary situations which arose from any association with him. This resistance upon my part, and my defence of my friend, annoyed my mother the more, and she wrote me several letters of remonstrance which certainly dealt rather faithfully with his character as it appeared to her. I was careless of my papers and these letters were read both by Cullingworth and his wife. I do them no injustice in saying this, for they finally admitted it. Apparently he imagined – he was a man of strange suspicions and secret plottings – that I was a party to such sentiments, whereas they were actually called forth by my defence of him. His manner changed, and more than once I caught his fierce grey eyes looking furtively at me with a strange sullen expression, so much so that I asked him what was the matter. He was actually scheming my ruin, which would be nothing financially, since I had nothing to lose, but would be much both to my mother and me if it touched my honour.

One day he came to me and told me that he thought my presence complicated his practice and that we had better part. I agreed in all good humour, assuring him that I had not come to hurt him and that I was very grateful for what he had done, even if it came to nothing. He then strongly advised me to go into practice myself. I replied that I had no capital. He answered that he would see to that, that he would allow me a pound a week until I got my feet under me, and that I could repay it at leisure. I thanked him warmly, and after looking at Tavistock I finally decided that Portsmouth would be a good place, the only reason being that I knew the conditions at Plymouth, and Portsmouth seemed analogous. I boarded an Irish steamer, therefore, and about July of 1882 I started off by sea, with one small trunk containing all my earthly possessions, to start practice in a town in which I knew no single soul. My cash balance was under ten pounds, and I knew not only that I had to meet all present expenses upon this, but that I had to furnish a house upon it. On the other hand the weekly pound should easily cover all personal needs, and I had the devil-may-care optimism of youth as to the future.

When I arrived at Portsmouth I went into lodgings for a week. On the very first night, with that curious faculty for running into dramatic situations which has always been with me, I became involved in a street fight with a rough who was beating (or rather kicking) a woman. It was a strange start, and after I began my practice one of the first people to whom I opened my door was this very rascal. I don't suppose he recognised me, but I could have sworn to him. I emerged from the fray without much damage, and was very glad to escape some serious scandal. It was the second time that I had got knocked about in defence of beauty in distress.

I spent a week in marking down the unoccupied houses, and finally settled at forty pounds a year into Bush Villa, which a kindly landlord has now called Doyle House. I was terrified lest the agent should ask for a deposit, but the name of my C.B. uncle as reference turned the scale in my favour. Having secured the empty house and its key, I went down to a sale in Portsea and for about four pounds secured quite a lot of second-hand – possibly tenth-hand – furniture. It met my needs and enabled me to make one room possible for patients with three chairs, a table and a central patch of carpet. I had a bed of sorts and a mattress upstairs. I fixed up the plate which I had brought from Plymouth, bought a red lamp on tick, and fairly settled down in receipt of custom. When all was done I had a couple of pounds in hand. Servants, of course, were out of the question, so I polished my own plate every morning, brushed down my front, and kept the house reasonably clean. I found that I could live quite easily and well on less than a shilling a day, so I could hold out for a long period.

I had at this time contributed several stories to *London Society*, a magazine now defunct but then flourishing under the editorship of a Mr Hogg. In the April 1882 number I had a story, now happily forgotten, called 'Bones', while in the preceding Christmas number I had had another, 'The Gully of Bluemansdyke', both of them feeble echoes of Bret Harte. These, with the stories already mentioned, made up my whole output at this time. I explained to Mr Hogg how I was situated, and wrote for him a new tale for his Christmas number entitled 'My Friend the Murderer'. Hogg behaved very well and sent me ten pounds, which I laid by for my first quarter's rent. I was not so pleased with him when, years later, he claimed the full copyright of all these immature stories, and published them in a volume with my name attached. Have a care, young authors, have a care, or your worst enemy will be your early self!

It was as well that I had that ten pounds, for Cullingworth, having learned that I was fairly committed, with my lease signed, now hurled his thunderbolt, which he thought would crush me. It was a curt letter – not a telegram for a wonder – in which he admitted that my letters had been read, expressed surprise that such a correspondence should have gone on while I was under his roof, and declared that he could have nothing more to do with me. He had, of course, no real grievance, but I am quite willing to admit that he honestly thought he had. But his method of revenge was a strange example of the schemings of a morbid mind.

For a moment I was staggered. But my boats were burned and I must go forward. I sent back a derisive reply to Cullingworth, and put him out of my head for ever – indeed, I heard of him no more until some five years later I read the news of his premature death. He was a remarkable man and narrowly escaped being a great one. I fear that he lived up to his great income and left his wife but poorly off.

7

My Start at Southsea

A Strange Life – Arrival of My Brother – I Buy up a Shop – Cheap
Servants – Queer Patients – Dangers of Medical Practice – Income-
Tax Joke – Tragedy in My House – My Marriage – A New Phase

What with cleaning up, answering the bell, doing my modest shopping,
which was measured in pennies rather than shillings, and perfecting my
simple household arrangements, the time did not hang heavily upon
my hands. It is a wonderful thing to have a house of your own for the
first time, however humble it may be. I lavished all my care upon
the front room to make it possible for patients. The back room was
furnished with my trunk and a stool. Inside the trunk was my larder,
and the top of it was my dining-room table. There was gas laid on, and I
rigged a projection from the wall by which I could sling a pan over the
gas jet. In this way I cooked bacon with great ease, and became expert in
getting a wonderful lot of slices from a pound. Bread, bacon and tea,
with an occasional saveloy – what could man ask for more? It is (or was)
perfectly easy to live well upon a shilling a day.

I had obtained a fair consignment of drugs on tick from a wholesale
house and these also were ranged round the sides of the back room.
From the very beginning a few stray patients of the poorest class, some
of them desirous of novelty, some disgruntled with their own doctors,
the greater part owing bills and ashamed to face their creditor, came to
consult me and consume a bottle of my medicine. I could pay for my
food by the drugs I sold. It was as well, for I had no other way of paying
for it, and I had sworn not to touch the ten golden pieces which
represented my rent. There have been times when I could not buy a
postage stamp and my letters have had to wait, but the ten golden coins
still remained intact.

It was a busy thoroughfare, with a church on one side of my house
and a hotel on the other. The days passed pleasantly enough, for it was
a lovely warm autumn, and I sat in the window of my consulting-room,
screened by the rather dingy curtain which I had put up, and watched

the passing crowd or read my book, for I had spent part of my scanty funds on making myself a member of a circulating library. In spite of my sparse food, or more probably on account of it, I was extraordinarily fit and well, so that at night when all hope of patients was gone for that day I would lock up my house and walk many miles to work off my energy. With its imperial associations it is a glorious place and even now if I had to live in a town outside London it is surely to Southsea, the residential quarter of Portsmouth, that I would turn. The history of the past carries on into the history of today, the new torpedo boat flies past the old *Victory* with the same white ensign flying from each, and the old Elizabethan culverins and sakers can still be seen in the same walk which brings you to the huge artillery of the forts. There is a great glamour there to anyone with the historic sense – a sense which I drank in with my mother's milk.

It had never entered my head yet that literature might give me a career, or anything beyond a little casual pocket money, but already it was a deciding factor in my life, for I could not have held on and must have either starved or given in but for the few pounds which Mr Hogg sent me, for they enabled all other smaller sums to be spent in nourishment. I have wondered sometimes as I look back that I did not contract scurvy, for most of my food was potted, and I had no means of cooking vegetables. However, I felt no grievance at the time, nor any particular perception that my mode of life was unusual, nor indeed any particular anxiety about the future. At that age everything seems an adventure – and there was always the novel pleasure of the house.

Once I had a moment of weakness during which I answered an advertisement which asked for a doctor to attend coolies in the tea gardens of the Terai. I spent a few unsettled days waiting for an answer, but none came and I settled down once more to my waiting and hoping. I had one avenue of success open of which I could not avail myself. My Catholic relatives had sent me an introduction to the bishop and I was assured that there was no Catholic doctor in the town. My mind, however, was so perfectly clear and I had so entirely broken away from the old faith that I could not possibly use it for material ends. I therefore burned the letter of introduction.

As the weeks passed and I had no one with whom to talk I began to think wistfully of the home circle at Edinburgh, and to wonder why, with my eight-roomed house, one or more of them should not come to keep me company. The girls were already governessing or preparing to do so, but there was my little brother Innes. It would relieve my mother and yet help me if he could join me. So it was arranged, and one happy evening the little knicker-bockered fellow, just ten years old, joined me as my comrade. No man could have had a merrier and brighter one. In a few weeks we had settled down to a routine life, I having found a good day-school for him. The soldiers of Portsmouth were already a great joy to him, and his future career was marked out by his natural tastes, for he was a born leader and administrator. Little did I foresee that he would win distinction in the greatest of all wars, and die in the prime of his manhood – but not before he knew that complete victory had been attained. Even then our thoughts were very military, and I remember how we waited together outside the office of the local paper that we might learn the result of the bombardment of Alexandria.

Turning over some old papers after these pages were written I came upon a letter written in straggling schoolboy script by my little brother to his mother at home which may throw an independent light upon those curious days. It is dated August 16, 1882. He says:

> The patients are crowding in. We have made three bob this week. We have vaxinated a baby and got hold of a man with consumtion, and today a gypsy's cart came up to the door selling baskets and chairs so we determined to let the man ring as long as he liked. After he had rong two or three times Arthur yelled out at the pitch of his voice, Go a way but the man rang again so I went down to the door and pulled open the letter box and cried out go a way. The man began to swere at me and say that he wanted to see Arthur. All this time Arthur thought that the door was open and was yelling Shut that door. Then I came upstairs and told Arthur what the man had said so Arthur went down and opened the door and we found out that the gypsy's child had measles . . . After all we got sixpence out of them and that is all ways something.

I remember the incident well, and certainly my sudden change of tone from the indignant householder, who is worried by a tramp, to my best bedside manner in the hopes of a fee, must have been very amusing. My recollection is, however, that it was the gypsy who got sixpence out of us.

For some time Innes and I lived entirely alone, doing the household tasks between us, and going long walks in the evening to keep ourselves fit. Then I had a brainwave and I put an advertisement in the evening paper that a ground floor was to let in exchange for services. I had numerous applicants in reply, and out of them I chose two elderly women who claimed to be sisters – a claim which they afterwards failed to make good. When once they were installed we became quite a civilised household and things began to look better. There were complex quarrels, however, and one of the women left. The other soon afterwards followed suit. As the first woman had seemed to me to be the most efficient, I followed her up and found that she had started a small shop. Her rent was weekly, so that was easily settled, but she talked gloomily about her stock. 'I will buy everything in your shop,' I said in a large way. It cost me exactly seventeen and sixpence, and I was loaded up for many months with matches, cakes of blacking and other merchandise. From then onwards our meals were cooked for us, and we became in all ways normal.

Month followed month and I picked up a patient here and a patient there until the nucleus of a little practice had been formed. Sometimes it was an accident, sometimes an emergency case, sometimes a new-comer to the town or one who had quarrelled with his doctor. I mixed with people so far as I could, for I learned that a brass plate alone will never attract, and people must see the human being who lies in wait behind it. Some of my tradespeople gave me their custom in return for mine, and mine was so small that I was likely to have the best of the bargain. There was a grocer who developed epileptic fits, which meant butter and tea to us. Poor fellow, he could never have realised the mixed feelings with which I received the news of a fresh outbreak. Then there was a very tall, horse-faced old lady with an extraordinary dignity of bearing. She would sit framed in the window of her little house, like the picture of a *grande dame* of the *ancien régime*. But every now and again she went on a wild burst, in the course of which she would skim plates out of the window at the passers-by. I was the only one who had influence over her at such times, for she was a haughty, autocratic old person. Once she showed an inclination to skim a plate at me also, but I quelled her by assuming a gloomy dignity as portentous as her own. She had some art treasures which she heaped upon me when she was what we will politely call 'ill', but claimed back again the moment she was well. Once when she had been particularly troublesome I retained a fine lava jug, in spite of her protests, and I have got it yet.

It is well that medical practice has its humorous side, for it has much to depress one. Most men never use their reasoning power at all on the religious side, but if they did they would find it difficult sometimes to reconcile the sights which a physician sees with the idea of a merciful providence. If one loses the explanation that this life is a spiritual chastening for another, and thinks that death ends all, and that this is our one experience, then it is impossible to sustain the goodness or the omnipotence of God. So I felt at the time, and it made me a Materialist, but now I know well that I was judging a story on the strength of one chapter.

Let me give an example. I was called in by a poor woman to see her daughter. As I entered the humble sitting-room there was a small cot at one side, and by the gesture of the mother I understood that the sufferer was there. I picked up a candle and walking over I stooped over the little bed, expecting to see a child. What I really saw was a pair of brown sullen eyes, full of loathing and pain, which looked up in resentment to mine. I could not tell how old the creature was. Long thin limbs were twisted and coiled in the tiny couch. The face was sane but malignant. 'What is it?' I asked in dismay when we were out of hearing. 'It's a girl,' sobbed the mother. 'She's nineteen. Oh! if God would only take her!' What a life for both! And how hard to face such facts and accept any of the commonplace explanations of existence!

Medical life is full of dangers and pitfalls, and luck must always play its part in a man's career. Many a good man has been ruined by pure bad luck. On one occasion I was called in to a lady who was suffering from what appeared to be dyspepsia of a rather severe type. There was absolutely nothing to indicate anything more serious. I therefore re-assured the family, spoke lightly of the illness, and walked home to make up a bismuth mixture for her, calling on one or two other cases on the way. When I got home I found a messenger waiting to say that the lady was dead. This is the sort of thing which may happen to any man at any time. It did not hurt me, for I was too lowly to be hurt. You can't ruin a practice when there is no practice. The woman really had a gastric ulcer, for which there is no diagnosis; it was eating its way into the lining of her stomach, it pierced an artery after I saw her, and she bled to death. Nothing could have saved her, and I think her relatives came to understand this.

I made £154 the first year, and £250 the second, rising slowly to £300, which in eight years I never passed, so far as the medical practice went. In the first year the Income Tax paper arrived and I filled it up to show that I was not liable. They returned the paper with 'Most unsatisfactory' scrawled across it. I wrote 'I entirely agree' under the words, and returned it once more. For this little bit of cheek I was had up before the assessors, and duly appeared with my ledger under my arm. They could make nothing, however, out of me or my ledger, and we parted with mutual laughter and compliments.

In the year 1885 my brother left me to go to a public school in Yorkshire. Shortly afterwards I was married. A lady named Mrs Hawkins, a widow of a Gloucestershire family, had come to Southsea with her son and daughter, the latter a very gentle and amiable girl. I was brought into contact with them through the illness of the son, which was of a sudden and violent nature, arising from cerebral meningitis. As the mother was very awkwardly situated in lodgings, I volunteered to furnish an extra bedroom in my house and give the poor lad, who was in the utmost danger, my personal attention. His case was a mortal one, and in spite of all I could do he passed away a few days later. Such a death under my own roof naturally involved me in a good deal of anxiety and trouble – indeed, if I had not had the foresight to ask a medical friend to see him with me on the day before he passed away, I should have been in a difficult position. The funeral was from my house. The family were naturally grieved at the worry to which they had quite innocently exposed me, and so our relations became intimate and sympathetic, which ended in the daughter consenting to share my fortunes. We were married on August 6, 1885, and no man could have had a more gentle and amiable life's companion. Our union was marred by the sad ailment which came after a very few years to cast its shadow over our lives, but it comforts me to think that during the time when we were together there was no single occasion when our affection was disturbed by any serious breach or division, the credit of which lies entirely with her own quiet philosophy, which enabled her to bear with smiling patience not only her own sad illness, which lasted so long, but all those other vicissitudes which life brings with it. I rejoice to think that though she married a penniless doctor, she was spared long enough to appreciate fully the pleasure and the material comforts which worldly success was able to bring us. She had some small income of her own which enabled me to expand my simple housekeeping in a way which gave her from the first the decencies, if not the luxuries, of life.

In many ways my marriage marked a turning-point in my life. A bachelor, especially one who had been a wanderer like myself, drifts easily into Bohemian habits, and I was no exception. I cannot look back upon those years with any spiritual satisfaction, for I was still in the valley of darkness. I had ceased to butt my head incessantly against what seemed to be an impenetrable wall, and I had resigned myself to ignorance upon that which is the most momentous question in life – for a voyage is bleak indeed if one has no conception to what port one is bound. I had laid aside the old charts as useless, and had quite despaired of ever finding a new one which would enable me to steer an intelligible course, save towards that mist which was all that my pilots, Huxley, Mill, Spencer and others, could see ahead of us. My mental attitude is correctly portrayed in *The Stark Munro Letters*. A dim light of dawn was to come to me soon in an uncertain fitful way which was destined in time to spread and grow brighter.

Up to now the main interest of my life lay in my medical career. But with the more regular life and the greater sense of responsibility, coupled with the natural development of brain-power, the literary side of me began slowly to spread until it was destined to push the other entirely aside. Thus a new phase had begun, part medical, part literary and part philosophical, which I shall deal with in another chapter.

8

My First Literary Success

New Outlook – *Cornhill* Dinner – James Payn – Genesis of Holmes –
A Study in Scarlet – *Micah Clarke* – Disappointments – Andrew
Lang – Oscar Wilde – His Criticism of Himself – *The White Company*

During the years before my marriage I had from time to time written
short stories which were good enough to be marketable at very small
prices – four pounds on an average – but not good enough to reproduce.
They are scattered about amid the pages of *London Society*, *All the Year
Round*, *Temple Bar*, *The Boy's Own Paper* and other journals. There let
them lie. They served their purpose in relieving me a little of that
financial burden which always pressed upon me. I can hardly have
earned more than ten or fifteen pounds a year from this source, so that
the idea of making a living by it never occurred to me. But though I was
not putting out I was taking in. I still have notebooks full of all sorts of
knowledge which I acquired during that time. It is a great mistake to
start putting out cargo when you have hardly stowed any on board. My
own slow methods and natural limitations made me escape this danger.

After my marriage, however, my brain seems to have quickened
and both my imagination and my range of expression were greatly
improved. Most of the short stories which appeared eventually in my
Captain of the Polestar were written in those years from 1885 to 1890.
Some of them are perhaps as good honest work as any that I have done.
What gave me great pleasure and for the first time made me realise that
I was ceasing to be a hack writer and was getting into good company
was when James Payn accepted my short story 'Habakuk Jephson's
Statement' for *Cornhill*. I had a reverence for this splendid magazine
with its traditions from Thackeray to Stevenson and the thought that I
had won my way into it pleased me even more than the cheque for
thirty pounds, which came duly to hand. It was, of course, anonymous –
such was the law of the magazine – which protects the author from
abuse as well as prevents his winning fame. One paper began its review:
'*Cornhill* opens its new number with a story which would have made

Thackeray turn in his grave.' A dear old gentleman who knew me hurried across the road to show me the paper with these cheering words. Another, more gracious, said, '*Cornhill* begins the New Year with an exceedingly powerful story in which we seem to trace the hand of the author of the *New Arabian Nights*.' It was great praise, but something less warm, which came straight to my own address, would have pleased me better.

I soon had two other stories in the *Cornhill* – 'John Huxford's Hiatus' and 'The Ring of Thoth'. I also penetrated the stout Scottish barrier of *Blackwood* with a story, 'The Physiologist's Wife', which was written when I was under the influence of Henry James. But I was still in the days of very small things – so small that when a paper sent me a woodcut and offered me four guineas if I would write a story to correspond I was not too proud to accept. It was a very bad woodcut and I think that the story corresponded all right. I remember writing a New Zealand story, though why I should have written about a place of which I knew nothing I cannot imagine. Some New Zealand critic pointed out that I had given the exact bearings of the farm mentioned as ninety miles to the east or west of the town of Nelson, and that in that case it was situated twenty miles out on the floor of the Pacific Ocean. These little things will happen. There are times when accuracy is necessary and others where the idea is everything and the place quite immaterial.

It was about a year after my marriage that I realised that I could go on doing short stories for ever and never make headway. What is necessary is that your name should be on the spine of a volume. Only so do you assert your individuality, and get the full credit or discredit of your achievement. I had for some time from 1884 onwards been engaged upon a sensational book of adventure which I had called 'The Firm of Girdlestone', which represented my first attempt at a connected narrative. Save for occasional patches it is a worthless book, and, like the first book of everyone else, unless he is a great original genius, it was too reminiscent of the work of others. I could see it then, and could see it even more clearly later. When I sent it to publishers and they scorned it I quite acquiesced in their decision and finally let it settle, after its periodical flights to town, a dishevelled mass of manuscript at the back of a drawer.

I felt now that I was capable of something fresher and crisper and more workmanlike. Gaboriau had rather attracted me by the neat dovetailing of his plots, and Poe's masterful detective, M. Dupin, had from boyhood been one of my heroes. But could I bring an addition of my own? I thought of my old teacher Joe Bell, of his eagle face, of his curious ways, of his eerie trick of spotting details. If he were a detective he would surely reduce this fascinating but unorganised business to something nearer to an exact science. I would try if I could get this effect. It was surely possible in real life, so why should I not make it plausible in fiction? It is all very well to say that a man is clever, but the reader wants to see examples of it – such examples as Bell gave us every day in the wards. The idea amused me. What should I call the fellow? I still possess the leaf of a notebook with various alternative names. One rebelled against the elementary art which gives some inkling of character in the name and creates Mr Sharps or Mr Ferrets. First it was Sherringford Holmes; then it was Sherlock Holmes. He could not tell his own exploits, so he must have a commonplace comrade as a foil – an educated man of action who could both join in the exploits and narrate them. A drab, quiet name for this unostentatious man. Watson would do. And so I had my puppets and wrote my *Study in Scarlet*.

I knew that the book was as good as I could make it, and I had high hopes. When 'Girdlestone' used to come circling back with the precision of a homing pigeon, I was grieved but not surprised, for I acquiesced in the decision. But when my little Holmes book began also to do the circular tour I was hurt, for I knew that it deserved a better fate. James Payn applauded but found it both too short and too long, which was true enough. Arrowsmith received it in May 1886 and returned it unread in July. Two or three others sniffed and turned away. Finally, as Ward, Lock & Co. made a speciality of cheap and often sensational literature, I sent it to them.

Dear Sir [they said] – We have read your story and are pleased with it. We could not publish it this year as the market is flooded at present with cheap fiction, but if you do not object to its being held over till next year, we will give you £25 for the copyright.

Yours faithfully,

WARD, LOCK & CO.
October 30, 1886

It was not a very tempting offer, and even I, poor as I was, hesitated to accept it. It was not merely the small sum offered, but it was the long delay, for this book might open a road for me. I was heart-sick, however, at repeated disappointments, and I felt that perhaps it was true wisdom to make sure of publicity, however late. Therefore I accepted, and the book became *Beeton's Xmas Annual* of 1887. I never at any time received another penny for it.

Having a long wait in front of me before this book could appear, and feeling large thoughts rise within me, I now determined to test my powers to the full, and I chose a historical novel for this end, because it seemed to me the one way of combining a certain amount of literary dignity with those scenes of action and adventure which were natural to my young and ardent mind. I had always felt great sympathy for the Puritans, who, after all, whatever their little peculiarities, did represent political liberty and earnestness in religion. They had usually been caricatured in fiction and art. Even Scott had not drawn them as they were. Macaulay, who was always one of my chief inspirations, had alone made them comprehensible – the sombre fighters, with their Bibles and their broadswords. There is a great passage of his – I cannot quote it verbally – in which he says that after the Restoration if ever you saw a carter more intelligent than his fellows, or a peasant who tilled his land better, you would be likely to find that it was an old pikeman of Cromwell's. This, then, was my inspiration in *Micah Clarke*, where I fairly let myself go upon the broad highway of adventure. I was well up in history, but I spent some months over details and then wrote the book very rapidly. There are bits of it – the picture of the Puritan household, and the sketch of Judge Jeffreys – which I have never bettered. When it was finished early in 1888 my hopes ran high and out it went on its travels.

But, alas! although my Holmes booklet was out, and had attracted some little favourable comment, the door still seemed to be barred. James Payn had first peep, and he began his letter of rejection with the sentence: 'How can you, can you, waste your time and your wits writing historical novels!' This was depressing after a year of work. Then came Bentley's verdict: 'It lacks in our opinion the one great necessary point for fiction, i.e. interest; and this being the case we do not think it could ever become popular with libraries and the general public.' Then *Blackwood* had its say: 'There are imperfections which would militate against success. The chances of the book proving a popular success do not seem to be strong enough to warrant us in publishing it.' There were others even mote depressing. I was on the point of putting the worn manuscript into hospital with its mangled brother 'Girdlestone' when as a last resource I sent it to Longmans, whose reader, Andrew

Lang, liked it and advised its acceptance. It was to 'Andrew of the brindled hair', as Stevenson called him, that I owe my first real opening, and I have never forgotten it. The book duly appeared in February 1889, and though it was not a boom book it had extraordinarily good reviews, including one special one all to itself by Mr Protheroe in the *Nineteenth Century*, and it has sold without intermission from that day to this. It was the first solid cornerstone laid for some sort of literary reputation.

British literature had a considerable vogue in the United States at this time for the simple reason that there was no copyright and they had not to pay for it. It was hard on British authors, but far harder on American ones, since they were exposed to this devastating competition. Like all national sins it brought its own punishment not only to American authors, who were guiltless, but to the publishers themselves, for what belongs to everyone belongs practically to no one, and they could not bring out a decent edition without being at once undersold. I have seen some of my early American editions which might have been printed on the paper that shopmen use for parcels. One good result, however, from my point of view was that a British author, if he had anything in him, soon won recognition over there, and afterwards, when the Copyright Act was passed, he had his audience all ready for him. My Holmes book had met with some American success and presently I learned that an agent of *Lippincott's* was in London and that he wished to see me, to arrange for a book. Needless to say that I gave my patients a rest for a day and eagerly kept the appointment.

Once only before had I touched the edge of literary society. That was when *Cornhill* was turned into a fully illustrated journal, an experiment which failed for it was quickly abandoned. The change was celebrated by a dinner at the Ship, at Greenwich, to which I was invited on the strength of my short contributions. All the authors and artists were there, and I remember the reverence with which I approached James Payn, who was to me the warden of the sacred gate. I was among the first arrivals, and was greeted by Mr Smith, the head of the firm, who introduced me to Payn. I loved much of his work and waited in awe for the first weighty remark which should fall from his lips. It was that there was a crack in the window and he wondered how the devil it had got there. Let me add, however, that my future experience was to show that there was no wittier or more delightful companion in the world. I sat next to Anstey that night, who had just made a most deserved hit with his *Vice Versa*, and I was introduced to other celebrities, so that I came back walking on air.

Now for the second time I was in London on literary business. Stoddart, the American, proved to be an excellent fellow, and had two others to dinner. They were Gill, a very entertaining Irish MP, and Oscar Wilde, who was already famous as the champion of aestheticism. It was indeed a golden evening for me. Wilde to my surprise had read *Micah Clarke* and was enthusiastic about it, so that I did not feel a complete outsider. His conversation left an indelible impression upon my mind. He towered above us all, and yet had the art of seeming to be interested in all that we could say. He had delicacy of feeling and tact, for the monologue man, however clever, can never be a gentleman at heart. He took as well as gave, but what he gave was unique. He had a curious precision of statement, a delicate flavour of humour, and a trick of small gestures to illustrate his meaning, which were peculiar to himself. The effect cannot be reproduced, but I remember how in discussing the wars of the future he said: 'A chemist on each side will approach the frontier with a bottle' – his upraised hand and precise face conjuring up a vivid and grotesque picture. His anecdotes, too, were happy and curious. We were discussing the cynical maxim that the good fortune of our friends made us discontented. 'The devil,' said Wilde, 'was once crossing the Libyan Desert, and he came upon a spot where a number of small fiends were tormenting a holy hermit. The sainted man easily shook off their evil suggestions. The devil watched their failure and then he stepped forward to give them a lesson. "What you do is too crude," said he. "Permit me for one moment." With that he whispered to the holy man, "Your brother has just been made Bishop of Alexandria." A scowl of malignant jealousy at once clouded the serene face of the hermit. "That," said the devil to his imps, "is the sort of thing which I should recommend." '

The result of the evening was that both Wilde and I promised to write books for *Lippincott's Magazine* – Wilde's contribution was *The Picture of Dorian Gray*, a book which is surely upon a high moral plane, while I wrote *The Sign of The Four*, in which Holmes made his second appearance. I should add that never in Wilde's conversation did I observe one trace of coarseness of thought, nor could one at that time associate him with such an idea. Only once again did I see him, many years afterwards, and then he gave me the impression of being mad. He asked me, I remember, if I had seen some play of his which was running. I answered that I had not. He said: 'Ah, you must go. It is wonderful. It is genius!' All this with the gravest face. Nothing could have been more different from his early gentlemanly instincts. I thought at the time, and still think, that the monstrous development which ruined him was pathological, and that a hospital rather than a police court was the place for its consideration.

When his little book came out I wrote to say what I thought of it. His letter is worth reproducing, as showing the true Wilde. I omit the early part in which he comments on my own work in too generous terms.

> Between me and life there is a mist of words always. I throw probability out of the window for the sake of a phrase, and the chance of an epigram makes me desert truth. Still I do aim at making a work of art, and I am really delighted that you think my treatment subtle and artistically good. The newspapers seem to me to be written by the prurient for the Philistine. I cannot understand how they can treat *Dorian Gray* as immoral. My difficulty was to keep the inherent moral subordinate to the artistic and dramatic effect, and it still seems to me that the moral is too obvious.

Encouraged by the kind reception which *Micah Clarke* had received from the critics, I now determined upon an even bolder and more ambitious flight. It seemed to me that the days of Edward III constituted the greatest epoch in English history – an epoch when both the French and the Scottish kings were prisoners in London. This result had been brought about mainly by the powers of a body of men who were renowned through Europe but who had never been drawn in British literature, for though Scott treated in his inimitable way the English archer, it was as an outlaw rather than as a soldier that he drew him. I had some views of my own, too, about the Middle Ages which I was anxious to set forth. I was familiar with Froissart and Chaucer and I was aware that the famous knights of old were by no means the athletic heroes of Scott but were often of a very different type. Hence came my two books *The White Company*, written in 1889, and *Sir Nigel*, written fourteen years later. Of the two I consider the latter the better book, but I have no hesitation in saying that the two of them taken together did thoroughly achieve my purpose, that they made an accurate picture of that great age, and that as a single piece of work they form the most complete, satisfying and ambitious thing that I have ever done. All things find their level, but I believe that if I had never touched Holmes, who has tended to obscure my higher work, my position in literature would at the present moment be a more commanding one. The work needed much research and I have still got my notebooks full of all sorts of lore. I cultivate a simple style and avoid long words so far as possible, and it may be that this surface of ease has sometimes caused the reader to underrate the amount of real research which lies in all my historical novels. It is not a matter which troubles me, however, for I have always felt that justice is done in the end, and that the real merit of any work is never permanently lost.

I remember that as I wrote the last words of *The White Company* I felt a wave of exultation and with a cry of 'That's done it!' I hurled my inky pen across the room, where it left a black smudge upon the duck's-egg wallpaper. I knew in my heart that the book would live and that it would illuminate our national traditions. Now that it has passed through fifty editions I suppose I may say with all modesty that my forecast has proved to be correct. This was the last book which I wrote in my days of doctoring at Southsea, and marks an epoch in my life, so I can now hark back to some other phases of my last years at Bush Villa before I broke away into a new existence. I will only add that *The White Company* was accepted by *Cornhill*, in spite of James Payn's opinion of historical novels, and that I fulfilled another ambition by having a serial in that famous magazine.

A new phase of medical experience came to me about this time, for I suddenly found myself a unit in the British army. The operations in the East had drained the Medical Service, and it had therefore been determined that local civilian doctors should be enrolled for temporary duty of some hours a day. The terms were a guinea a day, and a number of us were tempted to volunteer where there were only a few vacancies. When I was called before the board of selection a savage-looking old army doctor who presided barked out, 'And you, sir – what are you prepared to do?' To which I answered, 'Anything.' It seems that the others had all been making bargains and reservations, so my wholehearted reply won the job.

It brought me into closer contact with the savage-looking medico, who proved to be Sir Anthony Home VC – an honour which he had won in the Indian Mutiny. He was in supreme charge, and as he was as fierce in speech and in act as in appearance, everyone was terrified of him. On one occasion I had told the orderly to draw a man's tooth, knowing that he was a very much more skilful dentist than I. I was on my way home when I was overtaken by an excited soldier who told me that Sergeant Jones was being court-martialled and would certainly lose his stripes because he had done a minor operation. I hurried back and on entering the room found Sir Anthony glaring at the unhappy man, while several other orderlies stood round awaiting their own turn. Sir Anthony's glare was transferred to me when I said that whatever the sergeant had done was by my express order. He grunted, banged the book he was holding and broke up the meeting. He seemed a most disagreeable old man, and yet when I was married shortly afterwards he sent me a most charming message wishing me good fortune. Up to then I had never had anything from him save a scowl from his thick eyebrows, so I was most agreeably surprised. Soon afterwards the pressure ceased and we civilians were all dismissed.

9

Pulling up the Anchor

Psychic Studies – Experiments in Telepathy – My First Séances – A
Curious Test – General Drayson – Opinion on Theosophy –
A. P. Sinnett – W. T. Stead – Journey to Berlin – Koch's Treatment –
Brutality of Bergmann – Malcolm Morris – Literary Society –
Political Work – Arthur Balfour – Our Departure

It was in these years after my marriage and before leaving Southsea that
I planted the first seeds of those psychic studies which were destined to
revolutionise my views and to absorb finally all the energies of my life. I
had at that time the usual contempt which the young educated man
feels towards the whole subject which has been covered by the clumsy
name of Spiritualism. I had read of mediums being convicted of fraud, I
had heard of phenomena which were opposed to every known scientific
law, and I had deplored the simplicity and credulity which could
deceive good, earnest people into believing that such bogus happenings
were signs of intelligence outside our own existence. Educated as I had
been during my most plastic years in the school of medical materialism,
and soaked in the negative views of all my great teachers, I had no room
in my brain for theories which cut right across every fixed conclusion
that I had formed. I was wrong and my great teachers were wrong, but
still I hold that they wrought well and that their Victorian agnosticism
was in the interests of the human race, for it shook the old ironclad
unreasoning evangelical position which was so universal before their
days. For all rebuilding a site must be cleared. There were two separate
Victorian movements towards change, the one an attempt to improve
the old building and make it good enough to carry on – as shown in the
Oxford and High Church development, the other a knocking down of
ruins which could only end in some fresh erection springing up. As I
have shown, my own position was that of a respectful materialist who
entirely admitted a great central intelligent cause, without being able to
distinguish what that cause was, or why it should work in so mysterious
and terrible a way in bringing its designs to fulfilment.

From my point of view the mind (and so far as I could see the soul, which was the total effect of all the hereditary or personal functionings of the mind) was an emanation from the brain and entirely physical in its nature. I saw, as a medical man, how a spicule of bone or a tumour pressing on the brain would cause what seemed an alteration in the soul. I saw also how drugs or alcohol would turn on fleeting phases of virtue or vice. The physical argument seemed an overpowering one. It had never struck me that the current of events might really flow in the opposite direction, and that the higher faculties could only manifest themselves imperfectly through an imperfect instrument. The broken fiddle is silent and yet the musician is the same as ever.

The first thing which steadied me and made me reconsider my position was the question of telepathy, which was already being discussed by William Barrett and others, even before the appearance of Myers' monumental work on *Human Personality* – the first book which devoted to these psychic subjects the deep study and sustained brain power which they demand. It may, in my opinion, take a permanent place in human literature like the *Novum Organum* or *The Descent of Man* or any other great root-book which has marked a date in human thought. Having read some of the evidence I began to experiment in thought transference, and I found a fellow-researcher in Mr Ball, a well-known architect in the town. Again and again, sitting behind him, I have drawn diagrams, and he in turn has made approximately the same figures. I showed beyond any doubt whatever that I could convey my thoughts without words.

But if I could verify such conclusions up to six feet I could not well doubt them when they gave me the evidence that the same results could be obtained at a distance. With an appropriate subject, and some undefined sympathy between the two individuals, it was independent of space. So the evidence seemed to show. I had always sworn by science and by the need of fearless following wherever truth might lie. It was clear now that my position had been too rigid. I had compared the thought-excretion of the brain to the bile-excretion of the liver. Clearly this was untenable. If thought could go a thousand miles and produce a perceptible effect then it differed entirely not only in degree but in kind from any purely physical material. That seemed certain, and it must involve some modification of my old views.

About this time (1886), the family of a general whom I attended professionally became interested in table turning and asked me to come and check their results. They sat round a dining-room table which after a time, their hands being upon it, began to sway and finally got sufficient motion to tap with one leg. They then asked questions and received answers, more or less wise and more or less to the point. They were got by the tedious process of reciting the alphabet and writing down the letter which the tap indicated. It seemed to me that we were collectively pushing the table, and that our own wills were concerned in bringing down the leg at the right moment. I was interested but very sceptical. Some of these messages were not vague platitudes but were definite and from dead friends of the family, which naturally impressed them greatly, though it had not the same effect upon me, since I did not know them. I have the old records before me as I write. 'Don't tell the girls when you see them, but they will talk about me. Kiss my baby for me. I watch her always. Francie.' This was the style of message, mixed up with a good many platitudes. We held twenty or more of such meetings, but I never received anything evidential to my own address, and I was very critical as to the whole proceedings.

None the less there was a problem to be solved and I went on with its solution, reading the pros and the cons, and asking advice from those who had experience, especially from General Drayson, a very distinguished thinker and a pioneer of psychic knowledge, who lived at that time at Southsea. I had known Drayson first as an astronomer, for he had worked out a revolutionary idea by which there is a fatal mistake in our present idea as to the circle which is described in the heavens by the prolonged axis of the earth. It is really a wider circle round a different centre, and this correction enables us to explain several things now inexplicable, and to make astronomy a more exact science, with certain very important reactions upon geology and the recurrent glacial epochs, the exact date of which could be fixed. His views impressed me much at the time, and several books upholding them have appeared since his death, notably *Draysoniana* by Admiral de Horsey. If he makes good, as I think he will, Drayson will make a great permanent name. His opinion therefore was not negligible upon any subject, and when he told me his views and experiences on Spiritualism I could not fail to be impressed, though my own philosophy was far too solid to be easily destroyed. I was too poor to employ professional mediums, and to work on such subjects without a medium is as if one worked at astronomy without a telescope. Once only an old man with some reputed psychic power came for a small fee and gave us a demonstration. He went into a loud-breathing trance to the alarm of his audience, and then gave each of us a test. Mine was certainly a very remarkable one, for it was, 'Do not read Leigh Hunt's book.' I was hesitating at the time whether I should read his *Comic Dramatists of the Restoration* or not, for on the one hand it is literature and on the other the treatment repelled me. This then was a very final and excellent test so far as telepathy went, but I would not fully grant that it was more. I was so impressed, however, that I wrote an account of it to *Light*, the psychic weekly paper, and so in the year 1887 I actually put myself on public record as a student of these matters. That was thirty-seven years ago, as I write, so I am a very senior student now. From that time onwards I read and thought a great deal, though it was not until the later phase of my life that I realised whither all this was tending. This question I will treat in a final section by itself, so that those to whom it is of less interest can avoid it.

I was deeply interested and attracted for a year or two by Theosophy, because while Spiritualism seemed at that time to be chaos so far as philosophy went, Theosophy presented a very well thought-out and reasonable scheme, parts of which, notably reincarnation and karma, seemed to offer an explanation for some of the anomalies of life. I read Sinnett's *Occult World* and afterwards with even greater admiration I read his fine exposition of Theosophy in *Esoteric Buddhism*, a most notable book. I also met him, for he was an old friend of General Drayson's, and I was impressed by his conversation. Shortly afterwards, however, there appeared Dr Hodgson's report upon his investigation into Madame Blavatsky's proceedings at Adyar, which shook my confidence very much. It is true that Mrs Besant has since then published a powerful defence which tends to show that Hodgson may have been deceived, but the subsequent book, *A Priestess of Isis*, which contains many of her own letters, leaves an unpleasant impression, and Sinnett's posthumous work seems to show that he also had lost confidence. On the other hand, Colonel Olcott shows that the woman undoubtedly had real psychic powers, whatever their source. As to Spiritualism, it seems to have only interested her in its lower phenomenal aspect. Her books show extraordinary erudition and capacity for hard work, even if they represent the transfer of other people's conclusions, as they frequently do. It would be unjust, however, to condemn the old wisdom simply because it was introduced by this extraordinary and volcanic person. We have also had in our branch of the occult many dishonest mediums, but we have hastened to unveil them where we could do so, and Theosophy will be in a stronger position when it shakes off Madame Blavatsky altogether. In any case it could never have met my needs for I ask for severe proof, and if I have to go back to unquestioning faith I should find myself in the fold from which I wandered.

My life had been a pleasant one with my steadily-increasing literary success, my practice, which was enough to keep me pleasantly occupied, and my sport, which I treat in a later chapter. Suddenly, however, there came a development which shook me out of my rut, and caused an absolute change in my life and plans. One daughter, Mary, had been born to us, our household was a happy one, and as I have never had personal ambitions, since the simple things of life have always been the most pleasant to me, it is possible that I should have remained in Southsea permanently but for this new episode in my life. It arose when in 1890 Koch announced that he had discovered a sure cure for consumption and that he would demonstrate it upon a certain date in Berlin.

A great urge came upon me suddenly that I should go to Berlin and see him do so. I could give no clear reason for this, but it was an irresistible impulse and I at once determined to go. Had I been a well-known doctor or a specialist in consumption it would have been more intelligible, but I had, as a matter of fact, no great interest in the more recent developments of my own profession, and a very strong belief that much of the so-called progress was illusory. However, at a few hours' notice I packed up a bag and started off alone upon this curious adventure. I had had an interchange of letters with Mr W. T. Stead over some matter and I called upon him at the *Review of Reviews* office as I passed through London to ask him if he could give me an introduction to Koch or to Dr Bergmann, who was to give the demonstration. Mr Stead was very amiable to this big unknown provincial doctor, and he gave me a letter for the British ambassador – Sir Edward Malet, if I remember right – and for Mr Lowe, *The Times* correspondent. He also asked me to do a character sketch of Koch for him, adding that he would have Count Mattei as a feature of his magazine this month and Koch the next. I said, 'Then you will have the greatest man of science and the greatest quack in Europe following each other.' Stead glared at me angrily, for it seems that the Mattei treatment with its blue electricity and the rest of it was at that moment his particular fad. However, we parted amiably and all through his life we kept in distant touch, though we came into sharp collision at the time of the Boer War. He was a brave and honest man, and if he was impulsive at times it was only the sudden out-flame of that fire which made him the great force for good that he was. In psychic knowledge he was a generation before his time, though his mode of expressing it may sometimes have been injudicious.

I went on to Berlin that night and found myself in the Continental Express with a very handsome and courteous London physician bound upon the same errand as myself. We passed most of the night talking and I learned that his name was Malcolm Morris and that he also had been a provincial doctor, but that he had come to London and had made a considerable hit as a skin specialist in Harley Street. It was the beginning of a friendship which endured.

Having arrived at Berlin the great thing was to be present at Bergmann's demonstration, which was to be next day at twelve. I went to our ambassador, was kept long waiting, had a chilly reception and was dismissed without help or consolation. Then I tried *The Times* correspondent, but he could not help me either. He and his amiable wife showed me every courtesy and invited me to dinner that night. Tickets were simply not to be had and neither money nor interest could procure them. I conceived the wild idea of getting one from Koch himself and made my way to his house. While there I had the curious experience of seeing his mail arrive – a large sack full of letters, which was emptied out on the floor of the hall, and exhibited every sort of stamp in Europe. It was a sign of all the sad broken lives and wearied hearts which were turning in hope to Berlin. Koch remained a veiled prophet, however, and would see neither me nor anyone else. I was fairly at my wits' ends and could not imagine how I could attain my purpose.

Next day I went down to the great building where the address was to be given and managed by bribing the porter to get into the outer hall. The huge audience was assembling in a room beyond. I tried further bribing that I might be slipped in, but the official became abusive. People streamed past me, but I was always the waiter at the gate. Finally everyone had gone in and then a group of men came bustling across, Bergmann, bearded and formidable, in the van, with a tail of house surgeons and satellites behind him. I threw myself across his path. 'I have come a thousand miles,' said I. 'May I not come in?' He halted and glared at me through his spectacles. 'Perhaps you would like to take my place,' he roared, working himself up into that strange folly of excitement which seems so strange in the heavy German nature. 'That is the only place left. Yes, yes, take my place by all means. My classes are filled with Englishmen already.' He fairly spat out the word 'Englishmen' and I learned afterwards that some recent quarrel with Morel MacKenzie over the illness of the Emperor Frederick had greatly incensed him. I am glad to say that I kept my temper and my polite manner, which is always the best shield when one is met by brutal rudeness. 'Not at all,' I said. 'I would not intrude, if there was really no room.' He glared at me again, all beard and spectacles, and rushed on with his court all grinning at the snub which the presumptuous Englishman had received. One of them lingered, however – a kindly American. 'That was bad behaviour,' said he. 'See here! If you meet me at four this afternoon I will show you my full notes of the lecture, and I know the cases he is about to show, so we can see them together tomorrow.' Then he followed on.

So it came about that I attained my end after all, but in a roundabout way. I studied the lecture and the cases, and I had the temerity to disagree with everyone and to come to the conclusion that the whole thing was experimental and premature. A wave of madness had seized the world and from all parts, notably from England, poor afflicted people were rushing to Berlin for a cure, some of them in such advanced stages of disease that they died in the train. I felt so sure of my ground and so strongly about it that I wrote a letter of warning to the *Daily Telegraph*, and I rather think that this letter was the very first which appeared upon the side of doubt and caution. I need not say that the event proved the truth of my forecast.

Two days later I was back in Southsea, but I came back a changed man. I had spread my wings and had felt something of the powers within me. Especially I had been influenced by a long talk with Malcolm Morris, in which he assured me that I was wasting my life in the provinces and had too small a field for my activities. He insisted that I should leave general practice and go to London. I answered that I was by no means sure of my literary success as yet, and that I could not so easily abandon the medical career which had cost my mother such sacrifices and myself so many years of study. He asked me if there was any special branch of the profession on which I could concentrate so as to get away from general practice. I said that of late years I had been interested in eye work and had amused myself by correcting refractions and ordering glasses in the Portsmouth Eye Hospital under Mr Vernon Ford. 'Well,' said Morris, 'why not specialise upon the eye? Go to Vienna, put in six months' work, come back and start in London. Thus you will have a nice clean life with plenty of leisure for your literature.' I came home with this great suggestion buzzing in my head and as my wife was quite willing and Mary, my little girl, was old enough now to be left with her grandmother, there seemed to be no obstacle in the way. There were no difficulties about disposing of the practice, for it was so small and so purely personal that it could not be sold to another and simply had to dissolve.

The Portsmouth Literary and Scientific Society gave me a God-speed banquet. I have many pleasant and some comic reminiscences of this society, of which I had been secretary for several years. We kept the sacred flame burning in the old city with our weekly papers and discussions during the long winters. It was there I learned to face an audience, which proved to be of the first importance for my life's work. I was naturally of a very nervous, backward, self-distrustful disposition in such things and I have been told that the signal that I was about to join in the discussion was that the whole long bench on which I sat, with everyone on it, used to shake with my emotion. But once up I learned to speak out, to conceal my trepidation, and to choose my phrases. I gave three papers, one on the Arctic seas, one on Carlyle and one on Gibbon. The former gave me a quite unmerited reputation as a sportsman, for I borrowed from a local taxidermist every bird and beast that he possessed which could conceivably find its way into the Arctic Circle. These I piled upon the lecture table, and the audience, concluding that I had shot them all, looked upon me with great respect. Next morning they were back with the taxidermist once more. We had some weird people and incidents at these debates. I remember one very learned discussion on fossils and the age of the strata, which was ended by a cadaverous major-general of the Evangelical persuasion who rose and said in a hollow voice that all this speculation was vain, and indeed incomprehensible, since we knew on an authority which could not possibly be questioned that the world was made exactly five thousand eight hundred and ninety years ago. This put the lid on the debate and we all crept home to bed.

My political work also caused me to learn to speak. I was what was called a Liberal-Unionist, that is, a man whose general position was Liberal, but who could not see his way to support Gladstone's Irish policy. Perhaps we were wrong. However, that was my view at the time. I had a dreadful first experience of platform speaking on a large scale, for at a huge meeting at the Amphitheatre the candidate, Sir William Crossman, was delayed, and to prevent a fiasco I was pushed on at a moment's notice to face an audience of three thousand people. It was one of the tight corners of my life. I hardly knew myself what I said, but the Irish part of me came to my aid and supplied me with a torrent of more or less incoherent words and similes which roused the audience greatly, though it read to me afterwards more like a comic stump speech than a serious political effort. But it was what they wanted and they were mostly on their feet before I finished. I was amazed when I read it next day, and especially the last crowning sentence, which was: 'England and Ireland are wedded together with the sapphire wedding ring of the sea, and what God has placed together let no man pluck asunder.' It was not very good logic, but whether it was eloquence or rodomontade I could not even now determine.

I was acting secretary when Mr Balfour came down to address a great meeting, and, as such, when the hall was full, I waited on the curb outside to receive him. Presently his carriage drove up and out he stepped, tall, thin and aristocratic. There were two notorious partisans of the other side waiting for him and I warned them not to make trouble. However, the moment Balfour appeared one of them opened a huge mouth with the intention of emitting a howl of execration. But it never got out, for I clapped my hand pretty forcibly over the orifice while I held him by the neck with the other hand. His companion hit me on the head with a stick, and was promptly knocked down by one of my companions. Meanwhile Balfour got safely in, and we two secretaries followed, rather dishevelled after our adventure. I met Lord Balfour several times in after life but I never told him how I once had my hat smashed in his defence.

What with the Literary Society and the politicians I left a gap behind me in Portsmouth and so did my wife, who was universally popular for her amiable and generous character. It was a wrench to us to leave so many good friends. However, towards the end of 1890 the die was cast, and we closed the door of Bush Villa behind us for the last time. I had days of privation there, and days of growing success during the eight long years that I had spent in Portsmouth. Now it was with a sense of wonderful freedom and exhilarating adventure that we set forth upon the next phase of our lives.

10

The Great Break

We set forth upon a bitter winter day at the close of 1890 with every chance of being snowed up on our long trek. We got through all right, however, and found ourselves in Vienna, arriving on a deadly cold night, with deep snow under foot and a cutting blizzard in the air. As we looked from the station the electric lights threw out the shining silver drift of snowflakes against the absolute darkness of the sky. It was a gloomy, ominous reception, but half an hour afterwards when we were in the warm cosy crowded tobacco-laden restaurant attached to our hotel we took a more cheerful view of our surroundings.

We found a modest *pension* which was within our means, and we put in a very pleasant four months, during which I attended eye lectures at the Krankenhaus, but could certainly have learned far more in London, for even if one has a fair knowledge of conversational German it is very different from following accurately a rapid lecture filled with technical terms. No doubt 'has studied in Vienna' sounds well in a specialist's record, but it is usually taken for granted that he has exhausted his own country before going abroad, which was by no means the case with me. Therefore, so far as eye work goes, my winter was wasted, nor can I trace any particular spiritual or intellectual advance. On the other hand I saw a little of gay Viennese society. I received kind and welcome hospitality from Brinsley Richards, *The Times* correspondent, and his wife, and I had some excellent skating. I also wrote one short book, *The Doings of Raffles Haw*, not a very notable achievement, by which I was able to pay my current expenses without encroaching on the very few hundred pounds which were absolutely all that I had in the world. This money was invested on the advice of a friend, and as it was almost all lost – like so much more that I have earned – it is just as well that I was never driven back upon it.

With the spring my work at Vienna had finished, if it can be said to have ever begun, and we returned via Paris, putting in a few days there with Landolt, who was the most famous French oculist of his time. It was great to find ourselves back in London once more with the feeling that we were now on the real field of battle, where we must conquer or perish, for our boats were burned behind us. It is easy now to look back and think that the issue was clear, but it was by no means so at the time, for I had earned little, though my reputation was growing. It was only my own inward conviction of the permanent merits of *The White Company*, still appearing month by month in *Cornhill*, which sustained my confidence. I had come through so much in the early days at Southsea that nothing could alarm me personally, but I had a wife and child now, and the stern simplicity of life which was possible and even pleasant in early days was now no longer to be thought of.

We took rooms in Montague Place, and I went forth to search for some place where I could put up my plate as an oculist. I was aware that many of the big men do not find time to work out refractions, which in some cases of astigmatism take a long time to adjust when done by retinoscopy. I was capable in this work and liked it, so I hoped that some of it might drift my way. But to get it, it was clearly necessary that I should live among the big men so that the patient could be easily referred to me. I searched the doctors' quarters and at last found suitable accommodation at 2 Devonshire Place, which is at the top of Wimpole Street and close to the classical Harley Street. There for a hundred and twenty pounds a year I got the use of a front room with part use of a waiting-room. I was soon to find that they were both waiting-rooms, and now I know that it was better so.

Every morning I walked from the lodgings at Montague Place, reached my consulting-room at ten and sat there until three or four, with never a ring to disturb my serenity. Could better conditions for reflection and work be found? It was ideal, and so long as I was thoroughly unsuccessful in my professional venture there was every chance of improvement in my literary prospects. Therefore when I returned to the lodgings at teatime I bore my little sheaves with me, the first-fruits of a considerable harvest.

A number of monthly magazines were coming out at that time, notable among which was *The Strand*, then as now under the editorship of Greenhough Smith. Considering these various journals with their disconnected stories it had struck me that a single character running through a series, if it only engaged the attention of the reader, would bind that reader to that particular magazine. On the other hand, it had long seemed to me that the ordinary serial might be an impediment rather than a help to a magazine, since, sooner or later, one missed one number and afterwards it had lost all interest. Clearly the ideal compromise was a character which carried through, and yet instalments which were each complete in themselves, so that the purchaser was always sure that he could relish the whole contents of the magazine. I believe that I was the first to realise this and *The Strand Magazine* the first to put it into practice.

Looking round for my central character I felt that Sherlock Holmes, whom I had already handled in two little books, would easily lend himself to a succession of short stories. These I began in the long hours of waiting in my consulting-room. Greenhough Smith liked them from the first, and encouraged me to go ahead with them. My literary affairs had been taken up by that king of agents, A. P. Watt, who relieved me of all the hateful bargaining, and handled things so well that any immediate anxiety for money soon disappeared. It was as well, for not one single patient had ever crossed the threshold of my room.

I was now once more at a crossroads of my life, and providence, which I recognise at every step, made me realise it in a very energetic and unpleasant way. I was starting off for my usual trudge one morning from our lodgings when icy shivers passed over me, and I only got back in time to avoid a total collapse. It was a virulent attack of influenza, at a time when influenza was in its deadly prime. Only three years before my dear sister Annette, after spending her whole life on the family needs, had died of it at Lisbon at the very moment when my success would have enabled me to recall her from her long servitude. Now it was my turn, and I very nearly followed her. I can remember no pain or extreme discomfort, and no psychic experiences, but for a week I was in great danger, and then found myself as weak as a child and as emotional, but with a mind as clear as crystal. It was then, as I surveyed my own life, that I saw how foolish I was to waste my literary earnings in keeping up an oculist's room in Wimpole Street, and I determined with a wild rush of joy to cut the painter and to trust for ever to my power of writing. I remember in my delight taking the handkerchief which lay upon the coverlet in my enfeebled hand, and tossing it up to the ceiling in my exultation.

I should at last be my own master. No longer would I have to conform to professional dress or try to please anyone else. I would be free to live how I liked and where I liked. It was one of the great moments of exultation of my life. The date was in August 1891.

Presently I was about, hobbling on a stick and reflecting that if I lived to be eighty I knew already exactly how it would feel. I haunted house-agents, got lists of suburban villas, and spent some weeks, as my strength returned, in searching for a new home. Finally I found a suitable house, modest but comfortable, isolated and yet one of a row. It was 12 Tennison Road, South Norwood. There we settled down, and there I made my first effort to live entirely by my pen. It soon became evident that I had been playing the game well within my powers and that I should have no difficulty in providing a sufficient income. It seemed as if I had settled into a life which might be continuous, and I little foresaw that an unexpected blow was about to fall upon us, and that we were not at the end, but really at the beginning, of our wanderings.

I could not know this, however, and I settled down with a stout heart to do some literary work worthy of the name. The difficulty of the Holmes work was that every story really needed as clear-cut and original a plot as a longish book would do. One cannot without effort spin plots at such a rate. They are apt to become thin or to break. I was determined, now that I had no longer the excuse of absolute pecuniary pressure, never again to write anything which was not as good as I could possibly make it, and therefore I would not write a Holmes story without a worthy plot and without a problem which interested my own mind, for that is the first requisite before you can interest anyone else. If I have been able to sustain this character for a long time and if the public find, as they will find, that the last story is as good as the first, it is entirely due to the fact that I never, or hardly ever, forced a story. Some have thought there was a falling off in the stories, and the criticism was neatly expressed by a Cornish boatman who said to me, 'I think, sir, when Holmes fell over that cliff, he may not have killed himself, but all the same he was never quite the same man afterwards.' I think, however, that if the reader began the series backwards, so that he brought a fresh mind to the last stories, he would agree with me that, though the general average may not be conspicuously high, still the last one is as good as the first.

I was weary, however, of inventing plots and I set myself now to do some work which would certainly be less remunerative but would be more ambitious from a literary point of view. I had long been attracted by the epoch of Louis XIV and by those Huguenots who were the French equivalents of our Puritans. I had a good knowledge of the memoirs of that date, and many notes already prepared, so that it did not take me long to write *The Refugees*. It has stood the acid test of time very well, so I may say that it was a success. Soon after its appearance it was translated into French, and my dear old mother, herself a great French scholar, had the joy when she visited Fontainebleau to hear the official guide tell the drove of tourists that if they really wanted to know about the court of the great monarch, they would find the clearest and most accurate account in an Englishman's book, *The Refugees*. I expect the guide would have been considerably astonished had he then and there been kissed by an elderly English lady, but it was an experience which he must have narrowly missed. I used in this book, also, a great deal which was drawn from Parkman, that great but neglected historian, who was in my opinion the greatest serious writer that America has produced.

There was an amusing episode connected with *The Refugees*, when it was read aloud in some strict Irish convent, the innocent Reverend Mother having mistaken my name and imagined that I was a canon, and therefore of course a holy man. I am told that the reading was a tremendous success and that the good sisters rejoiced that the mistake was not found out until the story was completed. My first name has several times led to mistakes, as when, at a big dinner at Chicago, I was asked to say grace, as being the only ecclesiastic present. I remember that at the same dinner one of the speakers remarked that it was a most sinister fact that though I was a doctor no *living* patient of mine had ever yet been seen.

During this Norwood interval I was certainly working hard, for besides *The Refugees* I wrote *The Great Shadow*, a booklet which I should put near the front of my work for merit, and two other little books on a very inferior plane – *The Parasite* and *Beyond the City*. The latter was of a domestic type unusual for me. It was pirated in New York just before the new Copyright Act came into force, and the rascal publisher thinking that a portrait – any sort of portrait – of the author would look well upon the cover, and being quite ignorant of my identity, put a very pretty and over-dressed young woman as my presentment. I still preserve a copy of this most flattering representation. All these books had some decent success, though none of it was remarkable. It was still the Sherlock

Holmes stories for which the public clamoured, and these from time to time I endeavoured to supply. At last, after I had done two series of them I saw that I was in danger of having my hand forced, and of being entirely identified with what I regarded as a lower stratum of literary achievement. Therefore as a sign of my resolution I determined to end the life of my hero. The idea was in my mind when I went with my wife for a short holiday in Switzerland, in the course of which we saw there the wonderful falls of Reichenbach, a terrible place, and one that I thought would make a worthy tomb for poor Sherlock, even if I buried my banking account along with him. So there I laid him, fully determined that he should stay there – as indeed for some years he did. I was amazed at the concern expressed by the public. They say that a man is never properly appreciated until he is dead, and the general protest against my summary execution of Holmes taught me how devoted and how numerous were his friends. 'You Brute' was the beginning of the letter of remonstrance which one lady sent me, and I expect she spoke for others besides herself. I heard of many who wept. I fear I was utterly callous myself, and only glad to have a chance of opening out into new fields of imagination, for the temptation of high prices made it difficult to get one's thoughts away from Holmes.

That Sherlock Holmes was anything but mythical to many is shown by the fact that I have had many letters addressed to him with requests that I forward them. Watson has also had a number of letters in which he has been asked for the address or for the autograph of his more brilliant confrère. A press-cutting agency wrote to Watson asking whether Holmes would not wish to subscribe. When Holmes retired several elderly ladies were ready to keep house for him and one sought to ingratiate herself by assuring me that she knew all about bee-keeping and could 'segregate the queen'. I had considerable offers also for Holmes if he would examine and solve various family mysteries. Once the offer – from Poland – was that I should myself go, and my reward was practically left to my own judgement. I had judgement enough, however, to avoid it altogether.

I have often been asked whether I had myself the qualities which I depicted, or whether I was merely the Watson that I look. Of course I am well aware that it is one thing to grapple with a practical problem and quite another thing when you are allowed to solve it under your own conditions. I have no delusions about that. At the same time a man cannot spin a character out of his own inner consciousness and make it really lifelike unless he has some possibilities of that character within him – which is a dangerous admission for one who has drawn so many villains as I. In my poem 'The Inner Room', describing our multiplex personality, I say:

> There are others who are sitting,
>   Grim as doom,
> In the dim ill-boding shadow
>   Of my room.
> Darkling figures, stern or quaint,
> Now a savage, now a saint,
> Showing fitfully and faint
>   In the gloom.

Among those figures there may perhaps be an astute detective also, but I find that in real life in order to find him I have to inhibit all the others and get into a mood when there is no one in the room but he. Then I get results and have several times solved problems by Holmes's methods after the police have been baffled. Yet I must admit that in ordinary life I am by no means observant and that I have to throw myself into an artificial frame of mind before I can weigh evidence and anticipate the sequence of events

I I

Sidelights on Sherlock Holmes

The Speckled Band – Barrie's Parody on Holmes – Holmes on the
Screen – Methods of Construction – Problems – Curious Letters –
Some Personal Cases – Strange Happenings

I may as well interrupt my narrative here in order to say what may
interest my readers about my most notorious character.

The impression that Holmes was a real person of flesh and blood
may have been intensified by his frequent appearance upon the stage.
After the withdrawal of my dramatisation of *Rodney Stone* from a theatre
upon which I held a six months' lease, I determined to play a bold and
energetic game, for an empty theatre spells ruin. When I saw the
course that things were taking I shut myself up and devoted my whole
mind to making a sensational Sherlock Holmes drama. I wrote it in a
week and called it *The Speckled Band* after the short story of that name.
I do not think that I exaggerate if I say that within a fortnight of the
one play shutting down I had a company working upon the rehearsals
of a second one, which had been written in the interval. It was a
considerable success. Lyn Harding, as the half epileptic and wholly
formidable Doctor Grimesby Rylott, was most masterful, while
Saintsbury as Sherlock Holmes was also very good. Before the end of
the run I had cleared off all that I had lost upon the other play, and I
had created a permanent property of some value. It became a stock
piece and is even now touring the country. We had a fine rock boa to
play the title-role, a snake which was the pride of my heart, so one can
imagine my disgust when I saw that one critic ended his disparaging
review by the words, 'The crisis of the play was produced by the
appearance of a palpably artificial serpent.' I was inclined to offer him a
goodly sum if he would undertake to go to bed with it. We had several
snakes at different times, but they were none of them born actors and
they were all inclined either to hang down from the hole in the wall like
inanimate bell-pulls, or else to turn back through the hole and get even
with the stage carpenter who pinched their tails in order to make them

more lively. Finally we used artificial snakes, and everyone, including the stage carpenter, agreed that it was more satisfactory.

This was the second Sherlock Holmes play. I should have spoken about the first, which was produced very much earlier, in fact at the time of the African war. It was written and most wonderfully acted by William Gillette, the famous American. Since he used my characters and to some extent my plots, he naturally gave me a share in the undertaking, which proved to be very successful. 'May I marry Holmes?' was one cable which I received from him when in the throes of composition. 'You may marry or murder or do what you like with him,' was my heartless reply. I was charmed both with the play, the acting and the pecuniary result. I think that every man with a drop of artistic blood in his veins would agree that the latter consideration, though very welcome when it does arrive, is still the last of which he thinks.

Sir James Barrie paid his respects to Sherlock Holmes in a rollicking parody. It was really a gay gesture of resignation over the failure which we had encountered with a comic opera for which he undertook to write the libretto. I collaborated with him on this, but in spite of our joint efforts, the piece fell flat. Whereupon Barrie sent me a parody on Holmes, written on the fly leaves of one of his books. It ran thus:

THE ADVENTURE OF THE TWO COLLABORATORS

In bringing to a close the adventures of my friend Sherlock Holmes I am perforce reminded that he never, save on the occasion which, as you will now hear, brought his singular career to an end, consented to act in any mystery which was concerned with persons who made a livelihood by their pen. 'I am not particular about the people I mix among for business purposes,' he would say, 'but at literary characters I draw the line.'

We were in our rooms in Baker Street one evening. I was (I remember) by the centre table writing out 'The Adventure of the Man without a Cork Leg' (which had so puzzled the Royal Society and all the other scientific bodies of Europe), and Holmes was amusing himself with a little revolver practice. It was his custom of a summer evening to fire round my head, just shaving my face, until he had made a photograph of me on the opposite wall, and it is a slight proof of his skill that many of these portraits in pistol shots are considered admirable likenesses.

I happened to look out of the window, and perceiving two gentlemen advancing rapidly along Baker Street asked him who they were. He immediately lit his pipe, and, twisting himself on a chair into the figure 8, replied: 'They are two collaborators in comic opera, and their play has not been a triumph.'

I sprang from my chair to the ceiling in amazement, and he then explained: 'My dear Watson, they are obviously men who follow some low calling. That much even you should be able to read in their faces. Those little pieces of blue paper which they fling angrily from them are Durrant's *Press Notices*. Of these they have obviously hundreds about their person (see how their pockets bulge). They would not dance on them if they were pleasant reading.'

I again sprang to the ceiling (which is much dented), and shouted: 'Amazing! but they may be mere authors.'

'No,' said Holmes, 'for mere authors only get one press notice a week. Only criminals, dramatists and actors get them by the hundred.'

'Then they may be actors.'

'No, actors would come in a carriage.'

'Can you tell me anything else about them?'

'A great deal. From the mud on the boots of the tall one I perceive that he comes from South Norwood. The other is as obviously a Scotch author.'

'How can you tell that?'

'He is carrying in his pocket a book called (I clearly see) *Auld Licht Something*. Would anyone but the author be likely to carry about a book with such a title?'

I had to confess that this was improbable.

It was now evident that the two men (if such they can be called) were seeking our lodgings. I have said (often) that my friend Holmes seldom gave way to emotion of any kind, but he now turned livid with passion. Presently this gave place to a strange look of triumph.

'Watson,' he said, 'that big fellow has for years taken the credit for my most remarkable doings, but at last I have him – at last!'

Up I went to the ceiling, and when I returned the strangers were in the room.

'I perceive, gentlemen,' said Mr Sherlock Holmes, 'that you are at present afflicted by an extraordinary novelty.'

The handsomer of our visitors asked in amazement how he knew this, but the big one only scowled.

'You forget that you wear a ring on your fourth finger,' replied Mr Holmes calmly.

I was about to jump to the ceiling when the big brute interposed.

'That tommy-rot is all very well for the public, Holmes,' said he, 'but you can drop it before me. And, Watson, if you go up to the ceiling again I shall make you stay there.'

Here I observed a curious phenomenon. My friend Sherlock Holmes *shrank*. He became small before my eyes. I looked longingly at the ceiling, but dared not.

'Let us cut the first four pages,' said the big man, 'and proceed to business. I want to know why – '

'Allow me,' said Mr Holmes, with some of his old courage. 'You want to know why the public does not go to your opera.'

'Exactly,' said the other ironically, 'as you perceive by my shirt stud.' He added more gravely, 'And as you can only find out in one way I must insist on your witnessing an entire performance of the piece.'

It was an anxious moment for me. I shuddered, for I knew that if Holmes went I should have to go with him. But my friend had a heart of gold. 'Never,' he cried fiercely, 'I will do anything for you save that.'

'Your continued existence depends on it,' said the big man menacingly.

'I would rather melt into air,' replied Holmes, proudly taking another chair. 'But I can tell you why the public don't go to your piece without sitting the thing out myself.'

'Why?'

'Because,' replied Holmes calmly, 'they prefer to stay away.'

A dead silence followed that extraordinary remark. For a moment the two intruders gazed with awe upon the man who had unravelled their mystery so wonderfully. Then drawing their knives –

Holmes grew less and less, until nothing was left save a ring of smoke which slowly circled to the ceiling.

The last words of great men are often noteworthy. These were the last words of Sherlock Holmes: 'Fool, fool! I have kept you in luxury for years. By my help you have ridden extensively in cabs, where no author was ever seen before. *Henceforth you will ride in buses!*'

The brute sank into a chair aghast.

The other author did not turn a hair.

To A. Conan Doyle, from his friend, J. M. Barrie

This parody, the best of all the numerous parodies, may be taken as an example not only of the author's wit but of his debonair courage, for it was written immediately after our joint failure which at the moment was a bitter thought for both of us. There is indeed nothing more miserable than a theatrical failure, for you feel how many others who have backed you have been affected by it. It was, I am glad to say, my only experience of it, and I have no doubt that Barrie could say the same.

Before I leave the subject of the many impersonations of Holmes I may say that all of them, and all the drawings, are very unlike my own original idea of the man. I saw him as very tall – 'over 6 feet, but so excessively lean that he seemed considerably taller', said *A Study in Scarlet*. He had, as I imagined him, a thin razor-like face, with a great hawk's-bill of a nose, and two small eyes, set close together on either side of it. Such was my conception. It chanced, however, that poor Sidney Paget who, before his premature death, drew all the original pictures, had a younger brother whose name, I think, was Walter, who served him as a model. The handsome Walter took the place of the more powerful but uglier Sherlock, and perhaps from the point of view of my lady readers it was as well. The stage has followed the type set up by the pictures.

Films of course were unknown when the stories appeared, and when these rights were finally discussed and a small sum offered for them by a French Company it seemed treasure trove and I was very glad to accept. Afterwards I had to buy them back again at exactly ten times what I had received, so the deal was a disastrous one. But now they have been done by the Stoll Company with Eille Norwood as Holmes, and it was worth all the expense to get so fine a production. Norwood has since played the part on the stage and won the approbation of the London public. He has that rare quality which can only be described as glamour, which compels you to watch an actor eagerly even when he is doing nothing. He has the brooding eye which excites expectation and he has also a quite unrivalled power of disguise. My only criticism of the films is that they introduce telephones, motor cars and other luxuries of which the Victorian Holmes never dreamed.

People have often asked me whether I knew the end of a Holmes story before I started it. Of course I did. One could not possibly steer a course if one did not know one's destination. The first thing is to get your idea. Having got that key idea one's next task is to conceal it and lay emphasis upon everything which can make for a different explanation. Holmes, however, can see all the fallacies of the alternatives, and arrives more or less dramatically at the true solution by steps which he can describe and justify. He shows his powers by what the South Americans now call *Sherlockholmitos*, which means clever little deductions, which often have nothing to do with the matter in hand, but impress the reader with a general sense of power. The same effect is gained by his offhand allusion to other cases. Heaven knows how many titles I have thrown about in a casual way, and how many readers have begged me to satisfy their curiosity as to 'Rigoletto and his abominable wife', 'The Adventure of the Tired Captain' or 'The Curious Experience of the Patterson Family in the Island of Uffa'. Once or twice, as in 'The Adventure of the Second Stain', which in my judgement is one of the neatest of the stories, I did actually use the title years before I wrote a story to correspond.

There are some questions concerned with particular stories which turn up periodically from every quarter of the globe. In 'The Adventure of the Priory School' Holmes remarks in his offhand way that by looking at a bicycle track on a damp moor one can say which way it was heading. I had so many remonstrances upon this point, varying from pity to anger, that I took out my bicycle and tried. I had imagined that the observations of the way in which the track of the hind wheel overlaid the track of the front one when the machine was not running dead straight would show the direction. I found that my correspondents were right and I was wrong, for this would be the same whichever way the cycle was moving. On the other hand the real solution was much simpler, for on an undulating moor the wheels make a much deeper impression uphill and a more shallow one downhill, so Holmes was justified of his wisdom after all.

Sometimes I have got upon dangerous ground where I have taken risks through my own want of knowledge of the correct atmosphere. I have, for example, never been a racing man, and yet I ventured to write 'Silver Blaze', in which the mystery depends upon the laws of training and racing. The story is all right, and Holmes may have been at the top of his form, but my ignorance cries aloud to heaven. I read an excellent and very damaging criticism of the story in some sporting paper, written clearly by a man who *did* know, in which he explained the exact penalties which would have come upon everyone concerned if they had acted as I described. Half would have been in jail and the other half warned off the turf for ever. However, I have never been nervous about details, and one must be masterful sometimes. When an alarmed editor wrote to me once: 'There is no second line of rails at that point,' I answered, 'I make one.' On the other hand, there are cases where accuracy is essential.

I do not wish to be ungrateful to Holmes, who has been a good friend to me in many ways. If I have sometimes been inclined to weary of him it is because his character admits of no light or shade. He is a calculating machine, and anything you add to that simply weakens the effect. Thus the variety of the stories must depend upon the romance and compact handling of the plots. I would say a word for Watson also, who in the course of seven volumes never shows one gleam of humour or makes one single joke. To make a real character one must sacrifice everything to consistency and remember Goldsmith's criticism of Johnson that 'he would make the little fishes talk like whales.'

I do not think that I ever realised what a living actual personality Holmes had become to the more guileless readers, until I heard of the very pleasing story of the charabanc of French schoolboys who, when asked what they wanted to see first in London, replied unanimously that they wanted to see Mr Holmes's lodgings in Baker Street. Many have asked me which house it is, but that is a point which for excellent reasons I will not decide.

There are certain Sherlock Holmes stories, apocryphal I need not say, which go round and round the press and turn up at fixed intervals with the regularity of a comet.

One is the story of the cabman who is supposed to have taken me to a hotel in Paris. 'Dr Doyle,' he cried, gazing at me fixedly, 'I perceive from your appearance that you have been recently at Constantinople. I have reason to think also that you have been at Buda, and I perceive some indication that you were not far from Milan.' 'Wonderful. Five francs for the secret of how you did it?' 'I looked at the labels pasted on your trunk,' said the astute cabby.

Another perennial is of the woman who is said to have consulted Sherlock. 'I am greatly puzzled, sir. In one week I have lost a motor horn, a brush, a box of golf balls, a dictionary and a bootjack. Can you explain it?' 'Nothing simpler, madame,' said Sherlock. 'It is clear that your neighbour keeps a goat.'

There was a third about how Sherlock entered heaven, and by virtue of his power of observation at once greeted Adam, but the point is perhaps too anatomical for further discussion.

I suppose that every author receives a good many curious letters. Certainly I have done so. Quite a number of these have been from Russia. When they have been in the vernacular I have been compelled to take them as read, but when they have been in English they have been among the most curious in my collection.

There was one young lady who began all her epistles with the words 'Good Lord'. Another had a large amount of guile underlying her simplicity. Writing from Warsaw, she stated that she had been bed-ridden for two years, and that my novels had been her only, etc., etc. So touched was I by this flattering statement that I at once prepared an autographed parcel of them to complete the fair invalid's collection. By good luck, however, I met a brother author on the same day to whom I recounted the touching incident. With a cynical smile, he drew an identical letter from his pocket. His novels had also been for two years her only, etc., etc. I do not know how many more the lady had written to, but if, as I imagine, her correspondence had extended to several countries, she must have amassed a rather interesting library.

The young Russian's habit of addressing me as 'Good Lord' had an even stranger parallel at home which links it up with the subject of this article. Shortly after I received a knighthood, I had a bill from a trades-man which was quite correct and businesslike in every detail save that it was made out to Sir Sherlock Holmes. I hope that I can stand a joke as well as my neighbours, but this particular piece of humour seemed rather misapplied and I wrote sharply upon the subject.

In response to my letter there arrived at my hotel a very repentant clerk, who expressed his sorrow at the incident, but kept on repeating the phrase, 'I assure you, sir, that it was bona fide.'

'What do you mean by bona fide?' I asked.

'Well, sir,' he replied, 'my mates in the shop told me that you had been knighted, and that when a man was knighted he changed his name, and that you had taken that one.'

I need not say that my annoyance vanished, and that I laughed as heartily as his pals were probably doing round the corner.

A few of the problems which have come my way have been very similar to some which I had invented for the exhibition of the reasoning of Mr Holmes. I might perhaps quote one in which that gentleman's method of thought was copied with complete success. The case was as follows: A gentleman had disappeared. He had drawn a bank balance of £40 which was known to be on him. It was feared that he had been murdered for the sake of the money. He had last been heard of stopping at a large hotel in London, having come from the country that day. In the evening he went to a music-hall performance, came out of it about ten o'clock, returned to his hotel, changed his evening clothes, which were found in his room next day, and disappeared utterly. No one saw him leave the hotel, but a man occupying a neighbouring room declared that he had heard him moving during the night. A week had elapsed at the time that I was consulted, but the police had discovered nothing. Where was the man?

These were the whole of the facts as communicated to me by his relatives in the country. Endeavouring to see the matter through the eyes of Mr Holmes, I answered by return mail that he was evidently either in Glasgow or in Edinburgh. It proved later that he had, as a fact, gone to Edinburgh, though in the week that had passed he had moved to another part of Scotland.

There I should leave the matter, for, as Dr Watson has often shown, a solution explained is a mystery spoiled. At this stage the reader can lay down the book and show how simple it all is by working out the problem for himself. He has all the data which were ever given to me. For the sake of those, however, who have no turn for such conundrums, I will try to indicate the links which make the chain. The one advantage which I possessed was that I was familiar with the routine of London hotels – though I fancy it differs little from that of hotels elsewhere.

The first thing was to look at the facts and separate what was certain from what was conjecture. It was all certain except the statement of the person who heard the missing man in the night. How could he tell such a sound from any other sound in a large hotel? That point could be disregarded, if it traversed the general conclusions.

The first clear deduction was that the man had meant to disappear. Why else should he draw all his money? He had got out of the hotel during the night. But there is a night porter in all hotels, and it is impossible to get out without his knowledge when the door is once shut. The door is shut after the theatre-goers return – say at twelve o'clock. Therefore, the man left the hotel before twelve o'clock. He had come from the music-hall at ten, had changed his clothes, and had departed with his bag. No one had seen him do so. The inference is that he had done it at the moment when the hall was full of the returning guests, which is from eleven to eleven-thirty. After that hour, even if the door were still open, there are few people coming and going so that he with his bag would certainly have been seen.

Having got so far upon firm ground, we now ask ourselves why a man who desires to hide himself should go out at such an hour. If he intended to conceal himself in London he need never have gone to the hotel at all. Clearly then he was going to catch a train which would carry him away. But a man who is deposited by a train in any provincial station during the night is likely to be noticed, and he might be sure that when the alarm was raised and his description given, some guard or porter would remember him. Therefore, his destination would be some large town which he would reach as a terminus where all his fellow passengers would disembark and where he would lose himself in the crowd. When one turns up the timetable and sees that the great Scotch expresses bound for Edinburgh and Glasgow start about midnight, the goal is reached. As for his dress-suit, the fact that he abandoned it proved that he intended to adopt a line of life where there were no social amenities. This deduction also proved to be correct.

I quote such a case in order to show that the general lines of reasoning advocated by Holmes have a real practical application to life. In another case, where a girl had become engaged to a young foreigner who suddenly disappeared, I was able, by a similar process of deduction, to show her very clearly both whither he had gone and how unworthy he was of her affections.

On the other hand, these semi-scientific methods are occasionally laboured and slow as compared with the results of the rough-and-ready, practical man. Lest I should seem to have been throwing bouquets either to myself or to Mr Holmes, let me state that on the occasion of a burglary of the village inn, within a stone's throw of my house, the village constable, with no theories at all, had seized the culprit while I had got no further than that he was a left-handed man with nails in his boots.

The unusual or dramatic effects which lead to the invocation of Mr Holmes in fiction are, of course, great aids to him in reaching a conclusion. It is the case where there is nothing to get hold of which is the deadly one. I heard of such a one in America which would certainly have presented a formidable problem. A gentleman of blameless life starting off for a Sunday-evening walk with his family, suddenly observed that he had forgotten something. He went back into the house, the door of which was still open, and he left his people waiting for him outside. He never reappeared, and from that day to this there has been no clue as to what befell him. This was certainly one of the strangest cases of which I have ever heard in real life.

Another very singular case came within my own observation. It was sent to me by an eminent London publisher. This gentleman had in his employment a head of department whose name we shall take as Musgrave. He was a hard-working person, with no special feature in his character. Mr Musgrave died, and several years after his death a letter was received addressed to him, in the care of his employers. It bore the postmark of a tourist resort in the west of Canada, and had the note 'Conflfilms' upon the outside of the envelope, with the words 'Report Sy' in one corner.

The publishers naturally opened the envelope as they had no note of the dead man's relatives. Inside were two blank sheets of paper. The letter, I may add, was registered. The publisher, being unable to make anything of this, sent it on to me, and I submitted the blank sheets to every possible chemical and heat test, with no result whatever. Beyond the fact that the writing appeared to be that of a woman there is nothing to add to this account. The matter was, and remains, an insoluble mystery. How the correspondent could have something so secret to say to Mr Musgrave and yet not be aware that this person had been dead for several years is very hard to understand – or why blank sheets should be so carefully registered through the mail. I may add that I did not trust the sheets to my own chemical tests but had the best expert advice without getting any result. Considered as a case it was a failure – and a very tantalising one.

Mr Sherlock Holmes has always been a fair mark for practical jokers, and I have had numerous bogus cases of various degrees of ingenuity, marked cards, mysterious warnings, cypher messages and other curious communications. It is astonishing the amount of trouble which some people will take with no object save a mystification. Upon one occasion, as I was entering the hall to take part in an amateur billiard competition, I was handed by the attendant a small packet which had been left for me. Upon opening it I found a piece of ordinary green chalk such as is used in billiards. I was amused by the incident, and I put the chalk into my waistcoat pocket and used it during the game. Afterwards, I continued to use it until one day, some months later, as I rubbed the tip of my cue the face of the chalk crumbled in, and I found it was hollow. From the recess thus exposed I drew out a small slip of paper with the words 'From Arsène Lupin to Sherlock Holmes'.

Imagine the state of mind of the joker who took such trouble to accomplish such a result.

One of the mysteries submitted to Mr Holmes was rather upon the psychic plane and therefore beyond his powers. The facts as alleged are most remarkable, though I have no proof of their truth save that the lady wrote earnestly and gave both her name and address. The person, whom we will call Mrs Seagrave, had been given a curious second-hand ring, snake-shaped and dull gold. This she took from her finger at night. One night she slept with it on and had a fearsome dream in which she seemed to be pushing off some furious creature which fastened its teeth into her arm. On awakening, the pain in the arm continued, and next day the imprint of a double set of teeth appeared upon the arm, with one tooth of the lower jaw missing. The marks were in the shape of blue-black bruises which had not broken the skin.

'I do not know,' says my correspondent, 'what made me think the ring had anything to do with the matter, but I took a dislike to the thing and did not wear it for some months, when, being on a visit, I took to wearing it again.' To make a long story short, the same thing happened, and the lady settled the matter for ever by dropping her ring into the hottest corner of the kitchen range. This curious story, which I believe to be genuine, may not be as supernatural as it seems. It is well known that in some subjects a strong mental impression does produce a physical effect. Thus a very vivid nightmare dream with the impression of a bite might conceivably produce the mark of a bite. Such cases are well attested in medical annals. The second incident would, of course, arise by unconscious suggestion from the first. None the less, it is a very interesting little problem, whether psychic or material.

Buried treasures are naturally among the problems which have come to Mr Holmes. One genuine case was accompanied by a diagram reproduced overleaf. It refers to an Indiaman which was wrecked upon the South African coast in the year 1782. If I were a younger man, I should be seriously inclined to go personally and look into the matter.

The ship contained a remarkable treasure, including, I believe, the old crown regalia of Delhi. It is surmised that they buried these near the coast, and that this chart is a note of the spot. Each Indiaman in those days had its own semaphore code, and it is conjectured that the three marks upon the left are signals from a three-armed semaphore. Some record of their meaning might perhaps even now be found in the old papers of the India Office. The circle upon the right gives the compass

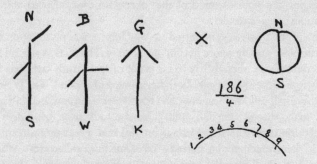

bearings. The larger semicircle may be the curved edge of a reef or of a rock. The figures above are the indications how to reach the X which marks the treasure. Possibly they may give the bearings as 186 feet from the 4 upon the semicircle. The scene of the wreck is a lonely part of the country, but I shall be surprised if sooner or later someone does not seriously set to work to solve the mystery – indeed at the present moment (1923) there is a small company working to that end.

I must now apologise for this digressive chapter and return to the orderly sequence of my career.

12

Norwood and Switzerland

The chief event of our Norwood life was the birth of my son Kingsley, who lived to play a man's part in the Great War, and who died shortly after its conclusion. My own life was so busy that I had little time for religious development, but my thoughts still ran much upon psychic matters, and it was at this time that I joined the Psychical Research Society, of which I am now one of the senior members. I had few psychic experiences myself, and my material philosophy, as expressed in *The Stark Munro Letters*, which were written just at the end of the Norwood period, was so strong that it did not easily crumble. Yet as year by year I read the wonderful literature of psychic science and experience, I became more and more impressed by the strength of the Spiritualist position and by the levity and want of all dignity and accurate knowledge which characterised the attitude of its opponents. The religious side of the matter had not yet struck me, but I felt more and more that the case for the phenomena vouched for by such men as Sir William Crookes, Barrett, Russel Wallace, Victor Hugo and Zöllner was so strong that I could see no answer to their exact record of observations. 'It is incredible but it is true,' said Crookes, and the aphorism seemed exactly to express my dawning convictions. I had a weekly impulse from the psychic paper, *Light*, which has, I maintain, during its long career and up to the present day, presented as much brain to the square inch as any journal published in these islands.

My pleasant recollection of those days from 1880 to 1893 lay in my first introduction, as a more or less rising author, to the literary life of London. It is extraordinary to remember that at that time there was a general jeremiad in the London press about the extinction of English literature, and the assumed fact that there were no rising authors to take the place of those who were gone. The real fact is that there was a most amazing crop, all coming up simultaneously, presenting perhaps no Dickens or Thackeray, but none the less so numerous and many sided and with so high an average of achievement that I think they would match for varied excellence any similar harvest in our literary history. It was during the years roughly from 1888 to 1893 that Rudyard Kipling, James Stephen Phillips, Watson, Grant Allen, Wells, Barrie, Bernard Shaw, H. A. Jones, Pinero, Marie Corelli, Stanley Weyman, Anthony Hope, Hall Caine and a whole list of others were winning their spurs. Many of these men I met in the full flush of their youth and their powers. Of some of them I will speak more fully later. As to the old school they were certainly somewhat of a declension, and the newcomers found no very serious opposition in gaining a hearing. Wilkie Collins, Trollope, George Eliot and Charles Reade had passed. I have always been a very great admirer of the last, who was really a great innovator as well as a most dramatic writer, for it was he who first introduced realism and founded his stories upon carefully arranged documents. He was the literary father of Zola. George Eliot has never appealed to me much, for I like my effects in a less leisurely fashion; but Trollope also I consider to be a very original writer, though I fancy he traces his ancestry through Jane Austen. No writer is ever absolutely original. He always joins at some point on to that old tree of which he is a branch.

Of the literary men whom I met at that time my most vivid recollections are of the group who centred round the new magazine *The Idler*, which had been started by Jerome K. Jerome, who had deservedly shot into fame with his splendidly humorous *Three Men in a Boat*. It has all the exuberance and joy of life which youth brings with it, and even now if I have ever time to be at all sad, which is seldom enough, I can laugh away the shadows when I open that book. Jerome is a man who, like most humorists, has a very serious side to his character, as all who have seen *The Passing of theThird Floor Back* will acknowledge, but he was inclined to be hotheaded and intolerant in political matters, from pure earnestness of purpose, which alienated some of his friends. He was associated in the editorship of *The Idler* with Robert Barr, a volcanic Anglo- or rather Scot-American, with a violent manner, a wealth of strong adjectives and one of the kindest of natures underneath it all. He was one of the best raconteurs I have ever known, and as a writer I have always felt that he did not quite come into his own. George Burgin, like some quaint gentle character from Dickens, was the sub-editor, and

Barrie, Zangwill and many other rising men were among the contributors who met periodically at dinner. I was not unfaithful to *The Strand*, but there were some contributions which they did not need, and with these I established my connection with *The Idler*. It was at this time and in this way that I met James Barrie, of whom I shall have more to say when I come to that chapter which treats of some eminent and interesting men whom I have known.

Two isolated facts stand out in my memory during that time at Norwood. One was that there seemed to be an imminent danger of war with France and that I applied for the Mediterranean war-correspondentship of the *Central News*, guessing that the chief centre of activity and interest would be in that quarter. I got the appointment and was all ready to start, but fortunately the crisis passed. The second was my first venture in the drama. I had written a short story called 'A Straggler of '15', which had seemed to me to be a moving picture of an old soldier and his ways. My own eyes were moist as I wrote it and that is the surest way to moisten those of others. I now turned this into a one-act play, and, greatly daring, I sent it to Henry Irving, of whose genius I had been a fervent admirer ever since those Edinburgh days when I had paid my sixpence for the gallery night after night to see him in *Hamlet* and *The Lyons Mail*. To my great delight I had a pleasing note from Bram Stoker, the great man's secretary, offering me a hundred pounds for the copyright. It was a good bargain for him, for it is not too much to say that Corporal Gregory Brewster became one of his stock parts and it had the enormous advantage that the older he got the more naturally he played it. The house laughed and sobbed, exactly as I had done when I wrote it. Several critics went out of their way to explain that the merit lay entirely with the great actor and had nothing to do with the indifferent play, but as a matter of fact the last time I saw it acted it was by a real corporal from a military camp, in the humble setting of a village hall and it had exactly the same effect upon the audience which Irving produced at the Lyceum. So perhaps there was something in the writing after all, and certainly every stage effect was indicated in the manuscript. I would add that with his characteristic largeness in money matters Irving always sent me a guinea for each performance in spite of his purchase of the copyright. Henry Irving the son carried on the part and played it, in my opinion, better than the father. I can well remember the flush of pleasure on his face when I uttered the word 'better' and how he seized my hand. I have no doubt it was trying for his great powers to be continually belittled by their measurement with those of his giant father, to whom he bore so remarkable a physical resemblance. His premature death was a great loss to the stage, as was that of his brother Lawrence, drowned with his wife in the great Canadian river of the same name as himself.

I now come to the great misfortune which darkened and deflected our lives. I have said that my wife and I had taken a tour in Switzerland. I do not know whether she had overtaxed herself in this excursion, or whether we encountered microbes in some inn bedroom, but the fact remains that within a few weeks of our return she complained of pain in her side and cough. I had no suspicion of anything serious, but sent for the nearest good physician. To my surprise and alarm he told me when he descended from the bedroom that the lungs were very gravely affected, that there was every sign of rapid consumption and that he thought the case a most serious one with little hope, considering her record and family history, of a permanent cure. With two children, aged four and one, and a wife who was in such deadly danger, the situation was a difficult one. I confirmed the diagnosis by having Sir Douglas Powell down to see her, and I then set all my energy to work to save the situation. The home was abandoned, the newly bought furniture was sold, and we made for Davos in the High Alps where there seemed the best chance of killing this accursed microbe which was rapidly eating out her vitals.

And we succeeded. When I think that the attack was one of what is called 'galloping consumption', and that the doctors did not give more than a few months, and yet that we postponed the fatal issue from 1893 to 1906, I think it is proof that the successive measures were wise. The invalid's life was happy too, for it was necessarily spent in glorious scenery. It was seldom marred by pain, and it was sustained by that optimism which is peculiar to the disease, and which came naturally to her quietly contented nature.

As there were no particular social distractions at Davos, and as our life was bounded by the snow and fir which girt us in, I was able to devote myself to doing a good deal of work and also to taking up with some energy the winter sports for which the place is famous. Whilst there I began the Brigadier Gerard series of stories, founded largely upon that great book *The Memoirs of General Marbot*. This entailed a great deal of research into Napoleonic days, and my military detail was, I think, very accurate – so much so that I had a warm letter of appreciation from

Archibald Forbes, the famous war correspondent, who was himself a great Napoleonic and military student. Before the end of the winter we were assured that the ravages of the disease had been checked. I dared not return to England, however, for fear of a relapse, so with the summer we moved on to Maloja, another health resort at the end of the Engadine valley, and there we endeavoured to hold all we had won – which, with occasional relapses, we succeeded in doing.

My sister Lottie, free at last from the work which she had so bravely done, had now joined us. Connie, the younger sister, had come back from Portugal earlier, and had joined us at Norwood, where she had met and eventually married E. W. Hornung the novelist. Of Hornung I will speak later. In the meantime Lottie's presence and the improvement of the invalid, which was so marked that no sudden crisis was thought at all possible, gave me renewed liberty of action. Before the catastrophe occurred I had given some lectures on literature at home, and the work with its movement and bustle was not distasteful to me. Now I was strongly pressed to go to America on the same errand, and in the late autumn of 1894 I set out on this new adventure.

My brother Innes, he who had shared my first days in Southsea, had since passed through Richmond Public School, and afterwards the Woolwich Academy, so that he was now just emerging as a subaltern. As I needed some companion, and as I thought that the change would do him good, I asked him to come with me to the States. We crossed on the ill-fated German liner *Elbe*, which a very short time afterwards was sunk after collision with a collier in the North Sea. Already I observed evidence of that irrational hatred of the British which in the course of twenty years was to lead to so terrific a result involving the destruction of the German Empire. I remember that on some fête day on board, the saloon was thickly decorated with German and American flags without one single British one, though a fair proportion of the passengers were British. Innes and I then and there drew a Union Jack and stuck it up aloft, where its isolation drew attention to our grievance.

Major Pond was my impresario in America, and a quaint character he was. He seemed the very personification of his country, huge, loose limbed, straggling, with a goat's beard and a nasal voice. He had fought in the Civil War and been mixed up with every historical American event of his lifetime.

He was a good, kind fellow and we formed a friendship which was never broken. He met us in the docks, and carried us off to a little hotel beside the Aldine Club, a small literary club, in which we had our meals.

I have treated America and my impression of that amazing and perplexing country in later pages of these memoirs, when I visited it under more detached conditions. At present it was all hard work with little time for general observations. Pond had fixed me up a pretty hard schedule, but on the other hand I had bargained to get back to Davos in time to spend Christmas with my wife, so that there was a limit to my servitude. My first reading was given in a fashionable Baptist Church, which was the usual launching slip for Pond's new lecturers. We had walked from the retiring-room and were just coming in sight of the audience when I felt something tickle my ear. I put up my hand and found that my collar was undone, my tie had fallen off, and my stud, the first cause of all the trouble, had disappeared. Standing there, on the edge of the platform, Pond dragged out his own stud. I replaced everything, and sailed on quite as I should be, while Pond retired to refit. It is strange, and possibly more than coincidence, how often one is prevented at the last moment from making some foolish appearance in public.

The readings went very well and the audience was generous in applause. I have my own theory of reading, which is that it should be entirely disassociated from acting and should be made as natural and also as audible as possible. Such a presentment is, I am sure, the less tiring for an audience. Indeed I read to them exactly as in my boyhood I used to read to my mother. I gave extracts from recent British authors, including some work of my own, and as I mixed up the grave and the gay I was able to keep them mildly entertained for an hour. Some papers maintained that I could not read at all, but I think that what they really meant was that I did not act at all. Others seemed to endorse my method. Anyhow I had an excellent first reception and Pond told me that he lay smiling all night after it. He had no difficulty afterwards in booking as many engagements as he could fit into the time. I visited every town of any size between Boston in the north and Washington in the south, while Chicago and Milwaukee marked my western limit.

Sometimes I found that it took me all my time to fit in the engagements, however fast I might travel. Once, for example, I lectured at Daly's Theatre in New York at a matinée, at Princetown College the same evening, some hundred miles away, and at Philadelphia next afternoon. It was no wonder that I got very tired – the more so as the exuberant hospitality in those pre-prohibition days was enough in itself to take the energies out of the visitor. It was all done in kindness, but it was dangerous for a man who had his work to do. I had one little break when I paid a pleasant visit to Rudyard Kipling, of which I shall speak later. Bar those few days I was going hard all the time, and it is no wonder that I was so tired out that I kept to my bunk most of the way from New York to Liverpool.

My memories are the confused ones of a weary man. I recall one amusing incident when as I bustled on to the stage at Daly's Theatre I tripped over the wooden sill of the stage door, with the result that I came cantering down the sloping stage towards the audience, shedding books and papers on my way. There was much laughter and a general desire for an encore.

Our visit was marred by one of those waves of anti-British feeling which sweep occasionally over the States, and which emanate from their own early history, every grievance being exaggerated and inflamed by the constant hostility of Irish pressmen and politicians. It all seems very absurd and contemptible to the travelling Briton, because he is aware how entirely one-sided it is, and how welcome, for example, is the American flag in every British public display. This was not known by the home-staying American, and probably he imagined that his own country was treated as rudely by us as ours by his. The Dunraven yacht race had given additional acerbity to this chronic ill-feeling, and it was very active at the time of our visit. I remember that a banquet was given to us at a club at Detroit at which the wine flowed freely, and which ended by a speech by one of our hosts in which he bitterly attacked the British Empire. My brother and I, with one or two Canadians who were present, were naturally much affronted, but we made every allowance for the lateness of the evening. I asked leave, however, to reply to the speech, and some of those who were present have assured me that they have never forgotten what I said. In the course of my remarks I said: 'You Americans have lived up to now within your own palings, and know nothing of the real world outside. But now your land is filled up, and you will be compelled to mix more with the other nations. When you do so you will find that there is only one which can at all under- stand your ways and your aspirations, or will have the least sympathy. That is the mother country which you are now so fond of insulting. She is an Empire, and you will soon be an Empire also, and only then will you understand each other, and you will realise that you have only one real friend in the world.' It was only two or three years later that there came the Cuban war, the episode of Manilla Bay where the British commander joined up with the Americans against the Germans, and several other incidents which proved the truth of my remarks.

A writer of average income is bound to lose pecuniarily upon a lecture tour, even in America, unless he prolongs it very much and works very hard indeed. By losing I do not mean that he is actually out of pocket, but that he could have earned far more if he had never gone outside his own study. In my own case I found after our joint expenses were paid that there was about £1,000 over. The disposal of this money furnished a curious example of the power of prayer, which, as Mr S. S. McClure has already narrated it, I have no delicacy in telling. He tells how he was endeavouring to run his magazine, how he was down to his last farthing, how he dropped on his knees on the office floor to pray for help, and how on the same day an Englishman who was a mere acquaintance walked into the office, and said: 'McClure, I believe in you and in the future of your magazine,' and put down £1,000 on the table. A critic might perhaps observe that under such circumstances to sell 1,000 shares at face value was rather hard upon the ignorant and trusting buyer. For a long time I could clearly see the workings of providence as directed towards Sam McClure, but could not quite get their perspective as regards myself, but I am bound to admit that in the long run, after many vicissitudes, the deal was justified both ways, and I was finally able to sell my holding twenty years later at a reasonable advance. The immediate result, however, was that I returned to Davos with all my American earnings locked up, and with no actual visible result of my venture.

The Davos season was in full blast when I returned, and my wife was holding her own well. It was at this time, in the early months of 1895, that I developed ski-running in Switzerland as described in my chapter on sport. We lingered late at Davos, so late that I was able to lay out a golf course, which was hampered in its start by the curious trick the cows had of chewing up the red flags. From Davos we finally moved to Caux, over the Lake of Geneva, where for some months I worked steadily at my writing. With the autumn I visited England, leaving the ladies at Caux, and it was then that events occurred which turned our road of life to a new angle.

Egypt in 1896

The wretched microbe which had so completely disorganised our lives, and which had produced all the sufferings so patiently borne, now seemed to be latent, and it was hoped that if we spent a winter in Egypt the cure might be complete. During this short visit to England, whither I had to rush every now and again in order to adjust my affairs, I met Grant Allen at luncheon, and he told me that he had also suffered from consumption and that he had found his salvation in the soil and air of Hindhead in Surrey. It was quite a new idea to me that we might actually live with impunity in England once more, and it was a pleasant thought after resigning oneself to a life which was unnatural to both of us at foreign health resorts. I acted very promptly, for I rushed down to Hindhead, bought an admirable plot of ground, put the architectural work into the hands of my old friend and fellow psychic researcher Mr Ball of Southsea, and saw the builder chosen and everything in train before leaving England in the autumn of 1895. If Egypt was a success, we should have a roof of our own to which to return. The thought of it brought renewed hope to the sufferer.

I then set forth, picked up my wife and my sister Lottie at Caux and took them on by easy stages through Italy, stopping a few days at Rome, and so to Brindisi, where we picked up a boat for Egypt. Once at Cairo we took up our quarters at the Mena Hotel, in the very shadow of the Pyramids, and there we settled down for the winter. I was still doing the Brigadier Gerard stories at the time, which required a good deal of historical research, but I had brought my materials with me, and all I lacked was the energy, which I found it most difficult to find in that enervating land.

On the whole it was a pleasant winter and led up to a most unforeseen climax. I ascended the Great Pyramid once, and was certainly never tempted to do so again, and was content to watch the struggles of the endless drove of tourists who attempted that uncomfortable and useless feat. There was golf of sorts and there was riding. I was still an immature horseman, but I felt that only practice would help me, so I set forth upon weird steeds provided by the livery stables opposite. As a rule they erred on the side of dullness, but I have a very vivid recollection of one which restored the average. If my right eyelid drops somewhat over my eye it is not the result of philosophic brooding, but it is the doing of a black devil of a horse with a varminty head, slab-sided ribs and restless ears. I disliked the look of the beast, and the moment I threw my leg over him he dashed off as if it were a race. Away we went across the desert, I with one foot in the stirrup, holding on as best I might. It is possible I could have kept on until he was weary, but he came suddenly on cultivated land and his forelegs sank in a moment over his fetlocks. The sudden stop threw me over his head, but I held on to the bridle, and he, pawing about with his front hoofs, struck me over the eye, and made a deep star-shaped wound which covered me with blood. I led him back and a pretty sight I presented as I appeared before the crowded verandah! Five stitches were needed, but I was thankful, for very easily I might have lost my sight.

My wife was well enough now to join in society, while my sister was just at an age to enjoy it, so that we saw a little of the very jovial life of Cairo, though the fact that Mena is some seven miles out, on the most monotonous road in the world, saved us from any excess. It was always a task to get in and out, so that only a great temptation would draw us. I joined in male society, however, a good deal and learned to know many of those great men who were shaping the new destinies of Egypt. I sketched some of them at the time in two paragraphs which may be quoted.

There is a broad and comfortable sofa in the hall of the Turf Club, and if you sit there about luncheon time you will see a fair sprinkling of Anglo-Egyptians, men who have helped to make, and are still helping to make, the history of our times. You have a view of the street from where you are, and perhaps in the brilliant sunshine a carriage flies past with two running syces before it and an English coachman upon the box. Within, one catches a glimpse of a strong florid face with a close-cropped soldierly grey moustache, the expression good-humoured and inscrutable. This is Lord Cromer, whom Egypt has changed from a major of gunners to a peer of the realm, while he in turn has changed it from a province of the East to one of the West. One has but to look at him to read the secret of his success as a diplomatist. His clear head, his brave heart, his physical health, and his nerves of iron are all impressed upon you even in that momentary glance at his carriage. And that lounging ennuyé attitude is characteristic also – most characteristic at this moment, when few men in the world can have more pressing responsibility upon their shoulders. It is what one could expect from the man who at the most critical moment of recent Egyptian history is commonly reported to have brought diplomatic interviews to an abrupt conclusion with the explanation that the time had come for his daily lawn-tennis engagement. It is no wonder that so strong a representative should win the confidence of his own countrymen, but he has made as deep an impression upon the native mind, which finds it difficult under this veiled Protectorate of ours to estimate the comparative strength of individuals. 'Suppose Khedive tell Lord Cromer go, Lord Cromer go?' asked my donkey-boy, and so put his chocolate finger upon the central point of the whole situation.

But this is a digression from the Turf Club, where you are seated upon a settee in the hall and watching the Englishmen who have done so much to regenerate Egypt. Of all the singular experiences of this most venerable land, surely this rebuilding at the hands of a little group of bustling, clear-headed Anglo-Saxons is the most extraordinary. There are Garstin and Wilcocks, the great water captains who have coaxed the Nile to right and to left, until the time seems to be coming when none of its waters will ever reach the Mediterranean at all. There is Kitchener, tall and straight, a grim silent soldier, with the weal of a Dervish bullet upon his face. There you may see Rogers, who stamped out the cholera, Scott, who reformed the law, Palmer, who relieved the over-taxed fellaheen, Hooker, who exterminated the locusts, Wingate, who knows more than any European of the currents of feeling in the Sudan – the same Wingate who reached his arm out a thousand miles and plucked Slatin out of Khartoum. And beside him the small man with the yellow-brown moustache and the cheery, ruddy face is Slatin himself, whose one wish in the world now is to have the Khalifa at his sword-point – that Khalifa at whose heels he had to run for so many weary years.

Shortly after the opening of the New Year of 1896 we went in one of Cook's boats up the river, getting as far as the outposts of civilisation at

Wady Halfa. The banks in the upper reaches were not too safe, as raiders on camels came down at times, but on the water one was secure from all the chances of fate. At the same time I thought that the managers of these tours took undue risks, and when I found myself on one occasion on the rock of Abousir with a drove of helpless tourists, male and female, nothing whatever between us and the tribesmen, and a river between us and the nearest troops, I could not but think what an appalling situation would arise if a little troop of these far-riding camel men were to appear. We had four negro soldiers as an escort, who would be helpless before any normal raiding party. It was the strong impression which I there received which gave me the idea of taking a group of people of different types and working out what the effect of so horrible an experience would be upon each. This became *The Tragedy of the Korosko*, published in America as *A Desert Drama* and afterwards dramatised with variations as *The Fires of Fate*. All went well as a matter of fact, but I thought then, and experienced British officers agreed with me, that it was unjustifiable. As the whole frontier force was longing for an excuse to advance, I am not sure that they would not have welcomed it if the Dervishes had risen to the ground bait which every week in the same place was laid in front of them.

I do not know how many temples we explored during that tour, but they seemed to me endless, some dating back to the mists of antiquity and some as recent as Cleopatra and the Roman period. The majestic continuity of Egyptian History seems to be its most remarkable feature. You examine the tombs of the First Dynasty at Abydos and there you see carved deep in the stone the sacred hawk, the goose, the plover, the signs of Horus and Osiris, of Upper and Lower Egypt. These were carved long before the Pyramids were built and can hardly be less ancient than 4000 BC. Then you inspect a temple built by the Ptolemies, after the date of Alexander the Great, and there you see the same old symbols cut in the same old way. There is nothing like this in the world. The Roman and the British Empires are mushrooms in comparison. Judged by Egyptian standards the days of Alfred the Great would be next door to our own, and our customs, symbols and way of thinking the same. The race seems to have petrified, and how they could do so without being destroyed by some more virile nation is hard to understand.

Their arts seem to have been high but their reasoning power in many ways contemptible. The recent discovery of the king's tomb near

Thebes – I write in 1924 – shows how wonderful were their decorations and the amenities of their lives. But consider the tomb itself. What a degraded intelligence does it not show! The idea that the body, the old outworn greatcoat which was once wrapped round the soul, should at any cost be preserved is the last word in materialism. And the hundred baskets of provisions to feed the soul upon its journey! I can never believe that a people with such ideas could be other than emasculated in their minds – the fate of every nation which comes under the rule of a priesthood.

It had been suggested that I should go out to the Salt Lakes in the desert some fifty miles from Cairo, and see the old Coptic monastery there. Those ancient monasteries, the abode alternately of saints and perverts – we saw specimens of each – have always aroused my keen interest, dating as they do to very early days of Christianity. Indeed, their date is often unknown, but everything betokens great age and the spirit which founded them seems to have been that of the hermits who in the third and fourth centuries swarmed in these wildernesses.

Leaving my wife at Mena, I went with Colonel Lewis of the Egyptian army, an excellent companion and guide. On arriving at a wayside station, we found a most amazing vehicle awaiting us, a sort of circus coach, all gilding and frippery. It proved to be the coach of state which had been prepared for Napoleon III on the chance that he would come to open the Suez Canal. It was surely a good bit of work, for here it was still strong and fit, but absurdly out of place in the majestic simplicity of the Libyan Desert.

Into this we got and set forth, the only guide being wheel-marks across the sand which in some of the harder places were almost invisible. The great sand waste rolled in yellow billows all around us, and far behind us the line of green trees marked the course of the Nile. Once a black dot appeared which, as it grew nearer, proved to be some sort of Oriental on foot. As he came up to us he opened a blackened mouth, pointed to it, and cried, 'Moya! Moya!' which means water. We had none and could only point encouragingly to the green belt behind us, on which with a curse he staggered upon his way.

A surprising adventure befell us, for the heavens suddenly clouded over and rain began to fall, an almost unknown thing in those parts. We lumbered on, however, with our two horses, while Colonel Lewis, who was keen on getting fit, ran behind. I remember saying to him that in my wildest dreams I never thought that I should drive across the Libyan Desert in an emperor's coach with a full colonel as carriage dog.

Presently in the fading light the horses slowed down, the Nubian driver descended, and began alternately scanning the ground and making gestures of despair. We realised then that he had lost the tracks and therefore that we had no notion where we were, though we had strong reasons to believe that we were to the south of the route. The difficulty was to know which was north and which south. It was an awkward business since we had no food or water and could see no end to our troubles. The farther we moved the deeper we should be involved. Night had closed in, and I was looking up at the drifting scud above us when in the chink of two clouds I saw for an instant a cluster of stars, and made sure that they were the four wheels of Charles's Wain. I am no astronomer, but I reasoned that this constellation would lie to the north of us, and so it proved, for when we headed that way, examining the ground every hundred yards or so with matches, we came across the track once more.

Our adventures, however, were not over, and it was all like a queer dream. We had great difficulty in keeping the track in the darkness, and the absurd coach lumbered and creaked while we walked with lanterns ahead of it. Suddenly to our joy we saw a bright light in the gloom. We quickened our pace, and came presently to a tent with a florid-bearded man seated outside it beside a little table where he was drawing by the light of a lamp. The rain had cleared now, but the sky was still overcast. In answer to our hail this man rather gruffly told us that he was a German surveyor at work in the desert. He motioned with his hand when we told him whither we were bound, and said it was close by. After leaving him we wandered on, and losing the tracks we were again very badly bushed. It seemed an hour or two before to our joy we saw a light ahead and prepared for a night's rest at the halfway house, which was our immediate destination. But when we reached the light what we saw was a florid-bearded man sitting outside a small tent with a lamp upon a table. We had moved in a circle. Fresh explanations – and this time we really did keep to the track and reached a big deserted wooden hut, where we put up the horses, ate some cold food, and tumbled, very tired, into two of the bunks which lined it.

The morrow made amends for all. It broke cold and clear and I have seldom felt a greater sense of exhilaration than when I awoke and walking out before dressing saw the whole endless desert stretching away on every side of me, yellow sand and black rock, to the blue shimmering horizon. We harnessed up and within a few hours came on the Natron Lake, a great salt lake, with a few scattered houses at one end where the workers dry out and prepare the salt. A couple of miles off was the lonely monastery which we had come to see – less lonely now, but before the saltworks were established one of the most inaccessible places one could imagine. It consisted of a huge outer wall, which seemed to be made of hardened clay. It had no doors or windows save one little opening which could be easily defended against the prowling Arabs, but I fear the garrison would not be very stout-hearted, for it was said to be the fear of military service which caused many of the monks to discover that they had a vocation. On being admitted I was conscious that we were not too welcome, though the military title of my companion commanded respect. We were shown round the inner courtyard, where there were palm trees and a garden, and then round the scattered houses within the wall. Near the latter there was, I remember, a barrel full of some substance which seemed to me, both by look and feel, to be rounded pieces of some light stone, and I asked if it were to hurl down at the Arabs if they attacked the door. It proved to be the store of bread for the monastery. We were treated to wine, which was sweet tent wine, which is still used, I believe, in the Holy Communion, showing how straight our customs come from the East. The Abbot seemed to me to be a decent man, but he complained of illness and was gratified when I overhauled him thoroughly, percussed his chest, and promised to send him out some medicine from Cairo. I did so, but whether it ever reached my remote patient I never learned. Some of the brothers, however, looked debauched, and there was a general air of nothing-to-do, which may have been deceptive but which certainly impressed me that day. As I looked from the walls and saw the desert on all sides, unbroken save for one blue corner of the salt lake, it was strange to consider that this was all these men would ever see of the world, and to contrast their fate with my own busy and varied existence. There was a library, but the books were scattered on the floor, all of them old and some no doubt rare. Since the discovery of the *Codex Sinaiticus* I presume that all these old Coptic libraries have been examined by scholars, but it certainly seemed to me that there might be some valuable stuff in that untidy heap.

Next evening Colonel Lewis and I were back in Cairo. We heard no news upon the way, and we had reached the Turf Club and were in the cloakroom washing our hands before dinner when some man came in and said: 'Why, Lewis, how is it you are not with your brigade?'

'My brigade!'

'Have you been away?'

'Yes, at the Natron Lake.'

'Good heavens! Have you heard nothing?'

'No.'

'Why, man, war is declared. We are advancing on Dongola. The whole army is concentrating on the frontier, and you are in command of an advanced brigade.'

'Good God!' Lewis's soap splashed into the water, and I wonder he did not fall plump on the floor. Thus it was that we learned of the next adventure which was opening up before both us and the British Empire.

14

On the Edge of a Storm

It is impossible to be near great historical events and not to desire to take part in them, or at the least to observe them. Egypt had suddenly become the storm centre of the world, and chance had placed me there at that moment. Clearly I could not remain in Cairo, but must get up by hook or by crook to the frontier. It was March and the weather would soon be too warm for my wife, but she was good enough to say that she would wait with my sister until April if I would promise to return by then. At that time the general idea was that some great event would at once occur, though looking back one can see that that was hardly possible. Anyhow I had a great urge to go south.

There was only one way to do it. The big morning papers had their men already upon the spot, but it was less likely that the evening papers were provided. I cabled to the *Westminster Gazette* asking to be made their honorary correspondent *pro tem*. I had a cable back assenting. Armed with this I approached the proper authority, and so within a day or two I was duly appointed and everything was in order.

I had to make my own way up and I had to get together some sort of kit. The latter was done hurriedly and was of fearsome quality. I bought a huge revolver of Italian make with a hundred cartridges, an ugly unreliable weapon. I bought also a water bottle, which was made of new resinous wood and gave a most horrible flavour of turpentine to everything put into it. It was like drinking varnish, but before I got back there were times when I was ready to drink varnish or anything else that was damp.

With a light khaki coat, riding breeches, a small valise, and the usual Christmas tree hung round me, I started off from Cairo by train to Asyut, where a small river boat was waiting. It was filled with officers going to the front, and we had a pleasant few days journeying to Aswan together. There were, I remember, several junior officers who have since made names in the world, Maxwell (now General Sir John Maxwell) and Hickman, who also rose to the top. There was a young cavalry lieutenant also, one Smythe, who seemed to me to be too gentle and quiet for such rough work as lay ahead. The next time I heard of him was when he was gazetted for the Victoria Cross. In soldiering there is nothing more deceptive than appearances. Your fierce, truculent man may always have a yellow streak where the gentle student has a core of steel. There lay one of the many mistakes which the Germans made later in judging those 'unwarlike islanders' the British.

The great question at the opening of the campaign was whether the native fellah troops would stand. The five negro battalions were as good as could be, but the record of the eight or nine Egyptian ones was not reassuring. The Arab of the Sudan is a desperate fanatic who rushes to death with the frenzy of a madman, and longs for close quarters where he can bury his spear in the body of his foeman, even though he carries several bullets in him before he reaches him. Would the Egyptians stand such onslaughts as these? It was thought improbable that they would, and so British battalions, the Connaughts, the Staffords and others, were brought up to stiffen their battle line. One great advantage the native soldiers had – and without it their case would have been hopeless – and that was that their officers were among the picked men of the British army. Kitchener would have none but the unmarried, for it was to be a wholehearted and if need be a desperate service, and, as the pay and life were good, he could accept or reject as he chose, so that his leaders were splendid. It was curious to see their fair faces and flaxen moustaches under the red tarbooshes, as they marched at the side of their men.

The relations between these officers and their men were paternal. If an officer of black troops came to Cairo he would go back with a pillow case stuffed with candies for his men. The Egyptians were more inscrutable, less sporting and less lovable, but none the less their officers were very loyal to them, and bitterly resented the distrust shown by the rest of the army. One British officer at some early battle seized the enemy's flag and cried: 'Well, the English shall not have this anyhow.' It is this spirit, whether in Egypt or in India, which makes the British officer an ideal leader of native troops. Even at the great Indian Mutiny they would not hear a word against their men until they were murdered by them.

At Aswan we were held up for a week, and no one was allowed to go farther. We were already well within the radius of the Arab raiders, for in the last year they had struck even farther north. The desert is like the sea, for if you have the camels, which correspond to the ships, your blow may fall anywhere and your attack is not suspected until the moment that you appear. The crowd of British officers who were waiting seemed little worried by any such possibility and were as unconcerned as if it was a Cook's tour and not a particularly dangerous expedition – so dangerous that of the last army which went south, that of Hicks Pasha, hardly one single man was ever seen again. Only once did I see them really excited. I had returned to the hotel which was the general headquarters, and as I entered the hall I saw a crowd of them all clustering round the notice board to read a telegram which had just been suspended. They were on the toes of their spurred boots, with their necks outstretched and every sign of quivering and eager interest. 'Ah,' thought I, 'at last we have got through the hide of these impenetrable men. I suppose the Khalifa is coming down, horse, foot and artillery, and we are on the eve of battle.' I pushed my way in, and thrust my head among all the bobbing sun-helmets. It was the account of the Oxford and Cambridge Boat Race.

I was struck by the splendid zeal of everyone. It was an inspiration. Hickman had been full of combative plans all the way on the boat. When we arrived there was a message for him to go down to Keneh and buy camels. Here was a drop down for a man all on fire for action. 'It is quite right,' said he, when I condoled with him. 'The force must have camels. I am the man to buy them. We all work for one end.' Self-abnegation of this sort is general. The British officer at his best is really a splendid fellow, a large edition of the public schoolboy, with his cheery slang overlying a serious purpose which he would usually die rather than admit. I heard of three of them at rail-end, all doing essential work and all with a degree of fever on them which might well have excused them from work altogether. Every evening each of them dropped a dollar into a hat, they then all took their temperatures and the highest got the pool.

Aswan is at the foot of the cataract, which extends for some thirty miles, and everything has to be transhipped and taken on a narrow toy railway to be reloaded on fresh steamers at Shellal. It was a huge task and I remember sympathising with Captain Morgan, who with fatigue parties of Egyptians and chain gangs of convicts was pushing the stuff through. Morgan had sold me a horse once and was shy of me in consequence, but he soon saw that I bore no grudge. *Caveat emptor!* I already saw in him those qualities of organisation which made him a real factor both in the Boer and in the European War. He has just died (1923) a general and full of honours. I remember seeing the 7th Egyptians after a long gruelling desert march working at those stores until they were so played out that it took four of them to raise a sixty-pound biscuit box.

The big pressmen had now arrived – 'Where the carcass is there shall the eagles, etc.' – and I had luckily made friends with them, so it was determined that we should all go on together. There were five of us who started out, led by Knight of the *Falcon*, representing *The Times*, and looking not unlike a falcon himself. He was a great man, tall and muscular, a famous yachtsman and treasure-seeker, traveller, fighter and scholar. He had just left the French in Madagascar. Next came Scudamore of the *Daily News*, small, Celtic, mercurial, full of wit and go. He was a great purchaser of camels, which were of course all paid for by the paper, so that when Robinson, the editor of the *Daily News*, heard of the Boer War his first comment was, 'Well, thank God, there are no camels in South Africa.' It was a study in Eastern ways to see Scudamore buying camels, and I learned from him how it is done. An Arab leads up the absurd-looking creature. You look depreciatingly at the beast – and you cannot take a better model than the creature's own expression as it looks at you. You ask how much is wanted for it. The owner says sixteen pounds. You then give a shriek of derision, sweep your arm across as if to wave him and his camel out of your sight for ever, and turning with a whisk you set off rapidly in the other direction. How far you go depends upon the price asked. If it is really very high, you may not get back for your dinner. But as a rule a hundred yards or so meet the case, and you shape your course so as to reach the camel and its owner. You stop in front of them and look at them with a disinterested and surprised look to intimate that you wonder that they should still be loitering there. The Arab asks how much you will give. You answer eight pounds. Then it is his turn to scream, whisk round, and do his hundred yards, his absurd chattel with its hornpipey legs trotting along behind him. But he returns to say that he will take fourteen, and off you go again with a howl and a wave. So the bargaining goes on, the circles continually shortening, until you have settled upon the middle price. But it is only when you have bought your camel that the troubles begin. It is the strangest and most deceptive animal in the world. Its appearance is so staid and respectable that you cannot give it credit for the black villany that lurks within. It approaches you with a mildly interested and superior expression, like a patrician lady in a Sunday school. You feel that a pair of glasses at the end of a fan is the one thing lacking. Then it puts its lips gently forward, with a faraway look in its eyes, and you have just time to say, 'The pretty dear is going to kiss me,' when two rows of frightful green teeth clash in front of you, and you give such a backward jump as you could never have hoped at your age to accomplish. When once the veil is dropped, anything more demoniacal than the face of a camel cannot be conceived. No kindness and no length of ownership seem to make them friendly. And yet you must make allowances for a creature which can carry six hundred pounds for twenty miles a day, and ask for no water and little food at the end of it.

This, however, is digression. The other pressmen were Beaman of the *Standard*, fresh from Constantinople, and almost an Eastern in his ways, and Julian Corbett, representing the *Pall Mall*, a gentle and amiable man who was destined later to be the naval historian of the Great War. Like myself he was an amateur among professionals, and had to return by a given date to Cairo.

As it was clear that nothing important could take place instantly, we determined to do part of the journey by road. A force of cavalry was going up, and we were ordered to join them and use them as an escort, but we thought we would be happier on our own, and so we managed to lose the Egyptians. There was some risk in our lonely journey along the right bank of the river with our left flank quite unprotected, but on the other hand the dust of a great body of horsemen would be insufferable. Therefore we set forth one evening, mounted upon our camels, with baggage camels in attendance, and quite a retinue of servants. In four or five days we reached Korosko, where we got boats which took us to the frontier at Wady Halfa, while the camels and servants came on by land.

I shall never forget those days, or rather those nights, for we rose at two in the morning and our longest march was before or during the dawn. I am still haunted by that purple velvet sky, by those enormous and innumerable stars, by the half-moon which moved slowly above us, while our camels with their noiseless tread seemed to bear us without effort through a wonderful dream world. Scudamore had a beautiful rolling baritone voice, and I can still hear it in my memory as it rose and fell in the still desert air. It was a wonderful vision, an intermezzo in real life, broken only once by my performing the unusual feat of falling off a camel. I have taken many tosses off horses, but this was a new experience. You have no proper saddle, but are seated upon a curved leather tray, so that when my brute suddenly threw himself down on his fore-knees – he had seen some green stuff on the path – I shot head foremost down his neck. It was like coming down a hose pipe in some acrobatic performance, and I reached the ground rather surprised but otherwise none the worse.

One or two pictures rise in mind. One was of some strange aquatic lizard – not a crocodile – lying on a sand bank. I cracked off my Italian revolver, which was more likely to hurt me than the lizard, and I saw the strange beast writhe into the stream. Once again, as I settled my couch at night, I saw a slug-like creature, with horned projections, the length about eighteen inches, which moved away and disappeared. It was a death adder – the sort perhaps which took Cleopatra to her fathers. Then again we went into a ruined hut to see if we could sleep there. In the dim light of our candle we saw a creature which I thought was a mouse rush round and round the floor, close to the wall. Then suddenly to my amazement it ran right up the wall and down again on to the floor. It was a huge spider, which now stood waving its forelegs at us. To my horror Scudamore sprang into the air, and came down upon it, squashing it into a square foot of filth. This was the real tarantula, a dangerous creature, and common enough in such places.

Yet another picture comes very clearly back to me. For some reason we had not started in the night, and the early dawn found us still resting in our small camp in a grove of palm trees near the path which led along the bank of the Nile. I awoke, and, lying in my blankets, I saw an amazing man riding along this path. He was a negroid Nubian, a huge, fierce, hollow-cheeked creature, with many silver ornaments upon him. A long rifle projected over his back and a sword hung from his side. A more sinister barbaric figure one could not imagine, and he was exactly the type of those Mahdi raiders against whom we had been warned. I never like to be an alarmist, especially among men who had seen much of war or danger, so I said nothing, but I managed to stir one of my companions, who sighted the newcomer with a muttered, 'My God!' The man rode past us and on northwards, never glancing at our grove. I have no doubt that he was really one of our own native tribesmen, for we had some in our pay; but had he been the other thing our fate would have been sealed. I wrote a short story, 'The Three Correspondents', which was suggested by the incident.

A strange wooden-faced Turkish soldier, Yussuf Bey, in the Egyptian service, commanding the troops at Korosko, had us up in audience, gave us long pink glasses of raspberry vinegar, and finally saw us on board the boat which in a day or two deposited us on the busy river-bank of Wady Halfa, where the same military bustle prevailed as we had left behind us at Aswan.

Halfa lies also at the base of a cataract, and again all the stuff had to be transhipped and sent on thirty miles by a little track to Sarras. I walked the first day to the small station where the track began, and I saw a tall officer in a white jacket and red tarboosh, who with a single orderly was superintending the work and watching the stores pass into the trucks. He turned a fierce red face upon me, and I saw that it was Kitchener himself, the commander of the whole army. It was characteristic of the man that he did not leave such vital things to chance, or to the assurance of some subordinate, but that he made sure so far as he could with his own eyes that he really had the tools for the job that lay before him. Learning who I was – we had met once before on the racecourse at Cairo – he asked me to dinner in his tent that night, when he discussed the coming campaign with great frankness. I remember that his chief-of-staff – Drage, I think, was the name – sat beside me and was so completely played out that he fell asleep between every course. I remember also the amused smile with which Kitchener regarded him. You had to go all out when you served such a master.

One new acquaintance whom I made in those days was Herbert Gwynne, a newly-fledged war correspondent, acting, if I remember right, for the *Chronicle*. I saw that he had much in him. When I heard of him next he was Reuter's man in the Boer War, and not very long afterwards he had become editor of the *Morning Post*, where he now is. Those days in Halfa were the beginning of a friendship of thirty years, none the less real because we are both too busy to meet. One of the joys of the hereafter is, I think, that we have time to cultivate our friends.

I was friendly also with a very small but gallant officer, one Anley, who had just joined the Egyptian army. His career was beginning and I foresaw that he would rise, but should have been very surprised had I known how we should meet again. I was standing in the ranks by the roadside as a private of Volunteers in the Great War when a red-tabbed, brass-hatted general passed. He looked along our ranks, his gaze fastened on me, and lo, it was Anley. Surprised out of all military etiquette, he smiled and nodded. What is a private in the ranks to do when a general smiles and nods? He can't formally stand to attention or salute. I fear that what I did was to close and then open my left eye. That was how I learned that my Egyptian captain was now a war brigadier.

We pushed on to Sarras and had a glimpse of the actual outpost of civilisation, all sandbags and barbed wire, for there was a Mahdi post at no distance up the river. It was wonderful to look south and to see distant peaks said to be in Dongola, with nothing but savagery and murder lying between. There was a whiff of real war in the little fortress but no sign of any actual advance.

Indeed, I had the assurance of Kitchener himself that there was no use my waiting and that nothing could possibly happen until the camels were collected – many thousands of them. I contributed my own beast to the army's need since I had no further use for it, and Corbett and I prepared to take our leave. We were warned that our only course was to be on the lookout and take a flying jump on to any empty cargo boat which was going downstream. This we did one morning, carrying our scanty belongings. Once on board we learned that there was no food and that the boat did not stop for several days. The rope had not been cast off, so I rushed to the only shop available, a Greek store of a type which spring up like mushrooms on the track of an army. They were sold out save for tinned apricots, of which I bought several tins. I rushed back and scrambled on board as the boat cast off. We managed to get some Arab bread from the boatmen, and that with the apricots served us all the way. I never wish to see another tinned apricot so long as I live. I associate their cloying sweetness with Rousseau's *Confessions*, a French edition of which came somehow into my hands and was my only reading till I saw Aswan once more. Rousseau also I never wish to read again.

So that was the end of our frontier adventure. We had been on the edge of war but not in it. It was disappointing, but it was late in April before I reached Cairo, and the heat was already becoming too much for an invalid. A week later we were in London, and I remember that, as I sat as a guest at the Royal Academy Banquet on May 1 of that year, I saw upon my wrists the ragged little ulcers where the poisonous jiggers which had burrowed into my skin while I lay upon the banks of the Nile were hatching out their eggs under the august roof of Burlington House.

15

An Interlude of Peace

Hindhead – *Rodney Stone* – *A Duet* – A Haunted House –
A Curious Society – Preternatural Powers – The
Little Doctor – The Shadow of Africa

When we returned to England I found that the house in which we hoped that the cure would be completed was not yet ready. It was a considerable mansion planned upon a large scale, so that it was not surprising that it had taken some time to build. We were compelled to take a furnished house at Haslemere until the early months of 1897, when we moved up to Moorlands, a boarding house on Hindhead close to the site of my building. There we spent some happy and busy months until the house was ready in the summer. I had taken up riding, and though I was never a great horseman I was able from that time onwards to get a good deal of health and pleasure out of it, for in that woody, heathy country there are beautiful rides in every direction, and the hunting, in which I joined, was at least picturesque. About June we moved into the new house, which I called Undershaw – a new word, I think, and yet one which described it exactly in good Anglo-Saxon, since it stood under a hanging grove of trees.

I have said little, during these years spent in the quest of health, concerning my literary production. The chief book which I had written since *The Refugees* was a study of the Regency with its bucks and prizefighters. I had always a weakness for the old fighting men and for the lore of the prize-ring, and I indulged it in this novel. At the time boxing had not gained the popular vogue which I have been told that this very book first initiated, and I can never forget the surprise of Sir George Newnes when he found out what the new serial was about. 'Why that subject of all subjects upon earth?' he cried. However, I think that the readers of *The Strand* found that I had not chosen badly, and the book is one which has held a permanent place as a picture of those wild old days. I wrote a considerable number of short tales during those years, and finally in 1898 a domestic study, *A Duet*, which was an attempt at quite a different form of literature – a picture in still life, as it were. It was partly imaginative and partly founded upon early experiences of my own and of friends. It led, I remember, to a public bickering with a man who has done good work as a critic, Dr Robertson Nicoll. He took exception to some passage in the book, which he had every right to do. But he wrote at that time for six or seven papers, under different names, so that it appeared as if a number of critics were all condemning me when it was really only one. I thought I had a grievance, and said so with such vehemence that he stated that he did not know whether to answer me in print or in the law courts. However, it all blew over and we became very good friends. Another book of those days was *Uncle Bernac*, which I never felt to be satisfactory, though I venture to claim that the two chapters which portray Napoleon give a clearer picture of him than many a long book has done, which is natural enough, since they are themselves the quintessence of a score of books.

So much for my work. I had everything in those few years to make a man contented, save only the constant illness of my partner. And yet my soul was often troubled within me. I felt that I was born for something else, and yet I was not clear what that something might be. My mind felt out continually into the various religions of the world. I could no more get into the old ones, as commonly received, than a man could get into his boy's suit. I still argued on materialist lines. I subscribed to the Rationalist Association and read all their literature carefully, but it was entirely destructive and one cannot permanently live on that alone. Besides, I was sure enough of psychic phenomena to be aware that there was a range of experience there which was entirely beyond any rational explanation, and that therefore a system which ignored a great body of facts, and was incompatible with them, was necessarily an imperfect system. On the other hand, convinced as I was of these abnormal happenings, and that intelligence, high or low, lay behind them, I by no means understood their bearing. I still confused the knocking at the door with the friend outside, or the ringing of the bell with the telephone message. Sometimes I had the peace of despair, when one felt that one could never possibly arrive at any conclusions save negative ones, and then again some fresh impulse of the soul would start one upon a new quest. In every direction I reached out, but never yet with any absolute satisfaction. I should have been relieved from all my troubles could I have given heartfelt adhesion to any form of orthodoxy – but my reason always barred the way.

During all the Egyptian and other periods of our exile I had never ceased to take the psychic subject very seriously, to read eagerly all that I could get, and from time to time to organise séances which gave indifferent but not entirely negative results, though we had no particular medium to help us. The philosophy of the subject began slowly to unfold, and it was gradually made more feasible, not only that life carried on, enclosed in some more tenuous envelope, but that the conditions which it encountered in the beyond were not unlike those which it had known here. So far I had got along the road, but the overwhelming and vital importance of it all had not yet been borne in upon me.

Now and then I had a psychic experience somewhat outside the general run of such events. One of these occurred when I was at Norwood in 1892 or 1893. I was asked by the Society of Psychical Research whether I would join a small committee to sit in and report upon a haunted house at Charmouth in Dorchester. I went down accordingly together with a Dr Scott and Mr Podmore, a man whose name was associated with such investigations. I remember that it took us the whole railway journey from Paddington to read up the evidence as to the senseless noises which had made life unendurable for the occupants, who were tied by a lease and could not get away. We sat up there two nights. On the first nothing occurred. On the second Dr Scott left us and I sat up with Mr Podmore. We had, of course, taken every precaution to checkmate fraud, putting worsted threads across the stairs, and so on.

In the middle of the night a fearsome uproar broke out. It was like someone belabouring a resounding table with a heavy cudgel. It was not an accidental creaking of wood, or anything of that sort, but a deafening row. We had all doors open, so we rushed at once into the kitchen, from which the sound had surely come. There was nothing there – doors were all locked, windows barred and threads unbroken. Podmore took away the light and pretended that we had both returned to our sitting-room, going off with the young master of the house, while I waited in the dark in the hope of a return of the disturbance. None came – or ever did come. What occasioned it we never knew. It was of the same character as all the other disturbances we had read about, but shorter in time. But there was a sequel to the story. Some years later the house was burned down, which may or may not have a bearing upon the sprite which seemed to haunt it, but a more suggestive thing is that the skeleton of a child about ten years old was dug up in the garden. This I give on the authority of a relation of the family who were so plagued. The suggestion was that the child had been done to death there long ago, and that the subsequent phenomena of which we had one small sample were in some way a sequence to this tragedy. There is a theory that a young life cut short in sudden and unnatural fashion may leave, as it were, a store of unused vitality which may be put to strange uses. The unknown and the marvellous press upon us from all sides. They loom above us and around us in undefined and fluctuating shapes, some dark, some shimmering, but all warning us of the limitations of what we call matter, and of the need for spirituality if we are to keep in touch with the true inner facts of life.

I was never asked for a report of this case, but Podmore sent one in, attributing the noises to the young man, though as a fact he was actually sitting with us in the parlour when the tumult broke out. A confederate was possible, though we had taken every step to bar it, but the explanation given was absolutely impossible. I learned from this, what I have often confirmed since, that while we should be most critical of all psychic assertions, if we are to get at the truth, we should be equally critical of all negatives and especially of so-called 'exposures' in this subject. Again and again I have probed them and found them to depend upon prejudice or upon an imperfect acquaintance with psychic law.

This brings me to another curious experience which occurred about this time, probably in 1898. There was a small doctor dwelling near me, small in stature, and also, I fear, in practice, whom I will call Brown. He was a student of the occult, and my curiosity was aroused by learning that he had one room in his house which no one entered except himself, as it was reserved for mystic and philosophic purposes. Finding that I was interested in such subjects, Dr Brown suggested one day that I should join a secret society of esoteric students. The invitation had been led up to by a good deal of preparatory enquiry. The dialogue between us ran somewhat thus:

'What shall I get from it?'

'In time, you will get powers.'

'What sort of powers?'

'They are powers which people would call supernatural. They are perfectly natural, but they are got by knowledge of deeper forces of nature.'

'If they are good, why should not everyone know them?'

'They would be capable of great abuse in the wrong hands.'

'How can you prevent their getting into wrong hands?'

'By carefully examining our initiates.'

'Should I be examined?'

'Certainly.'

'By whom?'

'The people would be in London.'

'Should I have to present myself?'

'No, no, they would do it without your knowledge.'

'And after that?'

'You would then have to study.'

'Study what?'

'You would have to learn by heart a considerable mass of material. That would be the first thing.'

'If this material is in print, why does it not become public property?'

'It is not in print. It is in manuscript. Each manuscript is carefully numbered and trusted to the honour of a passed initiate. We have never had a case of one going wrong.'

'Well,' said I, 'it is very interesting and you can go ahead with the next step, whatever it may be.'

Some little time later – it may have been a week – I awoke in the very early morning with a most extraordinary sensation. It was not a nightmare or any prank of a dream. It was quite different from that, for it persisted after I was wide awake. I can only describe it by saying that I was tingling all over. It was not painful, but it was queer and disagreeable, as a mild electric shock would be. I thought at once of the little doctor.

In a few days I had a visit from him. 'You have been examined and you have passed,' said he with a smile. 'Now you must say definitely whether you will go on with it. You can't take it up and drop it. It is serious, and you must leave it alone or go forward with a whole heart.'

It began to dawn upon me that it really was serious, so serious that there seemed no possible space for it in my very crowded and preoccupied life. I said as much, and he took it in very good part. 'Very well,' said he, 'we won't talk of it any more unless you change your mind.'

There was a sequel to the story. A month or two later, on a pouring wet day, the little doctor called, bringing with him another medical man whose name was familiar to me in connection with exploration and tropical service. They sat together beside my study fire and talked. One could not but observe that the famous and much-travelled man was very deferential to the little country surgeon, who was the younger of the two.

'He is one of my initiates,' said the latter to me. 'You know,' he continued, turning to his companion, 'Doyle nearly joined us once.' The other looked at me with great interest and then at once plunged into a conversation with his mentor as to the wonders he had seen and, as I understood, actually done. I listened amazed. It sounded like the talk of two lunatics. One phrase stuck in my memory.

'When first you took me up with you,' said he, 'and we were hovering over the town I used to live in, in Central Africa, I was able for the first time to see the islands out in the lake. I always knew they were there, but they were too far off to be seen from the shore. Was it not extra-ordinary that I should first see them when I was living in England?'

'Yes,' said Brown, smoking his pipe and staring into the fire. 'We had some fun in those days. Do you remember how you laughed when we made the little steamboat and it ran along the upper edge of the clouds?'

There were other remarks as wild. 'A conspiracy to impress a simpleton,' says the sceptic. Well, we can leave it at that if the sceptic so wills, but I remain under the impression that I brushed against something strange, and something which I am not sorry that I avoided. It was not Spiritualism and it was not Theosophy, but rather the acquisition of powers latent in the human organisation, after the alleged fashion of the old gnostics or of some modern fakirs in India, though some doubtless would spell fakirs with an 'e'. One thing I am very sure of, and that is that morals and ethics have to keep pace with knowledge, or all is lost. The Maori cannibals had psychic knowledge and power, but were man-eaters none the less. Christian ethics can *never* lose its place whatever expansion our psychic faculties may enjoy. But Christian theology can and will.

To return to the little doctor, I came across him again, as psychic as ever, in Portland, Oregon, in 1923. From what I learned I should judge that the powers of the society to which he belonged included that of loosening their own etheric bodies, in summoning the etheric bodies of others (mine, for example) and in making thought images (the steam-boat) in the way that we are assured is possible by willpower. But their line of philosophy or development is beyond me. I believe they represent a branch of the Rosicrucians.

All seemed placid at this time. My wife was holding her own in winter as well as in summer. The two children, Mary and Kingsley, were passing through the various sweet phases of human development, and brought great happiness into our lives. The country was lovely. My life was filled with alternate work and sport. As with me so with the nation. They were years of prosperity and success. But the shadow of South Africa was falling upon England, and before it passed my personal fortunes, as well as so many more, were destined to be involved in it. I had a deep respect for the Boers and some fear of their skill at arms, their inaccessible situation, and their sturdy Teutonic tenacity. I foresaw that they would be a most dangerous enemy, and I watched with horror the drift of events which from the time of the ill-judged Jameson Raid never ceased to lead to open war. It was almost a relief when at last it came and we could clearly see the magnitude of our task. And yet few people understood it at the time. On the very eve of war I took the chair at a dinner to Lord Wolseley at the Authors' Club and he declared that we could send two divisions to Africa. The papers next day were all much exercised as to whether such a force was either possible to collect or necessary to send. What would they have thought had they been told that a quarter of a million men, a large proportion of them cavalry, would be needed before victory could be won. The early Boer victories surprised no one who knew something of South African history, and they made it clear to every man in England that it was not a wine glass but a rifle which one must grasp if the health of the Empire was to be honoured.

16

The Start for South Africa

From December 10 to 17, 1899, was the black week for England. In that week General Gatacre lost a battle at Stormberg, Lord Methuen lost one at Magersfontein and General Buller lost one at Colenso. The three together would not have made more than a minor action in the Great War to come, but at the time it seemed portentous. There were ominous stirrings on the Continent also and rumours of a coalition. It was lucky for us that the German fleet was not yet in being and that our own was able to keep the ring, or we should soon have had some Lafayette in South Africa with perhaps a Yorktown to follow. However, it was bad enough as it was, but the nation as usual rose splendidly to the occasion, and everyone hastened to do what they could. Hence it was that I found myself early one morning at Hounslow – if I remember right – standing in a long queue of men who were waiting to enlist in the Middlesex Yeomanry. I had one or two friends in the regiment and hence my choice.

The colonel, a grizzled soldier, sat behind a deal table in an orderly room and dealt swiftly with the applicants. He had no idea who I was, but seeing a man of forty before him he intimated that I surely did not intend to go into the ranks. I said that I was prepared to take a commission. He asked if I could ride and shoot. I said that I could do both in moderation. He asked if I had had military experience. I said that I had led an adventurous life and seen a little of military operations in the Sudan, which was stretching it about as far as it would go. Two white lies are permitted to a gentleman – to screen a woman or to get into a fight when the fight is a rightful one. So I trust I may be forgiven.

However the colonel would only put me on his waiting list, took my name, still without recognising me, and passed on to the next case. I departed somewhat crestfallen and unsettled, not knowing whether I had heard the last of the matter or not. Almost immediately afterwards, however, I received an offer which took me out in a capacity which was less sporting but probably in my case and at my age a good deal more useful. This came from my friend John Langman, whose son Archie I had known well in Davos days. Langman was sending out a hospital of fifty beds at his own expense to Africa, and had already chosen his staff of surgeons but not his personnel. Archie Langman was to go with the hospital as general manager. Langman's idea was that I should help him to choose the personnel, that I should be a supplementary medico, and that I should exercise a general supervision over the whole in an unofficial capacity. To all this I agreed and spent a week at his house at Stanhope Terrace, choosing from many candidates those who seemed the most likely. On the whole they proved to be a worthy choice. There were many things to be done, and in the middle of them I received a note re-opening the question of the Yeomanry, but by this time I was entirely committed to the Langman Hospital.

When we were complete we were quite a good little unit, but our weakness was unfortunately at the head. Dr O'Callaghan had been a personal friend of Langman's and had thus got the senior billet, but he was in truth an excellent gynaecologist, which is a branch of the profession for which there seemed to be no immediate demand. He was a man too who had led a sedentary life and was not adapted, with all the will in the world, for the trying experience which lay before us. He realised this himself and returned to England after a short experience of South African conditions. We were compelled to have one military chief, as a bond with the War Office, and this proved to be one Major Drury, a most amusing Irishman who might have come right out of Lever. To leave the service and to 'marry a rich widow with a cough' was, he said, the height of his ambition. He was a very pleasant companion in civil life, but when it came to duties which needed tact and routine he was rather too Celtic in his methods, and this led to friction and occasional rows in which I had to sustain the point of view of Mr Langman. I have no doubt he thought me an insubordinate dog, and I thought him – well, he has passed away now, and I remember him best as a very amusing companion.

Under O'Callaghan and Drury were two really splendid younger surgeons, Charles Gibbs and Scharlieb, the latter the son of the well-known lady doctor. They were as good as they could be. Then we had our ward-masters, cooks, stewards, storekeepers and, finally, some fifteen to twenty orderlies. Altogether we numbered just fifty men, and were splendidly fitted out by the generosity of Mr Langman.

A month or two passed before we could get away, and I remember one amusing incident which occurred during that time. I had spent a good deal of thought over the problem how best to attack men who lay concealed behind cover. My conclusions were that it was useless to fire at them direct, since, if they knew their business, very little of them would be vulnerable. On the other hand, if one could turn a rifle into a portable howitzer and drop a bullet with any sort of rough general accuracy within a given area, then it seemed to me that life would hardly be possible within that area. If, for example, the position was twenty thousand square yards in size, and twenty thousand rifles were dropping bullets upon it, each square yard would sooner or later be searched and your mark would be a whole prostrate or crouching body. What I was really evolving, though I could not know it, was the machine-gun barrage of dropping or vertical fire as practised in the Great War. My principles were absolutely right and have not even yet received their full application. I wrote an article to *The Times* explaining my views, but so far as I know it had no results.

Meanwhile I was practising how to turn a rifle into a howitzer. I fastened a large needle at the end of a thread to the back sight. When the gun pointed straight up in the air the needle swung down across the stock and I marked the spot. Then the idea was to tilt the gun slowly forward, marking advances of 200, 400 and so on in the range, so that you had a dial marked on the stock and could always by letting the needle fall across the correct mark on the dial drop the bullet within a certain distance.

But the crux was to discover the exact ranges. To do this I went down to Frensham Pond and, standing among the reeds and tilting the gun very slightly forward, I pulled the trigger. The bullet very nearly fell upon my own head. I could not locate it, but I heard quite a loud thud. But what amazed me, and still amazes me, was the time it took. I counted fifty seconds on my watch between the discharge and the fall. I don't wonder if the reader is incredulous. I feel incredulous also, but such is the fact as I recorded it.

My idea was to mark the bullet splashes on the calm water of the lake, but though I fired and fired at various angles not a splash could I see. Finally a little man who may have been an artist broke in upon my solitude.

'Do you want to know where those bullets are going?'

'Yes, sir, I do.'

'Then I can tell you, sir, for they have been dropping all round *me*.'

I felt that unless my howitzer was to claim its first victim on the spot I had better stop. It was clear that the light bullet with so heavy a charge went so high into the atmosphere that one lost all command over it. Twice the weight and half the charge would have served my purpose better. Then came other calls and I could never work it out, but I am very sure that with a little care in detail I could have got a converging fire which would have cleared any kopje in South Africa.

As I was convinced that the idea was both practical and much needed I communicated full particulars to the War Office. Here is the letter I had in reply.

War Office,
February 16, 1900

Sir – With reference to your letter concerning an appliance for adapting rifles to high-angle fire I am directed by the Secretary of State for War to inform you that he will not trouble you in the matter.

I am, sir, your obedient servant,

(signature illegible)
Director General of Ordnance

Thus, whether my invention was nonsense or whether it was, as I believe, radical and epoch-making, I was given no chance to explain or to illustrate it. As I remarked in *The Times*: 'No wonder that we find the latest inventions in the hands of our enemies rather than ourselves if those who try to improve our weapons meet with such encouragement as I have done.' Our traditions were carried on in the Great War, for Pomeroy, the inventor of the inflammable bullet which brought down the Zeppelins, was about to return to New Zealand in despair, and it was, as I am assured, private and not official bullets which first showed how valuable was his discovery and forced a belated acceptance by the War Office.

At last our time drew near. My wife had gone to Naples, where it was hoped that the warmer climate would complete her cure. My affairs were all settled up. I was to go as an unpaid man, and I contributed my butler Cleeve, a good intelligent man, for the general use, paying him myself. In this way I retained my independence and could return when I felt that the time had come – which, as events turned out, proved to be very valuable to me.

We were reviewed by the old Duke of Cambridge in some drill-hall in London. There befell me on this occasion one of those quaint happenings which seem to me to have been more common in my life than in that of most other men. We were drawn up in our new khaki uniforms, and wearing our tropical helmets, for the royal duke's inspection. If we had been asked to form fours we should have broken down completely, but luckily we were placed in double line and so we remained. I was standing in front on the right flank. With my eyes fixed rigidly before me I was still able out of the corner of them to be aware that the old duke, with his suite, was coming across to begin at my end. Presently he halted in front of me, and stood motionless. I remained quite rigid, looking past him. He continued to stand, so near me that I could hear and almost feel his puffy breath. 'What on earth!' I wondered, but I gave no sign. At last he spoke. 'What is this?' he asked. Then louder, 'What is this?' and finally, in a sort of ecstasy, 'What *is* it?' I never moved an eyelash, but one of a group of journalists upon my right went into hysterical but subdued laughter. There was whispering among the suite, something was explained, and the funny old man passed on. But did ever Lever in his maddest moment represent that his hero on the first day of wearing uniform should have such an experience with the ex-commander-in-chief of the British army and the uncle of the Queen?

It seems that what was worrying the dear old gentleman – he was about eighty at the time – was that my tunic buttons had no mark upon them, a thing which he had never seen in Her Majesty's Army. Even a crown or a star would do, but no mark at all completely upset him, for he was a great stickler for correct military clothing. So, of course, was King Edward. A friend of mine at a ball in India (royalty being present) was swooped down upon by a very agitated aide-de-camp who began: 'His Royal Highness desires me to say . . . ' and went on to point out some defect in his dress kit. My friend answered: 'I will mention the matter to my tailor,' which was, I think, an admirable way of quietly putting the matter into its true perspective.

On this occasion we officers all filed up to be presented and the old duke made amends by blurting out some very kindly things, for it seems that he greatly approved of my wooden-soldier attitude, in spite of my reprehensible buttons. He had a day of agitations, for on the top of the buttons one of the curtains of the hotel took fire during our luncheon at Claridge's, and there was great excitement for a few moments. He made, I remember, an extremely indiscreet speech in which he said: 'They turned me off because they said I was too old, but old as I am I wouldn't have been such a fool as to – ' and then he strung off a number of things which Lord Wolseley, his successor, was supposed to have done. The press was merciful and did not report.

We sailed on February 28, 1900, from Tilbury, in the chartered transport *Oriental*, carrying with us a mixed lot of drafts, and picking up the Royal Scots Militia at Queenstown, where a noisy Irishwoman threw a white towel on board, crying, 'You may be afther finding it useful.' The Scots were a rather rough crowd with a number of territorial magnates, Lord Henry Scott, Lord Tewkesbury, Lord Newport, Lord Brackley and others among their officers. Colonel Garstin of the Middlesex was in general command of the whole of us. The monotony of the three weeks' voyage was broken only by a cricket match at the Cape de Verdes, by a lecture on the war which I delivered on deck under a tropical moon to all hands, and to an enteric inoculation, which was voluntary but should have been compulsory, for even as it was it saved many lives, and I am not sure that my own was not among them. The Great War has shown for ever how effective this treatment is. We lost more from enteric than from the bullet in South Africa, and it is sad to think that nearly all could have been saved had Almroth Wright's discovery been properly appreciated. His brother was on board, I remember – an officer of Sappers – and took the virus particularly badly, though all of us were quite bad enough, for the right dose had not yet been accurately determined.

On the evening of March 21 we reached Capetown and found the bay full of shipping. There were fifty large steamers at anchor – mostly empty. Some of us had a run ashore, but we had some trouble getting on board again, for there was a big swell and the little tug dared not come quite alongside. We had to jump therefore from the paddle-box as the roll favoured us, landing on a hanging ladder, where a quartermaster seized us. To some people such a feat is easy, while others evidently regarded it with horror, and I wondered that we escaped from having some tragedy. The only real mishap was a strange one. A row of soldier faces was looking down on us over the bulwarks, when I saw the grin upon one of them change to a look of horrible agony and he gave a wild scream. He still remained standing, but several men ran towards him, and then he disappeared. Only afterwards did I learn that a huge iron bar had in some way fallen upon his foot, pinning him to the place. He fainted as they disengaged him and was carried below with his bones crushed.

I spent next day ashore, with the Mount Nelson Hotel as my headquarters. It was full of a strange medley of wounded officers, adventuresses and cosmopolitans. Kitchener came down and cleared it out shortly afterwards, for the syrens were interfering with his fighting men. The general war news was very good. Paardeburg had been fought, Lord Roberts had made his way to Bloemfontein and Kimberley had been relieved by French, whose immediate return to head off Cronje was one of the inspired incidents of the war. It was a consolation to find that Boers really could be captured in large numbers, for their long run of successes while the conditions were in their favour was getting badly upon the public nerves and a legendary sort of atmosphere was beginning to build up around them.

Some money had been given me for charitable purposes when I was in London, so I went down to the camp of the Boer prisoners to see if I could spend some of it. It was a racecourse, pent in with barbed wire, and they were certainly a shaggy, dirty, unkempt crowd but with the bearing of free men. There were a few cruel or brutal faces, some of them half caste, but most were good honest fellows and the general effect was formidable. There were some who were maned like lions. I afterwards went into the tents of the sick Boers. Several were sitting sullenly round and one was raving in delirium, saying something in his frenzy which set all the others laughing in a mirthless way. One man sat in a corner with a proud dark face and brooding eagle eyes. He bowed with grave courtesy when I put down some money for cigarettes. A Huguenot, or I am mistaken.

We had been waiting for orders and now we suddenly left Capetown on March 26, reaching East London on the 28th. There we disembarked, and I was surprised to find Leo Trevor, of amateur theatrical fame, acting as transport officer. In spite of his efforts (I hope it was not through them) our hospital stuff was divided between two trains, and when we reached Bloemfontein after days of travel we found that the other half had wandered off and was engulfed in the general chaos. There were nights of that journey which I shall never forget – the great train roaring through the darkness, the fires beside the line, the dark groups silhouetted against the flames, the shouts of 'Who are you?' and the crash of voices as our mates cried back, 'The Camerons,' for this famous regiment was our companion. Wonderful is the atmosphere of war. When the millennium comes the world will gain much, but it will lose its greatest thrill.

It is a strange wild place, the veldt, with its vast green plains and peculiar flat-topped hills, relics of some extraordinary geological episode. It is poor pasture – a sheep to two acres – so it must always be sparsely inhabited. Little white farms, each with its eucalyptus grove and its dam, were scattered over it. When we crossed the Free State border by a makeshift bridge, beside the ruins of the old one, we noticed that many of these little houses were flying the white flag. Everyone seemed very good-humoured, burghers and soldiers alike, but the guerrilla war afterwards altered all that.

It was April 2 and 5 a.m. when we at last reached the capital of the Free State, and were dumped down outside the town in a great green expanse covered with all sorts of encampments and animals. There was said to be a large force of Boers close to the town, and they had cut up one of our columns a few days before at Sanna's Post. Some troops were moving out, so I, with Gwynne whom I had known in Egypt, and that great sportsman Claude de Crespigny, set forth to see what we could, an artilleryman lending me his led horse. There was nothing doing, however, for it was Brother Boer's way never to come when you wanted him and always when you didn't. Save for good company, I got nothing out of a long hot day.

Good company is always one of the solaces of a campaign. I ran across many old friends, some soldiers, some medicos, some journalists. Knight of the *Falcon* had, alas, been hit in an early battle and was in hospital. Julian Ralph, a veteran American correspondent, Bennett Burleigh the rugged old war horse, queer little Melton Prior who looked like the prim headmaster of a conventional school, dark-eyed Donohue of the *Chronicle*, Paterson the Australian, of Snowy River fame, they were a wonderful set of men. I had little time to enjoy their society, however, for among the miles of loaded trucks which lay at the endless sidings I had to my great joy discovered the missing half of our equipment and guided a fatigue party down to it. All day we laboured and before evening our beds were up and our hospital ready for duty. Two days later wagons of sick and wounded began to disgorge at our doors and the real work had begun.

We had been given the cricket field as our camp and the fine pavilion as our chief ward. Others were soon erected, for we had plenty of tents – one each for our own use and a marquee for the mess. We were ready for any moderate strain, but that which was put upon us was altogether beyond our strength and for a month we had a rather awful time. The first intimation of trouble came to me in a simple and dramatic way. We had a bath in the pavilion and I had gone up to it and turned the tap, but not a drop of water appeared, though it had been running freely the night before. This small incident was the first intimation that the Boers had cut the water supply of the town, which caused us to fall back upon the old wells, which in turn gave rise to an outbreak of enteric which cost us five thousand lives. The one great blot in Lord Roberts's otherwise splendid handling of the campaign was, in my opinion, that he did not buzz out at once with every man he could raise and relieve the waterworks, which were only twenty miles away. Instead of this he waited for his army to recuperate, and so exposed them to the epidemic. However, it is always easy to be wise after the event.

The outbreak was a terrible one. It was softened down for public consumption and the press messages were heavily censored, but we lived in the midst of death – and death in its vilest, filthiest form. Our accommodation was for fifty patients, but a hundred and twenty were precipitated upon us, and the floor was littered between the beds with sick and often dying men. Our linen and utensils were never calculated for such a number, and as the nature of the disease causes constant pollution, and this pollution of the most dangerous character and with the vilest effluvia, one can imagine how dreadful was the situation. The worst surgical ward after a battle would be a clean place compared to that pavilion. At one end was a stage with the scene set for *HMS Pinafore*. This was turned into latrines for those who could stagger so far. The rest did the best they could, and we did the best we could in turn. But a Vereshchagin would have found a subject in that awful ward, with the rows of emaciated men, and the silly childish stage looking down upon it all. In the very worst of it two nursing sisters appeared among us, and never shall I forget what angels of light they appeared, or how they nursed those poor boys, swaddling them like babies and meeting every want with gentle courage. Thank God, they both came through safe.

Four weeks may seem a short time in comfort, but it is a very long one under conditions such as those, amid horrible sights and sounds and smells, while a haze of flies spreads over everything, covering your food and trying to force themselves into your mouth – every one of them a focus of disease. It was bad enough when we had a full staff, but soon the men began to wilt under the strain. They were nearly all from the Lancashire cotton mills, little, ill-nourished fellows but with a great spirit. Of the fifteen twelve contracted the disease and added to the labours of the survivors. Three died. Fortunately we of the staff were able to keep going, and we were reinforced by a Dr Schwartz of Cape-town. The pressure was great, but we were helped by the thought that the greater the work the more we proved the necessity of our presence in Africa. Above all, our labours were lightened by the splendid stuff that we had for patients. It was really glorious to see the steady patience with which they bore their sufferings. The British soldier may grouse in days of peace, but I never heard a murmur when he was faced with this loathsome death.

Our hospital was no worse off than the others, and as there were many of them the general condition of the town was very bad. Coffins were out of the question, and the men were lowered in their brown blankets into shallow graves at the average rate of sixty a day. A sickening smell came from the stricken town. Once when I had ridden out to get an hour or two of change, and was at least six miles from the town, the wind changed and the smell was all around me. You could smell Bloemfontein long before you could see it. Even now if I felt that low deathly smell, compounded of disease and disinfectants, my heart would sink within me.

At last there came the turn. The army had moved on. Hospitals up the line absorbed some of the cases. Above all the water works had been retaken, and with hardly any resistance. I went out with the force which was to retake it, and slept for the night in a thin coat under a wagon, an experience which left me colder than I can ever remember being in my life – a cold which was not only on the surface, but like some solid thing within you. Next morning there was every prospect of a battle, for we had been shelled the night before and it looked as if the position would be held, so Ian Hamilton, who commanded, made a careful advance. However, there was no resistance, and save for some figures watching us from distant hills there was no sign of the enemy. He had slipped away in the night.

In the advance we passed over the Drift at Sanna's Post where the disaster had occurred some weeks before. The poor artillery horses were still lying in heaps where they had been shot down, and the place was covered with every kind of litter – putties, cholera belts, haversacks, and broken helmets. There were great numbers of Boer cartridge papers which were all marked 'Split Bullets. Manufactured for the Use of the British Government, London'. What the meaning of this was, or where they came from, I cannot imagine, for certainly our fellows had always the solid Lee-Metford bullet, as I can swear after inspecting many a belt. It sounded like some ingenious trick to excuse atrocities, and yet on the whole the Boer was a fair and good-humoured fighter until near the close of the war.

The move of Hamilton's was really the beginning of the great advance, and having cleared the waterworks he turned north and became the right wing of the army. On his left was Tucker's 7th Division, then Kelly Kenny's 6th Division, Pole-Carew's 1st Division, including the Guards, and finally a great horde of mounted infantry, including the Yeomanry, the Colonial and the Irregular Corps. This was the great line which set forth early in May to sweep up from Bloemfontein to Pretoria. Things had become more quiet at the hospital and presently Archie Langman and I found a chance to get away and to join the army at the first stage of its advance. I wrote our experience out while it was still fresh in my mind, and the reader will forgive me if I reproduce some of this, as it is likely to be more vivid and more detailed than the blurred impression now left in my memory after more than twenty years.

17

Days with the Army

Stand in the pass at Karee, and look north in the clear fresh morning
air! Before you lies a great plain, dull green, with white farmhouses
scattered here and there. One great donga slashes it across. Distant hills
bound it on all sides, and at the base of those in front, dimly seen, are a
line of houses and a steeple. This is Brandfort, ten miles off, and we are
advancing to attack it.

The troops are moving forward, line after line of red face and khaki,
with rumbling columns of guns. Two men sit their horses beside us on
a knoll, and stare with their glasses at the distant houses. Gallant figures
both of them: the one spruce, debonair, well groomed, with laughing
eyes and upward-curved moustache, a suggestion of schoolboy mischief
about his handsome face; the other, grim, fierce, all nose and eyebrow,
white scales of sun-dried skin hanging from his brick-red face. The first
is Pole-Carew, General of Division; the second is Brigadier Stephen-
son. We are finding our men, and these are among them.

Here is another man worth noting. You could not help noting him if
you tried. A burly, broad-shouldered man, with full, square, black beard
over his chest, his arm in a sling, his bearing a mediaeval knight-errant.
It is Crabbe, of the Grenadier Guards. He reins his horse for an instant
while his Guardsmen stream past him.

'I've had my share – four bullets already. Hope I won't get another
today.'

'You should be in hospital.'

'Ah, there I must venture to disagree with you.' He rides on with his
men.

Look at the young officers of the Guards, the dandies of Mayfair. No
carpet soldiers, these, but men who have spent six months upon the
veldt, and fought from Belmont to Bloemfontein. Their walk is dainty,

their putties are well rolled – there is still the suggestion of the West End.

If you look with your glasses on the left you may see movement on the farthest skyline. That is Hutton's Mounted Infantry, some thousands of them, to turn the flank of any resistance. As far as you can see to the right is Tucker's Division. Beyond that again are Ian Hamilton's Mounted Infantry and French's Cavalry. The whole front is a good thirty miles, and thirty-five thousand men go to the making of it.

Now we advance over the great plain, the infantry in extended order, a single company covering half a mile. Look at the scouts and the flankers – we should not have advanced like that six months ago. It is not our additional numbers so much as our new warcraft which makes us formidable. The big donga is only two thousand yards off now, so we halt and have a good look at it. Guns are unlimbered – just as well to be ready. Pole-Carew rides up like a schoolboy on a holiday.

'Who's seen old Tucker?' I hear him say, with his glasses to his eyes. He had sent a message to the scouts. 'There now, look at that aide of mine. He has galloped along the donga to see if any Boers are in it. What right had he to do that? When I ask him he will say that he thought I was there . . . Halloa, you, sir, why don't you come back straight?'

'I did, sir.'

'You didn't. You rode along that donga.'

'I thought you were there, sir.'

'Don't add lying to your other vices.'

The aide came grinning back. 'I was fired at, but I dare not tell the old man.'

Rap! Rap! Rap! Rifles in front. Everyone pricks up his ears. Is it the transient sniper or the first shot of a battle? The shots come from the farmhouse yonder. The 83rd Field Battery begin to fidget about their guns. The officer walks up and down and stares at the farmhouse. From either side two men pull out lines of string and give long, monotonous cries. They are the rangefinders. A gunner on the limber is deep in a sixpenny magazine, absorbed, his chin on his hand.

'Our scouts are past the house,' says an officer.

'That's all right,' says the major.

The battery limbers up and the whole force advances to the farm-house. Off-saddle and a halt for luncheon.

Halloa! Here are new and sinister developments. A Tommy drives a smart buggy and pair out of the yard, looted for the use of the army. The farm is prize of war, for have they not fired at our troops? They could not help the firing, poor souls, but still this sniping must be discouraged. We are taking off our gloves at last over this war. But the details are not pretty.

A frightened girl runs out.

'Is it right that they kill fowls?' Alas! the question is hardly worth debating, for the fowls are dead. Erect and indignant, the girl drives in her three young turkeys. Men stare at her curiously, but she and her birds are not molested.

Here is something worse. A fat white pig all smothered in blood runs past. A soldier meets it, his bayonet at the charge. He lunges and lunges again, and the pig screams horribly. I had rather see a man killed. Some are up in the loft throwing down the forage. Others root up the vegetables. One drinks milk out of a strange vessel, amid the laughter of his comrades. It is a grotesque and mediaeval scene.

The general rides up, but he has no consolation for the women. 'The farm has brought it upon itself.' He rides away again.

A parson rides up. 'I can't imagine why they don't burn it,' says he.

A little Dutch boy stares with large, wondering grey eyes. He will tell all this to his grandchildren when we are in our graves.

'War is a terrible thing,' says the mother, in Dutch. The Tommies, with curious eyes, cluster round the doors and windows, staring in at the family. There is no individual rudeness.

One Kaffir enters the room. 'A Kaffir!' cries the girl, with blazing eyes.

'Yes, a Kaffir,' says he defiantly – but he leaves.

'They won't burn the house, will they?' cries the mother.

'No, no,' we answer; 'they will not burn the house.'

We advance again after lunch, the houses and steeple much nearer.

Boom! Boom! Boom! Cannon at last!

But it is far away, over at Tucker's side. There are little white puffs on the distant green hills. Those are shells bursting. If you look through your glasses you will see – eight miles off – a British battery in action. Sometimes a cloud of dust rises over it. That is a Boer shell which has knocked up the dust. No Boers can be seen from here.

Boom! Boom! Boom!

It becomes monotonous. 'Old Tucker is getting it hot!' Bother old Tucker, let us push on to Brandfort.

On again over the great plain, the firing dying away on the right. We have had a gun knocked off its wheels and twelve men hit over there. But now Hutton's turning movement is complete, and they close in on the left of Brandfort. A pompom quacks like some horrid bird among the hills. Our horse artillery are banging away. White spurts of shrapnel rise along the ridge. The leading infantry bend their backs and quicken their pace. We gallop to the front, but the resistance has collapsed. The mounted men are riding forward and the guns are silent. Long, sunlit hills stretch peacefully before us.

I ride through the infantry again. 'The bloody blister on my toe has bust.' 'This blasted water-bottle!' Every second man has a pipe between his parched lips.

The town is to the right, and two miles of plain intervene. On the plain a horseman is rounding up some mares and foals. I recognise him as I pass – Burdett-Coutts – a well-known figure in society. Mr Maxwell of the *Morning Post* suggests that we ride to the town and chance it. 'Our men are sure to be there.' No sign of them across the plain, but we will try. He outrides me, but courteously waits, and we enter the town together. Yes, it's all right; there's a Rimington Scout in the main street – a group of them, in fact.

A young Boer, new caught, stands among the horsemen. He is discomposed – not much. A strong, rather coarse face; well dressed; might appear, as he stands, in an English hunting-field as a young yeoman farmer.

'Comes of being fond of the ladies,' said the Australian sergeant.

'Wanted to get her out of the town,' said the Boer.

Another was brought up. 'I'd have got off in a minute,' says he.

'You'd have got off as it was if you had the pluck of a louse,' says his captor. The conversation languished after that.

In came the Staff, galloping grandly. The town is ours.

A red-headed Irish-American is taken on the kopje. 'What the hell is that to you?' he says to every question. He is haled away to gaol – a foul-mouthed blackguard.

We find the landlady of our small hotel in tears – her husband in gaol, because a rifle has been found. We try to get him out, and succeed. He charges us four shillings for half a bottle of beer, and we wonder whether we cannot get him back into gaol again.

'The house is not my own. I find great burly men everywhere,' he cries, with tears in his eyes. His bar is fitted with pornographic pictures to amuse our simple farmer friends – not the first or the second sign which I have seen that pastoral life and a Puritan creed do not mean a high public morality.

We sit on the stoep and smoke in the moonlight.

There comes a drunken inhabitant down the main street. A dingy Tommy stands on guard in front.

'Halt! Who goes there?'

'A friend.'

'Give the countersign!'

'I'm a free-born Englishman!'

'Give the countersign!'

'I'm a freeborn – ' With a rattle the sentry's rifle came to his shoulder and the moon glinted on his bayonet.

'Hi, stop!' cries a senior correspondent. 'You juggins, you'll be shot! Don't fire, sentry!'

Tommy raised his rifle reluctantly and advanced to the man. 'What shall I do with him, sir?' he asked the correspondent.

'Oh, what you like!' He vanished out of history.

I talk politics with Free Staters. The best opening is to begin, in an enquiring tone, 'Why did you people declare war upon us?' They have got into such an injured-innocence state that it comes quite as a shock to them when they are reminded that they were the attackers. By this Socratic method one attains some interesting results. It is evident that they all thought they could win easily, and that they are very bitter now against the Transvaal. They are mortally sick of the war; but, for that matter, so are most of the British officers. It has seemed to me sometimes that it would be more judicious, and even more honourable, if some of the latter were less open about the extent to which they are 'fed-up'. It cannot be inspiriting for their men. At the same time there would be a mutiny in the army if any conditions short of absolute surrender were accepted – and in spite of their talk, if a free pass were given today, I am convinced that very few officers would return until the job was done.

Our railway engineers are great. The train was in Brandfort next day, in spite of broken bridges, smashed culverts, twisted metals, every sort of wrecking. So now we are ready for another twenty miles Pretoria-wards. The Vet River is our goal this time, and off we go with the early morning.

Another great green plain, with dotted farms and the huge khaki column slowly spreading across it. The day was hot, and ten miles out the Guards had had about enough. Stragglers lay thick among the grass, but the companies kept their double-line formation, and plodded steadily along. Ten miles sounds very little, but try it in the dust of a column on a hot day, with a rifle over your shoulder, a hundred rounds of ammunition, a blanket, a canteen, an empty water-bottle and a dry tongue.

A grey-bearded padre limped bravely beside his men.

'No, no,' says he, when offered my horse. 'I must not spoil my record.'

The men are silent on the march: no band, no singing. Grim and sullen, the column flows across the veldt. Officers and men are short in their tempers.

'Why don't you,' etc., etc., bleats a subaltern.

'Because I never can hear what you say,' says the corporal.

They halt for a midday rest, and it seems to me, as I move among them, that there is too much nagging on the part of the officers. We have paid too much attention to the German military methods. Our true model should have been the American, for it is what was evolved by the Anglo-Celtic race in the greatest experience of war which the Anglo-Celtic race has ever had.

On we go again over that great plain. Is there anything waiting for us down yonder where the low kopjes lie? The Boers have always held rivers. They held the Modder. They held the Tugela. Will they hold the Vet? Halloa, what's this?

A startled man in a nightcap on a dapple-grey horse. He gesticulates. 'Fifty of them – hot corner – lost my helmet.' We catch bits of his talk. But what's that on the dapple-grey's side? The horse is shot through the body. He grazes quietly with black streaks running down the reeking hair.

'A West Australian, sir. They shot turble bad, for we were within fifty yards before they loosed off.'

'Which kopje?'

'That one over yonder.'

We ride forward, and pass through the open ranks of the Guards' skirmishers. Behind us the two huge naval guns are coming majestically up, drawn by their thirty oxen, like great hock-bottles on wheels. In front a battery has unlimbered. We ride up to the side of it. Away in front lies a small, slate-roofed farm beside the kopje. The Mounted

Infantry have coalesced into one body and are moving towards us. 'Here's the circus. There is going to be a battle,' was an infantry phrase in the American War. Our circus was coming in, and perhaps the other would follow.

The battery (84th RFA) settles down to its work.

Bang! I saw the shell burst on a hillside far away. 'Three thousand five hundred,' says somebody. Bang! 'Three thousand two hundred and fifty,' says the voice. Bang! 'Three thousand three hundred.' A puff shoots up from the distant grey roof as if their chimney were on fire. 'Got him that time!'

The game seems to us rather one-sided, but who is that shooting in the distance?

'Wheeeeeee' – what a hungry whine, and then a dull muffled 'Ooof!' Up goes half a cartload of earth about a hundred yards ahead of the battery. The gunners take as much notice as if it were a potato.

'Wheeeeeee – ooof!' Fifty yards in front this time.

'Bang! Bang!' go the crisp English guns.

'Wheeeeee – ooof!' Fifty yards behind the battery. They'll get it next time as sure as fate. Gunners go on unconcernedly. 'Wheeeeee – ooof!' Right between the guns, by George! Two guns invisible for the dust. Good heavens, how many of our gunners are left? Dust settles, and they are all bending and straining and pulling the same as ever.

Another shell and another, and then a variety, for there comes a shell which breaks high up in the air – wheeeeee – tang – with a musical, resonant note, like the snapping of a huge banjo-string, and a quarter of an acre of ground spurted into little dust-clouds under the shrapnel. The gunners take no interest in it. Percussion or shrapnel, fire what you will, you must knock the gun off its wheels or the man off his pins before you settle the RFA.

But every shell is bursting true, and it is mere luck that half the battery are not down. Once only did I see a man throw back his head a few inches as a shell burst before him. The others might have been parts of an automatic machine. But the officer decided to shift the guns – and they are shifted. They trot away for half a mile to the right and come into action again.

The lonely hero is the man to be admired. It is easy to be collectively brave. A man with any sense of proportion feels himself to be such a mite in the presence of the making of history that his own individual welfare seems for the moment too insignificant to think of. The unit is lost in the mass. But now we find ourselves alone on the plain with the battery away to the right. The nerves of the novice are strung up by the sound of the shells, but there is something of exhilaration in the feeling also.

There is a fence about two hundred yards off, and to this we tether our horses, and we walk up and down trying with our glasses to spot where the Boer guns are. We have suspicions, but nothing more. Our gunners may know, but we do not feel confident about it. Surely the stealthy lurking gun is worth six guns which stand bravely forth in the open. These farmers have taught our riflemen their business, and they bid fair to alter the artillery systems of the world as well. Our guns and theirs are like a fight between a blind man and one who can see.

An artillery colonel is wandering loose, and we talk. He has no job of his own, so he comes, like the coachman on a holiday, to watch some other man's guns at work. A shell falls some distance short of us.

'The next one,' says the colonel, 'will go over our heads. Come and stand over here.' I do so, with many mental reservations. Wheeeeeeee –

'Here it comes!' says the colonel. 'Here I go!' think I. It burst on our level, but forty yards to the right. I secure a piece as a souvenir.

'Shall we wait for another?' I began to be sorry that I met the colonel.

But a new sensation breaks upon us. Looking back we see that two monster naval guns are coming into action not fifty yards from our tethered horses, which stand in a dead line before their huge muzzles. We only just got them clear in time. Bang! the father of all the bangs this time, and a pillar of white smoke with a black heart to it on the farther hill. I can see some riders, like ants, going across it – Boers on the trek. Our men take the huge brass cartridge-case out of the gun.

'Can I have that?'

'Certainly,' says the lieutenant.

I tie it on to my saddle, and feel apologetic towards my long-suffering horse. The great gun roars and roars and the malignant spouts of smoke rise on the farthest hill.

A line of infantry in very open order comes past the great guns and I advance a little way with them. They are Scots Guards. The first line goes forward, the second is halted and lying down.

'That's right! Show where you are!' cries the second line, derisively. I seem to have missed the point, but the young officer in the first line is very angry.

'Hold your tongues!' he shouts, with his red face looking over his shoulder. 'Too many orders. No one gives orders but me.' His men lie down. The sun is sinking low, and it is evident that the contemplated infantry assault will not come off. One of the great naval shells passes high over our heads. It is the sound of a distant train in a tunnel.

A man canters past with a stretcher over his shoulder. His bay horse lollops along, but the stretcher makes him look very top-heavy. He passes the guns and the infantry, and rides on along the edge of a maize field. He is half a mile out now, heading for the kopje. Every instant I expect to see him drop from his horse. Then he vanishes in a dip of the ground.

After a time the stretcher appears again.

This time two men are carrying it, and the horseman rides beside. I have bandages in my pocket, so I ride forward also.

'Has a surgeon seen him?'

'No, sir.' They lay the man down. There is a handkerchief over his face.

'Where is it?'

'His stomach and his arm.' I pull up his shirt, and there is the Mauser bullet lying obvious under the skin. It has gone round instead of penetrating. A slit with a penknife would extract it, but that had better be left for chloroform and the field hospital. Nice clean wound in the arm.

'You will do very well. What is your name?'

'Private Smith, sir. New Zealander.' I mention my name and the Langman Hospital at Bloemfontein.

'I've read your books,' says he, and is carried onwards.

There has been a lull in the firing and the sun is very low. Then after a long interval comes a last Boer shell. It is an obvious insult, aimed at nothing, a derisive good-night and goodbye. The two naval guns put up their long necks and both roared together. It was the last word of the Empire – the mighty angry voice calling over the veldt. The red rim had sunk and all was purple and crimson, with the white moon high in the west. What had happened? Who had won? Were other columns engaged? No one knew anything or seemed to care. But late at night as I lay under the stars I saw on the left front signal flashes from over the river, and I knew that Hutton was there.

So it proved, for in the morning it was over the camp in an instant that the enemy had gone. But the troops were early afoot. Long before dawn came the weird, muffled tapping of the drums and the crackling of sticks as the camp-kettles were heated for breakfast. Then with the first light we saw a strange sight. A monstrous blister was rising slowly from the veldt. It was the balloon being inflated – our answer to the lurking guns. We would throw away no chances now, but play every card in our hand – another lesson which the war has driven into our proud hearts. The army moved on, with the absurd windbag flapping over the heads of the column. We climbed the kopjes where the enemy had crouched, and saw the litter of empty Mauser cases and the sangars so cunningly built. Among the stones lay a packet of the venomous-looking green cartridges still unfired. They talk of poison, but I doubt it. Verdigris would be an antiseptic rather than a poison in a wound. It is more likely that it is some decomposition of the wax in which the bullets are dipped. Brother Boer is not a Bushman after all. He is a tough, stubborn fighter, who plays a close game, but does not cheat.

We say goodbye to the army, for our duty lies behind us and theirs in front. For them the bullets, for us the microbes, and both for the honour of the flag. Scattered trails of wagons, ambulance carts, private buggies, impedimenta of all kinds, radiate out from the army. It is a bad drift, and it will be nightfall before they are all over. We pass the last of them, and it seems strange to emerge from that great concourse and see the twenty miles of broad, lonely plain which lie between us and Brandfort. We shall look rather foolish if any Boer horsemen are hanging about the skirts of the army.

We passed the battlefield of last night, and stopped to examine the holes made by the shells. Three had fallen within ten yards, but the ant-heaps round had not been struck, showing how harmless the most severe shellfire must be to prostrate infantry. From the marks in the clay the shells were large ones – forty-pounders, in all probability. In a little heap lay the complete kit of a Guardsman – his canteen, water-bottle, cup, even his putties. He had stripped for action with a vengeance. Poor devil, how uncomfortable he must be today!

A Kaffir on horseback is rounding up horses on the plain. He gallops towards us – a picturesque, black figure on his shaggy Basuto mount. He waves his hand excitedly towards the east. 'Englishman there – on veldt – hurt – Dutchman shoot him.' He delivers his message clearly enough.

'Is he alive?'

He nods.

'When did you see him?'

He points to the sun and then farther east. About two hours ago apparently.

'Can you take us there?' We buy him for two shillings, and all canter off together.

Our road is through maize fields and then out on to the veldt. By Jove, what's that? There is a single black motionless figure in the middle of that clearing. We gallop up and spring from our horses. A short, muscular, dark man is lying there with a yellow, waxen face and a blood-clot over his mouth. A handsome man, black-haired, black-moustached, his expression serene – No. 410 New South Wales Mounted Infantry – shot, overlooked and abandoned. There are evident signs that he was not alive when the Kaffir saw him. Rifle and horse are gone. His watch lies in front of him, dial upwards, run down at one in the morning. Poor chap, he had counted the hours until he could see them no longer.

We examine him for injuries. Obviously he had bled to death. There is a horrible wound in his stomach. His arm is shot through. Beside him lies his water-bottle – a little water still in it, so he was not tortured by thirst. And there is a singular point. On the water-bottle is balanced a red chess pawn. Has he died playing with it? It looks like it. Where are the other chessmen? We find them in a haversack out of his reach. A singular trooper this, who carries chessmen on a campaign. Or is it loot from a farmhouse? I shrewdly suspect it.

We collect the poor little effects of No. 410 – a bandolier, a stylographic pen, a silk handkerchief, a clasp-knife, a Waterbury watch, £2 6s. 6d. in a frayed purse. Then we lift him, our hands sticky with his blood, and get him over my saddle – horrible to see how the flies swarm instantly on to the saddle-flaps. His head hangs down on one side and his heels on the other. We lead the horse, and when from time to time he gives a horrid dive we clutch at his ankles. Thank heaven, he never fell. It is two miles to the road, and there we lay our burden under a telegraph post. A convoy is coming up, and we can ask them to give him a decent burial. No. 410 holds one rigid arm and clenched fist in the air. We lower it, but up it springs, menacing, aggressive. I put his mantle over him; but still, as we look back, we see the projection of that raised arm. So he met his end – somebody's boy. Fair fight, open air, and a great cause – I know no better death.

A long, long ride on tired horses over an endless plain. Here and there mounted Kaffirs circle and swoop. I have an idea that a few mounted police might be well employed in our rear. How do we know what these Kaffirs may do among lonely farms held by women and children? Very certain I am that it is not their own horses which they are rounding up so eagerly.

Ten miles have passed, and we leave the track to water our horses at the dam. A black mare hard-by is rolling and kicking. Curious that she should be so playful. We look again, and she lies very quiet. One more has gone to poison the air of the veldt. We sit by the dam and smoke. Down the track there comes a Colonial corps of cavalry – a famous corps, as we see when our glasses show us the colour of the cockades. Good heavens, will we never have sense beaten into us? How many disasters and humiliations must we endure before we learn how to soldier? The regiment passes without a vanguard, without scouts, without flankers, in an enemy's country intersected by dongas. Oh, for a Napoleon who might meet such a regiment, tear the epaulettes of the colonel from his shoulders, Stellenbosch him instantly without appeal or argument. Only such a man with such powers can ever thoroughly reorganise our army.

Another six miles over the great plain. Here is a small convoy, with an escort of militia, only a mile or two out from Brandfort. They are heading wrong, so we set them right. The captain in charge is excited. 'There are Boers on that hill!' The hill is only half a mile or so away on our left, so we find the subject interesting. 'Kaffirs!' we suggest. 'No, no, mounted men with bandoliers and rifles. Why, there they are now.' We see moving figures, but again suggest Kaffirs. It ends by our both departing unconvinced. We thought the young officer jumpy over his first convoy, but we owe him an apology, for next morning we learned that the Mounted Infantry had been out all night chasing the very men whom we had seen. It is likely that the accidental presence of the convoy saved us from a somewhat longer journey than we had intended.

A day at Brandfort, a night in an open truck, and we were back at the Café Enterique, Boulevard des Microbes, which is our town address.

Final Experiences in South Africa

Military men are more full of jealousies and more prone to divide into
cliques than any set of men whom I have met. South Africa was rent
with their quarrels, and one heard on every side of how General This
was daggers drawn with General That. But the greatest cleavage of all
was between the Roberts men and the Buller men. The former were
certainly very bitter against the reliever of Ladysmith, and the comments
about the difference between his evening telegrams and those of next
morning were painful to hear. I had, however, less sympathy, as Buller
was a coarse-fibred man, though a brave soldier. Several authentic
anecdotes pointed to this want of perception. When, for example, he
entered Ladysmith the defenders had saved up a few cakes and other
luxuries for the day of their release. These they laid before Buller at the
welcoming lunch. 'I thought you were a starving city,' said he, looking
round at them. This story I heard from several men who claimed to
speak with knowledge as well as bitterness. It would have been sad had
Buller's long, meritorious, hard-fighting career gone down in clouds,
but it cannot be denied that in the French or I think in any other
service he could not have survived Colenso. The strange speech which
he made at a London luncheon after the war proved, I think, that his
mind had lost something of its grip of realities. Roberts, as usual,
played the noblest possible part in this unhappy controversy. 'I shall
handle Buller with all possible tenderness,' he said to one of his staff,
and he lived up to his words.

I found the hospital on my return to be in a very improved condition. I
fell ill myself, however, though it was not serious enough to incapacitate
me. I still think that if I had not been inoculated I should at that time
have had enteric, and there was surely something insidious in my system,
for it was a good ten years before my digestion recovered its tone. My

condition was not unproved by a severe bruising of the ribs caused by a foul in one of the inter-hospital football matches which we had organised in order to take the minds of the men from their incessant work. Charles Gibbs strapped me up with plaster, as in a corset, but I was getting too old for the rough handling which I could have smiled at in my youth.

One quaint memory of those days rises before me. There was a sharp quarrel between Drury, our military CO representing routine discipline, and our cooks and servants representing civilian ideas of liberty. It was mishandled and had reached such a point when I returned from the army that the men were on absolute strike, the work was disorganised and the patients were suffering. Drury was breathing fire and fury, which only made the men more obdurate. It really looked as if there might be a considerable scandal, and I felt that it was just such a case as Mr Langman would have wished me to handle. I asked leave of Major Drury, therefore, that I might take the matter up, and he was, I fancy, very glad that I should, for he was at the end of his resources, and a public exposure of a disorganised unit means also a discredited commander. I therefore sat behind the long mess table, and had the six ringleaders before me, all standing in a line with sullen mutiny in their faces. I talked to them gently and quietly, saying that I was in some sense responsible for them, since several of them had been enlisted by me. I sympathised with them in all they had gone through, and said that all our nerves had been a little overstrained, but that duty and discipline must rise above our bodily weakness. No doubt their superiors also had been strained and some allowance must be made on both sides. I then took a graver tone. 'This matter is just going forward for court martial and I have intervened at the last instant. You clearly understand your own position. You have disobeyed orders on active service in the presence of the enemy. There is only one punishment possible for such an offence. It is death.' Six pairs of eyes stared wildly in front of me. Having produced my effect I went into their grievances, promised that they should be considered, and demanded an apology to Major Drury as the condition for doing anything further. They were six chastened men who filed out of the marquee, the apology was forthcoming, and there were no more troubles in the camp.

An anxiety came to us about this time from a very unexpected cause, for Archie Langman, who had been my good comrade in my visit to the army, went off again, trekking up country with the Imperial Yeomanry, and ran right into the arms of De Wet, who had just raided the line and won a small victory at a place called Roodeval. The famous guerrilla leader was stern but just, and he treated the hospital men with consideration, so that Archie returned none the worse for his adventure. But there was a bad day or two for me between our learning of his capture and of his release.

The army had got forward with little fighting, and Pretoria was in our hands. It seemed to all of us that the campaign was over and that only cleaning-up remained to be done. I began to consider my own return to Europe, and there were two potent influences which drew me, apart from the fact that the medical pressure no longer existed. The first was that I had during all this time continued to write the history of the war, drawing my material very often from the eye-witnesses to these events. But there was a good deal which could only be got at the centre, and therefore if my book was to be ready before that of my rivals it was necessary for me to be on the spot. The second was that a political crisis and a general election were coming on, and it was on the cards that I might be a candidate. I could not, however, leave Africa until I had seen Pretoria, so, with some difficulty, I obtained leave and was off on the much-broken and precarious railway on June 22.

That journey was certainly the strangest railway journey of my life. From minute to minute one never knew what would happen. I was in the good company of Major Hanbury Williams, Lord Milner's secretary, who allowed me to share his special carriage, and we had with us a little alert man named Amery, then unknown to fame, but now deservedly in the seats of the mighty. There were others but I have forgotten them. When the train stopped in the middle of the veldt, which it continually did, one never knew whether it was for five minutes or for five hours, as did actually occur, and as it went on again without warning one had to sit tight. We met a down train with its windows shattered and heard that twenty folk had been injured in a Boer ambuscade. Every hour we expected to be attacked. Once during one of our long halts we saw a horseman come cantering over the great green expanse. We got out to see and interview him. He was a tall, slab-sided fellow, unarmed, but with a rakish debonair look to him. He said he was a loyal British farmer, but I had no doubt in my own mind that he was a Boer scout who wanted to see what our train was carrying. He sat easy in his saddle for some little time, chatting with us, and then suddenly wheeled his grey horse round and galloped away.

Some way farther down the line we saw a farm burning, and a fringe of our irregulars riding round it. I was told that it was one of De Wet's farms and that it was a punishment for cutting the line. The whole scene might have been from the Middle Ages – say a company of Moss troopers on a raid over the English border.

When we came to the place of the Roodeval disaster, where our Derbyshire militia had been sadly cut up by De Wet, the train had to stop, for the line was under repair, and we were able to go over the ground. The place was littered with shells for the heavy guns taken from some looted train. Then there were acres covered with charred or partly charred letters, blowing about in the wind, for De Wet had burned the mail bags – one of his less sportsmanlike actions. Napoleon went one better, however, on a certain occasion when he published an intercepted British mail, which led to a British reprisal of the same sort, not at all conducive to the peace of families. I picked up one letter which fluttered up to me, and I read in rough handwriting, 'I hope you have killed all them Boers by now,' with many x's (kisses) underneath. Among other things were some of the band instruments, across which De Wet had driven his heavy wagons.

It gave me a strange thrill when I looked out early one morning at a deserted platform and saw the word Pretoria printed upon a board. Here we were at last at the very centre of all things. The Transvaal Hotel was open and for several days it was my headquarters while I examined men and things. One of my first tasks was to see Lord Roberts, who desired to interview me on account of some sensational articles by Burdett-Coutts which had appeared in the London press upon the state of the hospitals. Of course that state had in many cases, possibly in all, been awful, but the reason lay in the terrible and sudden emergency. Everyone had done his best to meet it and had met it to a surprising degree, but cases of hardship were numerous all the same. This I explained to Lord Roberts – and also to the Royal Commission in London. As an unpaid independent volunteer my words may have had more weight than those of some far greater authority who was personally involved. I can see Roberts now as he sat behind a small desk in his room. His face looked red and engorged, but that was due no doubt to his life in the sun. He was urbane and alert, reminding me at once of our former meeting in London. His light blue eyes were full of intelligence and kindness, but they had the watery look of age. Indeed, I can hardly remember in all military history a case where a man over seventy had been called out from retirement to conduct so arduous a campaign, and it was his conception of the fine flank march to Paardeburg which had actually beaten the Boers, however long they might keep up appearances of resistance. We had a short vivid talk and I never saw him again until he came to my own house at Hindhead to inspect my rifle range in 1902.

Of Lord Kitchener I saw nothing at Pretoria, but on one occasion a big man on a huge bay horse went past me at a hand gallop on the veldt, and as he passed he waved his hand, and I knew it was the famous soldier. He had been under a cloud since Paardeburg, and indeed it is hard to see how his tactics can be justified, since he attacked the Boers and lost some two thousand men, when they were headed off and were bound to surrender in any case. There may be reasons unknown to a civilian, but I have heard soldiers speak warmly about it, for some of the attackers were mounted troops who had to gallop to the edge of the donga, and could do nothing when they got there. Colonel Hannay actually registered some protest before obeying the orders in which he and many of his men met their death. However, it was to Kitchener that all men turned now when the organisation of the lines of communication was the vital point, and that rather than actual battle was his forte. I have been told by some who have been in action with him that he became nervously restless and impatient in a fight, while Roberts, on the other hand, became cooler and more quiet the greater the danger grew. In organisation, however, Kitchener was inhuman in his cool accuracy. 'Regret to report great dynamite explosion. Forty Kaffirs killed,' was the report of one officer. 'Do you need more dynamite?' was the answering telegram from Lord Kitchener.

There was a bench outside my hotel on which a group of old bearded burghers used to smoke their pipes every day. I went down and sat among them with my Boer pipe filled with the best Magaliesburg. I said nothing, so soon they began to make advances, speaking excellent English in rough guttural fashion. Botha was not far from the town, and it was notorious that spies took him out the news every night. These old fellows were clearly a collecting station, so I thought it would be useful to give them something to ponder. After conversational remarks one of them said: 'Tell us, mister, when are we to have peace?' They were under the impression that the whole British nation was longing for peace, and it was this which encouraged the resistance. 'Oh,' said I, 'I hope not for a long time yet.' They all looked at each other, and then the spokesman said: 'Why do you say that, mister?' 'Well, it's this way,' said I. 'This country, you see, is going to be a British colony. It would be very awkward for us to have a colony which was full of dangerous men. We couldn't kill them then, could we? They would be fellow-citizens and under the law's protection, the same as we. Our only chance is to kill them now, and that's what we will do if we have the time.' The old fellows all grunted and puffed furiously at their pipes, but they could find no answer. Possibly some version of the matter may have reached the point I was aiming at.

Our longest excursion from Pretoria was to Waterval, whither Bennett Burleigh took me in his Cape cart. Once we got quite close to a Boer patrol, about a dozen horsemen. Burleigh could not believe that they were actually the enemy until I pointed out that several of the horses were white, which was hardly ever known in our service. He then examined them with his glass, and found I was right. They were clearly on some quest of their own, for they took no notice of us, though they could easily have cut us off. Our drive took us to the great prison camp where so many British and colonial soldiers had a humiliating experience. The prisoners had only got free a week or two before, and the whole place, many acres in size, was covered with every sort of souvenir. I contented myself with a Boer carbine which had been broken by a British prisoner, a band triangle, a half-knitted sock, the knitting needles being made from the barbed wire, and a set of leg fetters from the camp gaol. A tunnel had been bored just before the general delivery by some captive Hussars. It was a wonderful work, considering that it was done chiefly with spoons, and it had just been finished when relief came. I descended into it, and was photographed by Burleigh as I emerged. I dare say many of my friends have copies of it still, with my inscription: 'Getting out of a hole, like the British Empire.'

I spent a day in Johannesburg, walking its deserted streets and seeing its great mines now dead or at least in suspended animation. I descended one of the deep mines, the Robinson, but as the hoisting machinery was out of order, and we had to walk in darkness down hundreds (it seemed thousands) of slippery wooden steps, with buckets, which did the draining, clanking past our ears, it was certainly an overrated amusement. We got the usual tips as to which mines were going to boom – on all of which I acted, and all of which proved to be wrong.

On July 4, after an uneventful journey, which proved in itself that our grip was tightening upon the country, I found myself back in the Langman Hospital again. Times were quiet there, though another of our poor orderlies had just died of erysipelas, which had broken out in the wards – not traumatic erysipelas, but a variety which came without apparent cause. I mention the fact because enteric had been so universal that there really seemed no other disease, and this was the only appearance of any other ailment. If the army had all been inoculated, this would, I think, have been absolutely the healthiest war on record. Of surgical cases we had few, but I remember one operation which is perhaps rather technical for discussion and yet stands out very clearly in my memory. It was performed upon the Dutch military attaché with the Boers, who was picked up wounded and paralysed after some engagement. A shrapnel bullet had broken one of his cervical vertebrae, the bone pressed on the nerves, and they had ceased to function. Watson Cheyne of London was the operator. He had cut down on the bone with a free incision and was endeavouring with a strong forceps to raise the broken arch of bone, when an amazing thing happened. Out of the great crimson cleft there rose a column of clear water two feet high, feathering at the top like a little palm tree, which gradually dwindled until it was only a few inches long, and finally disappeared. I had, I confess, no idea what it was, and I think many of the assembled surgeons were as taken aback as I was. The mystery was explained by Charles Gibbs, my mentor in such matters, who said that the cerebro-spinal fluid, which is usually a mere moistening round the cord, had been greatly stimulated and increased by the pressure of the broken bone. It had finally distended the whole sheath. The forceps had punctured a small hole in the sheath and then the fluid had been pressed through and shot into the air as I had seen it. Perhaps the release was too sudden, for the patient died shortly after he was removed from the table.

Charles Gibbs is still in practice, and senior surgeon of Charing Cross Hospital, but he will forgive me if I remind him that his pupil did once score over him. One of my enteric patients was obviously dying and kept murmuring that he would like some solid food. Of course the first law in treating enteric is, or was, that diet must be fluid, as the intestine is ulcerated and puncture of it means death by peritonitis. I said to Gibbs: 'Do you consider that this man is sure to die?' 'He is certainly as bad as he can be,' said Gibbs. 'Well then,' said I, 'I propose to give him a solid meal.' Gibbs shook his head and was shocked. 'It is a great responsibility you take.' 'What's the odds,' I asked, 'if he has to die anyhow?' 'Well, it's just the difference whether you kill him or the disease does.' 'Well, I'll take the chance,' said I – and I did so. A year or so later I was attending a public meeting at Edinburgh when the following letter, which I copy from my book of curiosities, was handed up to me.

> *128 Royal Road, Kennington Park,*
> *London, SE*
> *October 1, 1900*
>
> Sir – As one who was under your care at Bloemfontein in Langman's Hospital I hope you will forgive me in taking the liberty of wishing you success at Edinburgh. I am actuated in this not only by political principles but by the fact that I (and others) owe my life to your kindness and care. You may not remember me, sir, but I can assure you the remembrance of you is written in my mind and can never be removed. Again wishing you success and hoping you will pardon this liberty,
>
> I remain, sir,
> Yours obediently,
>
> (PTE) M. HANLON, CIV

M. Hanlon was my enteric patient and he had never looked back from the day he had that square meal. But I don't say it was an example for the family practitioner to copy.

On July 11 I went on board the *Briton* at Capetown and we sailed for England once more. I called upon Sir Alfred Milner before I left, and found him a very much older man than when only a few years before I had met him on the eve of his African experience. His hair was grizzled and his shoulders bowed, but his brave heart was as steadfast as ever, nor did it ever fail until his hard and thankless task was done. He made one error, I think, when he desired to keep South Africa under martial law when the war was over, but who could have done better, or as well, under the intolerable conditions which he had to face?

It was a remarkable passenger list on the *Briton*, and a very joyous voyage. The Duke of Norfolk and his brother Lord Edward Talbot were two of the most cheery people on the ship. It was a weird sight to see the senior Baron of England and a lumpy Hollander sitting face to face on a spar, and slashing each other with bladders to see which could knock off the other. Blood told, if I remember right. Then there was Sir John Willoughby, of Jameson Raid fame, Lady Sarah Wilson from

Mafeking, the Duke of Marlborough, Lady Arthur Grosvenor, the Honourable Ivor Guest and many famous soldiers. Especially was I fortunate in my friendship with Fletcher Robinson and with Nevinson, which was cemented by this closer association. Only one cloud marred the serenity of that golden voyage. There was a foreign officer on board, whose name I will not mention, who had been with the Boers and who talked with great indiscretion as to his experiences and opinions. He stated in my presence that the British had habitually used Dum-Dum bullets, on which I lost my temper and told him he was a liar. I must say that he behaved very well, for after thinking it over he saw that he was in the wrong and he sent down my friend Robinson to my cabin with a query as to whether I would accept an apology. I answered that I would not, since it was the army, and not me, which had been insulted. In an hour Robinson reappeared with the following letter, which ended what might have been a serious incident.

DEAR SIR – Allow me to tell you that I regret lively what I said about expanding bullets – which I said but after hear saying evidence I request you to let everybody know that I strongly wish on the contrary that I desire to be on best terms with every Englishman and beg you for that to be my interpreter.

Yours very truly.

The first days of August saw me in London once more, and soon all that strange episode – the green expanse of the veldt, the flat-topped hills, the enteric wards – had become the vision of a dream.

19

An Appeal to the World's Opinion

Misrepresentation – Sudden Resolve – Reginald Smith – A Week's
Hard Work – *The Cause and Conduct of the War* – Translations –
German Letter – Complete Success – Surplus

One of the most pleasing and complete episodes in my life was connected with the pamphlet which I wrote upon the methods and
objects of our soldiers in South Africa. It was an attempt to stem the
extraordinary outbreak of defamation which had broken out in every
country – or nearly every country – in Europe, and which had attained
such a height that it really seemed that on this absolutely fictitious
basis might be built up a powerful political combination which would
involve us in a serious war.

I can well remember the inception of my enterprise! The date was
January 7, 1902. The day was a Tuesday. Sir Henry Thompson was
holding that evening one of those charming 'octave' dinners at which it
was my occasional privilege to attend, and I was going up to town from
Hindhead to keep the engagement. Sitting alone in a carriage I read the
foreign correspondence of *The Times*. In a single column there were
accounts of meetings in all parts of Europe – notably one of some
hundreds of Rhineland clergymen – protesting against our brutalities to
our enemies. There followed a whole column of extracts from foreign
papers, with grotesque descriptions of our barbarities. To anyone who
knew the easy-going British soldier or the character of his leaders the
thing was unspeakably absurd; and yet, as I laid down the paper and
thought the matter over, I could not but admit that these Continental
people were acting under a generous and unselfish motive which was
much to their credit. How could they help believing those things, and,
believing them, was it not their duty, by meeting, by article, by any
means, to denounce them? Could we accuse them of being credulous?
Would we not be equally so if all our accounts of any transaction came
from one side, and were supported by such journalists and, above all,
such artists as lent their pens and pencils, whether venally or not, to the

Boer cause? Of course we would. And whose fault was it that our side of the question was not equally laid before the jury of the civilised world? Perhaps we were too proud, perhaps we were too negligent – but the fact was obvious that judgement was being given against us by default. How *could* they know our case? Where could they find it? If I were asked what document they could consult, what could I answer? *Blue-books* and state papers are not for the multitude. There were books like Fitz-Patrick's *Transvaal from Within* or E. T. Cook's *Rights and Wrongs*, but these were expensive volumes, and not readily translated. Nowhere could be found a statement which covered the whole ground in a simple fashion. Why didn't some Briton draw it up? And then like a bullet through my head, came the thought, 'Why don't you draw it up yourself?'

The next instant I was on fire with the idea. Seldom in my life have I been so conscious of a direct imperative call which drove every other thought from the mind. If I were a humble advocate, it was all the better, since I could have no axe to grind. I was fairly well posted in the facts already, as I had written an interim history of the war. I had seen something of the campaign, and possessed many documents which bore upon the matter. My plans widened every instant. I would raise money from the public and by the sale of the book at home. With this I would translate it into every language. These translations should be given away wholesale. Every professor, every clergyman, every journalist, every politician, should have one put under his nose in his own language. In future, if they traduced us, they could no longer plead ignorance that there was another side to the question. Before I reached London all my programme was sketched out in my head. There was no item of it, I may add, which was not eventually carried through.

Fortune was my friend. I have said that I was dining that night with Sir Henry Thompson. My neighbour at dinner was a gentleman whose name I had not caught. My mind being full of the one idea, my talk soon came round to it, and instead of my neighbour being bored, my remarks were received with a courteous and sympathetic attention which caused me to make even greater demands upon his patience. Having listened from the soup to the savoury (often has my conscience rebuked me since), he ended by asking me mildly how I proposed to raise the money for these wide-reaching schemes. I answered that I would appeal to the public. He asked me how much would suffice. I answered that I could make a start with a thousand pounds. He remarked that it would take much more than that. 'However,' he added, 'if a thousand pounds would go any way towards it, I have no doubt that sum could be got for you.' 'From whom?' I asked. He gave me his name and address and said: 'I have no doubt that if you carry out the scheme on the lines you suggest, I could get the money. When you have done your work, come to me, and we will see how it is best to proceed.' I promised to do so, and thanked him for his encouragement. Sir Eric Barrington of the Foreign Office was the name of this fairy godfather.

This was my first stroke of good luck. A second came next morning. I had occasion to call upon the publishing house of Smith, Elder & Co., over some other business, and during the interview I told Mr Reginald Smith the plan that I had formed. Without a moment's hesitation he placed the whole machinery of his worldwide business at my disposal, without payment of any kind. From that moment he became my partner in the enterprise, and I found his counsel at every stage of as great help to me as the publishing services which he so generously rendered. Not only did he save heavy costs to the fund, but he arranged easily and successfully those complex foreign transactions which the scheme entailed.

That morning I called at the War Office and was referred by them to the Intelligence Department, where every information which they possessed was freely put at my disposal. I then wrote to *The Times* explaining what I was trying to do, and asking those who sympathised with my object to lend me their aid. Never was an appeal more generously or rapidly answered. My morning post on the day after brought me a hundred and twenty-seven letters, nearly all of which contained sums drawn from every class of the community, varying from the fifty pounds of Lord Rosebery to the half-crown of the widow of a private soldier. Most of the remittances were accompanied by letters which showed that, however they might pretend in public to disregard it, the attitude of the foreign critics had really left a deep and bitter feeling in the hearts of our people.

It was on January 9 that I was able to begin my task. On the 17th I had finished it. When the amount of matter is considered, and the number of researches and verifications which it entailed, I need not say that I had been absorbed in the work, and devoted, I dare say, sixteen hours a day to its accomplishment. So far as possible I kept my individual opinions in the background, and made a more effective case by marshalling the statements of eye-witnesses, many of them Boers, on the various questions of farm-burnings, outrages, concentration camps, and other contentious subjects. I made the comments as simple and as short as I could, while as to the accuracy of my facts, I may say that, save as to the exact number of farmhouses burned, I have never heard of one which has been seriously questioned. It was a glad day for me when I was able to lay down my pen with the feeling that my statement was as full and as effective as it was in me to make it.

Meanwhile the subscriptions had still come steadily in, until nearly £1,000 more had been banked by the time that the booklet was finished. The greater number of contributions were in small sums from people who could ill afford it. One notable feature was the number of governesses and others residing abroad whose lives had been embittered by their inability to answer the slanders which were daily uttered in their presence. Many of these sent their small donations. A second pleasing feature was the number of foreigners resident in England who supported my scheme, in the hope that it would aid their own people to form a juster view. From Norwegians alone I received nearly fifty pounds with this object. If Britain's own children too often betrayed her at a crisis of her fate, she found at least warm friends among the strangers within her gates. Another point worth noting was that a disproportionate sum was from clergymen, which was explained by several of them as due to the fact that since the war began they had been pestered by anti-national literature, and took this means of protesting against it.

The proofs having been printed, I sent them to my Foreign Office friend as I had promised, and presently received an invitation to see him. He expressed his approval of the work, and handed me a banknote for five hundred pounds, at the same time explaining that the money did not come from him. I asked if I might acknowledge it as from an anonymous donor. 'The donor would not object,' said my friend. So I was able to head my list with 'A Loyal Briton', who contributed five hundred pounds. I dare say the Secret Service knew best whence the money came.

By this time the banking account had risen to some two thousand pounds, and we were in a position to put our foreign translations in hand. The British edition had in the meantime been published, the distribution being placed in the hands of Messrs Newnes, who gave the enterprise whole-hearted aid. The book was retailed at sixpence, but as it was our desire that the sale should be pushed it was sold to the trade at about threepence. The result was to leave the main profit of the enterprise in the hands of the retailer. The sale of the pamphlet was very large – in fact, I should imagine that it approached a record for the time. Some two hundred and fifty thousand copies were sold in Great Britain very quickly, and about three hundred thousand within a couple of months. This great sale enabled us to add considerably to the fund by the accumulation of the small rebate which had been reserved upon each copy. Our financial position was very strong, therefore, in dealing with the foreign translations.

The French edition was prepared by Professor Sumichrast of Harvard University, who was a French-Canadian by birth. This gentleman patriotically refused to take any payment for his work, which was admirably done. It was published without difficulty by Galignani, and several thousands were given away where they would do most good, in France, Belgium and Switzerland. Twenty thousand copies of this edition were printed.

The German edition was a more difficult matter. No German publisher would undertake it, and the only courtesy which we met with in that country was from Baron von Tauchnitz, who included the volume in his well-known English library. Our advances were met with coldness, and occasionally with insult. Here, for example, is a copy of an extreme specimen of the kind of letter received.

January 1902

Messrs Smith, Elder & Co.

GENT – Doyle's book makes the impression as if it was ordered or influenced by the English Jingo party.

Now, you know, this English war party (as well as the English officers and soldiers in Transvaal) are contempted by the whole civilised world as coward scoundrels and vile brutes who murder women and children.

It would be for me, as an importer of English literature to Germany, Austria and Russia, in the highest degree imprudent to do anything that could awake the suspicion I was in connection with so despised a party.

I have shown your letter to several persons. Nobody was inclined to take up the matter.

There is a mixture of venom and smugness about this epistle which gives it a high place in my collection. In spite of rebuffs, however, I found an Anglo-German publishing house in Berlin to undertake the work, and with the assistance of Herr Kurt von Musgrave, who gave me an excellent translation, I was able to work off more than one very large edition, which had a perceptible effect in modifying the tone of that portion of the German press which was open to reason. Altogether twenty thousand copies were distributed in the Fatherland and German-speaking Austria.

I remember one whimsical incident at this time. Somewhat tired, after the book was in the press, I went down to Seaford for a rest. While there, a message reached me that a Pan-German officer of Landwehr had come over to London, and desired to see me. I wired that I could not come up, but that I should be happy to see him if he came down. Down he came accordingly, a fine, upstanding, soldierly man, speaking excellent English. The German proofs had passed through his hands, and he was much distressed by the way in which I had spoken of the hostility which his countrymen had shown us, and its effect upon our feelings towards them. We sat all day and argued the question out. His great point, as a Pan-German, was that someday both Germany and Britain would have to fight Russia – Britain for India, and Germany perhaps for the Baltic Provinces. Therefore they should keep in close touch with each other. I assured him that at the time the feeling in this country was much more bitter against Germany than against Russia. He doubted it. I suggested as a test that he should try the question upon any bus driver in London as a fair index of popular opinion. He was very anxious that I should modify certain paragraphs, and I was equally determined not to do so, as I was convinced they were true. Finally, when he left me on his return to London, he said, 'Well, I have come eight hundred miles to see you, and I ask you now as a final request that in the translation you will allow the one word "Leider" [Alas] to be put at the opening of that paragraph.' I was perfectly ready to agree to this. So he got one word in exchange for sixteen hundred miles of travel, and I think it was a very sporting venture.

One charming incident connected with this German translation was that a small group of Swiss (and in no country had we such warm-hearted friends as among the minority in Switzerland) were so keen upon the cause that they had a translation and an edition of their own, with large print and maps. It was published independently at Zurich, Dr Angst, the British Consul in that town, helping to organise it. Amongst other good friends who worked hard for the truth, and exposed themselves to much obloquy in doing so, were Professor Naville, the eminent Egyptologist of Geneva, and Monsieur Talichet, the well-known editor of the *Bibliothèque Universelle* of Lausanne, who sacrificed the circulation of his old-established magazine in upholding our cause.

So much for the French and German editions. The American and Canadian had arranged themselves. There remained the Spanish, Portuguese, Italian, Hungarian and Russian, all of which were rapidly prepared and circulated without a hitch, save that in the case of the Russian, which was published at Odessa, the censor suppressed it at the last instant. We were successful, however, in getting his veto removed. In each of these countries several thousands of the booklet were given away. In every case we found a larger sale for these foreign editions than we expected, arising no doubt from the eagerness of English residents abroad to make their neighbours understand our position.

The Dutch edition was a stumbling-block. This gallant little nation felt a most natural sympathy for their kinsfolk in arms against us, and honestly believed that they had been very badly used. We should certainly have felt the same. The result was that we were entirely unable to find either publisher or distributor. The greater the opposition the more obvious was the need for the book, so Mr Reginald Smith arranged that a large edition should be printed here, and sent direct to all leaders of Dutch opinion. I believe that out of some five thousand copies not more than twenty were sent back to us.

The Norwegian edition also presented some difficulties which were overcome by the assistance of Mr Thomassen of the *Verdensgang*. This gentleman's paper was entirely opposed to us, but in the interests of fair play he helped me to get my book before the public. I hope that some relaxation in his attitude towards us in his paper may have been due to a fuller comprehension of our case, and a realisation of the fact that a nation does not make great sacrifices extending over years for an ignoble cause. One other incident in connection with the Norwegian edition is pleasant for me to recall. I had prefaced each Continental version with a special foreword, designed to arrest the attention of the particular people whom I was addressing. In this case, when the book was going to press in Christiania, the preface had not arrived from the translator (the accomplished Madame Brockmann), and as she lived a hundred miles off, with all the passes blocked by a phenomenal snowstorm, it looked as if it must be omitted. Finally, however, my short address to the Scandinavian people was heliographed across from snow-peak to snow-peak, and so found its way to the book.

There was one other language into which the book needed to be translated, and that was the Welsh, for the vernacular press of the Principality was almost entirely pro-Boer, and the Welsh people had the most distorted information as to the cause for which their fellow-countrymen fought so bravely in the field. The translation was done by Mr W. Evans, and some ten thousand copies were printed for distribution through the agency of the Cardiff *Western Mail*. This finished our labours. Our total output was three hundred thousand of the British edition, about fifty thousand in Canada and the United States, twenty thousand in Germany, twenty thousand in France, five thousand in Holland, ten thousand in Wales, eight thousand in Hungary, five thousand in Norway and Sweden, three thousand five hundred in Portugal, ten thousand in Spain, five thousand in Italy, and five thousand in Russia. There were editions in Tamil and Kanarese, the numbers of which I do not know. In all, I have seen twenty different presentments of my little book. The total sum at our disposal amounted to about five thousand pounds, of which, speaking roughly, half came from subscriptions and the other half was earned by the book itself.

It was not long before we had the most gratifying evidence of the success of these efforts. There was a rapid and marked change in the tone of the whole Continental press, which may have been a coincidence, but was certainly a pleasing one. In the case of many important organs of public opinion there could, however, be no question of coincidence, as the arguments advanced in the booklet and the facts quoted were cited in their leading articles as having modified their former anti-British views. This was the case with the *Tagblatt* of Vienna, whose London representative, Dr Maurice Ernst, helped me in every way to approach the Austrian public. So it was also with the *National Zeitung* in Berlin, the *Indépendance Belge* in Brussels, and many others. In the greater number of cases, however, it was unreasonable to suppose that a journal would publicly eat its own words, and the best result for which we could hope was that which we often attained, an altered and less acrimonious tone.

Mr Reginald Smith and I now found ourselves in the very pleasant position of having accomplished our work so far as we could do it, and yet of having in hand a considerable sum of money. What were we to do with it? To return it to subscribers was impossible, and indeed at least half of it would have to be returned to ourselves since it had been earned by the sale of the book. I felt that the subscribers had given me a free hand with the money, to use it to the best of my judgement for national aims.

Our first expense was in immediate connection with the object in view, for we endeavoured to supplement the effect of the booklet by circulating a large number of an excellent Austrian work, *Recht und Unrecht im Burenkrieg*, by Dr Ferdinand Hirz. Six hundred of these were distributed where they might do most good.

Our next move was to purchase half a dozen very handsome gold cigarette cases. On the back of each was engraved, 'From Friends in England to a Friend of England'. These were distributed to a few of those who had stood most staunchly by us. One went to the eminent French publicist, Monsieur Yves Guyot, a second to Monsieur Talichet of Lausanne, a third to Mr Sumichrast, and a fourth to Professor Naville. By a happy coincidence the latter gentleman happened to be in this country at the time, and I had the pleasure of slipping the small souvenir into his hand as he put on his overcoat in the hall of the Athenaeum Club. I have seldom seen anyone look more surprised.

There remained a considerable sum, and Mr Reginald Smith shared my opinion that we should find some permanent use for it, and that this use should bring benefit to natives of South Africa. We therefore forwarded a thousand pounds to Edinburgh University, to be so invested as to give a return of forty pounds a year, which should be devoted to the South African student who acquitted himself with most distinction. There are many Afrikander students at Edinburgh, and we imagined that we had hit upon a pleasing common interest for Boer and for Briton; but I confess that I was rather amazed when at the end of the first year I received a letter from a student expressing his confidence that he would win the bursary, and adding that there could be no question as to his eligibility, as he was a full-blooded Zulu.

The fund, however, was by no means exhausted, and we were able to make contributions to the Civilian Rifleman's movement, to the Union Jack Club, to the Indian famine, to Japanese nursing, to the Irish old soldiers' institute, to the fund for distressed Boers, and to many other deserving objects. These donations varied from fifty guineas to ten. Finally we were left with a residuum which amounted to £309 0s. 4d. Mr Reginald Smith and I sat in solemn conclave over this sum, and discussed how it might best be used for the needs of the Empire. The fourpence presented no difficulty, for we worked it off upon the crossing-sweeper outside, who had helped to relieve Delhi. Nine pounds went in tobacco for the Chelsea veterans at Christmas. There remained the good round sum of three hundred pounds. We bethought us of the saying that the safety of the Empire might depend upon a single shot from a twelve-inch gun, and we devoted the whole amount to a magnificent cup, to be shot for by the various ships of the Channel Squadron, the winner to hold it for a single year. The stand of the cup was from the oak timbers of the *Victory*, and the trophy itself was a splendid one in solid silver gilt. By the kind and judicious cooperation of Admiral Sir Percy Scott, the Inspector of Target Practice, through whose hands the trophy passed to the senior admiral afloat, Sir Arthur Wilson VC, in command of the Channel Squadron, all difficulties were overcome and the cup was shot for that year, and has since produced, I am told, great emulation among the various crews. Our one condition was that it should not be retained in the mess-room, but should be put out on the deck where the winning bluejackets could continually see it. I learn that the *Exmouth* came into Plymouth Harbour with the cup on the top of her fore turret.

The one abiding impression left upon my mind by the whole episode is that our government does not use publicity enough in stating and defending its own case. If a private individual could by spending three thousand pounds and putting in a month's work make a marked impression upon the public opinion of the world, what could be done by a really rich and intelligent organisation? But the first requisite is that you should honestly have a just cause to state. Who is there outside England who really knows the repeated and honest efforts made by us to settle the eternal Irish question and hold the scales fair between rival Irishmen? We certainly do, as a great Frenchman said, 'defend ourselves very badly'. If we let cases go by default how can we imagine that the verdict can be in our favour?

20

My Political Adventures

I have twice stood for Parliament, though if anyone were to ask me my
real reasons for doing so I should find it difficult to give them an
intelligible answer. It certainly was from no burning desire to join that
august assembly, for in each case I deliberately contested seats which
every expert considered to be impossible, and though on one occasion
I very nearly proved the experts to be wrong, my action is none the less
a sign that I had no great wish to be at the head of the poll, for other
and easier seats had been offered me. In the case of Central Edinburgh,
for which I stood in the 1900 election, there may have been some
sentimental call, for it was the section of the city where I was educated
and where much of my boyhood was spent. It was said to be the
premier Radical stronghold of Scotland, and to carry it would be a fine
exploit, for though I was a good deal of a Radical myself in many ways,
I knew that it would be a national disgrace and possibly an imperial
disaster if we did not carry the Boer War to complete success, and that
was the real issue before the electors.

I believe that providence one way or another gets a man's full powers
out of him, but that it is essential that the man himself should co-
operate to the extent of putting himself in the way of achievement. Give
yourself the chance always. If it is so fated, you will win through. If your
path lies elsewhere, then you have got your sign through your failure.
But do not put yourself in the position later in life of looking back and
saying, 'Perhaps I might have had a career there had I tried.' Deep in
my bones I felt that I was on earth for some big purpose, and it was only
by trying that I could tell that the purpose was not political, though I
could never imagine myself as fettered to a party or as thinking that all
virtues lay with one set of men.

My political work was not wasted. I stood in the two most heckling
constituencies in Scotland, and through that odious and much-abused

custom I gained a coolness on the platform and a disregard for interruption and clamour, which have stood me in good stead since. Indeed,
I hold that it was to fashion me more perfectly for my ultimate work
that I was twice passed through this furnace. I remember that once at
Hawick my soldier brother came to see how I was getting on, and was
struck by the effect which I had upon my audience. 'It would be strange,
Arthur,' said he, 'if your real career should prove to be political and not
literary.' 'It will be neither. It will be religious,' said I. Then we looked
at each other in surprise and both burst out laughing. The answer
seemed quite absurd and pointless, for no remote possibility of such a
thing suggested itself. It was a curious example of that unconscious
power of prophecy which is latent within us.

I had hardly landed from South Africa when I flung myself into the
Edinburgh contest. Mr Cranston, later Sir Robert Cranston, a well-
known citizen, was my chairman. When I arrived a small meeting was
held, and I, a weary man, listened while it was gravely debated, with
much weighing of pros and cons, what my view was to be on each of the
vital questions. Finally it was all settled to their satisfaction and written
down, preparatory to forming the election address. I had listened with
some amusement, and when it was all over I said: 'Gentlemen, may I
ask who is going to honour these promises that you are making?' 'Why,
you, of course,' said they. 'Then I think it would be better if I made
them,' said I, and, crumpling up their document, I picked up a pen and
wrote out my own views and my own address. It was well received and
would have won the election against enormous odds – some thousands
of votes at the last trial – were it not for a very unexpected intervention.

Those who remember the election will bear me out that it was an
exciting affair. My opponent was a Mr Brown, a member of Nelson's
publishing firm, which had large works in the constituency. I was fresh
from the scene of war and overflowing with zeal to help the army, so I
spared myself in no way. I spoke from barrels in the street or any other
pedestal I could find, holding many wayside meetings besides my big
meetings in the evening, which were always crowded and uproarious.
There was nothing which I could have done and did not do. My
opponent was not formidable, but I had against me an overwhelming
party machine with its registered lists and record of unbroken victory.
It was no light matter to change the vote of a Scotsman, and many of
them would as soon think of changing their religion. One serious
mischance occurred. I was determined to do and say nothing which I

did not heartily mean, and this united Ireland, North and South, for the first time in history. The Irish vote was considerable, so that this was important. The South quarrelled with me because, though I favoured some devolution, I was not yet converted to Home Rule. The North was angry because I was in favour of a Catholic University for Dublin. So I had no votes from Ireland. When I went down to hold a meeting in a hall in the Cowgate, which is the Irish quarter, I was told that it had been arranged to break my platform up. This seems to have been true, but fortunately I got on good human terms with my audience, and indeed moved some of them to tears by telling them of the meeting between the two battalions of the Royal Dublin Fusiliers at Ladysmith. So it happened that when a sinister-looking figure, a local horse-slaughterer, appeared on the edge of the stage, he was received in silence. He moved slowly across and said something about free speech. I felt that if I or my people were violent there would be a riot, so I simply said: 'Trot along, sonny, trot along!' He did trot along and disappeared on the other side of the stage. After the transit of this sinister star, and my temporary eclipse, all went well to the end.

As the day of the election approached, it became more and more evident that I was getting dangerous, but I was knocked out – fortunately for myself, as I now discern – by a curious interference. There was an Evangelical fanatic named Plimmer living at Dunfermline who thought it his special mission in life to keep Roman Catholic candidates out of Parliament. Therefore at the eleventh hour, the very night before the voting, the whole district was placarded with big sheets to say that I was a Roman Catholic, that I had been educated by Jesuits, and in fact that my whole candidature was an attack upon Kirk and Covenant and Lesser Catechism and everything dear to the Scottish heart. It was very cleverly done, and of course this fanatic alone could not have paid the expenses, though I cannot believe that Mr Brown knew anything of the matter. My unhappy supporters saw crowds of workmen reading these absurd placards and calling out, 'I've done with him!' As it was I very narrowly missed the seat, being only beaten by a few hundred votes. The question of an appeal came along, but the thing was so clever that it really was difficult to handle, since it was true enough that I had been educated by Jesuits and yet absurdly untrue that this education influenced my present frame of mind. Therefore we had to leave it alone.

Looking back, I am inclined to look upon Mr Plimmer as one of the great benefactors of my life. He altered the points at the last moment

My mother aged
seventeen

Lady Conan Doyle in
1920

The steam-whaler *Hope*

The staff of the Langman Hospital, South Africa, 1900

Kingsley Conan Doyle

On the French front
The family in the wilds of Canada

and prevented me from being shunted on to a sideline which would perhaps have taken me to a dead end. I could never have been a party man, and there seems no place under our system for anyone else. At the moment I was a little sore, and I wrote a letter to the *Scotsman* which defined my religious position as it was then, and caused, I believe, no little comment. I had the following letter from Sir John Boraston, who was the party organiser. The first sentence refers to the possibility of lodging a legal protest.

> *6 Great George Street,*
> *Westminster, London, SW*
> *October 18, 1900*

DEAR DR DOYLE – Probably your Edinburgh advisers are right, but it is undoubtedly a misfortune that the perpetrators of attacks such as that which was made upon you should be allowed to go unpunished. Your fight was indeed a phenomenal one, and you have the consolation of knowing that if you did not actually win a seat for yourself, you did materially contribute to the Liberal Unionist victories in two other Edinburgh constituencies – this is generally admitted.

I am sure you will feel that your first entry into active political life promises a full measure of success at no distant date, and I hope I may see you again before long to talk matters over.

Yours very truly, (*sgd*) JOHN BORASTON

I had no further urge to try political adventures, but when the Tariff Reform election of 1905 came round I felt that I should make some sacrifice for the faith that was in me. Mr 'Tommy' Shaw, as he was called – now Lord Shaw – was one of the most energetic Radicals in Scotland, and was reputed to be most firmly established in his seat, which was called 'The Border Burghs', consisting of the small towns of Hawick, Galashiels and Selkirk, all of them engaged in the woollen trade, and all of them hard hit by German competition. It seemed to me that if there was a good field anywhere for Mr Joseph Chamberlain's views on a protective tariff it should be there, where an open market had caused such distress and loss. My reasoning was sound enough, but I had not reckoned upon the innate conservatism of the Scottish character, which cannot readjust its general principles to meet the particular case – a noble trait, but occasionally an unpractical one. Party politics are not a divine law, but simply a means to an end, which must adjust itself as the end varies.

This time I really expended a good deal of work as well as money upon the attempt, for if you stand for others besides yourself you have no choice but to work up to the last pound of steam. I might have added my neck to the other things which I risked, for in an endeavour to get into comradeship with the people I joined in what is known as the 'common-riding' at Hawick, where a general holiday is proclaimed while the bounds of the common are ridden over and defined. Part of the proceedings was that each mounted man had to gallop full-split down the high road over a measured course of half a mile or so, the burghers lining the way and helping him by waving sticks and umbrellas. I was mounted on a hunter which I had never seen before, and which was full of spirit. Fortunately this monstrous road performance came off late in the afternoon, and I had taken some of the spirit out of him by our ride round the common. I do not profess to be a great horseman, and I certainly nearly made the acquaintance of the Hawick turnpike. Sooner or later someone will be killed at that game, and horses must be lamed every year. Afterwards an interminable ballad was recited with a sort of jingling chorus to which all who are near the reciter keep time with their feet. As it would seem unsympathetic not to join in, I also kept time with the rhythm, and was amused and amazed when I got back to London to see in the papers that I had danced a hornpipe in public before the electors. Altogether I had no desire to face another Hawick common-riding.

The trouble in dealing with a three-town constituency, each town very jealous of the others, is that whatever you do has to be done thrice or you give offence. I was therefore heartily sick of the preparation and only too pleased when the actual election came off. I thought then, and I think now, that a sliding tariff, if only as an instrument for bargaining, would be altogether to our interest in this country, and would possibly cause some of our rivals to cease closing their markets to us, while they freely use the open market which we present. I still think that Chamberlain's whole scheme was an admirable one, and that it was defeated by a campaign of misrepresentation and actual lying, in which Chinese labour and dear food played a chief part. I stood among the ruins of a dismantled factory in the Border Burghs and I showed how it had been destroyed by German competition, and how while we let their goods in free they were levying taxes on ours and spending the money so gained upon warships with which we might someday have to reckon. The answer to my arguments consisted largely of coloured cartoons of

Chinamen working in chains in the mines of the Transvaal, and other nonsense of the sort. I worked very hard, so hard that on the last night of the election I addressed meetings in each of the three towns, which, as they are separated by many miles of hilly roads, is a feat never done, I understand, before or since. However, it was of no avail and I was beaten, though I believe I am right in saying that the party showed a less decrease of votes than in any constituency in Scotland. The thing which annoyed me most about the election was that my opponent, Tommy Shaw, only appeared once, so far as I remember, in the constituency, and did everything by deputy, so that I found myself like a boxer who is punching his rival's second instead of himself all the time. I had the melancholy satisfaction of noting that the Radical chairman who was so engrossed in the wrongs of Chinamen in the Transvaal went into liquidation within a few months, giving as his reason the pressure of foreign competition in the woollen trade.

It is a vile business this electioneering, though no doubt it is chastening in its effects. They say that mud-baths are healthy and purifying, and I can compare it to nothing else. This applies particularly, I think, to Scotland, where the art of heckling has been carried to extremes. This asking of questions was an excellent thing so long as it was honest in its desire to know the candidate's opinion upon a public measure. But the honest questions are the exception and the unfortunate man is baited by all sorts of senseless trick questions from mischievous and irresponsible persons, which are designed to annoy him and make him seem foolish or ignorant. Some reform is badly needed in this matter. Often, after a speech of an hour, I had an hour of questions, one more absurd than another. The press records will show, I hope, that I held my own, for I knew my subject well, and by this time I had had a good schooling on the platform. Sometimes I countered heavily. I remember one robust individual coming down with a carefully prepared question which he shouted from the back of the hall. I had been speaking of retaliation in commercial tariffs, and his question was: 'Mr Candidate, how do you reconcile retaliation with the Sermon on the Mount?' I answered: 'We cannot in life always reach the highest ideals. Have you sold all and given to the poor?' The man was locally famous as having done nothing of the sort, and there was a howl of delight at my answer which fairly drove him out of the hall.

There is a peculiar dry Scottish wit which is very effective when you get it on your side. I remember one solemn person who had a loaf on the end of a pole which he protruded towards me, as if it were a death's-head, from the side box of the theatre in which I spoke. The implication was, I suppose, that I would raise the price of bread. It was difficult to ignore the thing and yet puzzling how to meet it, but one of my people in broad Doric cried: 'Tak' it hame and eat it!' which quite spoilt the effect. Usually these interpolations are delivered in a dreamy impersonal sort of voice. When, in talking of the Transvaal War, I said with some passion, 'Who is going to pay for this war?' a seedy-looking person standing against the side wall said, 'I'm no' carin'!' which made both me and the audience laugh. Again I remember my speech being quite interrupted by a joke which was lost upon me. I had spoken of the self-respect and decent attire of American factory hands. 'Gang and look at Broon's,' said the dreamy voice. I have never yet learned whether Brown's factory was famous for tidiness or the reverse, but the remark convulsed the audience.

The Radicals used to attend my meetings in great numbers, so that really, I think, they were often hostile audiences which I addressed. Since their own candidate held hardly any meetings I was the only fun to be had. Before the meeting the packed house would indulge in cries and counter-cries with rival songs and slogans, so that as I approached the building it sounded like feeding-time at the zoo. My heart often sank within me as I listened to the uproar, and I would ask myself what on earth I meant by placing myself in such a position. Once on the platform, however, my fighting blood warmed up, and I did not quail before any clamour. It was all a great education for the future, though I did not realise it at the time, but followed blindly where some strange inward instinct led me on. What tired me most was the personal liberties taken by vulgar people, which is a very different thing from poor people, whom I usually find to be very delicate in their feelings. I take a liberty with no man, and there is something in me which rises up in anger if any man takes a liberty with me. A candidate cannot say all he thinks on this matter, or his party may suffer. I was always on my guard lest I should give offence in this way, and I well remember how on one occasion I stood during a three days' campaign a good many indignities with exemplary patience. I was on edge, however, and, as luck would have it, at the very last moment, as I stood on the platform waiting for the London train, one of my own people, an exuberant young bounder, came up with a loud familiar greeting and squeezed my right hand until my signet ring nearly cut me. It opened the sluice and out came a torrent of whaler language which I had hoped that I had long ago forgotten. The blast seemed to blow him bodily across the platform, and formed a strange farewell to my supporters.

Thus ended my career in politics. I could say with my friend Kendrick Bangs: 'The electors have returned me – to the bosom of my family.' A very pleasant constituency it is. I had now thoroughly explored that path, and had assured myself that my life's journey did not lie along it. And yet I was deeply convinced that public service was waiting for me somewhere. One likes to feel that one has some small practical influence upon the affairs of one's time, but I encourage myself by the thought that though I have not been a public man, yet my utterances in several pamphlets and numerous letters in the press may have had more weight with the public since I was disassociated from any political interest which could sway my judgement.

Post-War Campaigns

When I returned from South Africa, I found that my wife had improved in health during her stay at Naples, and we were able to settle
down once more at Hindhead, where, what with work, cricket and
hunting, I had some pleasant years. A few pressing tasks were awaiting
me, however. Besides the barren contest at Edinburgh I had done a
history of the war, but the war still continued, and I had to modify it
and keep it up to date in successive editions, until in 1902 it took final
shape. I called it *The Great Boer War*, not because I thought the war
'great' in the scale of history, but to distinguish it from the smaller Boer
War of 1881. It had the good fortune to please both friend and foe, for
there was an article from one of the Boer leaders in the *Cornhill* com-
mending its impartial tone. It has been published now by Nelson in a
cheap edition, and shows every sign of being the permanent record of
the campaign. No less than twenty-seven thousand pounds was spent
upon an official history, but I cannot find that there was anything in it
which I had not already chronicled, save for those minute details of
various forces which clog a narrative. I asked the chief official historian
whether my book had been of use to him, and he very handsomely
answered that it had been the spine round which he built.

This history, which is a large-sized book, is not to be confused with
the pamphlet *The Cause and Conduct of the War in South Africa*, which
was a small concise defence of the British position. The inception and
result of this I have already described. I have no doubt that it was to the
latter that my knighthood and my appointment as Deputy-Lieutenant
of Surrey, both of which occurred in 1902, were due.

I remember that on going down to Buckingham Palace to receive the
accolade, I found that all who were waiting for various honours were
herded into funny little pens, according to their style and degree,
there to await their turn. It chanced that Professor Oliver Lodge, who

was knighted on the same morning, was penned with me, and we plunged at once into psychic talk, which made me forget where I was, or what I was there for. Lodge was really more advanced and certain in his views than I was at that time, but I was quite sure about the truth of the phenomena, and only doubtful whether some alternative explanation might be found for a discarnate intelligence as the force at the back of them. This possibility I weighed for years before the evidence forced me to the Spiritist conclusion. But when, among the cloud of lies with which we are constantly girt, I read that Lodge and I were converted to our present views by the death of our respective sons, my mind goes back very clearly to that exchange of thought in 1902. At that time we had both studied the subject for many years.

Among the many congratulations which I had on my knighthood there were few which I valued more highly than that of my old comrade, H. A. Gwynne, who knew so much about South African affairs. He was good enough to say: 'I look upon your work during this terrible South African business as quite equal to that of a successful general.' This may well be the exaggeration of friendship, but it is at least pleasing to know that those who were in a position to judge did not look upon me as a mere busybody who butts in without due cause.

There is one incident at this period which comes back to my memory, and seems very whimsical. I had taken a course of muscular development with Mr Sandow, the strong man, and in that way had formed an acquaintance with him. In the winter of 1901 Mr Sandow had a laudable desire to do something for the British wounded, and with that idea he announced a competition at the Albert Hall. He was himself to show feats of strength and then there was to be a muster of strong men who should exhibit their proportions and receive prizes. There were to be three prizes, a golden statue about two feet high, a silver replica, and a bronze. Sandow asked Lawes the sculptor and myself to be the two judges, he being referee.

It proved to be a very big event. The Albert Hall was crowded. There were eighty competitors, each of whom had to stand on a pedestal, arrayed only in a leopard's skin. Lawes and I put them up ten at a time, chose one here and one there, and so gradually reduced the number until we only had six left. Then it became excessively difficult, for they were all perfectly developed athletes. Finally the matter was simplified by three extra prizes, and then we got down to the three winners, but had still to name their order, which was all-important since the value of the three prizes was so very different. The three men were all wonderful specimens, but one was a little clumsy and another a little short, so we gave the valuable gold statue to the middle one, whose name was Murray, and who came from Lancashire. The vast audience was very patient during our long judgement, and showed that it was in general agreement. After the meeting Sandow had invited the prize-winners, the judges and a chosen company to a late supper, which was very sumptuous, with champagne flowing freely. When we had finished it was early in the morning. As I left the place of banquet I saw in front of me the winning athlete going forth into the London night with the big golden statue under his arm. I had seen that he was a very simple countryman, unused to London ways, so I overtook him and asked him what his plans were. He confided to me that he had no money, but he had a return ticket to Bolton or Blackburn, and his idea was to walk the streets until a train started for the North. It seemed to me a monstrous thing to allow him to wander about with his treasure at the mercy of any murderous gang, so I suggested that he should come back with me to Morley's Hotel, where I was residing. We could not get a cab, and it seemed to me more grotesque than anything of Stevenson's London imaginings that I should be wandering round at three in the morning in the company of a stranger who bore a great golden statue of a nude figure in his arms. When at last we reached the hotel I told the night porter to get him a room, saying at the same time, 'Mind you are civil to him, for he has just been declared to be the strongest man in England.' This went round the hotel, and I found that in the morning he held quite a reception, all the maids and waiters paying homage while he lay in bed with his statue beside him. He asked my advice as to selling it, for it was of considerable value and seemed a white elephant to a poor man. I told him he should open a gymnasium in his native town and have the statue exhibited as an advertisement. This he did, and I believe he has been very successful.

A post-African task was the building up of rifle clubs, for I was enormously impressed by the power of the rifle as shown in the recent war. A soldier was no longer a specialised creature, but every brave man who could hold a rifle-barrel straight was a dangerous man. I founded the Undershaw Club, which was the father of many others, and which was inspected by Lord Roberts, Mr Seeley and other great men. Within a year or two England was dotted with village clubs, though I fear that few of them still hold their own.

I was so struck by the factors in modern warfare and I had thought so much about them in Africa that I wrote about them with some freedom and possibly even with some bitterness, so that I speedily found myself involved in hot controversy with Colonel Lonsdale Hale, *The Times* expert, and also with Colonel Maude, a well-known military writer. Perhaps as a civilian I should have expressed my views in a more subdued way, but my feelings had been aroused by the conviction that the lives of our men, and even the honour of our country, had been jeopardised by the conservatism of the military and that it would so happen again unless more modern views prevailed. I continued to advance my theories for the next ten years, and I have no doubt, when I judge them by the experience of the Great War, that in the main I was right. The points which I made were roughly as follows:

* That the rifle (or machine-gun, which is a modified rifle) is the supreme arbiter in war, and that therefore everything must be sacrificed to concentrate upon that.
* That the only place for swords, lances and all the frippery of the past was a museum. Bayonets also are very questionable.
* That cavalry could not divide their allegiance between rifle and sword since entirely different ground and tactics are needed for each, the swordsman looking for level sward, the rifleman looking for cover. Therefore all cavalry should at once become mounted rifles.
* That the very heaviest guns of our fortresses or battleships would be transported by road and used in the field in our next campaign.
* That field guns must take cover exactly as riflemen do.
* That the Yeomanry, a very expensive force, should be turned into a cyclist organisation.

In view of the fine work done by the Yeomanry, especially in the Eastern deserts, I should reconsider the last item, and the bayonet question is debatable, but all the rest will stand. I stressed the fact also that the period of military training is placed too high, and that an excellent army could be rapidly vamped up if you had the right men. This also was proved by the war.

I remember a debate which I attended as to the proper arms and use of cavalry. The cavalry were there in force, all manner of gallant fellows, moustached and debonair, inclined to glare at those who would disarm them. Sir Taubman-Goldie was in the chair. Three of us, all civilians, upheld the unpopular view that they should lose all their glory and become sombre but deadly riflemen. It is curious now to record that the three men were Erskine Childers, Lionel Amery and myself. Childers was shot at dawn as a traitor to Ireland as well as to Britain, Amery became First Lord of the Admiralty, and I write this memoir. I remember Amery's amusing comparison when he twitted the cavalry with wishing to retain the *arme blanche* simply because their Continental antagonists would have it. 'If you fight a rhinoceros,' he said, 'you don't want to tie a horn on your nose.' It is an interesting commentary upon this discussion that on one morning during the war there were duels between two separate squadrons of British and German cavalry. The first two squadrons, who were Lancers, rode through each other's ranks twice with loss on either side and no conclusive result. In the second case German Lancers charged British Hussars, who dismounted, used their carbines, and simply annihilated the small force which attacked them.

When my immediate preoccupations after the war had been got rid of, I settled down to attempt some literary work upon a larger and more ambitious scale than the Sherlock Holmes or Brigadier Gerard stories which had occupied so much of my time. The result was *Sir Nigel*, in which I reverted to the spacious days of *The White Company*, and used some of the same characters. *Sir Nigel* represents in my opinion my high-water mark in literature, and though that mark may be on sand, still an author knows its comparative position to the others. It received no particular recognition from critics or public, which was, I admit, a disappointment to me. In England versatility is looked upon with distrust. You may write ballad tunes or you may write grand opera, but it cannot be admitted that the same man may be master of the whole musical range and do either with equal success.

In 1906 my wife passed away after the long illness which she had borne with such exemplary patience. Her end was painless and serene. The long fight had ended at last in defeat, but at least we had held the vital fort for thirteen years after every expert had said that it was untenable. For some time after these days of darkness I was unable to settle to work, until the Edalji case came suddenly to turn my energies into an entirely unexpected channel.

It was in the year 1907 that this notorious case took up much of my time, but it was not wasted as it ended, after much labour, in partially rectifying a very serious miscarriage of justice. The facts of the case are a little complex and became more so as the matter proceeded. George

Edalji was a young law student, son of the Reverend S. Edalji, the Parsee vicar of the parish of Great Wyrley, who had married an English lady. How the vicar came to be a Parsee, or how a Parsee came to be the vicar, I have no idea. Perhaps some catholic-minded patron wished to demonstrate the universality of the Anglican Church. The experiment will not, I hope, be repeated, for though the vicar was an amiable and devoted man, the appearance of a coloured clergyman with a half-caste son in a rude, unrefined parish was bound to cause some regrettable situation.

But no one could have foreseen how serious that situation would become. The family became the butt of certain malicious wags in the neighbourhood and were bombarded with anonymous letters, some of them of the most monstrous description. There was worse, however, to come. A horrible epidemic of horse-maiming had broken out, proceeding evidently from some blood-lusting lunatic of Sadic propensities. These outrages continued for a long time, and the local police were naturally much criticised for doing nothing. It would have been as well had they continued to do nothing, for they ended by arresting George Edalji for the crime, the main evidence being that there were signs that the writer of the anonymous letters knew something about the crimes, and that it was thought that young Edalji had written the anonymous letters which had plagued his family so long. The evidence was incredibly weak, and yet the police, all pulling together and twisting all things to their end, managed to get a conviction at the Stafford Quarter Sessions in 1903. The prisoner was sentenced to seven years' penal servitude.

There were some murmurs among discerning people at the time, and Mr Voules, of *Truth*, has an honourable record for having kept some sort of agitation going, but nothing practical was done until the unhappy youth had already served three years of his sentence. It was late in 1906 that I chanced to pick up an obscure paper called *The Umpire*, and my eye caught an article which was a statement of his case, made by himself. As I read, the unmistakable accent of truth forced itself upon my attention and I realised that I was in the presence of an appalling tragedy, and that I was called upon to do what I could to set it right. I got other papers on the case, studied the original trial, went up to Staffordshire and saw the family, went over the scene of the crimes and finally wrote a series of articles on the case, which began in the *Daily Telegraph* of January 12, 1907. As I bargained that they should be non-copyright they were largely transferred to other papers, sold for a penny at street-curbs and generally had a very wide circulation, so that England soon rang with the wrongs of George Edalji.

These wrongs would have been almost comic had they not had so tragic an upshot. If the whole land had been raked, I do not think that it would have been possible to find a man who was so unlikely, and indeed so incapable, of committing such actions. He was of irreproachable character. Nothing in his life had ever been urged against him. His old schoolmaster with years of experience testified to his mild and tractable disposition. He had served his time with a Birmingham solicitor, who gave him the highest references. He had never shown traits of cruelty. He was so devoted to his work that he had won the highest honours in the legal classes, and he had already at the age of twenty-seven written a book upon Railway Law. Finally he was a total abstainer, and so blind that he was unable to recognise anyone at the distance of six yards. It was clear that the inherent improbability of such a man committing a long succession of bloody and brutal crimes was so great that it could only be met by the suggestion of insanity. There had never, however, been any indication even of eccentricity in George Edalji. On the contrary, his statements of defence were measured and rational, and he had come through a series of experiences which might well have unhinged a weaker intellect.

The original theory at the trial had been that Edalji had committed the particular mutilations with which he was charged some time in the evening. This line of attack broke down completely, and he was able to advance a certain alibi. In the middle of the case, therefore, the police prosecution shifted its ground and advanced the new theory that it was done in the early hours of the morning. George Edalji, as it happened, slept in the same room as his father, the parish vicar. The latter is a light sleeper and is accustomed, as many people are, to assure privacy by turning the key of his room. He swore that George never left the room during the night. This may not constitute an absolute alibi in the eye of the law, but it is difficult to imagine anything nearer to one unless a sentinel had been placed outside the door all night. It is so near an alibi that nothing but the most cogent considerations could shake it, but far from there being any such considerations, the case was such a thing of threads and patches that one cannot imagine how any sane jury could have accepted it, even though the defence was weakly conducted. So bad was this defence that in the whole trial no mention, so far as I could ascertain, was ever made of the fact that the man was practically blind, save in good light, while between his house and the place where the mutilation was committed lay the full breadth of the London and North-Western Railway, an expanse of rails, wires and other obstacles, with hedges to be forced on either side, so that I, a strong and active man, in broad daylight found it a hard matter to pass.

What aroused my indignation and gave me the driving force to carry the thing through was the utter helplessness of this forlorn little group of people, the coloured clergyman in his strange position, the brave blue-eyed, grey-haired wife, the young daughter, baited by brutal boors and having the police, who should have been their natural protectors, adopting from the beginning a harsh tone towards them and accusing them, beyond all sense and reason, of being the cause of their own troubles and of persecuting and maligning themselves. Such an exhibition, sustained, I am sorry to say, by Lord Gladstone and all the forces of the Home Office, would have been incredible had I not actually examined the facts.

The articles caused a storm of indignation through the country. *Truth*, Sir George Lewis and other forces joined in the good work. A committee was formed by the government to examine and report. It consisted of Sir Arthur Wilson, the Honourable John Lloyd Wharton and Sir Albert de Rutzen. Their finding, which came to hand in June, was a compromise document, for though they were severe upon the condemnation of Edalji and saw no evidence which associated him with the crime, they still clung to the theory that he had written the anonymous letters, that he had therefore been himself contributory to the miscarriage of justice, and that for this reason all compensation for his long period of suffering should be denied him.

It was a wretched decision, and the Law Society at the prompting of Sir George Lewis showed what they thought of it by at once readmitting Edalji to the roll of solicitors with leave to practise, which they would never have done had they thought him capable of dishonourable con-duct. But the result stands. To this day this unfortunate man, whose humble family has paid many hundreds of pounds in expenses, has never been able to get one shilling of compensation for the wrong done. It is a blot upon the record of English justice, and even now it should be wiped out. It is to be remembered that the man was never tried for writing the letters – a charge which could not have been sustained – so that as the matter stands he has got no redress for three years of admitted false imprisonment, on the score that he did something else for which he has never been tried. What a travesty of justice! The *Daily Telegraph* got up a subscription for him which ran to some three hundred pounds. The first use that he made of the money was to repay an old aunt who had advanced the funds for his defence. He came to my wedding reception, and there was no guest whom I was prouder to see.

So far, my work had been satisfactory. Where I caused myself great trouble was that in my local exploration at Wyrley I had come across what seemed to me a very direct clue as to both the writer, or rather writers, of the letters, and also of the identity of the mutilator – though the latter word may also have been in the plural. I became interested, the more so as the facts were very complex and I had to do with people who were insane as well as criminal. I have several letters threatening my life in the same writing as those which assailed the Edaljis – a fact which did not appear to shake in the least the Home Office conviction that George Edalji had written them all. Mentally I began to class the Home Office officials as insane also. The sad fact is that officialdom in England stands solid together, and that when you are forced to attack it you need not expect justice, but rather that you are up against an unavowed trade union the members of which are not going to act the blackleg to each other, and which subordinates the public interest to a false idea of loyalty. What confronts you is a determination to admit nothing which inculpates another official, and as to the idea of punishing another official for offences which have caused misery to helpless victims, it never comes within their horizon. Even now, after the lapse of so many years, I can hardly think with patience of the handling of this case.

The mistake that I made, so far as my own interests were concerned, was that having got on the track of the miscreant I let the police and the Home Office know my results before they were absolutely completed. There was a strong *prima facie* case, but it needed the goodwill and co-operation of the authorities to ram it home. That cooperation was wanting, which was intelligible in the case of the local police, since it traversed their previous convictions and conclusions, but was inexcusable in the Home Office. The law officers of the crown upheld their view that there was not a *prima facie* case, but I fear that consciously or unconsciously the same trade-union principle was at work. Let me briefly state the case that the public may judge. I will call the suspect 'X'. I was able to show:

1 That X had shown a peculiar knife or horse-lancet to someone and had stated that this knife did the crimes. I had this knife in my possession.

2 That this knife or a similar knife must have been used in some of the crimes, as shown by the shallow incision.

3 That X had been trained in the slaughter-yard and the cattle-ship, and was accustomed to brutal treatment of animals.

4 That he had a clear record both of anonymous letters and of destructive propensities.

5 That his writing and that of his brother exactly fitted into the two writings of the anonymous letters. In this I had strong independent evidence.

6 That he had shown signs of periodical insanity, and that his household and bedroom were such that he could leave unseen at any hour of the night.

There were very many corroborative evidences, but those were the main ones, coupled with the fact that when X was away for some years the letters and outrages stopped, but began again when he returned. On the other hand, when Edalji was put in prison the outrages went on the same as before.

It will hardly be believed that after I had laid these facts before the Home Office they managed to present the House of Commons with the official legal opinion that there was not a *prima facie* case, while a high official of the government said to me: 'I see no more evidence against these two brothers than against myself and my brother.' The points I mention are taken from the paper I laid before the law officers of the crown, which lies before me as I write, so the facts are exactly as stated.

I had one letter in sorrow and also in anger from the Staffordshire police complaining that I should be libelling this poor young man whose identity could easily be established.

I do not know what has become of X or how often he has been convicted since, but on the last occasion of which I have notes the magistrate said in condemning him to six months' imprisonment with hard labour: 'His character was extremely bad, he having been convicted of arson, of stealing on three occasions and of damage. On his own confession he had committed a deliberate and cruel theft from his aged mother and it was impossible to overlook the seriousness of the case.' So much for the inoffensive youth whom I had libelled! But what about Edalji's three years of gaol?

On September 18, 1907, I married Miss Jean Leckie, the younger daughter of a Blackheath family whom I had known for years, and who was a dear friend of my mother and sister. There are some things which one feels too intimately to be able to express, and I can only say that the years have passed without one shadow coming to mar even for a moment the sunshine of my Indian summer which now deepens to a golden autumn. She and my three younger children with the kindly sympathy of my two elder ones have made my home an ideally happy one.

My wife's people had a house at Crowborough, and there they had gone to reside. As they were very attached I thought it would be a happy arrangement not to separate them, so I bought a house close by, named 'Windlesham'. As I paid for it by a sum of money which I recovered after I had been unjustly defrauded of it, my friends suggested 'Swindlesham' as a more appropriate name. Thus it came about that in 1907 I left Undershaw, Hindhead, after ten years' residence, and moved myself and my belongings to the highlands of Sussex, where I still dwell in the few months of settled life which give me a rest between my wanderings.

Very soon after my marriage, having just got clear of the Edalji case, I became entangled in that of Oscar Slater. The one was in a way the cause of the other, for since I was generally given credit for having got Edalji out of his troubles, it was hoped by those who believed that Slater's condemnation was a miscarriage of justice that I might be able to do the same for him. I went into the matter most reluctantly, but when I glanced at the facts, I saw that it was an even worse case than the Edalji one, and that this unhappy man had in all probability no more to do with the murder for which he had been condemned than I had. I am convinced that when on being convicted he cried out to the judge that he never knew that such a woman as the murdered woman existed he was speaking the literal truth.

In one respect the Oscar Slater case was not so serious as the Edalji one, because Slater was not a very desirable member of society. He had never, so far as is known, been in trouble as a criminal, but he was a gambler and adventurer of uncertain morals and dubious ways – a German Jew by extraction, living under an alias. Edalji, on the other hand, was a blameless youth. But in another aspect Slater's case was worse than that of Edalji, since the charge was murder. He was very nearly hanged, and finally the life sentence was actually carried out, so that the wrong was never righted and at the present moment the unfortunate man is in gaol. It is a dreadful blot upon the administration of justice in Scotland, and such judicial crimes are not, I am convinced, done with impunity even to the most humble. Somehow – somewhere, there comes a national punishment in return.

The case was roughly this: an elderly woman, Miss Gilchrist, was done to death most brutally in her flat, while her servant-maid, Helen Lambie, was absent for ten minutes on an errand. Her head was beaten to pieces by some hard instrument. The neighbours were alarmed by the noise, and one of them, together with the maid, actually saw the murderer, a young man, leave the flat and passed him at the door. The police description at the time was by no means in agreement with Slater's appearance. Robbery did not appear to be the motive of the crime, for nothing was missing unless it was a single diamond brooch. On the other hand, a box of papers had been broken into and left in disorder. The date was December 21, 1908.

And now comes the great fact which is admitted by all, and which makes the whole case wildly improbable if not utterly impossible. It was thought that a diamond brooch had been taken. It was found out that a diamond brooch had also been pawned by the Bohemian Slater, who had started for America. Was it not clear that he was the murderer? New York was warned. Slater was arrested and in due time was returned to Glasgow. Then came the fiasco. It was found beyond all doubt that the brooch in question had been in Slater's possession for years, and that it had nothing to do with Miss Gilchrist at all.

This should have been the end of the case. It was too preposterous to suppose that out of all the folk in Glasgow the police had arrested the right man by pure chance – for that was what it amounted to. But the public had lost its head, and so had the police. If the case had completely gone to pieces surely it could be reconstructed in some fresh form. Slater was poor and friendless. He had lived with a woman, which shocked Scotch morality. As one writer boldly said in the press: 'Even if he did not do it, he deserved to be condemned, anyhow.' A case was made up in the most absurd manner. A half-crown card of tools was found in his box with the sort of tools which are found on such cards. The frail hammer was evidently the instrument which had beaten in the woman's skull. The handle might have been cleaned. Then surely there had been blood on it. The police description was already amended so as to be nearer to Slater. He, a sallow, dark-haired Jew, was picked out by witnesses from among a group of fair Scotsmen. Someone had been seen waiting in the street for some nights before. This someone was variously described by many witnesses. Some descriptions would fit Slater, some were his very opposite. The people who saw the murderer leave thought it might be Slater, but were not sure. The chief witness, Adams, was very short-sighted and had not his glasses. A clear alibi was proved by Slater, but as his mistress and his servant girl were the witnesses, it was not allowed. Whom could he produce save the inmates of his house? No attempt was ever made to show that Slater had any connection with Miss Gilchrist, or with the maid, Lambie, and as Slater was really a stranger in Glasgow, it was impossible to see how he could have known anything about this retired old maid. But he was not too well defended, while Mr Ure, the Advocate-General of Scotland, prosecuting for the state, thundered away in a most violent speech in which several statements were made, uncorrected by Judge Guthrie, which were very inexact, and which must have powerfully swayed the jury. Finally, the crown got a conviction by nine votes to six (five 'not proven') – which, of course, would have meant a new trial in England, and the wretched foreigner was condemned to death. The scaffold was actually erected, and it was only two mornings before his execution that the order came which prevented a judicial murder. As it was, the man became a convict – and is one still.

It is an atrocious story, and as I read it and realised the wickedness of it all, I was moved to do all I could for the man. I was aided by the opinion of Sir Herbert Stephen, who read the evidence and declared that there was not even a *prima facie* case against the man. I, therefore, started a newspaper agitation and wrote a small book with an account of the whole matter. The consciences of some people responded, and finally we got up sufficient pressure to induce the government to appoint a commissioner, Sheriff Miller, to examine the case. It was all to no purpose, and the examination was a farce. The terms of reference were so narrow that the conduct of the police was entirely excluded, which was really the very thing at issue, since we held that where their original evidence failed them, they had strained many points in trying to build up a case and to obtain a verdict. It was also decided that evidence should not be on oath. The result was that there was no result, nor could there be with such limitations. None the less, some fresh evidence was put forward which further weakened the already very weak case for the prosecution. For example, at the trial it had been stated that Slater, on reaching Liverpool from Glasgow, had gone to a Liverpool hotel under a false name, as if he were trying to throw the police off his track. It was shown that this was not true, and that he had signed the register with his own Glasgow name. I say his Glasgow name, for he had several pseudonyms in the course of his not too reputable career, and, as a fact, he took his actual passage under a false name, showing that he intended to make a clear start in America. He was, according to his own account, pursued by some woman – probably his lawful wife – and this covering of tracks was to escape this huntress. The fact that he used his own name at the hotel showed that the new name was for American rather than for British use, and that he had no fear of Glasgow pursuit.

We could do no more, and there the matter rested. There was a very ugly aftermath of the case, which consisted of what appeared to be persecution of Mr Trench, a detective who had given evidence at the inquiry which told in favour of our view. A charge was shortly after-wards made against both him and a solicitor, Mr Cook, who had been conspicuous upon Slater's side, which might well have ruined them both. As it was, it caused them great anxiety and expense. There had been a most unpleasant political flavour to the whole proceedings; but on this occasion the case came before a Conservative Judge, Mr Scott Dickson, who declared that it should never have been brought into court, and dismissed it forthwith with contempt. It is a curious circum-stance that as I write, in 1924, Judge Guthrie, Cook, Trench, Helen Lambie, Miller and others have all passed on. But Slater still remains, eating out his heart at Peterhead.

One strange psychic fact should be mentioned which was brought to my notice by an eminent English KC. There was a Spiritualist circle which used to meet at Falkirk, and shortly after the trial messages were received by it which purported to come from the murdered woman. She was asked what the weapon was which had slain her. She answered that it was an iron box-opener. Now I had pondered over the nature of certain wounds in the woman's face, which consisted of two cuts with a little bridge of unbroken skin between. They might have been caused by the claw end of a hammer, but on the other hand, one of the woman's eyes had been pushed back into her brain, which could hardly have been done by a hammer, which would have burst the eyeball first. I could think of no instrument which would meet the case. But the box-opener would exactly do so, for it has a forked end which would make the double wound, and it is also straight so that it might very well penetrate to the brain, driving the eye in front of it. The reader will reasonably ask why did not the Spiritualists ask the name of the criminal. I believe that they did and received a reply, but I do not think that such evidence could or should ever be used or published. It could only be useful as the starting point of an inquiry.

There was one intervention during those years to which I look back with satisfaction, and that was my protest against the King's Oath before the Coronation of King Edward VII. The Oath was actually changed, and though my protest may have had no effect upon that historic fact, it was none the less the first letter in *The Times* upon the subject.

It ran thus:

Sir – Surely Colonel Sandys and the members of the Protestant Reformation Society should, looking at the matter simply from their own point of view, recognise that the surest way to strengthen any creed is, as the whole history of the world has proved, to persecute it. And it is mere juggling with words to attempt to show that it is anything other than persecution to hold up the Roman Catholic faith to obloquy in the Coronation Oath, while every other creed, Christian or non-Christian, is left unassailed. Is it not a shocking thing that, while Roman Catholic chapels throughout the whole Empire are still draped in black for a deceased monarch, his successor should be compelled by law to insult the most intimate convictions of these same mourners?

And is it not a most narrow and foolish policy, unworthy of this tolerant age, that a young king should be forced to offend the feelings of great numbers of Irishmen, Canadians and other subjects? I feel sure that, apart from Catholics, the great majority of broadminded thinkers of any or of no denomination in this country are of opinion that the outcry of fanatics should be disregarded, and that all creeds should receive the same courteous and respectful treatment so long as their adherents are members of the common Empire. To bring these mediaeval rancours to an end would indeed be an auspicious opening of a new reign.

Yours faithfully,
Arthur Conan Doyle

22

The Years between the Wars

Years of peaceful work followed my marriage, broken only by two
journeys to the Mediterranean, in the course of which we explored
some out-of-the-way portions of Greece, and visited Egypt, where I
found hardly one single man left of all the good fellows whom I had
once known. In the course of our travels we visited Constantinople,
looking at the great guns in the forts on the Dardanelles, with little
thought of all the British lives which were to be sacrificed upon those
low, dark, heather-clad hills which slope down to the northern shore. In
Constantinople we attended the weekly *selamlik* of Abdul Hamid, and
saw him with his dyed beard and the ladies of his harem as they passed
down to their devotions. It was an incredible sight to Western eyes to
see the crowd of officers and officials, many of them fat and short of
wind, who ran like dogs behind his carriage in the hope that they might
catch the imperial eye. It was Ramadan, and the old Sultan sent me a
message that he had read my books and that he would gladly have seen
me had it not been the holy month. He interviewed me through his
chamberlain and presented me with the Order of the Medjedie, and,
what was more pleasing to me, he gave the Order of the Chevekat to
my wife. As this is the Order of Compassion, and as my wife ever since
she set foot in Constantinople had been endeavouring to feed the horde
of starving dogs who roamed the streets, no gift could have been more
appropriate.

We were admitted secretly and by very special favour into the great
Mosque of Sophia during the sacred festival which is known as the
Night of Power. It was a most marvellous spectacle as from the upper
circle of pillared arches we looked down upon sixty thousand lighted
lamps and twelve thousand worshippers, who made, as they rose and
fell in their devotions, a sound like the wash of the sea. The priests in

their high pulpits were screaming like seagulls, and fanaticism was in the air. It was at this moment that I saw a woman – I will not call her a lady – young and flighty, seat herself jauntily on the edge of the stone parapet, and look down at the twelve thousand men who were facing us. No unbeliever should be tolerated there, and a woman was the abomination of abominations. I heard a low deep growl and saw fierce bearded faces looking up. It only needed one fiery spirit to head the rush and we should have been massacred – with the poor consolation that some of us at least had really asked for it. However, she was pulled down, and we made our way as quickly and as quietly as possible out of a side door. It was time, I think.

One curious incident of our journey stands out in my memory. We were steaming past Aegina on a lovely day with calm water around us. The captain, a courteous Italian, had allowed us to go upon the bridge, and we – my wife and I – were looking down into the transparent depths when we both clearly saw a creature which has never, so far as I know, been described by science. It was exactly like a young ichthyo-saurus, about four feet long, with thin neck and tail, and four marked side-flippers. The ship had passed it before we could call any other observer. I was interested to notice that Admiral Anstruther in the *Evening News* some years later described, and drew, an exactly similar creature which he had seen underwater off the Irish coast. This old world has got some surprises for us yet.

Here and there, as I look back at those long and happy years, some particular episode flashes vividly into my memory. I do not often do journalistic work – why should one poach upon the preserves of others? – but on the occasion of the Olympic Games of 1908 I was tempted, chiefly by the offer of an excellent seat, to do the Marathon Race for the *Daily Mail*. It was certainly a wonderful experience, for it will be known to history as the Dorando Race. Perhaps a few short paragraphs from my description may even now recapture the thrill of it. The huge crowd – some fifty thousand people – were all watching the entrance to the stadium, the dark gap through which the leader must appear. Then –

At last he came. But how different from the exultant victor whom we expected! Out of the dark archway there staggered a little man, with red running-drawers, a tiny boylike creature. He reeled as he entered and faced the roar of the applause. Then he feebly turned to the left and wearily trotted round the track. Friends and encouragers were pressing round him.

Suddenly the whole group stopped. There were wild gesticulations. Men stooped and rose again. Good heavens! he has fainted; is it possible that even at this last moment the prize may slip through his fingers? Every eye slides round to that dark archway. No second man has yet appeared. Then a great sigh of relief goes up. I do not think in all that great assembly any man would have wished victory to be torn at the last instant from this plucky little Italian. He has won it. He should have it.

Thank God, he is on his feet again – the little red legs going incoherently, but drumming hard, driven by a supreme will within. There is a groan as he falls once more and a cheer as he staggers to his feet. It is horrible, and yet fascinating, this struggle between a set purpose and an utterly exhausted frame. Again, for a hundred yards, he ran in the same furious and yet uncertain gait. Then again he collapsed, kind hands saving him from a heavy fall.

He was within a few yards of my seat. Amid stooping figures and grasping hands I caught a glimpse of the haggard, yellow face, the glazed, expressionless eyes, the lank black hair streaked across the brow. Surely he is done now. He cannot rise again.

From under the archway has darted the second runner, Hayes, Stars and Stripes on his breast, going gallantly, well within his strength. There is only twenty yards to do if the Italian can do it. He staggered up, no trace of intelligence upon his set face, and again the red legs broke into their strange automatic amble.

Will he fall again? No, he sways, he balances, and then he is through the tape and into a score of friendly arms. He has gone to the extreme of human endurance. No Roman of the prime ever bore himself better than Dorando of the Olympic of 1908. The great breed is not yet extinct.

Of course the prize went to the American, as his rival had been helped, but the sympathy of the crowd, and I am sure of every sporting American present, went out to the little Italian. I not only wrote Dorando up, but I started a subscription for him in the *Daily Mail*, which realised over £300 – a fortune in his Italian village – so that he was able to start a baker's shop, which he could not have done on an Olympic medal. My wife made the presentation in English, which he could not understand; he answered in Italian, which we could not understand; but I think we really did understand each other all the same.

There is no denying that the American team were very unpopular in London, though the unpopularity was not national, for the stadium was thick with American flags. Everyone admitted that they were a splendid lot of athletes, but they were not wisely handled and I saw with my own eyes that they did things which would not have been tolerated if done by an English team in New York. However, there may well have been some want of tact on both sides, and causes at work of which the public knew nothing. When I consider the Dunraven Yacht race, and then these Olympic Games, I am by no means assured that sport has that international effect for good which some people have claimed for it. I wonder whether any of the old Grecian wars had their real origin in the awards at Olympia. I may add that we had a dozen or so of the American boys down to 'Windlesham', where we had a very pleasant day together. I found them all excellent fellows. I put up a billiard Olympic prize, and one of them bore it off with him. The whole incident was very pleasant.

My work for a few years after my marriage ran largely in the direction of drama, and if it was not lucrative it at least provided us with a good deal of amusement and excitement. In the case of one venture this excitement became a little too poignant, though all ended well in the end. I had dramatised *Rodney Stone* under the name of *The House of Temperley*, with all the ring scenes and prize fights included and treated in the most realistic fashion. We had an excellent boxing instructor who took one of the smaller parts and who not only fought himself but trained the others to a remarkable degree of skill. So realistic was it that when on the first night the bully, Berks, after a long encounter, went down with a crash from a fine raking uppercut, there was an involuntary groan from the whole house, which meant as clearly as could be, 'There now, you have killed a man for our amusement.' It was really incredibly well done and I could never have believed that such scenes could be so cleverly faked, though it was not always done with impunity, for Rex Davies, who played Gloucester Dick, assured me that he lost a tooth and broke both a finger and a rib during his engagement. The play itself was unequal, but was so very novel and sensational in its best scenes that it should have been a considerable success. I found no manager who would take the risk, and I had myself to take the Adelphi Theatre for a six months' lease, at a rent which with the company worked out at about six hundred pounds a week. As on the top of this the production cost about two thousand pounds, it will be seen that I was plunging rather deep.

And luck did not favour us. The furore for boxing had not yet set in. Ladies were afraid to come, and imagined it would be a brutal spectacle. Those who did come were exhilarated beyond measure, but the prejudice still weighed heavily against us. Then there came one of those theatrical slumps when everything goes wrong, and finally King Edward died and that killed it outright. It was a very serious situation. I still had the theatre upon my hands. I might sublet it, or I might not. If I did not, the expense was simply ruinous.

It was under these circumstances that, as I have already said, I wrote and rehearsed *The Speckled Band* in record time, and so saved the situation. The real fault of this play was that in trying to give Holmes a worthy antagonist I overdid it and produced a more interesting personality in the villain. The terrible ending was also against it. However, it was a considerable success and saved a difficult – almost a desperate – situation.

Yet another theatrical venture was my *Fires of Fate*, some of which is certainly the best dramatic work that I have ever done. It was unlucky, as it was produced in a very hot summer. I carried it at my own expense through the two impossible holiday months, but when Lewis Waller, who played the hero, returned from a provincial tour to London, he was keen on some new play and my *Fires* were never really burned out. I fancy sometimes that they might even now flame up again if given a chance. I stage managed most of this play myself, and with curious results. There are certain dramatic conventionalities which can only be broken through by one who is not himself an actor. There was a scene where a number of helpless tourists, men and women, were brutally ill-treated by Arabs. The brutality in rehearsal was conventional. I made the Arabs get imitation whips and cudgels and really savage the poor travellers. The effect was novel and appalling. There was a young Welsh officer in the front of the stalls who was a friend of my brother's. He held both the VC and the DSO. So stirred was he by the sight that he could hardly be restrained from clambering on to the stage in order to help the unhappy tourists. The end of that act, when the drove of bleeding captives is led away and you hear the monotonous song of the Arabs as they march, and you see Lewis Waller, who has been left for dead, struggle up on his elbow and signal across the Nile for assistance, was one which brought the whole house to its feet. Such moments to a dramatist give a thrill of personal satisfaction such as the most successful novelist never can feel. There is no more subtle pleasure if you are really satisfied with your work than to sit in the shadow of a box and watch not the play but the audience.

I had one other dramatic venture, *Brigadier Gerard*, which also was mildly successful. In fact, I have never known failure on the stage save in the case of the unfortunate 'Jane Annie'. Lewis Waller played the Brigadier and a splendid dashing Hussar he made. It was a glorious performance. I remember that in this play also I ran up against the conventionalities of the stage. I had a group of Hussar officers, the remnants of the regiment which had gone through Napoleon's last campaign. When it came to the dress rehearsal, I found them, to my horror, dressed up in brand new uniforms of chestnut and silver. 'Good heavens!' I cried. 'This is not a comic opera!' 'What do you want done?' asked Waller. 'Why,' said I, 'these men are warriors, not ballet dancers. They have been out in all weathers day and night for months. Every scrap of truth goes out of the play if they appear like that.' The uniforms had cost over a hundred pounds, but I covered them with mud and dust and tore holes in them. The result was that, with begrimed faces, I got a band of real Napoleonic soldiers. Waller himself insisted on retaining his grease paint and his nice new clothes, but I am sure every man in the audience, if not every woman, would have liked him better as I had made the others. Poor Willie Waller! There was some strange and wonderful blood in his veins. He was a glorious fellow, and his premature death a great blow to our stage. What virility! What a face and figure! They called him the 'Flappers' idol', and it reflects credit on the flapper, for where could she find a less sickly and more manly type? He caught his fatal illness in serving the soldiers. One of his greatest possessions was his voice. He came down to 'Windlesham' once, and as he was reciting in the music-room that wonderful resonant voice chanced to catch the exact note which corresponded to the curve of all the glass lampshades on the walls. They all started thrilling as a wineglass does when it is touched. I could quite believe after that that matter could be disintegrated by sound if the sound were strong enough. I am not clear what blood ran in Waller's veins, Hebrew or Basque or both. I only know that it went to make a very wonderful man. His intense feeling about everything that he did was one of his characteristics and no doubt, a cause of his success. It did not carry him far in golf, however. I remember hearing him as he approached the last tee mutter, 'God, give me one good drive.' I fear, however, that the betting was against it.

In 1910 a fresh task opened up before me. It arose from my being deeply moved by reading some of the evidence concerning the evil rule in the Congo of the former King of the Belgians, Leopard II. I examined this evidence carefully before I accepted it, and I assured myself that it was supported by five British consuls and by Lord Cromer, as well as by travellers of many races, Belgian, French, American, Swedish and others. An attempt has been made since to minimise the facts and to pretend that Roger Casement had been at the back of the agitation for sinister purposes of his own. This contention is quite untenable and the evidence for the atrocities is overwhelming and from very many sources, the Belgians themselves being among the best witnesses. I put in some two years working with Mr Morel and occasionally lecturing in the country upon this question, and it was certainly the efforts of the Congo Association, which we represented, that eventually brought the question to the notice of that noble man King Albert which meant setting it right so that the colony is now, so far as I know, very well managed. Casement, whom I shall always regard as a fine man afflicted with mania, has met his tragic end, and Morel's views upon the war have destroyed the feelings which I had for him, but I shall always maintain that they both did noble work in championing the wrongs of those unhappy and helpless negroes. My own book *The Crime of the Congo*, which was translated into all European languages, had also, I hope, some influence towards that end.

In the early summer of 1912 I had a telegram from Lord Northcliffe which let me in for about as much trouble as any communication which I have ever received. It was to the effect that Britain must regain her place among the athletic nations which had been temporarily eclipsed by the Olympic Games at Stockholm, and that I was the one man in Great Britain who could rally round me the various discordant forces which had to be united and used. This was very complimentary, but it was Lord Northcliffe's sole contribution to the matter for a very long time, and I was left to my own devices entirely in carrying out a complex task. So badly co-ordinated were Northcliffe's papers that I had some of them actually attacking me while I was working on their chief's suggestion.

When I examined I found chaos. On the one hand was the British

Olympic Committee, a most sound and respectable body, under Lord Desborough. In some way they had lost touch with press and public and were generally in disfavour, though really they had done their best. On the other hand was *The Times*, which had worked itself into a fury about the misdeeds of the Committee, and had set a tone which poisoned the whole press against them. Lord Northcliffe would have nothing to do with anything which emanated from the Committee; the Committee defied Lord Northcliffe. It was clear that this had to be cleared up as a preliminary, and the matter took enough diplomacy to have settled the Balkan question. I called upon the Committee and suggested that an independent body be formed on which they could be represented. To this they agreed. I then called on *The Times* and said: 'You are no longer dealing with the old Olympic Committee, but with a new body. Do you agree to this?' Yes, that was all in order. I may have omitted the trifling fact that the new body did not yet exist. I then asked Mr Studd, the famous cricketer of old and head of the Polytechnic to help me to form the new body. We soon had a very effective one, including several leading athletes and Lord Forster, now Governor-General of Australia. I served, of course, on the committee, and soon we were in touch with everyone and all promised to go smoothly.

But presently a huge mistake was made. I don't wish to represent myself as the fount of all wisdom, and no doubt I make as many slips as my fellows, but that particular one would never have been made had I been present, but I was called away and was out of the country at that crucial committee meeting. It had been already determined that an appeal to the public over all our names should be issued. The amount had not been discussed, but in my own mind I had thought that ten thousand pounds would suffice. I was horrified, therefore, when I returned from my holiday to find that they had appealed for a hundred thousand pounds. The sum was absurd, and at once brought upon us from all sides the charge of developing professionalism. My position was very difficult. If I protested now it would go far to ruin the appeal. After all it might succeed. I could only fall into line with the others and do my best for the sake of the cause to defend a policy which I looked upon as mistaken. We actually collected about seven thousand pounds, and finally, as we found that the general feeling was either hostile or apathetic, we handed over this sum to the Olympic Committee. Then came the war, and so in any case our labour was in vain, for the Games were to be in Berlin in 1916. We were all playing another game by then. This matter was spread over a year of my life and was the most barren thing that I ever touched, for nothing came of it, and I cannot trace that I ever received one word of thanks from any human being. I was on my guard against Northcliffe telegrams after that.

I remember one curious episode about that time. I was staying in a Northumberland Avenue Hotel, and I walked out at night in pensive mood, strolling down the Embankment and watching the great dark river with the gleam of the lights upon it. Suddenly a man passed me, walking very rapidly and muttering in an incoherent way. He gave me an impression of desperation and I quickened my pace and followed him. With a rush he sprang up on the parapet and seemed to be about to throw himself into the river. I was just in time to catch his knees and to pull him down. He struggled hard to get back up, but I put my arm through his and led him across the road. There I reasoned with him and examined into the cause of his troubles. He had had some domestic quarrel, I believe, but his main worry was his business, which was that of a baker. He seemed a respectable man and the case seemed genuine, so I calmed him down, gave him such immediate help as I could, and made him promise to return home and to keep in touch with me afterwards.

When the excitement of the incident was over, I had grave doubts as to whether I had not been the victim of a clever swindler. I was considerably relieved, therefore, to get a letter a few days later giving name and address and obviously genuine. I lost sight of the case after that.

Another matter which preoccupied me much in the years before the war, and preoccupies me still, is the Reform of our Divorce Laws. I was president of the Reform Union for ten years and have only just vacated the position in order to make room for a far more efficient successor in Lord Birkenhead. I am quite alive to all the arguments of our opponents, and quite understand that laxity in the marriage tie is an evil, but I cannot understand why England should lag behind every other Protestant country in the world, and even behind Scotland, so that unions which are obviously disgusting and degrading are maintained in this country while they can be dissolved in our colonies or abroad. As to morality I cannot, I fear, admit that our morality here is in the least better than in Scandinavia, Holland or Germany, where they have more rational laws. I think that in some states in America they have pushed divorce to an extreme, but even in America I should say that married happiness and morality generally are quite as high as with us. The House of Lords has shown itself to be more liberal in this matter than the Commons, possibly because the latter have a fear of organised Church influence in their constituencies. It is one of several questions which makes me not sorry to see Labour, with its larger outlook, in power for a time in this country. Our marriage laws, our land laws, the cheapening of justice and many other things have long called out for reform, and if the old parties will not do it then we must seek some new one which will.

During these long and happy years, when the smooth current of our national life was quietly sliding toward Niagara, I did not lose my interest in psychic matters, but I cannot say that I increased my grasp of the religious or spiritual side of the subject. I read, however, and investigated whenever the chance arose. A gentleman had arranged a series of physical seances in a large studio in North London, and I attended them, the mediums being Cecil Husk and Craddock. They left a very mixed impression upon my mind, for in some cases I was filled with suspicion and in others I was quite sure that the result was genuine. The possibility that a genuine medium may be unscrupulous and that when these very elusive forces fail to act he may simulate them is one which greatly complicates the whole subject, but one can only concentrate upon what one is sure is true and try to draw conclusions from that. I remember that many sheeted ghosts walked about in the dim light of a red lamp on these occasions, and that some of them came close to me, within a foot of my face, and illuminated their features by the light of a phosphorescent slate held below them. One splendid Arab, whom the medium called Abdullah, came in this fashion. He had a face like an idealised W. G. Grace, swarthy, black-bearded and dignified, rather larger than human. I was looking hard at this strange being, its nose a few inches from my own, and was wondering whether it could be some very clever bust of wax, when in an instant the mouth opened and a terrific yell was emitted. I nearly jumped out of my chair. I saw clearly the gleaming teeth and the red tongue. It certainly seemed that he had read my thought and had taken this very effective way of answering it.

Some of the excitements of my life during these and the subsequent years were due to financial entanglements which arose from a certain speculative element in my own nature, depending rather upon the love of adventure than upon any hope of gain. If when I earned money I had dug a hole in the garden and buried it there I should be a much richer man today. I can hardly blame the punter on the racecourse when I remember the outside chances which I have taken in the past in every possible form of speculation. But I have the advantage over the mere gambler in this, that every pound of my money went to develop something or other and lined the pocket of the working man, who, by the way, when he grumbles over the profits of the capitalist never even alludes to his losses. If a balance sheet were struck it would be interesting to see what, if any, is the exact margin of profit.

It is true that sometimes I have indulged in a pure gamble but never for any sum which would hurt me. I have painful memories of a guano island off South Africa on which our treasure seekers were not even allowed to land, though every bird's nest was rumoured to contain a diamond. The Spanish galleon in the bay of Tobermory also took treasure rather than gave it, and the return for my shares was a lump of glass and a rusted bar. That was more than ever I had from certain spots in Kalgurli and Coolgardie and other alleged gold-bearers, which have nearly all been gold consumers so far as I am concerned. I fear some of those mines were like that legendary one where the manager, getting a cable which ordered him to start crushing, replied, 'I have nothing to crush until you return samples.'

I have played my involuntary part also in the development of the Rand and Rhodesia, from those early and unsophisticated days when I misread the quotation and meaning to invest sixty pounds was faced next morning with a bill for nine hundred pounds. Occasionally it is true that I backed a winner, but as a rule I must confess that I was not judicious in my selections.

But it was at home that I expended myself most freely. I saw the enormous possibilities of Kent coal, which even now are not fully understood; but I did not sufficiently weigh the impossibilities, which are that an enterprise can be successful which is wildly financed and extravagantly handled. I and many others lost our money sinking the shafts which may bring fortunes to our successors. I even descended a thousand feet through the chalk to see with my own eyes that the coal was *in situ*. It seems to have had the appearance and every other quality of coal save that it was incombustible, and when a dinner was held by the shareholders which was to be cooked by local coal, it was necessary to send out and buy something which would burn. There were, however, lower strata which were more sensitive to heat. Besides Kent Coal I lost very heavily in running a manufacturing plant in Birmingham, into which I was led by those successive stages in which you are continually trying to save what you have already invested until the situation becomes so serious that you drop it in terror. We turned from bicycles to munitions during the war, and actually worked hard the whole four years, with a hundred artisans making needful war material, without ever declaring a penny of dividend. This, I should think, must be a record, and at least no one could call us profiteers. The firm was eventually killed dead by the successive strikes of the moulders and the miners. It is amazing how one set of workmen will ruin another set without apparently any remonstrance from the sufferers. Another bad egg was a sculpture machine for architectural work, which really had great possibilities, but we could not get the orders. I was chairman of this company, and it cost me two years of hard work and anxiety, ending up by my paying the balance out of my own pocket, so that we might wind up in an honourable way. It was a dismal experience, with many side adventures attached to it, which would make a sensational novel.

Such are some of the vicissitudes which cannot be disregarded in a retrospect of life, for they form a very integral and absorbing part of it. I have had my ill luck and I have had my good. Amid the latter I count the fact that I have been for twenty-one years a director of Raphael Tuck & Co., without the least cloud to darken the long and pleasant memory. I have also been for many years chairman of Besson's famous brass instrument firm. I think a man should know all sides of life, and he has missed a very essential side if he has not played his part in commerce. In investments, too, I would not imply that I have always been unfortunate. My speculative adventures are over, and I can at least say that unless the British Empire goes down I shall be able to retain enough for our modest needs.

23

Some Notable People

President Roosevelt – Lord Balfour – Mr Asquith – Lord Haldane –
George Meredith – Rudyard Kipling – James Barrie – Henry Irving –
Bernard Shaw – R. L. S. – Grant Allen – James Payn –
Henry Thompson – Royalty – Lights of the Law

When I have chanced during my life to come in contact with notable people, I have often made some short record at the time of what they said and how they impressed me. It is difficult, however, to use these notes for publication when you happen to have been a guest, and it can only be done, I think, by using one's judgement and never consciously harming one's host. If everyone were altogether silent upon such occasions the most pleasing side of great contemporaries would never be chronicled, for the statesman in slippers is a very much more human and lovable person than the politician on the platform.

Among the great men that I have known President Roosevelt occupied a prominent place. He was not a big, nor, so far as one could see, a powerful man, but he had tremendous dynamic force and an iron will which may account for his reputation as an athlete. He had all the simplicity of real greatness, speaking his mind with great frankness and in the clearest possible English. He had in him a great deal of the boy, a mischievous, adventurous, high-spirited boy, with a deep, strong, thoughtful manhood in the background. We were present, my wife and I, at the Guildhall when he made his memorable speech about Egypt, in which he informed a gathering, which contained the Foreign Secretary, Sir Edward Grey, and many of our Cabinet, that we should either rule more strictly or clear out altogether. It was, of course, a most unwarrantable intrusion into our affairs, but it was a calculated indiscretion, and very welcome, I believe, to those who were dealing with Egypt. As he made his way through the dense crowd afterwards he passed me and said with a grin: 'I say, I let them have it that time, didn't I?' There was the mischievous boy coming out.

He had a quick blunt wit which showed itself often in his metaphors.

He spoke to me, I remember, of someone who had a nine-guinea-pig-power brain. One of his entourage told me how the president had been awakened once to address some prairie folk at a wayside station. 'They have come sixty miles to see you,' said his secretary. 'They would have come a hundred to see a cat with two heads,' said the ruffled president.

I met him once at a small luncheon party at the invitation of Lord Lee, who had soldiered with him in Cuba. He was extremely talkative – in fact, I can hardly remember anyone else saying anything. Thinking it over afterwards I concluded that two ideas were running through his mind, and every now and then coming to the surface. They were formidable ideas, and may have been some temporary wave of feeling, but they were certainly in his thoughts. The one was that there would be another civil war in the States. The second, that if you had the farmer class on your side they presented the best military material. From this I gathered that it was not a geographical but an economic struggle that was in his mind. *Absit omen*, but great men are often pessimists, and the Duke of Wellington was deeply convinced that Britain could not long survive his death.

When Roosevelt was shot I sent him a cable to express that sympathy which every Englishman felt. I have his answer before me, written only a day or so after the event:

> *Mercy Hospital, Chicago*
> *October 19, 1912*

DEAR MR DOYLE – Many thanks for your kind message of sympathy. As you know, a bullet wound is rather a serious thing, but all conditions seem to be favourable, and I hope in a few days we will all be relieved from anxiety.

Sincerely yours,

THEODORE ROOSEVELT

It is typewritten, but signed by his own hand. I do not think that a more brave and detached letter was ever written by a sufferer.

Roosevelt was a very loud hearty man, with a peculiar wild-beast toothy grin, and an explosive habit of slapping his hand down for emphasis. I jotted down a few of his *obiter dicta* after our conversation. He had no good word for Henry James. 'He is not a whole man. All that subtlety is really decadence.' He was very virile, not to say heroic in his views. 'A man should guard particularly against being led from his duty, especially a dangerous duty, by his women. I guess a woman would have had a bad time if she had tried to lead Leonidas from the pass.' Of the German emperor he said that he was jealous of the king's dog at the king's funeral because he attracted the more notice. Altogether he was one of the raciest talkers I have ever met.

Among the occasional great ones of earth whom I have met there is hardly anyone who stands out more clearly than Arthur Balfour, with his willowy figure, his gentle intellectual face, and, as I read it, his soul of steel. I should think that of all men of our day he was the last who would be turned from any path which he had deliberately taken, but, on the other hand, he was capable of standing a most unconscionable time at the place where paths divide, for his mind was so subtle and active that he would always see the two sides of every question and waver between them. He could never have been a pioneer.

The occasion of our first meeting was a most ridiculous one. Old Lord Burnham, the first of his line, had invited me down to his country house at Beaconsfield – a wonderful house which had been built originally by Waller, the royalist poet. Burke had lived close by, and the dagger which, in a melodramatic moment, he threw upon the floor of the house, in order to show the dangers of French Republican propaganda, is still on exhibition. I can remember the party well, though nearly all of them are now on the farther side. I see Lady Dorothy Nevill with her mittened hands and her prim pussy-cat manner, retailing gossip about Disraeli's flirtations. Sir Henry James walks under the trees with bended head, talking to the rising barrister who is destined as Lord Reading to be Viceroy of India. Lady Cleveland, mother of Lord Rosebery, is listening with her old face wreathed in smiles to Lady Dorothy's scandal. Young Harry Irving looks unutterably bored as Lord Burnham explains golf to him, bending his head over to get a glimpse of the ball round the curve of his goodly waistcoat. Mr Asquith stands smiling beside them. As one looks back they seem all to have been shadows in a world of shadow.

Lord Burnham's hobby was Turkish baths, and he had an excellent one in the front of the house, the drying room being the first door on the right as one entered, and being a simple sitting-room as far as appearance went. With his usual kind hospitality Lord Burnham had urged me to try his bath, and having done so I was placed, arrayed in a long towel, and with another towel screwed round my head, in the drying room. Presently the door opened, and entered Arthur Balfour, Prime Minister of England. He knew nothing of the house or its ways, and I can remember the amazement with which he gazed at me. Lord Burnham following at his heels introduced me, and I raised the towel on my head. There were no explanations, and I felt that he went away with the impression that this was my usual costume.

I did not see him after that weekend – he kept his room, I remember, until midday on the Sunday – until some years later when, after heavy domestic loss, I was endeavouring to collect myself again in a little inn near Dunbar. He heard of my presence, and in his kindness sent a car over from Whittingehame, only a few miles away, with a request that I should come over for a couple of days. There was present his brother, Gerald Balfour, a man with a beautifully refined face and manner, not unlike that of Andrew Lang. His wife is the famous Lady Betty Balfour, the daughter of Lord Lytton. When one thinks of that group of inter-allied families – the Balfours, Cecils, Sedgwicks and Lyttons – it seems a sort of nerve ganglion of British life. There was also Lady Frances Balfour, who was a daughter of the Duke of Argyle, and not unlike him, as I can remember him. Her husband was Arthur Balfour's brother, an architect and antiquary, while another brother was Colonel of the London Scottish. Finally, there was Miss Alice Balfour, a very sweet and gently intellectual person, who was my actual hostess.

I found Arthur Balfour in great spirits because he had just won a golf medal at North Berwick. He seemed as pleased as any schoolboy, and his sister told me that no political success ever gave him the keen pleasure which he had from his golf victory. He was an average player, orthodox in style, and about ten or twelve in handicap. He proved to be a charming host, for he was a good listener, seeming to be really eager to hear your opinion, laughed heartily at small provocation, and talked always very frankly and modestly of himself. After my long solitude I was more loquacious, I remember, than is my way, but he bore it with good humour.

Every night – or at least on the Sunday night – the whole staff of the large rambling establishment, maids and grooms, some twenty in all, came in for prayers, which were read by the head of the house. It was fine to hear groom and statesman praying humbly together that they be forgiven the sins of the day, and merging all earthly distinctions in the presence of that which is above us all.

He was very interesting when he spoke of the outrage which the Russian fleet had committed when, on their way to Japan, they opened fire at the British trawlers on the Dogger Bank. It was curious to hear his gentle voice and to note his listless impersonal manner while he spoke in this fashion: 'I was very angry, really very angry about that affair. If our fleet had been at home I should have been inclined to have stopped them in the Straits. Of course, one would not do that unless one had overpowering force, so as to avoid bloodshed and save the Russian face. Their ambassador called that morning and gave complete assurances, or really I should have had to do something. He got himself into trouble with his own government, who felt that he had given away their case.'

I asked him how Cabinet councils were worked. He said that they voted upon points and went by majorities, unless it was a vital thing, when of course the dissenters must resign.

I observed in his character a very great horror of cowardice. Nothing seemed to arouse such scorn in him. He grew quite red, I remember, as he spoke of Lord George Sackville, and recalled that though he had been broken and should have been shot at the Battle of Minden in 1759, he was none the less Minister of War during the American campaign. He was also, as I reminded him, a most debauched man; and the murder of his mistress, Miss Reay, the actress, by her true lover, the clergyman Hackman, was one of the *causes célèbres* of that century.

I shall always carry away the memory of that visit – a bright gleam in a dark passage of life. I see very clearly the old house, the huge broken tree outside, inside which a state conspiracy was once hatched, the fine library with its wealth of French memoirs, and above all the remarkable man who stood for so much in the life of the country. I was not at that time so convinced of the primary importance of psychic things as I became later, and I regret it, as this would have been my one opportunity to explore a knowledge which at that time was certainly greater than my own. Years later, when the fight was heavy upon me, and when I was almost alone in the polemical arena, I wrote to Mr Balfour, and charged him with sharing all my convictions and yet leaving me to defend them single-handed. His answer was: 'Surely my opinions upon this subject are already sufficiently well known,' which is surely an admission that I was right in my description of them, and yet was not much of a prop to me in my time of need.

I cast my mind back to other statesmen whom I have known, and Mr Asquith's kindly personality comes into my memory. I remember playing a round of golf with him once – and a very bad player he was – but his conversation as we went round was plus four. He was a naturally sweet-natured man, but under that gentleness there lay judgement and firmness, as was shown at the great crisis of history. He never said too much, but what he did say he lived up to. In conducting us safely through those first two years of war he did that for which he has never had sufficient credit, and the more light we have had since, the more clear it has been that Lord Kitchener and he were really doing all that men could do, in munition work and all other ways. Because he had the solid Yorkshire stolidity, more nervous and excitable people thought that he did not take the war sufficiently seriously, while the constant lies about the pro-German tendencies of his wife increased the evil impression. We owe him a reparation which is second only to that which is due to Lord Haldane.

And that is indeed a heavy one. If one man could be named who was absolutely indispensable to victory it was Haldane. He it was who built up the whole splendid weapon which flashed so swiftly from its sheath, and which Germany was so amazed to find directed at its breast as it rushed forward upon its furious course. He could not work miracles; he could not introduce conscription when a candidate with such a programme would have been chased from the hustings; he could not prepare the public mind in some dramatic way which would have pre-cipitated the very crash which there was still some chance of avoiding. But all we had he gave us – the eight divisions which saved France, the Territorials who carried on the good work until the new armies were ready, and the Officers' Training Corps, which strengthened us where we should have been fatally weak. There has never been so foolish and ungrateful a clamour as that which has been raised against Haldane. I remember that when he took the chair for me in the first war lecture which I gave in London there were cries of 'Traitor!' from people, chiefly women, among the audience. I had never seen Haldane before, and have never seen him since, so I have no personal bias in the matter, but I am proud that it was in my first volume of the *History of the War*, published in 1915, that I first put forward the unpopular view which will now be more fully accepted.

With George Meredith I had several interesting connections. I have the greatest possible admiration for him at his best, while his worst is such a handicap that I think it will drag four-fifths of his work to oblivion. If his own generation finds him hard to understand, what will our descendants make of him? He will be a cult among a few – a precious few in every sense. And yet I fully recognise that his was the most active original brain and the most clever pen of any man, novelist or otherwise, of my time. Knowing this well, it is strange that I can see so limited a future for him. His subtle and intricate mind seemed unable to realise the position of the plain outsiders who represent the world. He could not see how his stained-glass might be less effective than the plain transparent substance as a medium for vision. The first requisite is to be intelligible. The second is to be interesting. The third is to be clever. Meredith enormously filled the third, but he was unequal upon the other two. Hence he will never, in spite of the glories of *Richard Feverel*, be on an equality with Dickens or Thackeray, who filled all three. He had simply no idea how his words would strike a less complex mind. I remember that once in the presence of Barrie, Quiller-Couch and myself, he read out a poem which he had inscribed 'To the British Working-Man' in the *Westminster Gazette*. I don't know what the British working-man made of it, but I am sure that we three were greatly puzzled as to what it was about.

I had written some articles on his work, which had been one of my youthful cults, and that led to his inviting me to see him at his villa at Box Hill – the first of several such visits. There had been a good deal in the papers about his health, so that I was surprised when, as I opened the garden gate, a slight but robust gentleman in a grey suit and a red tie swung out of the hall door and came singing loudly down the path. I suppose he was getting on to seventy at the time but he looked younger, and his artistic face was good to the eye. Greeting me he pointed to a long steep hill behind the house and said: 'I have just been up to the top for a walk.' I looked at the sharp slope and said: 'You must be in good trim to do it.' He looked angry and said: 'That would be a proper compliment to pay to an octogenarian.' I was a little nettled by his touchiness, so I answered: 'I understood that I was talking to an invalid.' It really seemed as if my visit would terminate at the garden gate, but presently he relented, and we soon became quite friendly.

He had in his youth been a judge of wine, and had still a reverence for a good vintage, but unfortunately some nervous complaint from which he suffered had caused the doctors to prohibit it absolutely. When lunch came round he asked me with a very earnest air whether I could undertake to drink a whole bottle of Burgundy. I answered that I saw no insuperable difficulty. A dusty old bottle was tenderly carried up, which I disposed of, Meredith taking a friendly interest in its dispatch. 'The fact is,' said he, 'I love my wine, and my little cellar was laid down with care and judgement, so that when some guest comes and drinks a glass and wastes the rest of the bottle it goes to my heart. It really did me good to see you enjoy that one.' I need not say that I intimated that I was always prepared to oblige.

His conversation was extraordinarily vivid and dramatic, uttered in a most vehement tone. It may have been artificial, and it may have been acting, but it was very arresting and entertaining. The talk got upon Napoleon's marshals, and you would have thought that he knew them intimately, and he did Murat's indignation at being told to charge *au bout*, as if he ever charged any other way, in a fashion which would have brought down the house. Every now and then he brought out a Meredithian sentence which sounded comic when applied to domestic matters. When the jelly swayed about as the maid put it on the table he said: 'The jelly, Mary, is as treacherous as the Trojan Horse.' He laughed when I told him how my groom, enlisted as a waiter for some special dinner, said, 'Huddup, there,' to the jelly under similar circumstances.

After lunch we walked up a steep path to the little chalet or summer-house where he used to write. He wished to read me a novel which he had begun twenty years before, but which he had not had the heart to go on with. I liked it greatly – and we roared with laughter at his description of an old sea-dog who turned up the collar of his coat when he went into action as if the bullets were rain. He said that my hearty enjoyment encouraged him to go on with it, and it has since appeared as *The Amazing Marriage*, but whether I really had anything to do with it I do not know. I should be proud to think so.

The nervous complaint from which he suffered caused him to fall down occasionally. As we walked up the narrow path to the chalet I heard him fall behind me, but judged from the sound that it was a mere slither and could not have hurt him. Therefore I walked on as if I had heard nothing. He was a fiercely proud old man, and my instincts told me that his humiliation in being helped up would be far greater than any relief I could give him. It was certainly a nice point to decide.

George Meredith's religious convictions were very difficult to decide. He certainly had no glimmering so far as I could see of any psychic element in life, and I should imagine that on the whole he shared the opinions of his friend, John Morley, which were completely negative. And yet I remember his assuring me that prayer was a very necessary thing, and that one should never abandon prayer. 'Who rises from prayer a better man, his prayer is granted,' says the Aphorist in *Richard Feverel*. How far these positions can be harmonised I do not know. I suppose that one may say that God is unknown, and yet rear a mental temple to the unknown God.

Rudyard Kipling I know far less than I should, considering how deeply I admire his writings and that we live in the same county; but we are both absorbed in work, and both much away from home, which may explain it. I can well remember how eagerly I bought his first book, *Plain Tales*, in the old Southsea days, when buying a book was a rare strain upon my exchequer. I read it with delight, and realised not only that a new force had arisen in literature, but that a new method of story writing had appeared which was very different from my own adherence to the careful plot artfully developed. This was go-as-you-please take-it-or-leave-it work, which glowed suddenly up into an incandescent phrase or paragraph, which was the more effective for its sudden advent. In form his stories were crude, and yet in effect – which, after all, is every-thing – they were superb. It showed me that methods could not be stereotyped, and that there was a more excellent way, even if it were beyond my reach. I loved the *Barrack Room Ballads* also, and such poems as 'The Bolivar', 'East and West' and above all the badly named 'L'Envoi' became part of my very self. I always read the last one aloud to my little circle before we start on any fresh expedition, because it contains the very essence of travel, romance and high adventure.

I saw Kipling most nearly in his very early days when he lived at Brattleboro', a little village in Vermont, in a chivalrous desire to keep his newly married wife in touch with her own circle. In 1894, as I have recorded, there was a good deal of tail-twisting going on in the States, and Kipling pulled a few feathers out of the Eagle's tail in retaliation, which caused many screams of protest, for the American was far more sensitive to such things than the case-hardened Briton. I say 'was', for I think as a nation with an increased assurance of their own worth and strength they are now more careless of criticism. The result at the time was to add oil to flames, and I, as a passionate believer in Anglo-American union, wrote to Kipling to remonstrate. He received my protest very good-humouredly, and it led to my visit to his country home. As a matter of fact, the concern shown in America, when the poet lay at death's door a few years later, showed that the rancour was not very deep. Perhaps he was better known at that time in America than in England, for I remember sitting beside a busman in London, who bowed his red face to my ear and said: 'Beg your pardon, sir, but 'oo is this 'ere Kilpin?'

I had two great days in Vermont, and have a grateful remembrance of Mrs Kipling's hospitality. The poet read me 'McAndrew's Hymn', which he had just done, and surprised me by his dramatic power which enabled him to sustain the Glasgow accent throughout, so that the angular Scottish greaser simply walked the room. I had brought up my golf clubs and gave him lessons in a field while the New England rustics watched us from afar, wondering what on earth we were at, for golf was unknown in America at that time. We parted good friends, and the visit was an oasis in my rather dreary pilgrimage as a lecturer.

My glimpses of Kipling since then have been few and scattered, but I had the pleasure several times of meeting his old father, a most delightful and lovable person, who told a story quite as well as his famous son. As the mother was also a very remarkable woman, it is no wonder that he carried such a cargo.

James Barrie is one of my oldest literary friends, and I knew him within a year or two of the time when we both came to London. He had just written his *A Window in Thrums*, and I, like all the world, acclaimed it. When I was lecturing in Scotland in 1893 he invited me to Kirriemuir, when I stayed some days with his family – splendid types of the folk who have made Scotland great. His father was a fine fellow, but his mother was wonderful with a head and a heart – rare combinations – which made me class her with my own mother. Kirriemuir could by no means understand Barrie's success, and looked upon their great son as an inexplicable phenomenon. They were acutely aware, however, that tourists were arriving from all parts to see the place on account of Barrie's books. 'I suppose you have read them,' I said to the wife of the local hotel man. 'Aye, I've read them, and steep, steep, weary work it was,' said she. She had some theory that it was a four-horse coach which her good man was running and not the books at all which accounted for the boom.

Great as are Barrie's plays – and some of them I think are very great – I wish he had never written a line for the theatre. The glamour of it and the – to him – easy success have diverted from literature the man with the purest style of his age. Plays are always ephemeral, however good, and are limited to a few, but Barrie's unborn books might have been an eternal and a universal asset of British literature. He has the chaste clarity which is the great style, which has been debased by a generation of wretched critics who have always confused what is clear with what is shallow, and what is turbid with what is profound. If a man's thought is precise, his rendering of it is precise, and muddy thoughts make obscure paragraphs. If I had to make my choice among modern stylists, I should pick Barrie for the lighter forms of expression and our British Winston Churchill for the more classical.

Barrie's great play – one of the finest in the language – is of course *The Admirable Crichton*. I shall always hope that I had a hand in the fashioning of it. I say this not in complaint but in satisfaction, for we all drop seeds into each other, and seldom know whence they come. We were walking together on the heath at Kirriemuir when I said: 'I had a quaint thought in the night, Barrie. It was that a king was visiting India and was wrecked on the way on some island far from the track of ships. Only he and one rather handy sailor were saved. They settled down to spend their lives together. Of course the result would be that the sailor would become the king and the king the subject.' We chuckled over the idea, and when Crichton appeared, I seemed to see the fine plant which had grown from the tiny seed.

Barrie and I had one unfortunate venture together, in which I may say that the misfortune was chiefly mine, since I had really nothing to do with the matter, and yet shared all the trouble. However, I should have shared the honour and profit in case of success, so that I have no right to grumble. The facts were that Barrie had promised Mr D'Oyley Carte that he would provide the libretto of a light opera for the Savoy. This was in the Gilbert days, when such a libretto was judged by a very high standard. It was an extraordinary commission for him to accept, and I have never yet been able to understand why he did so, unless, like Alexander, he wanted fresh worlds to conquer. On this occasion, however, he met with a disastrous repulse, and the opera, *Jane Annie*, to which I alluded in an early chapter, was one of the few failures in his brilliant career.

I was brought into the matter because Barrie's health failed on account of some family bereavement. I had an urgent telegram from him at Aldburgh, and going there I found him very worried because he had bound himself by this contract and he felt in his present state unable to go forward with it. There were to be two acts, and he had written the first one, and had the rough scenario of the second, with the complete sequence of events – if one may call it a sequence. Would I come in with him and help him to complete it as part author? Of course

I was very happy to serve him in any way. My heart sank, however, when, after giving the promise, I examined the work. The only literary gift which Barrie has not got is the sense of poetic rhythm, and the instinct for what is permissible in verse. Ideas and wit were there in abundance. But the plot itself was not strong, though the dialogue and the situations also were occasionally excellent. I did my best and wrote the lyrics for the second act, and much of the dialogue, but it had to take the predestined shape. The result was not good. However, the actual comradeship of production was very amusing and interesting, and our failure was mainly painful to us because it let down the producer and the caste. We were well abused by the critics, but Barrie took it all in the bravest spirit.

I find, in looking over my papers, a belated statement of account from Barrie which is good reading.

In Account with J. M. Barrie

	*Wh*y	*Cause of delay*	*Remarks*
A	£1 lent at Station.	Object moving too fast.	Doyle *says* he lent it.
B	£12 *Jane Annie* on tour.	Moving or swaying of Kodak.	Better late than never.
C	£80 6s. 4d. Heaven knows.	Failure to pull cord.	Doyle gets ⅖ of a penny beyond his share.

Our association was never so closely renewed, but through all my changing life I have had a respect and affection for Barrie which were, I hope, mutual. How I collaborated with him at cricket as well as at work is told in my chapter on sport.

Henry Irving is one of the other great men whom I have met at close quarters, for his acting of Gregory Brewster brought us in contact. When he was producing *Coriolanus* he came down to Hindhead and used to drop in of an evening. He was fond of a glass of port – indeed, he was one of the four great men who were stated (probably untruly) by the Honourable G. Russell to drink a bottle each night – being the only trait which these great men had in common. The others, I remember, were Tennyson, Gladstone and Moses Montefiore, and the last I believe was really true. Like all bad habits, it overtook the sinner at last, and he was cut off at the age of a hundred and sixteen.

Irving had a curious dry wit which was occasionally sardonic and ill-natured. I can well believe that his rehearsals were often the occasion for heart-burnings among the men and tears among the ladies. The unexpectedness of his remarks took one aback. I remember when my friend Hamilton sat up with me into the 'wee sma' hours' with the famous man he became rather didactic on the subject of the Deity or the Universe or some other tremendous topic, which he treated very solemnly, and at great length. Irving sat with his intense eyes riveted upon the speaker's face, which encouraged Hamilton to go on and on. When at last he had finished, Irving remarked: '*What* a low comedian you would have made!' He wound up his visit by giving me his copy of *Coriolanus* with all his notes and stage directions – a very precious relic.

Many visions of old times rise before my eyes as I write, but my book would lose all proportion should I dwell upon them. I see Henley, the formidable cripple, a red-bearded, loud-voiced buccaneer of a man who could only crawl, for his back appeared to be broken. He was a great poet and critic who seemed to belong to the roaring days of Marlowe of the mighty line and the pot-house fray. I see Haggard too, first as the young spruce diplomatist, later as the worn and bearded man with strange vague tendencies to mysticism. Shaw, too, I see with the pleasant silky voice and the biting phrase. It was strange that all the mild vegetables which formed his diet made him more pugnacious and, I must add, more uncharitable than the carnivorous man – I have known no literary man who was more ruthless to other people's feelings. And yet to meet him was always to like him. He could not resist a bitter jest or the perverted pleasure of taking up an unpopular attitude. As an example I remember Henry Irving's son telling me that when Shaw was invited to his father's funeral he wrote in reply: 'If I were at Westminster Henry Irving would turn in his grave, just as Shakespeare would turn in his grave were Henry Irving at Stratford.' I may not have it verbally exact, but that was near enough. It was the kind of outrageous thing that he would say. And yet one can forgive him all when one reads the glorious dialogue of some of his plays. He seems subhuman in emotion and superhuman in intellect.

Shaw was always a thorn in Irving's side, and was usually the one jarring note among the chorus of praise which greeted each fresh production. At a first night at the Lyceum – those wonderful first nights which have never been equalled – the lanky Irishman with his greenish face, his red beard and his sardonic expression must have been like the death's-head at the banquet to Irving. Irving ascribed this animosity to

Shaw's pique because his plays were not accepted, but in this I am sure that he did an injustice. It was simply that contrary twist in the man which made him delight in opposing whatever anyone else approved. There is nothing constructive in him, and he is bound to be in perpetual opposition. No one for example was stronger for peace and for non-militarism than he, and I remember that when I took the chair at a meeting at Hindhead to back up the Tsar's peace proposals at The Hague, I thought to myself as I spied Shaw in a corner of the room: 'Well, this time at any rate he must be in sympathy.' But far from being so he sprang to his feet and put forward a number of ingenious reasons why these proposals for peace would be disastrous. Do what you could he was always against you.

Perhaps it is no bad thing to have the other point of view continually stated, and the British stand that sort of thing better than other nations. Had Shaw said in America what he said in England about the war whilst it was in progress he would have been in personal danger. There were times, however, when his queer contrary impulses became perfectly brutal in their working. One was at the time of the *Titanic* disaster, when he deliberately wrote a letter at a time when the wounds were raw, overwhelming everyone concerned with bitter criticism. I was moved to write a remonstrance, and we had a sharp debate in public, which did not in any way modify our kindly personal relations. I can recall a smaller but even more unjustifiable example of his sour nature when he was staying at Hindhead. A garden-party had been got up for some charity, and it included the woodland scenes from *As You Like It*, which were done by amateurs, and very well done too. Shaw with no provocation wrote a whole column of abuse in the local paper, spattering all the actors and their performance with ridicule, and covering them with confusion, though indeed they had nothing to be ashamed of. One mentions these things as characteristic of one side of the man, and as a proof, I fear, that the adoption by the world of a vegetarian diet will not bring unkind thoughts or actions to an end. But with it all Shaw is a genial creature to meet, and I am prepared to believe that there is a human kindly side to his nature though it has not been presented to the public. It took a good man to write *Saint Joan*.

Wells, too, I have known long, and indeed I must have often entered the draper's shop in which he was employed at Southsea, for the proprietor was a patient of mine. Wells is one of the great fruits which popular education has given us, since he came, as he is proud to state, from the heart of the people. His democratic frankness and complete absence of class feeling are occasionally embarrassing. I remember his asking me once if I had played cricket at Liphook. I said that I had. He said: 'Did you notice an old fellow who acts as professional and ground-keeper?' I said that I had. 'That was my father,' said Wells. I was too much surprised to answer, and could only congratulate myself that I had made no unpleasant comments before I knew the identity of the old man.

I have always had my doubts as to those elaborate forecasts of the future in which Wells indulges. He has, it is true, made a couple of good shots which have already materialised in the tanks and in the machine which would deliver news in our own houses. But he has never shown any perception of the true meaning of the psychic, and for want of it his history of the world, elaborate and remarkable as it was, seemed to me to be a body without a soul. However, this also may be given him, and it will make his equipment complete. I remember discussing the matter with him, when George Gissing, Hornung, he and I foregathered in Rome early in this century, but apparently my words had no effect.

Willie Hornung, my brother-in-law, is another of my vivid memories. He was a Dr Johnson without the learning but with a finer wit. No one could say a neater thing, and his writings, good as they are, never adequately represented the powers of the man, nor the quickness of his brain. These things depend upon the time and the fashion, and go flat in the telling, but I remember how, when I showed him the record of someone who claimed to have done a hundred yards under ten seconds, he said: 'It is a sprinter's error.' Golf he could not abide, for he said it was 'unsportsmanlike to hit a sitting ball'. His criticism upon my Sherlock Holmes was: 'Though he might be more humble, there is no police like Holmes.' I think I may claim that his famous character Raffles was a kind of inversion of Sherlock Holmes, Bunny playing Watson. He admits as much in his kindly dedication. I think there are few finer examples of short-story writing in our language than these, though I confess I think they are rather dangerous in their suggestion. I told him so before he put pen to paper, and the result has, I fear, borne me out. You must not make the criminal a hero.

Jerome, too, is an old friend. He is an adventurous soul, and at one time started a four-in-hand. I remember sitting on the top of it, and when one of the leaders turned right round and took a good look at the driver I thought it was time to get down. Maxwell also is an old friend. He is, of course, the son of Miss Braddon, who married a publisher of that name. I respect him for doing a man's work in the war when, though he was fifty years of age, and had led a sedentary life, he volunteered for a fighting battalion, a credit which he shares with A. E. W. Mason. Maxwell's work has always greatly appealed to me, and I have long looked upon him as the greatest novelist that we possess.

I never met Robert Louis Stevenson in the flesh, though I owe so much to him in the literary spirit. Never can I forget the delight with which I read those early stories of his in the *Cornhill*, before I knew the name of the author. I still think that 'The Pavilion on the Links' is one of the great short stories of the world, though there were alterations in the final form which were all for the worse, and showed prudery upon the part of the publishers. Stevenson's last year at Edinburgh University must have just about coincided with my first one, and Barrie must also have been in that grey old nest of learning about the year 1876. Strange to think that I probably brushed elbows with both of them in the crowded portal.

From his faraway home in Samoa he seemed to keep a quick eye upon literary matters in England, and I had most encouraging letters from him in 1893 and 1894. 'O frolic fellow-spookist' was his curious term of personal salutation in one of these, which showed that he shared my interest in psychic research but did not take it very seriously. I cannot guess how at that time he had detected it, though I was aware that he had himself in early days acted as secretary to a psychic research or rather to a spiritualist society in Edinburgh, which studied the remarkable mediumship of Duguid. His letters to me consisted of kind appreciation of my work. 'I have a great talent for compliment,' he said, 'accompanied by a hateful, even a diabolic, frankness.' He had been retailing some of my Sherlock Holmes yarns to his native servants – I should not have thought that he needed to draw upon anyone else – and he complained to me in a comical letter of the difficulty of telling a story when you had to halt every moment to explain what a railway was, what an engineer was, and so forth. He got the story across in spite of all difficulties, and, said he, 'If you could have seen the bright feverish eyes of Simite you would have tasted glory.' But he explained that the natives took everything literally, and that there was no such thing as an imaginary story for them. 'I, who write this, have had the indiscretion to perpetuate a trifling piece of fiction, "The Bottle Imp". Parties who come up to visit my mansion, after having admired the ceiling by Vanderputty and the tapestry by Gobbling, manifest towards the end a certain uneasiness which proves them to be fellows of an infinite delicacy. They may be seen to shrug a brown shoulder, to roll up a speaking eye, and at last the secret bursts from them: "Where is the bottle?" ' In another letter he said that as I had written of my first book in *The Idler* he also would do so. 'I could not hold back where the white plume of Conan Doyle waved in front of me.' So, at least, I may boast that it is to me that the world owes the little personal sketch about *Treasure Island* which appeared in that year. I cannot forget the shock that it was to me when driving down the Strand in a hansom cab in 1896 I saw upon a yellow evening poster 'Death of Stevenson'. Something seemed to have passed out of my world.

I was asked by his executors to finish the novel *St Ives*, which he had left three-quarters completed, but I did not feel equal to the task. It was done, however, and, I understand, very well done, by Quiller-Couch. It is a desperately difficult thing to carry on another man's story, and must be a more or less mechanical effort. I had one experience of it when my neighbour at Hindhead, Grant Allen, was on his deathbed. He was much worried because there were two numbers of his serial, *Hilda Wade*, which was running in *The Strand Magazine*, still uncompleted. It was a pleasure for me to do them for him, and so relieve his mind, but it was difficult collar work, and I expect they were pretty bad. Some time afterwards a stranger, who evidently confused Allen and me, wrote to say that his wife had given him a baby girl, and that in honour of me he was calling her Hilda Wade. He was really nearer the truth than appeared at first sight.

I well remember that deathbed of Grant Allen's. He was an agnostic of a type which came very near atheism, though in his private life an amiable and benevolent man. Believing what he did, the approach of death must have offered rather a bleak prospect, and as he had paroxysms of extreme pain the poor fellow seemed very miserable. I had often argued the case with him, I from a theistic and he from a negative point of view, but I did not intrude my opinions or disturb his mind at that solemn moment. Deathbed changes, though some clergy may rejoice in them, are really vain things. His brain, however, was as clear as ever, and his mind was occupied with all manner of strange knowledge, which he imparted in the intervals of his pain, in the curious high nasal voice which was characteristic. I can see him now, his knees drawn up to ease internal pain and his long thin nose and reddish-grey goatee protruding over the sheet, while he creaked out: 'Byzantine art, my dear Doyle, was of three periods, the middle one roughly coinciding with the actual fall of the Roman Empire. The characteristics of the first period – ' and so on, until he would give a cry, clasp his hands across his stomach, and wait till the pain passed before resuming his lecture. His dear little wife nursed him devotedly, and mitigated the gloom of those moments which can be made the very happiest in life if one understands what lies before one. One thinks, as a contrast, of Dr Hodgson's impatient cry, 'I can hardly wait for death!'

Grant Allen's strong opinions in print, and a certain pleasure he took in defending outside positions, gave quite a false view of his character, which was gentle and benignant. I remember his coming to a fancy dress ball which we gave in the character of a cardinal, and in that guise all the quiet dignity of the man seemed to come out and you realised how much our commonplace modern dress disguises the real man. He used to tell with great amusement how a couple, who afterwards became close friends, came first to call, and how as they waited on the doorstep the wife said to the husband: 'Remember, John, if he openly blasphemes, I leave the room.' He had, I remember, very human relations with the maids, who took a keen interest in their employer's scientific experiments. On one occasion these were connected with spiders, and the maid rushed into the drawing-room and cried: 'Oh, sir, Araminta has got a wasp.' Araminta was the name given to the big spider which he was observing at the time.

Grant Allen had no actual call to write fiction, but his brain was agile enough to make some sort of job of anything to which it turned. On the other hand, as a popular scientist he stood alone, or shared the honour with Samuel Laing. His only real success in fiction was the excellent short story 'John Creedy', where he combined science with fiction, with remarkable results.

At the time when I and so many others turned to letters there was certainly a wonderful vacancy for the newcomer. The giants of old had all departed. Thackeray, Dickens, Charles Reade and Trollope were memories. There was no great figure remaining save Hardy rising. The novelist was Mrs Humphrey Ward, who was just beginning her career with *Robert Elsmere*, the first of that series of novels which will illuminate the later Victorian era more clearly than any historian ever can do. I think it was Hodgkin who said, when he read *Count Robert of Paris*: 'Here have I been studying Byzantium all my life, and I never understood it until this blessed Scotch lawyer came along.' That is the special prerogative of imagination. Trollope and Mrs Ward have the whole Victorian civilisation dissected and preserved.

Then there were Meredith, unintelligible to most, and Walter Besant. There was Wilkie Collins, too, with his fine stories of mystery, and finally there was James Payn.

Payn was much greater than his books. The latter were usually rather mechanical, but to get at the real man one has to read such articles as his 'Literary Reminiscences', and especially his 'Backwater of Life'. He had all that humorous view which nature seems to give as a compensation to those whose strength is weak. Had Payn written only essays he would have rivalled Charles Lamb. I knew him best in his latter days, when he was crippled with illness, and his poor fingers so twisted with rheumatic arthritis that they seemed hardly human. He was intensely pessimistic as to his own fate. 'Don't make any mistake, Doyle, death is a horrible thing – horrible! I suffer the agonies of the damned!' But five minutes later he would have his audience roaring with laughter, and his own high treble laugh would be the loudest of all.

His own ailments were frequently a source of mirth. I remember how he described the breaking of a blood vessel in Bournemouth and how they carried him home on a litter. He was dimly conscious of the fir-woods through which he passed. 'I thought it was my funeral, and that they had done me well in the matter of plumes.' When he told a story he was so carried away by his sense of humour that he could hardly get the end out, and he finished up in a kind of scream. An American had called upon him at some late hour and had discoursed upon Assyrian tablets. 'I thought they were something to eat,' he screamed. He was an excellent whist player, and the Baldwin Club used to send three members to his house on certain days so that the old fellow should not go without his game. This game was very scientific. He would tell with delight how he asked some novice: 'Do you play the penultimate?' To which the novice answered: 'No – but my brother plays the American organ.'

Many of my generation of authors had reason to love him, for he was a human and kindly critic. His writing, however, was really dreadful. It was of him that the story was told than an author handed one of his letters to a chemist for a test. The chemist retired for a time and then returned with a bottle and demanded half a crown. Better luck attended the man who received an illegible letter from a railway director. He used it as a free pass upon the line. Payn used to joke about his own writing, but it was a very real trouble when one could not make out whether he had accepted or rejected one's story. There was one letter in which I could only read the words 'infringement of copyright'. He was very funny when he described the work of the robust younger school. 'I have received a story from — ' he said. 'Five thousand words, mostly damns.'

I knew Sir Henry Thompson, the famous surgeon, very well, and was frequently honoured by an invitation to his famous octave dinners, at which eight carefully chosen male guests were always the company. They always seemed to me to be the most wonderful exhibitions of unselfishness, for Thompson was not allowed any alcohol, or anything save the most simple viands. Possibly, however, like Meredith and the bottle of burgundy, he enjoyed some reflex pleasure from the enjoyment of others. He had been a wonderful viveur and judge of what was what, and I fear that I disappointed him, for I was much more interested in the conversation than the food, and it used to annoy me when some argument was interrupted in order to tell us that it was not ordinary ham but a Westphalian wild boar that we were eating and that it had been boiled in wine for precisely the right time prescribed by the best authorities. But it was part of his wonderful unselfish hospitality to make his guests realise exactly what it was that was set before them. I have never heard more interesting talk than at these male gatherings, for it is notorious that though ladies greatly improve the appearance of a feast they usually detract from the quality of the talk. Few men are ever absolutely natural when there are women in the room.

There was one special dinner, I fancy it was the hundredth of the series, which was particularly interesting as the Prince of Wales, now George V, was one of the eight, and gave us a most interesting account of the voyage round the world from which he had just returned. Of the rest of the company I can only recall Sir Henry Stanley, the traveller, and Sir Crichton Browne. Twenty years later I met the king when he visited a trade exhibition and I attended as one of the directors of Tuck's famous postcard firm. He at once said: 'Why, I have not seen you since that pleasant dinner when you sat next to me at Sir Henry Thompson's.' It seemed to me to be a remarkable example of the royal gift of memory.

I have not often occupied a chair among the seats of the mighty. My life has been too busy and too preoccupied to allow me to stray far from my beaten path. The mention of the prince, however, reminds me of the one occasion when I was privileged to entertain – or to attempt to entertain – the present queen. It was at a small dinner to which I was invited by the courtesy of Lord Middleton whose charming wife, once Madeleine Stanley daughter of Lady Helier, I could remember since her girlhood. Upon this occasion the prince and princess came in after dinner, the latter sitting alone at one end of the room with a second chair beside her own, which was occupied successively by the various gentlemen who were to be introduced to her. I was led up in due course, made my bow, and sat down at her request. I confess that I found it heavy going at first, for I had heard somewhere that royalty has to make the first remark, and had it been the other way there was such a gulf between us that I should not have known where to begin. However she was very pleasant and gracious and began asking me some questions about my works which brought me on to very easy ground. Indeed, I became so interested in our talk that I was quite disappointed when Mr John Morley was led up, and I realised that it was time for me to vacate the chair.

There was another amusing incident on that eventful evening. I had been asked to take in Lady Curzon, whose husband, then Viceroy of India, had been unable to attend. The first couple had passed in and there was a moment's hesitation as to who should go next, but Lady Curzon and I were nearest the door, so possibly with some little encouragement from the lady we filed through. I thought nothing of the incident but some great authority upon these matters came to me afterwards in great excitement. 'Do you know,' he said, 'that you have established a precedent and solved one of the most difficult and debatable matters of etiquette that has ever caused ill-feeling in British society? The Lord Chancellor and the College of Heralds should be much obliged to you, for you have given them a definite lead. There has never been so vexed a question as to whether a vice-reine when she is away from the country where she represents royalty shall take precedence over a duchess. There was a duchess in the room, but you by your decided action have settled the matter for ever.' So who shall say that I have done nothing in my life?

Of the distinguished lights of the law whom I have met from time to time I think that Sir Henry Hawkins – then become Lord Bampton – made the most definite impression. I met him at a weekend gathering at

Cliveden, when Mr Astor was our host. On the first night at dinner, before the party had shaken down into mutual acquaintance, the ex-judge, very old and as bald as an ostrich egg, was seated opposite, and was wreathed in smiles as he made himself agreeable to his neighbour. His appearance was so jovial that I remarked to the lady upon my left: 'It is curious to notice the appearance of our *vis-à-vis* and to contrast it with his reputation,' alluding to his sinister record as an inexorable judge. She seemed rather puzzled by my remark, so I added: 'Of course you know who he is.' 'Yes,' said she; 'his name is Conan Doyle and he writes novels.' I was hardly middle-aged at the time and at my best physically, so that I was amused at her mistake, which arose from some confusion in the list of guests. I put my dinner card up against her wineglass, so after that we got to know each other.

Hawkins was a most extraordinary man, and so capricious that one never knew whether one was dealing with Jekyll or with Hyde. It was certainly Hyde when he took eleven hours summing up in the Penge case, and did all a man could do to have all four of the prisoners condemned to death. Sir Edward Clarke was so incensed at his behaviour on this occasion that he gave notice when Hawkins retired from the bench that if there were the usual complimentary ceremonies he would protest. So they were dropped.

I might, on the other hand, illustrate the Jekyll side of him by a story which he told me with his own lips. A prisoner had a pet mouse. One day the brute of a warder deliberately trod upon it. The prisoner caught up his dinner knife and dashed at the warder, who only just escaped, the knife stabbing the door as it closed behind him. Hawkins as judge wanted to get the man off, but the attempt at murder was obvious and the law equally clear. What was he to do? In his charge to the jury he said: 'If a man tries to kill another in a way which is on the face of it absurd, it becomes a foolish rather than a criminal act. If, for example, a man in London discharged a pistol to hurt a man in Edinburgh, we could only laugh at such an offence. So also when a man stabs an iron-plated door while another man is at the other side of it we cannot take it seriously.' The jury, who were probably only too glad to follow such a lead, brought in a verdict of 'Not guilty'.

Another distinguished man of the law who left a very clear impression upon my mind was Sir Francis Jeune, afterwards Lord St Helier. I attended several of Lady Jeune's famous luncheon parties, which were quite one of the outstanding institutions of London, like Gladstone's breakfasts, in the last quarter of the nineteenth century. I am indebted to this lady for very many kind actions. Her husband always impressed me with his gentle wisdom and with his cultivated taste. He told me that if every copy of Horace were destroyed he thought that he could reconstruct most of it from memory. He presided over the Divorce Courts, and I remember upon one occasion I said to him: 'You must have a very low opinion of human nature, Sir Francis, since the worst side of it is forever presented towards you.' 'On the contrary,' said he very earnestly, 'my experience in the Divorce Courts has greatly raised my opinion of humanity. There is so much chivalrous self-sacrifice and so much disposition upon the part of everyone to make the best of a bad business that it is extremely edifying.' This view seemed to me to be worth recording.

24

Some Recollections of Sport

It is here – before we approach what Maxwell has called 'The Great
Interruption' – that I may perhaps break my narrative in order to inter-
polate a chapter upon the general subject of my experiences of sport,
which have taken up an appreciable part of my life, added greatly to its
pleasure, and which can be better treated as a whole than recounted
seriatim. It may best be fitted in at this spot as my sporting life one way
and another may be said to have reached its modest zenith about that
time.

As one grows old one looks back at one's career in sport as a thing
completed. Yet I have at least held on to it as long as I could, for I
played a hard match of Association football at forty-four, and I played
cricket for ten years more. I have never specialised, and have therefore
been a second-rater in all things. I have made up for it by being an all-
rounder, and have had, I dare say, as much fun out of sport as many an
adept. It would be odd if a man could try as many games as I for so
many years without having some interesting experiences or forming a
few opinions which would bear recording and discussion.

And first of all let me 'damn the sins I have no mind to' by recording
what most of my friends will regard as limitation. I never could look
upon flat-racing as a true sport. Sport is what a man does, not what a
horse does. Skill and judgement are shown, no doubt, by the professional jockeys, but I think it may be argued that in nine cases out of
ten the best horse wins, and would have equally won, could his head be
kept straight, had there been a dummy on his back. But making every
allowance, on the one side, for what human qualities may be called

forth, and for any improvement of the breed of horses (though I am told that the same pains in other directions would produce infinitely more fruitful and generally useful results), and putting on the other side the demoralisation from betting, the rascality among some bookmakers, and the collection of undesirable characters brought together by a race meeting, I cannot avoid the conclusion that the harm greatly outweighs the good from a broadly national point of view. Yet I recognise, of course, that it is an amusement which lies so deeply in human nature – the oldest, perhaps, of all amusements which have come down to us – that it must have its place in our system until the time may come when it will be gradually modified, developing, perhaps, some purifying change, as prizefighting did when it turned to contests with the gloves.

I have purposely said 'flat-racing', because I think a stronger case, though not, perhaps, an entirely sound one, could be made out for steeplechasing. Eliminate the mob and the money, and then, surely, among feats of human skill and hardihood there are not many to match that of the winner of a really stiff point-to-point, while the man who rides at the huge barriers of the Grand National has a heart for any-thing. As in the old days of the ring, it is not the men nor the sport, but it is the followers who cast a shadow on the business. Go down to Waterloo and meet any returning race train, if you doubt it.

If I have alienated half my readers by my critical attitude to the Turf, I shall probably offend the other half by stating that I cannot persuade myself that we are justified in taking life as a pleasure. To shoot for the pot must be right, since man must feed, and to kill creatures which live upon others (the hunting of foxes, for example) must also be right, since to slay one is to save many; but the rearing of birds in order to kill them, and the shooting of such sensitive and inoffensive animals as hares and deer, cannot, I think, be justified. I must admit that I shot a good deal before I came to this conclusion. Perhaps the fact, while it prevents my assuming any airs of virtue, will give my opinion greater weight, since good shooting is still within my reach, and I know nothing more exhilarating than to wait on the borders of an autumn-tinted wood, to hear the crackling advance of beaters, to mark the sudden whirr and the yell of 'Mark over', and then, over the topmost branches, to see a noble cock pheasant whizzing downwind at a pace which pitches him a hundred yards behind you when you have dropped him. But when your moment of exultation is over, and you note what a beautiful creature he is and how one instant of your pleasure has wrecked him, you feel that you had better think no longer if you mean to slip two more cartridges into your gun and stand by for another. Worse still is it when you hear the childlike wail of the wounded hare. I should think that there are few sportsmen who have not felt a disgust at their own handiwork when they have heard it. So, too, when you see the pheasant fly on with his legs showing beneath him as sign that he is hard hit. He drops into the thick woods and is lost to sight. Perhaps it is as well for your peace of mind that he should be lost to thought also.

Of course, one is met always by the perfectly valid argument that the creatures would not live at all if it were not for the purposes of sport, and that it is presumably better from their point of view that they should eventually meet a violent death than that they should never have existed. No doubt this is true. But there is another side of the question as to the effect of the sport upon ourselves – whether it does not blunt our own better feelings, harden our sympathies, brutalise our natures. A coward can do it as well as a brave man; a weakling can do it as well as a strong man. There is no ultimate good from it. Have we a moral right, then, to kill creatures for amusement? I know many of the best and most kind-hearted men who do it, but still I feel that in a more advanced age it will no longer be possible.

And yet I am aware of my own inconsistency when I say I am in sympathy with fishing, and would gladly have a little if I knew where to get it. And yet, is it wholly inconsistent? Is a cold-blooded creature of low organisation like a fish to be regarded in the same way as the hare which cries out in front of the beagles, or the deer which may carry the rifle bullet away in its side? If there is any cruelty it is surely of a much less degree. Besides, is it not the sweet solitude of nature, the romantic quest, rather than the actual capture which appeals to the fisherman? One thinks of the stories of trout and salmon which have taken another fly within a few minutes of having broken away from a former one, and one feels that their sense of pain must be very different from our own.

I once had the best of an exchange of fishing stories, which does not sound like a testimonial to my veracity. It was in a Birmingham inn, and a commercial traveller was boasting of his successes. I ventured to back the weight of the last three fish which I had been concerned in catching against any day's take of his lifetime. He closed with the bet and quoted some large haul, a hundred pounds or more. 'Now, sir,' he asked triumphantly, 'what was the weight of your three fish?' 'Just over two hundred tons,' I answered. 'Whales?' 'Yes, three Greenland whales.' 'I give you best,' he cried; but whether as a fisherman, or as a teller of fish stories, I am not sure. As a matter of fact, I had only returned that year from the Arctic seas, and the three fish in question were, in truth, the last which I had helped to catch.

My experiences during my Arctic voyage both with whales and bears I have already touched upon, so I will not refer to them again, though it was the greatest period of sport which has ever come my way.

I have always been keen upon the noble old English sport of boxing, and, though of no particular class myself, I suppose I might describe my form as that of a fair average amateur. I should have been a better man had I taught less and learned more, but after my first tuition I had few chances of professional teaching. However, I have done a good deal of mixed boxing among many different types of men, and had as much pleasure from it as from any form of sport. It stood me in good stead aboard the whaler. On the very first evening I had a strenuous bout with the steward, who was an excellent sportsman. I heard him afterwards, through the partition of the cabin, declare that I was 'the best sur–r–r–geon we've had, Colin – he's blacked my ee'. It struck me as a singular test of my medical ability, but I dare say it did no harm.

I remember when I was a medical practitioner going down to examine a man's life for insurance in a little Sussex village. He was the gentleman farmer of the place, and a most sporting and jovial soul. It was a Saturday, and I enjoyed his hospitality that evening, staying over till Monday. After breakfast it chanced that several neighbours dropped in, one of whom, an athletic young farmer, was fond of the gloves. Conversation soon brought out the fact that I had a weakness in the same direction. The result was obvious. Two pairs of gloves were hunted from some cupboard, and in a few minutes we were hard at it, playing light at first and letting out as we warmed. It was soon clear that there was no room inside a house for two heavyweights, so we adjourned to the front lawn. The main road ran across the end of it, with a low wall of just the right height to allow the village to rest its elbows on it and enjoy the spectacle. We fought several very brisk rounds, with no particular advantage either way, but the contest always stands out in my memory for its queer surroundings and the old English picture in which it was set. It is one of several curious bye-battles in my career. I recollect another where another man and I, returning from a ball at five of a summer morning, went into his room and fought in our dress clothes several very vigorous rounds as a wind-up to the evening's exercise.

They say that every form of knowledge comes useful sooner or later. Certainly my own experience in boxing and my very large acquaintance with the history of the prize-ring found their scope when I wrote *Rodney Stone*. No one but a fighting man would ever, I think, quite understand or appreciate some of the detail. A friend of mine read the scene where Boy Jim fights Berks to a prizefighter as he lay in what proved to be his last illness. The man listened with growing animation until the reader came to the point where the second advises Boy Jim, in technical jargon, how to get at his awkward antagonist. 'That's it! By God, he's got him!' shouted the man in the bed. It was an incident which gave me pleasure when I heard it.

I have never concealed my opinion that the old prize-ring was an excellent thing from a national point of view – exactly as glove-fighting is now. Better that our sports should be a little too rough than that we should run a risk of effeminacy. But the ring outlasted its time. It was ruined by the villainous mobs who cared nothing for the chivalry of sport or the traditions of British fair play as compared with the money gain which the contest might bring. Their blackguardism drove out the good men – the men who really did uphold the ancient standards, and so the whole institution passed into rottenness and decay. But now the glove contests carried on under the discipline of the National Sporting or other clubs perpetuate the noble old sport without a possibility of the more evil elements creeping into it once more. An exhibition of hardihood without brutality, of good-humoured courage without savagery, of skill without trickery, is, I think, the very highest which sport can give. People may smile at the mittens, but a twenty-round contest with four-ounce gloves is quite as punishing an ordeal as one could wish to endure. There is as little room for a coward as in the rougher days of old, and the standard of endurance is probably as high as in the average prizefight.

One wonders how our champions of today would have fared at the hands of the heroes of the past. I know something of this end of the question, for I have seen nearly all the great boxers of my time, from J. L. Sullivan down to Tommy Burns, Carpentier, Bombardier Wells, Beckett and that little miracle Jimmy Wilde. But how about the other end – the men of old? Wonderful Jem Mace was the only link between them. On the one hand, he was supreme in the 1860s as a knuckle-fighter; on the other, he gave the great impetus to glove-fighting in America, and more especially in Australia, which has brought over such champions as Frank Slavin and Fitzsimmons, who, through Mace's teaching, derive straight from the classic line of British boxers. He of all men might have drawn a just comparison between the old and the new. But even his skill and experience might be at fault, for it is notorious that many of the greatest fighters under the old regime were poor hands with the mittens. Men could bang poor Tom Sayers all round the ring with the gloves, who would not have dared to get over the ropes had he been without them. I have seen Mace box, and even when over sixty it is wonderful how straight was his left, how quick his feet, and how impregnable his guard.

After the Great War, one can see that those of us who worked for the revival of boxing wrought better than we knew, for at the supreme test of all time – the test which has settled the history of the future – it has played a marked part. I do not mean that a man used his fists in the war, but I mean – and every experienced instructor will, I am sure, endorse it – that the combative spirit and aggressive quickness gave us the attacking fire and helped especially in bayonet work. But it was to our allies of France that the chief advantage came. I believe that Carpentier, the boxer, did more to win the war for France than any other man save the actual generals or politicians. The public proof that a Frenchman could be at the very head of his class, as Ledoux was also at a lighter weight, gives a physical self-respect to a nation which tinges the spirit of every single member of it. It was a great day for France when English sports, boxing, Rugby football and others came across to them, and when a young man's ideal ceased to be amatory adventure with an occasional duel. England has taught Europe much, but nothing of more value than this.

To return to my own small experiences of the game, I might have had one very notable one, for I was asked to referee the great contest when the champions of the white and black races fought for what may prove to be almost the last time.

My first intimation was a cable followed by a letter:

New York
December 9, 1909

MY DEAR SIR – I hope you will pardon the liberty I took as a stranger in cabling to you asking if you would act at the championship battle between Jeffries and Johnson. The fact is that when the articles were signed recently your name was suggested for referee, and Tex Rickard, promoter of the fight, was greatly interested, as were many others. I believe it will interest you to know that the opinion was unanimous that you would do admirably in the position. In a voting contest several persons sent in your name as their choice. Believe me among sporting men of the best class in America you have many strong admirers; your splendid stories of the ring, and your avowed admiration for the great sport of boxing have made you thousands of friends.

It was because of this extremely friendly feeling for you in America that I took the liberty of cabling to you. I thank you for your reply.

It would indeed rejoice the hearts of the men in this country if you were at the ringside when the great negro fighter meets the white man Jeffries for the world's championship.

I am, my dear sir,
Yours sincerely,

IRVING JEFFERSON LEWIS
Managing Editor *New York Morning Telegraph*

I was much inclined to accept this honourable invitation, though my friends pictured me as winding up with a revolver at one ear and a razor at the other. However, the distance and my engagements presented a final bar.

If boxing is the finest single-man sport, I think that Rugby football is the best collective one. Strength, courage, speed and resource are great qualities to include in a single game. I have always wished that it had come more my way in life, but my football was ruined, as many a man's is, by the fact that at my old school they played a hybrid game peculiar to the place, with excellent points of its own, but unfitting the youngster for any other. All these local freak games, wall games, Winchester games, and so on are national misfortunes, for while our youths are wasting their energies upon them – those precious early energies which make the instinctive players – the young South African or New Zealander is brought up on the real universal Rugby, and so comes over to pluck a few more laurel leaves out of our depleted wreath. In Australia I have seen in Victoria a hybrid though excellent game of their own, but they have had the sense in other parts to fall into line, and are already taking the same high position which they hold in other branches of sport. I hope that our headmasters will follow the same course.

In spite of my wretched training I played for a short time as a forward in the Edinburgh University team, but my want of knowledge of the game was too heavy a handicap. Afterwards I took to Association, and played first goal and then back for Portsmouth, when that famous club was an amateur organisation. Even then we could put a very fair team in the field, and were runners-up for the County Cup the last season that I played. In the same season I was invited to play for the county. I was always too slow, however, to be a really good back, though I was a long and safe kick. After a long hiatus I took up football again in South Africa and organised a series of inter-hospital matches in Bloemfontein which helped to take our minds away from enteric. My old love treated me very scurvily, however, for I received a foul from a man's knee which buckled two of my ribs and brought my games to a close. I have played occasionally since, but there is no doubt that as a man grows older a brisk charge shakes him up as it never did before. Let him turn to golf, and be thankful that there is still one splendid game which can never desert him. There may be objections to the 'Royal and Ancient' – but a game which takes four miles of country for the playing must always have a majesty of its own.

Personally I was an enthusiastic, but a very inefficient golfer – a ten at my best, and at my worst outside the pale of all decent handicaps. But surely it is a great testimony to the qualities of a game when a man can be both enthusiastic and inefficient. It is a proof at least that a man plays for the game's sake and not for personal kudos. Golf is the coquette of games. It always lures one on and always evades one. Ten years ago I thought I had nearly got it. I hope so today. But my scoring cards will show, I fear, that the coquette has not yet been caught. The elderly lover cannot hope to win her smile.

I used in my early golfing days to practise on the very rudimentary links in front of the Mena Hotel, just under the Pyramids. It was a weird course, where, if you sliced your ball, you might find it bunkered in the grave of some Rameses or Thothmes of old. It was here, I believe, that the cynical stranger, after watching my energetic but ineffectual game, remarked that he had always understood that there was a special tax for excavating in Egypt. I have a pleasant recollection of Egyptian golf in a match played with the late Sirdar, then head of the Intelligence Department. When my ball was teed I observed that his negro caddie pointed two fingers at it and spat, which meant, as I was given to understand, that he cursed it for the rest of the game. Certainly I got into every hazard in the course, though I must admit that I have accomplished that when there was no Central African curse upon me. Those were the days before the reconquest of the Sudan, and I was told by Colonel Wingate – as he then was – that his spies coming down from Omdurman not infrequently delivered their messages to him while carrying his golf clubs, to avoid the attention of the Kalipha's spies, who abounded in Cairo. On this occasion the Sirdar beat me well, but with a Christian caddie I turned the tables on him at Dunbar, and now we have signed articles to play off the rubber at Khartoum, no cursing allowed. When that first match was played we should as soon have thought of arranging to play golf on the moon.

Every now and then I give up the game in disgust at my own in-competence, but only to be lured on once more. Hunting in an old desk I came upon an obituary which I had written for my game at some moment of special depression. It ran, 'Sacred to the memory of my golf. It was never strong, being permanently afflicted with a deformed stance and an undeveloped swing. After long weakness cheerfully borne it finally succumbed, and was buried in the eighteenth hole, regretted by numerous caddies.' However it is out and about once more, none the worse for this premature interment.

There is said to be a considerable analogy between golf and billiards, so much so that success in the one generally leads to success in the other. Personally, I have not found it so, for though I may claim, I suppose, to be above the average amateur at billiards, I am probably below him in golf. I have never quite attained the three-figure break, but I have so often topped the eighty, and even the ninety, that I have lived in constant hope. My friend, the late General Drayson, who was a great authority on the game, used to recommend that every player should ascertain what he called his 'decimal', by which he meant how many innings it took him, whether scoring or not, to make 100. The number, of course, varies with the luck of the balls and the mood of the player; but, taken over a dozen or twenty games, it gives a fair average idea of the player's form, and a man by himself can in this way test his own powers. If, for example, a player could, on an average, score one hundred in twenty innings then his average would be five, which is very fair amateur form. If a man finds his 'decimal' rise as high as ten over a sequence of games, he may be sure that he can hold his own against most players that he is likely to meet. I dare say my own decimal when I was in practice would be from six to eight.

I was never good enough for the big matches, and though I once went in for the amateur championship it was not out of any illusions about my game, but because I was specially asked to do so, as it was advisable to strengthen the undoubted amateur element in the contest. By the luck of a bye, and by beating a player who was about my own form, I got into the third round, when I ran across Mr Evans, who eventually reached the final with my scalp as well as several others at his girdle. I made six hundred and fifty against his one thousand, which, as I was not helped by a bad fall from a motor bike a few days before, was as much as I could expect. Forty-two off the red was my best effort. Surely billiards is the king of all indoor games, and should have some writer who would do for it in prose what John Nyren did for cricket. I have never seen any worthy appreciation of its infinite varieties from the forcing losing hazard which goes roaring into a top pocket with a clash upon the rail, to the feather stroke so delicate that it is only the quiver of reflected light upon the object ball which shows that it has indeed been struck. Greatest of all is the ball heavily loaded with side which drifts down the long cushion and then is sucked against every apparent law into the pocket as though it were the centre of a whirlpool. Mr E. V. Lucas is one who could do it with discernment.

I have one funny recollection of billiards, when I wandered into some small hotel in a south-coast watering place, and for want of something to do played the marker. He was a pompous person in a frock coat with a very good opinion of his own game, which was really ruined by a habit he had of jerking. I won the match, which was not difficult to do, and then I thought it a kindness to point out to the man how he could improve his game. He took this badly, however, and hinted that he allowed gentlemen who played him to get the better of him. This in turn annoyed me, so I said: 'Look here. I will come in after dinner and you can show all you can do, and you shall have a sovereign if you win.' After dinner his game was worse than ever, while I had amazing luck and made the 100 in about three shots. As I put on my coat and was leaving the room the queer little fellow sidled up to me and said: 'I beg pardon, sir, but is your name Roberts?'

My earliest recollection of cricket is not a particularly pleasant one. When I was a very small boy at a preparatory school I was one of a group of admirers who stood around watching a young cricketer who had just made his name hitting big hits off the school bowlers. One of the big hits landed on my kneecap and the cricketer in his own famous arms carried me off to the school infirmary. The name, Tom Emmett, lingers in my memory, though it was some years before I appreciated exactly what he stood for in the game. I think, like most boys, I would rather have been knocked down by a first-class cricketer than picked up by a second-rater.

That was the beginning of my acquaintance with a game which has on the whole given me more pleasure during my life than any other branch of sport. I have ended by being its victim, for a fast bowler some years ago happened to hit me twice in the same place under my left knee, which has left a permanent weakness. I have had as long an innings as one could reasonably expect, and carry many pleasant friendships and recollections away with me.

I was a keen cricketer as a boy, but in my student days was too occupied to touch it. Then I took it up again, but my progress was interrupted by work and travel. I had some cause, therefore, to hold on to the game as I had lost so much of it in my youth. Finally, I fulfilled a secret ambition by getting into the fringe of first-class cricket, though rather, perhaps, through the good nature of others than my own merits. However, I can truly say that in the last season when I played some first-class cricket, including matches against Kent, Derbyshire and the London County, I had an average of thirty-two for those games, so I may claim to have earned my place. I was more useful, however, in an amateur team, for I was a fairly steady and reliable bowler, and I could generally earn my place in that department, while with the MCC the professional talent is usually so strong that the amateur who fails in batting and is not a particularly good field has no chance of atoning with the ball. Yet even with the MCC I have occasionally had a gleam of success. Such a one came some years ago, when the team presented me with a little silver hat for getting three consecutive clean-bowled wickets against the Gentlemen of Warwick. One of my victims explained his downfall by assuring me that he had it thoroughly in his head that I was a left-handed bowler, and when the ball came from my right hand he was too bewildered to stop it. The reason is not so good as that of an artist who, when I had bowled him out, exclaimed: 'Who can play against a man who bowls in a crude pink shirt against an olive-green background?'

A bowler has many days when everything is against him, when a hard, smooth wicket takes all the spin and devil out of him, when he goes all round and over the wicket, when lofted balls refuse to come to hand, or, if they do come, refuse to stay. But, on the other hand, he has his recompense with many a stroke of good fortune. It was in such a moment that I had the good luck to get the wicket of W. G. Grace, the greatest of all cricketers.

W. G. had his speedy revenge. There was nothing more childlike and bland than that slow, tossed-up bowling of his, and nothing more subtle and treacherous. He was always on the wicket or about it, never sent down a really loose ball, worked continually a few inches from the leg, and had a perfect command of length. It was the latter quality which was my downfall. I had made some thirty or forty, and began to relax in the deep respect with which I faced the doctor's deliveries. I had driven him for four, and jumped out at him again the next ball. Seeing my intention, as a good bowler does, he dropped his ball a foot or two shorter. I reached it with difficulty, but again I scored four. By this time I was very pleased with myself, and could see no reason why every one of these delightful slows should not mean a four to me. Out I danced to reach the next one on the half volley. It was tossed a little higher up in the air, which gave the delusion that it was coming right up to the bat, but as a matter of fact it pitched well short of my reach, broke sharply across and Lilley, the wicketkeeper, had my bails off in a twinkling. One feels rather cheap when one walks from the middle of the pitch to the pavilion, longing to kick oneself for one's own foolishness all the way. I have only once felt smaller, and that was when I was bowled by A. P. Lucas, by the most singular ball that I have ever received. He propelled it like a quoit into the air to a height of at least thirty feet, and it fell straight and true on to the top of the bails. I have often wondered what a good batsman would have made of that ball. To play it one would have needed to turn the blade of the bat straight up, and could hardly fail to give a chance. I tried to cut it off my stumps, with the result that I knocked down my wicket and broke my bat, while the ball fell in the midst of this general chaos. I spent the rest of the day wondering gloomily what I ought to have done – and I am wondering yet.

I have had two unusual experiences upon Lord's ground. One was that I got a century in the very first match that I played there. It was an unimportant game, it is true, but still the surprising fact remained. It was a heavy day, and my bat, still encrusted with the classic mud, hangs as a treasured relic in my hall. The other was less pleasant and even more surprising. I was playing for the Club against Kent, and faced for the first time Bradley, who was that year one of the fastest bowlers in England. His first delivery I hardly saw, and it landed with a terrific thud upon my thigh. A little occasional pain is one of the chances of cricket, and one takes it as cheerfully as one can, but on this occasion it suddenly became sharp to an unbearable degree. I clapped my hand to the spot, and found to my amazement that I was on fire. The ball had landed straight on a small tin vesta box in my trousers pocket, had splintered the box, and set the matches ablaze. It did not take me long to turn out my pocket and scatter the burning vestas over the grass. I should have thought this incident unique, but Alec Hearne, to whom I told it, assured me that he had seen more than one accident of the kind. W. G. was greatly amused. 'Couldn't get you out – had to set you on fire!' he cried, in the high voice which seemed so queer from so big a body.

There are certain matches which stand out in one's memory for their peculiar surroundings. One was a match played against Cape de Verde at that island on the way to South Africa. There is an Atlantic telegraph station there with a large staff, and they turn out an excellent eleven. I understand that they played each transport as it passed, and that they had defeated all, including the Guards. We made up a very fair team, however, under the captaincy of Lord Henry Scott, and after a hard fight we defeated the islanders. I don't know how many of our eleven left their bones in South Africa: three at least – Blasson, Douglas Forbes (who made our top score) and young Maxwell Craig never returned. I remember one even more tragic match in which I played for the Incogniti against Aldershot Division a few months before the African War. The regiments quartered there were those which afterwards saw the hardest service. Major Ray, who made the top score, was killed at Magersfontein. Young Stanley, who went in first with me, met his death in the Yeomanry. Taking the two teams right through, I am sure that half the men were killed or wounded within two years. How little we could have foreseen it that sunny summer day!

It is dangerous when an old cricketer begins to reminisce, because so much comes back to his mind. He has but to smell the hot rubber of a bat handle to be flooded with memories. They are not always glorious. I remember three ladies coming to see me play against one of the Bedford schools. The boys politely applauded as I approached the wicket. A very small boy lobbed up the first ball which I played at. It went up into the air, and was caught at point by the very smallest boy I have ever seen in decent cricket. It seemed to me about a mile as I walked back from the wicket to the pavilion. I don't think those three ladies ever recovered their confidence in my cricketing powers.

As a set-off to this confession of failure let me add a small instance of success, where by 'taking thought' I saved a minor international match. It was at The Hague in 1892, and the game was a wandering British team against Holland. The Dutch were an excellent sporting lot, and had one remarkable bowler in Posthuma, a left-hander, who had so huge a break with his slow ball that it was not uncommon for him to pitch the ball right outside the matting on which we played and yet bring it on to the wicket. We won our various local matches without much difficulty, but we were aware that we should have a stiff fight with United Holland, the more so as Dutch hospitality was almost as dangerous to our play as Dutch cricket.

So it proved, and we were in the position that with four wickets in hand they had only fifteen runs to make with two batsmen well set. I had not bowled during the tour, for as we were a scratch team, mostly from the schoolmaster class, we did not know each other's capacity. Seeing, however, that things were getting desperate, I went the length of asking our skipper to give me a chance.

I had observed that the batsmen had been very well taught by their English professional, and that they all played in most orthodox fashion with a perfectly straight bat. That was why I thought I might get them out. I brought every fielder round to the off, for I felt that they would not think it correct to pull, and I tossed up good length balls about a foot on the offside. It came off exactly as I expected. The pro had not told them what to do with that particular sort of tosh, and the four men were all caught for as many runs by mid-off or cover. The team in their exultation proceeded to carry me into the pavilion, but whether it was my sixteen stone or the heat of the weather, they tired of the job midway and let me down with a crash which shook the breath out of me – so Holland was avenged. I played against them again when they came to England, and made sixty-seven, but got no wickets, for they had mastered the offside theory.

Some of my quaintest cricket reminiscences are in connection with J. M. Barrie's team – the 'Allah-Akbarries', or 'Lord help us' as we were called. We played in the old style, caring little about the game and a good deal about a jolly time and pleasant scenery. Broadway, the country home of Mr Navarro and his wife, formerly Mary Anderson, the famous actress, was one of our favourite haunts, and for several years in succession we played the Artists there. Bernard Partridge, Barrie, A. E. W. Mason, Abbey the Academician, Blomfield the architect, Marriott Watson, Charles Whibley, and others of note took part, and there were many whimsical happenings, which were good fun if they were not good cricket. I thought all record of our games had faded from human ken, but lately a controversy was raised over Mr Armstrong, the Australian captain, bowling the same man from opposite ends on consecutive overs. This led to the following paragraph in a Birmingham paper, which, I may say, entirely exaggerates my powers but is otherwise correct.

Barrie and Armstrong

I am not surprised that in the matter of Mr Armstrong's conduct in bowling two consecutive overs from different ends, no reference has been made to the important precedent which on a similar occasion Sir James Barrie failed to establish (writes a correspondent of the *Nation*). The occasion was his captaincy (at Broadway, in Worcestershire) of an eleven of writers against a strong team of alleged artists. The circumstances were these. One side had compiled seventy-two runs, chiefly, if not wholly, contributed by Sir Arthur Conan Doyle.

The sun-worshippers had thereupon responded with an equal number of runs for the loss of all but their last wicket. The ninth wicket had fallen to the last ball of Sir Arthur's over, the other eight having succumbed to the same performer, then in his prime. Actuated, apparently, by the belief that Sir Arthur was the only bowler of his side capable of taking or reaching a wicket, even in Worcestershire, Sir James thereupon put him on at the opposite end. Before, however, he could take a practice ball, a shout was heard from the artists' pavilion, and the nine unengaged players were seen issuing from it to contest our captain's decision. After an exciting contest, it was ultimately given in their favour, with the result that the first ball of the new bowler was hit for two, assisted by overthrows, and the innings and match were won by the artists.

Of Barrie's team I remember that it was printed at the bottom of our cards that the practice ground was in the *National Observer* office. Mr Abbey, the famous artist, usually captained against Barrie, and it was part of the agreement that each should have a full pitch to leg just to start his score. I remember my horror when by mistake I bowled a straight first ball to Abbey, and so broke the unwritten law as well as the wicket. Abbey knew nothing of the game, but Barrie was no novice. He bowled an insidious left-hand good-length ball coming from leg which was always likely to get a wicket.

Talking of bowling, I have twice performed the rare feat of getting all ten wickets. Once it was against a London club, and once I ran through the side of a Dragoon regiment at Norwich. My best performance at Lord's was seven wickets for fifty-one against Cambridgeshire in 1904.

Of fencing my experience has been limited, and yet I have seen enough to realise what a splendid toughening exercise it is. I nearly had an ugly mishap when practising it. I had visited a medical man in Southsea who was an expert with the foils, and at his invitation had a bout with him. I had put on the mask and glove, but was loath to have the trouble of fastening on the heavy chest plastron. He insisted, however, and his insistence saved me from an awkward wound, for, coming in heavily upon a thrust, his foil broke a few inches from the end, and the sharp point thus created went deeply into the pad which covered me. I learned a lesson that day.

On the whole, considering the amount of varied sport which I have done, I have come off very well as regards bodily injury. One finger broken at football, two at cricket (one after the other in the same season), the disablement of my knee – that almost exhausts it. Though a heavy man and quite an indifferent rider, I have never hurt myself in a fair selection of falls in the hunting field and elsewhere. Once, as I have narrated, when I was down, the horse kicked me over the eye with his forefoot, but I got off with a rather ragged wound, though it might have been very much more serious.

Indeed, when it comes to escapes, I have had more than my share of luck. One of the worst was in a motor accident, when the machine, which weighed over a ton, ran up a high bank, threw me out on a gravel drive below, and then, turning over, fell upon the top of me. The steering wheel projected slightly from the rest, and thus broke the impact and undoubtedly saved my life, but it gave way under the strain, and the weight of the car settled across my spine just below the neck, pinning my face down on the gravel, and pressing with such terrific force as to make it impossible to utter a sound. I felt the weight getting heavier moment by moment, and wondered how long my vertebrae could stand it. However, they did so long enough to enable a crowd to collect and the car to be levered off me. I should think there are few who can say that they have held up a ton weight across their spine and lived unparalysed to talk about it. It is an acrobatic feat which I have no desire to repeat.

There is plenty of sport in driving one's own motor and meeting the hundred and one unexpected roadside adventures and difficulties which are continually arising. These were greater a few years ago, when motors were themselves less solidly and accurately constructed, drivers were less skilled, and frightened horses were more in evidence. No invention of modern civilisation has done so much for developing a man's power of resource and judgement as the motor. To meet and overcome a sudden emergency is the best of human training, and if a man is his own driver and mechanician on a fairly long journey he can hardly fail to have some experience of it.

I well remember in the early days of motoring going up to Birmingham to take delivery of my new twelve-horsepower Wolseley. I had invested in the sort of peaked yachting cap which was considered the correct badge of the motorist in those days, but as I paced the platform of New Street Station a woman removed any conceit I might have over my headgear, by asking me peremptorily how the trains ran to Walsall. She took me for one of the officials. I got the car safely home, and no doubt it was a good car as things went at that time, but the secret of safe brakes had not yet been discovered, and my pair used to break as if they were glass. More than once I have known what it is to steer a car when it is flying backwards under no control down a winding hill. Looking back at those days it seems to me that I was under the car nearly as much as on the top of it, for every repair had to be done from below. There were few accidents, from smashing my differential, seizing my engines and stripping my gears, which I have not endured. It was a chain-driven machine, and I can well remember one absurd incident when the chain jumped the cogs and fell off. We were on a long slope of three miles and ran on with the engine turned off quite unconscious of what had occurred. When we reached level ground the car naturally stopped, and we got out, opened the bonnet, tested the electricity and were utterly puzzled as to what was amiss, when a yokel in a cart arrived waving our motive power over his head. He had picked it up on the road.

Our descendants will never realise the terror of the horses at this innovation, nor the absurd scenes which it caused. On one occasion I was motoring down a narrow lane in Norfolk, with my mother in the open tonneau. Coming round a curve we came upon two carts, one behind the other. The leading horse, which had apparently never seen a motor before, propped his forelegs out, his ears shot forward, his eyes stared rigidly and then in a moment he whirled round, ran up the bank, and tried to escape behind his comrade. This he could have done but for the cart, which he also dragged up the bank. Horse and cart fell sideways on the other horse and cart, and there was such a mixture that you could not disentangle it. The carts were full of turnips and these formed a top dressing over the interlaced shafts and the struggling horses. I sprang out and was trying to help the enraged farmer to get something right end up, when I glanced at my own car which was almost involved in the pile. There was my dear old mother sitting calmly knitting in the midst of all the chaos. It was really like something in a dream.

My most remarkable motor-car experience was when I drove my own sixteen-horsepower Dietrich-Lorraine in the International Road Competition organised by Prince Henry of Prussia in 1911. This affair is discussed later, when I come to the preludes of war. I came away from it with sinister forebodings. The impression left on my mind by the whole incident is shown by the fact that one of the first things I did when I got to London was to recommend a firm of which I am director to remove a large sum which it had lying in Berlin. I have no doubt that it would have continued to lie there and that we might have lost it. As to the contest itself it ended in a British victory, which was owing to the staunch way in which we helped each other when in difficulties, while the Germans were more a crowd of individuals than a team. Their cars were excellent and so was their driving. My own little car did very well and only dropped marks at Sutton Bank in Yorkshire, that terrible hill, one in three at one point, with a hairpin bend. When we finally panted out our strength I put my lightweight chauffeur to the wheel, ran round, and fairly boosted her up from behind, but we were fined so many marks for my leaving the driving wheel. Not to get up would have meant three times the forfeit, so my tactics were well justified.

No doubt the coming science of aviation will develop the same qualities as motor driving to an even higher degree. It is a form of sport in which I have only aspirations and little experience. I had one balloon ascent in which we covered some twenty-five miles and ascended six thousand feet, which was so delightful an expedition that I have always been eager for another and a longer one. A man has a natural trepidation the first time he leaves the ground, but I remember that, as I stood by the basket with the gas bag swinging about above me and the assistants clinging to the ropes, someone pointed out an elderly gentleman and said: 'That is the famous Mr So-and-So, the aeronaut.' I saw a venerable person and I asked how many ascents he had made. 'About a thousand,' was the answer. No eloquence or reasoning could have convinced me so completely that I might get into the basket with a cheerful mind, though I will admit that for the first minute or so one feels very strange, and keeps an uncommonly tight grip of the side-ropes. This soon passes, however, and one is lost in the wonder of the prospect and the glorious feeling of freedom and detachment. As in a ship, it is the moment of nearing land once more which is the moment of danger – or, at least, of discomfort; but beyond a bump or two, we came to rest very quietly in the heart of a Kentish hop-field.

I had one aeroplane excursion in rather early days, but the experience was not entirely a pleasant one. Machines were under-engined in those days and very much at the mercy of the wind. We went up at Hendon – May 25, 1911, the date – but the machine was a heavy biplane, and though it went downwind like a swallow it was more serious when we turned and found, looking down, that the objects below us were stationary or even inclined to drift backwards. However, we got back to the field at last, and I think the pilot was as relieved as I. What impressed me most was the terrible racket of the propeller, comparing so unfavourably with the delicious calm of the balloon journey.

There is one form of sport in which I have, I think, been able to do some practical good, for I can claim to have been the first to introduce skis into the Grisons division of Switzerland, or at least to demonstrate their practical utility as a means of getting across in winter from one valley to another. It was in 1894 that I read Nansen's account of his crossing of Greenland, and thus became interested in the subject of skiing. It chanced that I was compelled to spend that winter in the Davos valley, and I spoke about the matter to Tobias Branger, a sporting tradesman in the village, who in turn interested his brother. We sent for skis from Norway, and for some weeks afforded innocent amusement to a large number of people who watched our awkward movements and complex tumbles. The Brangers made much better progress than I. At the end of a month or so we felt that we were getting more expert, and determined to climb the Jacobshorn, a considerable hill just opposite the Davos Hotel. We had to carry our unwieldy skis upon our backs until we had passed the fir trees which line its slopes, but once in the open we made splendid progress, and had the satisfaction of seeing the flags in the village dipped in our honour when we reached the summit. But it was only in returning that we got the full flavour of skiing. In ascending you shuffle up by long zigzags, the only advantage of your footgear being that it is carrying you over snow which would engulf you without it. But coming back you simply turn your long toes and let yourself go, gliding delightfully over the gentle slopes, flying down the steeper ones, taking an occasional cropper, but getting as near to flying as any earthbound man can. In that glorious air it is a delightful experience.

Encouraged by our success with the Jacobshorn, we determined to show the utility of our accomplishment by opening up communications with Arosa, which lies in a parallel valley and can only be reached in winter by a very long and roundabout railway journey. To do this we had to cross a high pass, and then drop down on the other side. It was a most interesting journey, and we felt all the pride of pioneers as we arrived in Arosa.

I have no doubt that what we did would seem absurdly simple to Norwegians or others who were apt at the game, but we had to find things out for ourselves and it was sometimes rather terrifying. The sun had not yet softened the snow on one sharp slope across which we had to go, and we had to stamp with our skis in order to get any foothold. On our left the snow slope ended in a chasm from which a blue smoke or fog rose in the morning air. I hardly dared look in that direction, but from the corner of my eye I saw the vapour of the abyss. I stamped along and the two gallant Switzers got on my left, so that if I slipped the shock would come upon them. We had no rope by which we could link up. We got across all right and perhaps we exaggerated the danger, but it was not a pleasant experience.

Then I remember that we came to an absolute precipice, up which no doubt the path zigzags in summer. It was not of course perpendicular, but it seemed little removed from it, and it had just slope enough to hold the snow. It looked impassable, but the Brangers had picked up a lot in some way of their own. They took off their skis, fastened them together with a thong, and on this toboggan they sat, pushing themselves over the edge and going down amid a tremendous spray of flying snow. When they had reached safety they beckoned to me to follow. I had done as they did and was sitting on my skis preparatory to launching myself when a fearsome thing happened, for my skis shot from under me, flew down the slope and vanished in huge bounds among the snow mounds beyond. It was a nasty moment, and the poor Brangers stood looking up at me some hundreds of feet below me in a dismal state of mind. However, there was no possible choice as to what to do, so I did it. I let myself go over the edge, and came squattering down, with legs and arms extended to check the momentum. A minute later I was rolling covered with snow at the feet of my guides, and my skis were found some hundreds of yards away, so no harm was done after all.

I remember that when we signed the hotel register Tobias Branger filled up the space after my name, in which the new arrival had to describe his profession, by the word 'Sportesmann', which I took as a compliment. It was at any rate more pleasant than the German description of my golf clubs, which went astray on the railway and turned up at last with the official description of 'Kinderspieler' (child's toys) attached to them. To return to the skis they are no doubt in very general use, but I think I am right in saying that these and other excursions of ours first demonstrated their possibilities to the people of the country and have certainly sent a good many thousands of pounds since then into Switzerland. If my rather rambling career in sport has been of any practical value to anyone, it is probably in this matter, and also, perhaps, in the opening up of miniature rifle-ranges in 1901, when the idea was young in this country, and when my Hindhead range was the pioneer and the model for many others.

A pleasing souvenir of my work on rifle clubs is to be found in the Conan Doyle Cup, which was presented by my friend Sir John Langman and is still shot for every year at Bisley by civilian teams.

On the whole as I look back there is no regret in my mind for the time that I have devoted to sport. It gives health and strength, but above all it gives a certain balance of mind without which a man is not complete. To give and to take, to accept success modestly and defeat bravely, to fight against odds, to stick to one's point, to give credit to your enemy and value your friend – these are some of the lessons which true sport should impart.

25

To the Rocky Mountains in 1914

New York – Baseball – Francis Parkman – Ticonderoga – Prairie Towns –
Procession of Ceres – Relics of the Past – A Moose – Prospects for
Emigrants – Jasper Park – The Great Divide – Algonquin Park

In 1914, with little perception of how near we were to the greatest event
of the world's history, we accepted an invitation from the Canadian
government to inspect the National Reserve at Jasper Park in the
Northern Rockies. The Grand Trunk Railway (Canadian) made matters
easy for us by generously undertaking to pass us over their system and to
place a private railroad car at our disposal. This proved to be a gloriously
comfortable and compact little home consisting of a parlour, a dining-
room and a bedroom. It belonged to Mr Chamberlin, the president of
the line, who allowed us the use of it. Full of anticipation we started off in
May upon our long and pleasant journey. Our first point was New York,
where we hoped to put in a week of sightseeing, since my wife had never
been to America. Then we were to go north and meet our kind hosts of
Canada. At the Plaza Hotel of New York we found ourselves in pleasant
quarters for a hectic week. Here are a few impressions.

We went to see a baseball game at New York – a first-class match, as
we should say – or 'some ball', as a native expert described it. I looked
on it all with the critical but sympathetic eyes of an experienced though
decrepit cricketer. The men were fine fellows, harder looking than
most of our professionals – indeed they train continually, and some of
the teams had even before the days of prohibition to practise complete
abstinence, which is said to show its good results not so much in
physical fitness as in the mental quickness which is very essential in the
game. The catching seemed to me extraordinarily good, especially the
judging of the long catches by the 'bleachers', as the outfields who are
far from any shade are called. The throwing in is also remarkably hard
and accurate, and, if applied to cricket, would astonish some of our
batsmen. The men earn anything from a thousand to fifteen hundred
pounds in the season. This money question is a weak point of the game,

as it is among our own soccer clubs, since it means that the largest purse has the best team, and there is no necessary relation between the player and the place he plays for. Thus we looked upon New York defeating the Philadelphia Athletics, but there was no more reason to suppose that New York had actually produced one team than that Philadelphia had produced the other. For this reason the smaller matches, such as are played between local teams or colleges, seem to me to be more exciting, as they do represent something definite.

The pitcher is the man who commands the highest salary and has mastered the hardest part of the game. His pace is remarkable, far faster, I should say, than any bowling; but of course it is a throw, and as such would not be possible in the cricket field. I had one uneasy moment when I was asked in Canada to take the bat and open a baseball game. The pitcher fortunately was merciful, and the ball came swift but true. I steadied myself by trying to imagine that it was a bat which I held in my grasp and that this was a full toss, which asked to be hit over the ropes. Fortunately, I got it fairly in the middle and it went on its appointed way, whizzing past the ear of a photographer, who expected me to pat it. I should not care to have to duplicate the performance – nor would the photographer.

I took the opportunity when I was in New York to inspect the two famous prisons, The Tombs and Sing Sing. The Tombs is in the very heart of the city, and a gloomy, ill-boding place it is when seen from without. Within it is equally dismal. I walked round in a somewhat shamefaced way, for it makes you feel so when you encounter human suffering which you cannot relieve. Warders and prisoners seemed however to be cheerful enough, and there was an off-hand way of doing things which seemed strange after our rigid methods. A Chinese prisoner, for example, was standing at the bottom of the lift, and I heard the warder shout through the tube, 'Have you got room for another Chink in number three?' I had a talk with one strange Englishman who was barred in like a wild beast. He spoke of the various prisons, of which he had a wide acquaintance, exactly as if they were hotels which he was recommending or condemning. 'Toronto is a very poor show. The food is bad. I hope I may never see Toronto Gaol again. Detroit is better. I had quite a pleasant time in Detroit.' And so on. He spoke and looked like a gentleman, but I could quite imagine, in spite of his genial manner, that he was a dangerous crook. When I left him he said: 'Well, bye-bye! Sorry you have to go! We can't all be out and about, can we?'

In the same week I went to Sing Sing, the State Penitentiary, which is some twenty miles from the city on the banks of the Hudson. It is an ancient building, dating from the middle of last century, and it certainly should be condemned by a rich and prosperous community. By a strange coincidence the convicts were having one of their few treats in the year that day, and I was able to see them all assembled together in the great hall, listening to a music-hall troupe from New York. Poor devils, all the forced, vulgar gaiety of the songs and the antics of half-clad women must have provoked a terrible reaction in their minds! Many of them had, I observed, abnormalities of cranium or of features which made it clear that they were not wholly responsible for their actions. There was a good sprinkling of coloured men among them. Here and there I noticed an intelligent and even a good face. One wondered how they got there.

I was locked up afterwards in one of the cells – seven feet by four – and I was also placed in the electrocution chair, a very ordinary, stout, cane-bottomed seat, with a good many sinister wires dangling round it. I had a long talk with the governor, who seemed in himself to be a humane man, but terribly hampered by the awful building which he had to administer.

One morning of early June my 'Lady Sunshine' and I – (if I may be allowed to quote the charmingly appropriate name which the New York press had given to my wife) left New York for Parkman land, which I had long wished to explore. We were glad to get away as we had been considerably harassed by the ubiquitous and energetic American reporter.

This individual is really, in nine cases out of ten, a very good fellow, and if you will treat him with decent civility he will make the best of you with the public. It is absurd for travellers to be rude to him, as is too often the attitude of the wandering Briton. The man is under orders from his paper, and if he returns without results it is not a compliment upon his delicacy which will await him. He is out to see you and describe you, and if he finds you an ill-tempered, cantankerous curmudgeon, he very naturally says so and turns out some excellent spicy reading at your expense. The indignant Briton imagines that this is done in revenge. The reporter would not be human if it did not amuse him to do it, but it very often represents the exact impression which the vituperative traveller has made upon the pressman, himself as often as not an overworked and highly strung man.

Reminiscences of interviews are occasionally amusing. I can remember that on my previous visit I was approached one night by an interviewer in a very marked state of intoxication. He was so drunk that I wondered what in the world he would make of his subject, and I bought his paper next day to see. To my amusement I found that I had made the worst possible impression upon him. He had found no good in me at all. He may even have attributed to me his own weakness, like the Scotch toper who said: 'Sandy drank that hard that by the end of the evening I couldn't see him.'

To return to Parkman land. I am surprised to find how few Americans and fewer Canadians there are who appreciate that great historian at his true worth. I wonder whether any man of letters has ever devoted himself to a task with such wholehearted devotion as Francis Parkman. He knew the old bloody frontier as Scott knew the border marches. He was soaked in New England tradition. He prepared himself for writing about Indians by living for months in their wigwams. He was intimate with old French life, and he spent some time in a religious house that he might catch something of the spirit which played so great a part in the early history of Canada. On the top of all this he had the well-balanced, unprejudiced mind of the great chronicler, and he cultivated a style which was equally removed from insipidity and from affectation. As to his industry and resolution, they are shown by the fact that he completed his volumes after he had been stricken by blindness. It is hard to name any historian who has such an equipment as this. From his *Pioneers of France in the New World* to his *Conspiracy of Pontiac* I have read his twelve volumes twice over, and put some small reflection of them into my *Refugees*.

We explored not only the beautiful, tragic Lake George, but also its great neighbour Lake Champlain, almost as full of historical reminiscence. Upon this, level with the head of the smaller lake, stood Ticonderoga, the chief seat of the French-Canadian power. Some five miles separate it from Lake George, up which the British came buzzing whenever they were strong enough to do so. Once in front of the palisades of Ticonderoga, they met with heavy defeat, and yet once again, by the valour of the newly enrolled Black Watch, they swept the place off the map. I wonder if Stevenson had actually been there before he wrote his eerie haunting ballad – the second finest of the sort, in my opinion, in our literature. It is more than likely, since he spent some time in the neighbouring Adirondacks. Pious hands were restoring the old fort of Ticonderoga, much of which has been uncovered. All day we skirted Lake Champlain, into which the old French explorer first found his way, and where he made the dreadful mistake of mixing in Indian warfare, which brought the whole blood-thirsty vendetta of the five nations upon the young French settlements. Up at the head of the lake we saw Plattsburg, where the Americans gained a victory in the war of 1812. The sight of these battlefields, whether they mark British or American successes, always fills me with horror. If the war of 1776 was, as I hold, a glorious mistake, that of 1812 was a senseless blunder. Had neither occurred, the whole of North America would now be one magnificent undivided country, pursuing its own independent destiny, and yet united in such unblemished ties of blood and memory to the old country that each could lean at all times upon the other. It is best for Britishers, no doubt, that we should never lean upon anything bigger than ourselves. But I see no glory in these struggles, and little wisdom in the statesmen who waged them. Among them they split the race from base to summit, and who has been the gainer? Not Britain, who was alienated from so many of her very best children. Not America, who lost Canada and had on her hands a civil war which a united empire could have avoided. Ah well, there is a controlling force some-where, and the highest wisdom is to believe that all things are ordered for the best.

About evening we crossed the Canadian frontier, the Richelieu River, down which the old Iroquois scalping parties used to creep, gleaming coldly in the twilight. There is nothing to show where you have crossed that border. There is the same sort of country, the same cultivation, the same plain wooden houses. Nothing was changed save that suddenly I saw a little old ensign flying on a gable, and it gives you a thrill when you have not seen it for a time.

It is not until he has reached the prairie country that the traveller meets with new conditions and new problems. He traverses Ontario with its prosperous mixed farms and its fruit-growing villages, but the general effect is the same as in Eastern America. Then comes the enormous stretch of the Great Lakes, those wonderful inland seas, with great ocean-going steamers. We saw the newly built *Noronic*, destined altogether for passenger traffic, and worthy to compare, both in internal fittings and outward appearance, with many an Atlantic liner. The Indians looked in amazement at La Salle's little vessel. I wondered what La Salle and his men would think of the *Noronic*! For two days in great comfort we voyaged over the inland waters. They lay peaceful for our passage, but we heard grim stories of winter gusts and of ships which were never heard of more. It is not surprising that there should be accidents, for the number of vessels is extraordinary, and being constructed with the one idea of carrying the maximum of cargo, they appeared to be not very stable. I am speaking now of the whale-back freight carriers and not of the fine passenger service, which could not be beaten.

I have said that the number of vessels is extraordinary. I have been told that the tonnage passing through Sault Sainte Marie, where the lakes join, is greater than that of any port in the world. All the supplies and manufactures for the West move one way, while the corn of the great prairie, and the ores from the Lake Superior copper and iron mines move the other. In the autumn there comes the triumphant procession of the harvest. Surely in more poetic days banners might have waved and cymbals clashed and priests of Ceres sung their hymns in the vanguard as this flotilla of mercy moved majestically over the face of the waters to the aid of hungry Europe. However, we have cut out the frills, to use the vernacular, though life would be none the worse could we tinge it a little with the iridescence of romance.

We stopped at Sault Sainte Marie, the neck of the hourglass between the two great lakes of Huron and Superior. There were several things there which are worthy of record. The lakes are of a different level, and the lock which avoids the dangerous rapids is on an enormous scale; but beside it, unnoticed save by those who know where to look and what to look for, there is a little stone-lined cutting no larger than an uncovered drain – it is the detour by which for centuries the *voyageurs*, trappers and explorers moved their canoes round the *sault* or fall on their journey to the great solitudes beyond. Close by it is one of the old Hudson Bay log forts, with its fireproof roof, its loop-holed walls and every other device for Indian fighting. Very small and mean these things look by the side of the great locks and the huge steamers within them. But where would locks and steamers have been had these others not taken their lives in their hands to clear the way?

The twin cities of Fort William and Port Arthur, at the head of Lake Superior, form the most growing community of Canada. They call them twin cities, but I expect, like their Siamese predecessors, they will grow into one. Already the suburbs join each other, though proximity does not always lead to amalgamation or even to cordiality, as in the adjacent towns of St Paul and Minneapolis. When the little American boy was asked in Sunday school who persecuted St Paul, he 'guessed it was Minneapolis'. But in the case of Fort William and Port Arthur they are so evidently interdependent that it is difficult to believe that they will fail to coalesce; when they do, I am of opinion that they may grow to be a Canadian Chicago, and possibly become the greatest city in the country. All lines converge there, as does all the lake traffic, and everything from east to west must pass through it. If I were a rich man and wished to become richer, I should assuredly buy land in the twin cities. Though they lie in the very centre of the broadest portion of the continent, the water communications are so wonderful that an ocean-going steamer from Liverpool or Glasgow can now unload at their quays.

The grain elevators of Fort William are really majestic erections, and with a little change of their construction might be aesthetic as well. Even now the huge cylinders into which they are divided look at a little distance not unlike the columns of Luxor. This branch of human ingenuity has been pushed at Fort William to its extreme. The last word has been said there upon every question covering the handling of grain. By some process, which is far beyond my unmechanical brain, the stuff is even divided automatically according to its quality, and there are special hospital elevators where damaged grain can be worked up into a more perfect article.

By the way, it was here, while lying at a steamship wharf on the very edge of the city, that I first made the acquaintance of one of the original inhabitants of Canada. A cleared plain stretched from the ship to a wood some hundreds of yards off. As I stood upon deck I saw what I imagined to be a horse wander out of the wood and begin to graze in the clearing. The creature seemed ewe-necked beyond all possibility, and looking closer I saw to my surprise that it was a wild hornless moose. Could anything be more characteristic of the present condition of Canada – the great mechanical developments of Fort William within gunshot of me on one side, and this shy wanderer of the wilderness on the other? In a few years the dweller in the great city will read of my experience with the same mixture of incredulity and surprise with which we read the occasional correspondent's whose grandfather shot a wood-cock in Maida Vale.

The true division between the east and west of Canada is not the Great Lakes, which are so valuable as a waterway, but the five hundred miles of country between the lakes and Winnipeg. It is barren, but beautiful, covered with forest which is not large enough to be of value as lumber. It is a country of rolling plains covered with low trees with rivers in the valleys. The soil is poor. It is really a problem what to do with this belt, which is small according to Canadian distance, but is none the less broader than the distance between London and Edinburgh. Unless minerals are found in it, I should think that it will be to Canada what the Highlands of Scotland are to Britain – a region set apart for sport because it has no other economic use. The singular thing about this barren tree-land is that it quite suddenly changes to the fertile prairie at a point to the east of Winnipeg. I presume that there is some geological reason, but it was strange to see the fertile plain run up to the barren woods with as clear a division as there is between the sea and the shore.

And now one reached the west of Winnipeg and was on that prairie which means so much both to Canada and to the world. It was wonderfully impressive to travel swiftly all day from the early summer dawn to the latest evening light, and to see always the same little clusters of houses, always the same distant farms, always the same huge expanse stretching to the distant skyline, mottled with cattle, or green with the half-grown crops. You think these people are lonely. What about the people beyond them and beyond them, again each family in its rude barracks in the midst of the hundred and sixty acres which form the minimum farm? No doubt they are lonely, and yet there are alleviations. When men or women are working on their own property and seeing their fortune growing, they have pleasant thoughts to bear them company. It is the women, I am told, who feel it most, and who go prairie-mad. Now they have rigged telephone circles which connect up small groups of farms and enable the women to relieve their lives by a little friendly gossip, when the whole district thrills to the news that Mrs Jones has been in the cars to Winnipeg and bought a new bonnet. At the worst the loneliness of the prairie can never, one would think, have the soul-killing effect of loneliness in a town. 'There is always the wind on the heath, brother.' Besides, the wireless has now arrived, and that is the best friend of the lonely man.

Land is not so easily picked up by the emigrant as in the old days, when a hundred and sixty acres beside the railroad were given away free. There was still in 1914 free land to be had, but it was in the back country. However, this back country of today is always liable to be opened up by the branch railway lines tomorrow. On the whole, however, it seems to be more economical, if the emigrant has the money, to buy a partially developed well-situated farm than to take up a virgin homestead. That is what the American emigrants do who have been pouring into the country, and they know best the value of such farms, having usually come from exactly similar ones just across the border, the only difference being that they can get ten acres in Canada for the price of one in Minnesota or Iowa. They hasten to take out their papers of naturalisation, and make, it is said, most excellent and contented citizens. Their energy and industry are remarkable. A body of them had reached the land which they proposed to buy about the time that we were in the West; they had come over the border with their wagons, their horses, and their ploughs. Being taken to the spot by the land agent, the leader of the party tested the soil, cast a rapid glance over the general prairie, and then cried: 'I guess this will do, boys. Get off the ploughs.'

The agent who was present told me that they had broken an acre of the prairie before they slept that night. These men were German Lutherans from Minnesota, and they settled in the neighbourhood of Scott. The gains on the farms are very considerable. It is not unusual for a man to pay every expense which he has incurred, including the price of the land, within the first two years. After that, with decent luck, he should be a prosperous man, able to bring up a family in ease and comfort. If he be British, and desires to return to the Old Country, it should not be difficult for him to save enough in ten or twelve years to make himself, after selling his farm, more or less independent for life. That is, as it seems to me, an important consideration for many people who hesitate to break all the old ties and feel that they are leaving their motherland for ever.

So much about farms and farming. I cannot see how one can write about this western part and avoid the subject which is written in green and gold from sky to sky. There is nothing else. Nowhere is there any sign of yesterday – not a cairn, not a monument. Life has passed here, but has left no footstep behind. But stay, the one thing which the old life still leaves is just this one thing – footsteps. Look at them in the little narrow black paths which converge to the water – little dark ruts which wind and twist. Those are the buffalo runs of old. Gone are the Cree and Blackfoot hunters who shot them down. Gone, too, the fur-traders who bought the skins. Chief Factor MacTavish, who entered into the great Company's service as a boy, spent his life in slow promotion from Fort This to Fort That and made a decent Presbyterian woman of some Indian squaw, finally saw with horror in his old age that the world was crowding his wild beasts out of their pastures. Gone are the great herds upon which both Indian hunter and fur-trader were parasitical. Indian, trader and buffalo all have passed, and here on the great plains are these narrow runways as the last remaining sign of a vanished world.

Edmonton is the capital of the western side of the prairie, even as Winnipeg is of the eastern. I do not suppose the average Briton has the least conception of the amenities of Winnipeg. He would probably be surprised to hear that the Fort Garry Hotel there is nearly as modern and luxurious as any hotel in Northumberland Avenue. There were no such luxuries in 1914 in Edmonton. The town was in a strangely half-formed condition, rude and raw, but with a great atmosphere of energy, bustle and future greatness. With its railway connections and water-ways it is bound to be a large city. At the time of our visit the streets were full of out-of-works, great husky men, some of them of magnificent physique, who found themselves at a loss, on account of cessations in railroad construction. They told me that they would soon be re-absorbed, but meantime the situation was the rudest object-lesson in economics that I have ever witnessed. Here were these splendid men, ready and willing to work. Here was a new country calling in every direction for labour. How came the two things to be even temporarily disconnected? There could be but one word. It was want of capital. And why was the capital wanting? Why was the work of the railroads held up? Because the money market was tight in London – London which finds, according to the most recent figures, seventy-three per cent of all the moneys with which Canada is developed. Such was the state of things. What will amend it? How can capital be made to flow into the best channels? By encouragement and security and the hope of good returns. I never heard of any system of socialism which did not seem to defeat the very object which it had at heart. And yet it was surely deplorable that the men should be there, and that the work should be there, and that none could command the link which would unite them.

A line of low distant hills broke the interminable plain which has extended with hardly a rising for fifteen hundred miles. Above them was, here and there, a peak of snow. Shades of Thomas Mayne Reid, they were the Rockies – my old familiar Rockies! Have I been here before? What an absurd question, when I lived here for about ten years of my life in all the hours of dreamland. What deeds have I not done among redskins and trappers and grizzlies within their wilds! And here they were at last, glimmering bright in the rising morning sun. At least, I have seen my dream mountains. Most boys never do.

Jasper Park is one of the great national playgrounds and health resorts which the Canadian government with great wisdom has laid out for the benefit of the citizens. When Canada has filled up and carries a large population, she will bless the foresight of the administrators who took possession of broad tracts of the most picturesque land and put them for ever out of the power of the speculative dealer. The National Park at Banff has for twenty years been a Mecca for tourists. That at Algonquin gives a great pleasure-ground to those who cannot extend their travels beyond Eastern Canada. But this new Jasper Park is the latest and the wildest of all these reserves. Some years ago it was absolute wilderness, and much of it impenetrable. Now, through the energy of Colonel Rogers, trails have been cut through it in various directions, and a great number of adventurous trips into country which is practically unknown can be carried out with ease and comfort. The packer plays the part of a dragoman in the East, arranging the whole expedition, food, cooking and everything else on inclusive terms; and once in the hands of a first-class Rocky Mountain packer, a man of the standing of Fred Stephens or the Otto Brothers, the traveller can rely upon a square deal and the companionship of one whom he will find to be a most excellent comrade. There is no shooting in the park – it is a preserve for all wild animals – but there is excellent fishing, and everywhere there are the most wonderful excursions, where you sleep at night under the stars upon the balsamic fir branches which the packer gathers for your couch. I could not imagine an experience which would be more likely to give a freshet of vitality when the stream runs thin. For a week we lived the life of simplicity and nature.

The park is not as full of wild creatures as it will be after a few years of preservation. The Indians who lived in this part rounded up everything that they could before moving to their reservation. But even now, the bear lumbers through the brushwood, the eagle soars above the lake, the timber wolf still skulks in the night, and the deer graze in the valleys. Above, near the snow-line, the wild goat is not uncommon, while at a lower altitude are found the mountain sheep. On the last day of our visit the rare cinnamon bear exposed his yellow coat upon a clearing within a few hundred yards of the village. I saw his clumsy good-humoured head looking at me from over a dead trunk, and I thanked the kindly Canadian law which has given him a place of sanctuary. What a bloodthirsty baboon man must appear to the lower animals! If any superhuman demon treated us exactly as we treat the pheasants, we should begin to reconsider our views as to what is sport.

The porcupine is another creature which abounded in the woods. I did not see any, but a friend described an encounter between one and his dog. The creature's quills are detachable when he wishes to be nasty, and at the end of the fight it was not easy to say which was the dog and which the porcupine.

Life in Jasper interested me as an experience of the first stage of a raw Canadian town. It will certainly grow into a considerable place, but at that time, bar Colonel Rogers' house and the station, there were only log-huts and small wooden dwellings. Christianity was apostolic in its simplicity and in its freedom from strife – though one has to go back remarkably early in apostolic times to find those characteristics. Two churches were being built, the pastor in each case acting also as head mason and carpenter. One, the cornerstone of which I had the honour of laying, was to be used in turn by several nonconformist bodies. To the ceremony came the Anglican parson, grimy from his labours on the opposition building, who prayed for the well-being of his rival. The whole function, with its simplicity and earnestness, carried out by a group of ill-clad men standing bareheaded in a drizzle of rain, seemed to me to have in it the essence of religion. As I ventured to remark to them, Kikuyu and Jasper can give some lessons to London.

We made a day's excursion by rail to the Tête Jaune Cache, which is across the British Columbian border and marks the watershed between East and West. Here we saw the Fraser, already a formidable river, rushing down to the Pacific. At the head of the pass stands the village of the railway workers, exactly like one of the mining townships of Bret Harte, save that the bad man is never allowed to be too bad. There is a worse man in a red serge coat and a stetson hat, who is told off by the state to look after him, and does his duty in such fashion that the most fire-eating desperado from across the border falls into the line of law. But apart from the gunman, this village presented exactly the same queer cabins, strange signs and gambling-rooms which the great American master has made so familiar to us.

And now we were homeward bound! Back through Edmonton, back through Winnipeg, back through that young giant, Fort William – but not back across the Great Lakes. Instead of that transit we took train, by the courtesy of the Canadian Pacific, round the northern shore of Superior, a beautiful wooded desolate country, which, without minerals, offers little prospect for the future. Some two hundred miles north of it, the Grand Trunk, that enterprising pioneer of empire, has opened up another line which extends for a thousand miles, and should develop a new corn and lumber district. Canada is like an expanding flower; wherever you look you see some fresh petal unrolling.

We spent three days at Algonquin Park. This place is within easy distance of Montreal or Ottawa, and should become a resort of British fishermen and lovers of nature. After all, it is little more than a week from London, and many a river in Finland takes nearly as long to reach. There is good hotel accommodation, and out of the thousand odd lakes in this enormous natural preserve one can find all sorts of fishing, though the best is naturally the most remote. I had no particular luck myself, but my wife caught an eight-pound trout, which Mr Bartlett, the courteous superintendent of the park, mounted, so as to confound all doubters. Deer abound in the park, and the black bear is not uncommon, while wolves can often be heard howling in the night-time.

What will be the destiny of Canada? Some people talk as if it were in doubt. Personally, I have none upon the point. Canada will remain exactly as she is for two more generations. At the end of that time there must be reconsideration of the subject, especially on the part of Great Britain, who will find herself with a child as large as herself under the same roof.

I see no argument for the union of Canada with the United States. There is excellent feeling between the two countries, but they could no more join at this period of their history than a great oak could combine with a well-rooted pine to make one tree. The roots of each are far too deep. It is impossible.

Then there is the alternative of Canada becoming an independent nation. That is not so impossible as a union with the States, but it is in the last degree improbable. Why should Canada wish her independence? She has it now in every essential. But her first need is the capital and the population which will develop her enormous territory and resources. This capital she now receives from the Mother Country to the extent in 1914 of seventy-three per cent, the United States finding fourteen per cent and Canada herself the remaining thirteen. Her dependence upon the Mother Country for emigrants, though not so great as her financial dependence, is still the greatest from any single source. Besides all this, she has the vast insurance policy which is called the British Navy presented to her for nothing – though honour demands some premium from her in the future – and she has the British diplomatic service for her use unpaid. Altogether, looking at it from the material side, Canada's interests lie deeply in the present arrangement. But there is a higher and more unselfish view which works even more strongly in the same direction. Many of the most representative Canadians are descendants of those United Empire Loyalists who in 1782 gave up everything and emigrated from the United States in order to remain under the flag. Their imperialism is as warm or warmer than our own. And everywhere there is a consciousness of the glory of the Empire, its magnificent future, and the wonderful possibilities of these great nations all growing up under the same flag with the same language and destinies. This sentiment joins with material advantages, and will prevent Canada from having any aspiration towards independence.

Yes, it will remain exactly as it is for the remainder of this century. At the end of that time her population and resources will probably considerably exceed those of the Mother Land, and problems will arise which our children's children may have some difficulty in solving. As to the French-Canadian, he will always be a conservative force – let him call himself what he will. His occasional weakness for flying the French flag is not to be resented, but is rather a pathetic and sentimental tribute to a lost cause, like that which adorns every year the pedestal of Charles at Whitehall.

I had some presentiment of coming trouble during the time we were in Canada, though I never imagined that we were so close to the edge of a world war. One incident which struck me forcibly was the arrival at Vancouver of a ship full of Sikhs who demanded to be admitted to Canada. This demand was resisted on account of the immigration laws. The whole incident seemed to me to be so grotesque – for why should sun-loving Hindus force themselves upon Canada – that I was convinced some larger purpose lay behind it. That purpose was, as we can now see, to promote discord among the races under the British flag. There can be no doubt that it was German money that chartered that ship.

I had several opportunities of addressing large and influential Canadian audiences, and I never failed to insist upon the sound state of the home population. The Canadians judge us too often by our ne'er-do-weels and remittance men, who are the sample Englishmen who come before them. In defence even of these samples it should be stated that they bulked very large in the first Canadian Division. I told the Canadians of our magnificent Boy Scout movement, and also of the movement of old soldiers to form a national guard. 'A country where both the old and the young can start new, unselfish, patriotic movements is a live country,' I said, 'and if we are tested we will prove just as good as ever our fathers were.' I did not dream how near the test would be, how hard it would press, or how gloriously it would be met.

And now I turn to the war, the physical climax of my life as it must be of the life of every living man and woman. Each was caught as a separate chip and swept into that fearsome whirlpool, where we all gyrated for four years, some sinking for ever, some washed up all twisted and bent, and all of us showing in our souls and bodies some mark of the terrible forces which had controlled us so long. I will show presently how the war reacted upon me, and also if one may speak without presumption, how in a minute way I in turn reacted upon the war.

26

The Eve of War

For a long time I never seriously believed in the German menace. Frequently I found myself alone, in a company of educated Englishmen, in my opinion that it was non-existent – or at worst greatly exaggerated. This conclusion was formed on two grounds. The first was that I knew it to be impossible that we could attack Germany save in the face of monstrous provocation. By the conditions of our government, even if those in high places desired to do such a thing, it was utterly impracticable, for a foreign war could not be successfully carried on by Great Britain unless the overwhelming majority of the people approved of it. Our foreign, like our home, politics are governed by the vote of the proletariat. It would be impossible to wage an aggressive war against any power if the public were not convinced of its justice and necessity. For this reason we could not attack Germany. On the other hand, it seemed to be equally unthinkable that Germany should attack us. One failed to see what she could possibly hope to gain by such a proceeding. She had enemies already upon her eastern and western frontiers, and it was surely unlikely that she would go out of her way to pick a quarrel with the powerful British Empire. If she made war and lost it, her commerce would be set back and her rising colonial empire destroyed. If she won it, it was difficult to see where she could look for the spoils. We could not give her greater facilities for trade than she had already. We could not give her habitable white colonies, for she would find it impossible to take possession of them in the face of the opposition of the inhabitants. An indemnity she could never force from us. Some coaling stations and possibly some tropical colonies, of which latter she already possessed abundance, were the most that she could hope for. Would such a prize as that be worth the risk attending such a war? To me it seemed that there could be only one answer to such a question.

I am still of the same opinion. But unhappily the affairs of nations are not always regulated by reason, and occasionally a country may be afflicted by a madness which sets all calculations at defiance. Then, again, I had looked upon the matter too much as between Great Britain and Germany. I had not sufficiently considered the chance of our being drawn in against our will in order to safeguard Belgium, or in order to stop the annihilation of France. It was so perfectly clear that Britain by her treaty obligations, and by all that is human and honourable, would fight if Belgium were invaded, that one could not conceive Germany taking such a step with any other expectation. And yet what we could not conceive is exactly what happened, for it is clear that the delusions as to our degeneration in character had really persuaded the Germans that the big cowardly fellow would stand by with folded arms and see his little friend knocked about by the bully. The whole idea showed an extraordinary ignorance of the British psychology, but absurd as it was, it was none the less the determining influence at the critical moment of the world's history. The influence of the lie is one of the strangest problems of life – that which is not continually influences that which is. Within one generation imagination and misrepresentation have destroyed the Boer republics and Imperial Germany.

One of my most remarkable pre-war experiences, which influenced my mind deeply, was my participation in the amateur motor race called the Prince Henry Competition. It was rather a reliability test than a race, for the car had to go some hundred and fifty miles a day on an average at its own pace, but marks were taken off for all involuntary stoppages, breakdowns, accidents, etc. Each owner had to drive his own car, and I had entered my little sixteen-horsepower landaulette. There were about forty British cars and fifty German, so that the procession was a very considerable one. Starting from Hamburg, the watering-place, our route ran through North Germany, then by steamer to Southampton, up to Edinburgh and back to London by devious ways.

The competition had been planned in Germany, and there can be no doubt in looking back that a political purpose underlay it. The idea was to create a false *entente* by means of sport, which would react upon the very serious political development in the wind, namely, the occupation of Agadir on the south-west coast of Morocco, which occurred on our second day out. As Prince Henry, who organised and took part in the competition, was also head of the German navy, it is of course obvious that he knew that the *Panther* was going to Agadir, and that there was a direct connection between the two events, in each of which he was a leading actor. It was a clumsy bit of stage management and could not possibly have been effective.

The peculiarity of the tour was that each car had an officer of the army or navy of the other nation as a passenger, to check the marks. Thus my wife and I had the enforced company for nearly three weeks of Count Carmer, Rittmeister of Breslau Cuirassiers, who began by being stiff and inhuman, but speedily thawed and became a very good fellow. The arrangements were very peculiar. Some British paper – the *Mail* if I remember right – had stated that the competition was really a device to pass a number of German officers through Great Britain in order to spy out the land. I think there may have been some truth in this, as our good count when we reached London went off to a hotel down in the East End, which seemed a curious thing for a wealthy *junker* to do. This criticism seems to have annoyed the Kaiser, and he said – or so it was reported – that none but junior officers should go as observers. I should think that ours was the senior of the lot, and the others were mostly captains and lieutenants. On the other hand, the British government, out of compliment to Prince Henry, had appointed the very best men available as observers. If there had been a sudden crisis over Agadir, and Germany had impounded us all, it would have been a national disaster and would have made a difference in a European war. Speaking from an imperfect memory, I can recall that we had General Grierson, Charles Munro, Rawlinson, I think, Captain – now General – Swinton of Tanks fame, Delme Ratcliffe, Colonel – now General – Holman, Major – now General – Thwaites, and many other notables both of the army and navy.

From the first relations were strained. There was natural annoyance when these senior officers found that their opposite numbers were youngsters of no experience. Then, again, at Cologne and Munster I understand that the German military did not show the proper courtesies, and certainly the hospitality which the whole party received until we reached England was negligible. The Germans themselves must have felt ashamed of the difference. Personally the competitors were not a bad set of fellows, though there were some bounders among them. We were not all above criticism ourselves.

Of the competition itself little need be said, as I have treated the sporting side of it elsewhere. Some of the Germans seemed to me to be a little mad, for they seemed consumed by the idea that it was a race, whereas it mattered nothing who was at the head of the procession or who at the tail, so long as you did the allotted distance in the allotted time. I saw a German bound into his car after some stoppage: 'How many ahead? Three Englishmen! Forwards! Forwards!' he cried. They barged into each other, dashed furiously round corners, and altogether behaved in a wild fashion, while our sedate old fellows pursued their course in a humdrum fashion and saved their marks. There were, however, some good fellows among the Germans. I have not forgotten how one of them, anonymously, used to place flowers in my wife's corner every morning.

But as an attempt at an *entente* it was a great failure. The British officer who was compelled to spend weeks with a carload of Germans was not expansive and refused to be digested. Some of the Germans, too, became disagreeable. I saw a large German car – they were all Benz and Mercedes, generally seventy to eighty horsepower – edge a little British car right off the road on to the grass track beside it. The driver of the British car was a pretty useful middle-weight boxer, but he kept his temper or there might have been trouble. There was very little love lost on either side, though I, as one of the few German-speaking competitors, did my very best to bring about a more cordial atmosphere. But war was in the air. Both sides spoke of it. Several of the British officers were either of the Intelligence branch, or had special German experience, and they were unanimous about it. My attempts towards peace were rejected. 'The only thing I want to do with these people is to fight them,' said Colonel Holman. 'Same here,' said the officer with him. It was a deep antagonism on either side. They were not only sure of the war, but of the date. 'It will be on the first pretext after the Kiel Canal is widened.' The Kiel Canal was finished in June 1914 and war came in August, so they were not far wrong. There was some little German chaff on the subject. 'Wouldn't you like one of these little islands?' I heard a German say as we steamed out past Heligoland and the Frisian Belt.

It was this experience which first made me take the threat of war seriously, but I could have persuaded myself that I was misled had it not been that I read soon afterwards Bernhardi's book *Germany and the Next War*. I studied it carefully and I put my impression of it into print in an article called 'England and the Next War', which appeared in the

Fortnightly Review in the summer of 1913. It lies before me now, as I write, and it is interesting to see how, as I projected my mind and my imagination over the possibilities of the future, I read much aright and some little wrong.

I began by epitomising Bernhardi's whole argument, and showing that, however we might disagree with it, we were bound to take it seriously, since he was undoubtedly a leader of a certain class of thought in his own country – that very military class which was now predominant. I demurred at his assumption that the German army in equal numbers must overcome the French. 'It is possible,' I remarked, 'that even so high an authority as General Bernhardi has not entirely appreciated how Germany has been the teacher of the world in military matters and how thoroughly her pupils have responded to that teaching. That attention to detail, perfection of arrangement for mobilisation, and careful preparation which have won German victories in the past may now be turned against her, and she may find that others can equal her in her own virtues.' I then examined Bernhardi's alleged grievances against Great Britain, and showed how baseless they were, and how little they could hope to gain by victory. I quoted one poisonous sentence: 'Even English attempts at a *rapprochement* must not blind us to the real situation. We may at most use them to delay the necessary and inevitable war until we may fairly imagine that we have some prospect of success.' 'This last sentence,' I remarked, 'must come home to some of us who have worked in the past for a better feeling between the two countries.'

I then gave an epitome of Bernhardi's plan of campaign as outlined in charming frankness in his volume, and I sketched out how far we were in a position to meet it and what were the joints in our armour. My general conclusions may be given as follows:

1   That invasion was not a serious danger and that the thought of it should not deflect our plans.
2   That if invasion becomes impossible then any force like the Territorials unless it is prepared to go abroad becomes useless.
3   That we should not have conscription save as a very last resource, since it is against the traditions of our people.
4   That our real danger lay in the submarine and in the airship, which could not be affected by blockade.

In discussing the submarine I said: 'What exact effect a swarm of submarines, lying off the mouth of the Channel and the Irish Sea, would produce upon the victualling of these islands is a problem which is beyond my conjecture. Other ships besides the British would be likely to be destroyed, and international complications would probably follow. I cannot imagine that such a fleet would entirely, or even to a very large extent, cut off our supplies. But it is certain that they would have the effect of considerably raising the price of whatever did reach us. Therefore, we should suffer privation, though not necessarily such privation as would compel us to make terms. From the beginning of the war every home source would naturally be encouraged, and it is possible that before our external supplies were seriously decreased, our internal ones might be well on the way to make up the deficiency.'

This did, I think, roughly outline the actual course of events.

5. That the submarines would affect military operations should we send a force to France or Belgium.
6. That therefore the Channel Tunnel was a vital necessity.
7. That all unnecessary expenses should be at once cut down, so that British credit should stand at its highest when the strain came.

These are only the general conclusions. The article attracted some attention, but I do not suppose that it had any actual influence upon the course of events. To reinforce it I wrote an imaginary episode called 'Danger' in *The Strand Magazine*, to show how even a small power might possibly bring us to our knees by the submarine. It was singularly prophetic, for not only did it outline the actual situation as it finally developed, but it contained many details – the zigzagging of the merchant ships, the use of submarine guns, the lying for the night on sandy bottoms, and so forth – exactly as they occurred. The article was sent round in proof to a number of high naval officers, mostly retired, for their opinions. I am afraid that the printed results, which I will not be so cruel as to quote, showed that it was as well they were retired, since they had no sense of the possibilities of the naval warfare of the future.

One result of my *Fortnightly* article was that General Henry Wilson, late Chief of the Staff College as he then was, desired to see me to cross-question me, and a meeting was arranged at the house of Colonel

Sackville-West, Major Swinton being also present. There, after luncheon, General Wilson machine-gunned me with questions for about an hour. He was fierce and explosive in his manner, and looked upon me, no doubt, as one of those pestilential laymen who insist upon talking of things they don't understand. As I could give reasons for my beliefs, I refused to be squashed, and when the interview was over I went straight down to the Athenaeum Club and wrote it all down from memory. It makes such curious reading that I give it exactly as I reported it that day, in dialogue, with one or two comments from Colonel Sackville-West. After saying with some asperity that I had made many statements which I could not substantiate, and so might give the public far too optimistic a view of the position, he said: 'Why do you say that we would never pay an indemnity to Germany?'

A. C. D.　　It is a matter of individual opinion. I go upon history and upon the spirit of our people.

GEN. W.　　Had not France equal spirit in 1870? How is it that they paid an indemnity?

A. C. D.　　Because Germany was sitting on the top of them, and she had to pay to get from under.

GEN. W.　　Why may she not sit on the top of us?

A. C. D.　　Because we live on an island and she cannot occupy us in the same way.

COL S.-W.　I believe a little pressure on London would cause us to pay an indemnity.

A. C. D.　　The man who suggested it would get hanged.

COL S.-W.　They would hang the man who made the war.

A. C. D.　　No, they would back him but hang the traitor.

GEN. W.　　You say that they would gain nothing by war. What about the carrying trade of the world?

A. C. D.　　The carrying trade depends on economic questions and upon geographical situation. For example, the Norwegians, who have no fleet, are one of the principal carriers.

GEN. W.　　At least they could starve us out if they held the seas.

A. C. D.　　Well, that is where my tunnel would come in; but of course I am entirely with you as to the need of holding the seas.

GEN. W.　　Well, now, you admit that we must go to the help of France?

A. C. D.　　Certainly.

GEN. W.　　But what can six divisions do?

A. C. D.   Well, my point is that six divisions with a tunnel are better than six divisions without a tunnel.

Col S.-W.   If we have a tunnel we must have a force worth sending to send through it.

A. C. D.   If you are going to couple the tunnel with compulsory service, you will get neither one nor the other.

Gen. W.   I think, so far as submarines go, that the British patrols would make it a very desperate service. Some desperate man might get his boat through.

A. C. D.   Some desperate man might command a flotilla and get it through.

Gen. W.   Many things seem possible theoretically which cannot be done in practice, but no doubt there is a danger there. In your view the Territorials are simply a support for the fighting army?

A. C. D.   Yes.

Gen. W.   But they are too untrained to go into action.

A. C. D.   They would be reserves and have time to train.

Gen. W.   Your idea of troops coming back in case of a raid through the tunnel is impossible. You could not withdraw troops in that way from their positions.

A. C. D.   Well, with all respect, I do not believe either in a raid or in an invasion.

Gen. W.   A war with Germany would be short and sharp – seven months would see it finished.

A. C. D.   You mean, no doubt, the continental part. I could imagine the naval part lasting ten years.

Col S.-W.   If your fleet was crushed, you would have to give in.

A. C. D.   A fleet can never be annihilated as an army is. There always remain scattered forces which can go on fighting. I don't think we need give in because the fleet is crushed.

Gen. W.   You don't suppose that the Englishman is a better soldier by nature than the Frenchman or the German?

A. C. D.   At least he is a volunteer.

Gen. W.   How would that affect the matter?

A. C. D.   I think he would rally better if he were beaten. There would be no end to his resistance, like the North in the American War.

Gen. W.   Don't you think, if war were declared with Germany, that the public, fearing an invasion, would clamour against any regular troops going abroad at all?

A. C. D.   I think the public would leave it to the War Office. In the South African War they allowed our troops to go six thousand miles away, and yet there was a danger of a European coalition.

Col S.-W.   But our navy was supreme then.

A. C. D.   Not against a coalition.

Gen. W.   When Cervera's fleet got loose, the Americans would not allow their troops to embark.

Col S.-W.   Even the Pacific coast was terrified.

A. C. D.   Well, surely that is the *reductio ad absurdum*.

Col S.-W.   Still, the fact remains.

Gen. W.   If we could send fifteen divisions we could stop a war.

A. C. D.   But that means compulsory service.

Gen. W.   Why not?

A. C. D.   Because I am convinced that you could not get it. I have twice stood for Parliament, and I am sure no candidate would have a chance on such a platform.

Gen. W.   Out descendants will say, 'Well, you saw the danger, and yet you made no effort.'

A. C. D.   Well, we have doubled our estimates. Surely that is an effort and must represent power somewhere.

We parted quite good friends, but the general's evident desire to rope me in as a compulsory-service man was vain. I venture to think that Lord Roberts's efforts in that direction were a great mistake, and that if he had devoted the same great energy to the line of least resistance, which was the Territorial force, we could have had half a million in the ranks when war broke out.

From the time that I was convinced by my experiences at the Prince Henry race and by carefully reading German literature that a war was really brewing, I naturally began to speculate as to the methods of attack and of defence. I have an occasional power of premonition, psychic rather than intellectual, which exercises itself beyond my own control, and which when it really comes is never mistaken. The danger seems to be that my own prejudice or reasonings may interfere with it. On this occasion I saw as clearly as possible what the course of a naval war between England and Germany would be. I had no doubt at all that our greatest danger – a desperately real one – was that they would use their submarines in order to sink our food ships, and that we might be starved into submission. Even if we won every fleet action, this unseen enemy would surely bring us to our knees. It all worked out in exact detail in my mind – so much so that Admiral Capelle mentioned my name afterwards in the Reichstag, and said that only I had accurately seen the economic form which the war would assume. This was perhaps true, so far as the economic side went, but Sir Percy Scott had spoken with far more authority than I on the growing power of the submarines in warfare.

I was made very uneasy by this line of thought, and all the more so because I asked several naval officers for some reassurance and could get none. One of them, I remember, said that it was all right because we should put a boom across the Channel, which seemed to me like saying that you could keep eels from going down a river by laying a plank across it. Among others I spoke to Captain Beatty, as he then was, whom I met at a weekend party at Knole, and though he could give me no reassurance about submarines he impressed me by his vivid and alert personality, and I felt that a navy with such men in command was safe enough where fighting was concerned. It could not, however, fill the platter if there was no loaf to place upon it. I pondered the matter, and could only see three palliatives, and no cure.

The first was to encourage home growth by a bonus or by a tariff. But here our accursed party politics barred the way, as I had learned only too clearly after spending a thousand pounds in fighting the Hawick Burghs in order to get some form of agricultural protection.

The second was to meet submarines by submarine food-carriers. I think that this may prove the final solution, but the ships were not yet planned, far less launched.

The third and most obvious was the Channel Tunnel, or tunnels for preference. I had supported this scheme for years, and felt that as a nation we had made fools of ourselves over it, exactly as we did over the Suez Canal. If we were an island the size of the Wight such timidity would be intelligible, but the idea of a great country being invaded through a hole in the ground twenty-seven miles long seemed to me the most fantastic possible, while the practical use of the tunnel both for trade and for tourists was obvious. But now I saw that far more serious issues were at stake, for if we were held up by submarines, and if France was either neutral or our ally, we could land all the Eastern portion of our supplies, which is not inconsiderable, at Marseilles and so run them safely to London without breaking bulk. When I put this forward in the press some military critic said: 'But if the submarines could hold up the Channel they could hold up the Mediterranean also.' This did not seem a good argument, because Germany was the possible enemy and it had no port in the Mediterranean, while the radius of submarine action at that time was not great enough to allow them to come so far. So strongly did I feel about the need for a Channel Tunnel in view of the coming war that I remember writing three memoranda and sending one to the army, one to the navy, and one to the Council of Imperial Defence. Of course I got no satisfaction of any kind, but Captain – now General – Swinton, who was acting as secretary to the latter body, told me that he had read my paper and that it had 'set him furiously thinking'. I wrote to Lord Northcliffe also, without avail. I felt as if, like Solomon Eagle, I could go through London with a burning brazier on my head if I could only get people to understand the need for the tunnel. The whole discussion had taken the utterly impossible and useless turn towards compulsory service, and the things which were practical and vital were being missed.

I spoke in public about the tunnel when I could, and on one occasion, just a year before the war, I raised a discussion in *The Times*, Mr Ronald McNeill giving me an opening by declaring in the House that the project was a crazy one. There was also about that time a meeting in the City at the Cannon Street Hotel, where a very influential body of men supported the scheme. My speech, as reported next day in *The Times* in a very condensed form, ran thus:

Sir A. Conan Doyle said there were possibilities in a future war that rendered it a matter of vital national importance that the tunnel should be constructed without delay. The danger was that we were getting five-sixths of our food supplies from abroad, and submarine craft were developing remarkable qualities which were not generally realised. They were able to avoid a blockade squadron, and to pass under a patrol line of torpedo boats without their existence being even suspected. If they were sent to the line of our commerce and told to sink a ship, they would torpedo that ship for a certainty. What would be the condition of our food supplies if there were twenty-five hostile submarines off the Kent coast and twenty-five in the Irish Channel? The price of food would reach an almost prohibitive figure. The military correspondent of *The Times* was a great opponent of the

Channel Tunnel and was always running it down and mocking at it. But the other day he wrote an article on the Mediterranean, and, forgetting the Channel Tunnel, he said: 'We must remember that more than half the food supply of this country now comes from the Mediterranean.' If it came through the Mediterranean, and if it got to Marseilles and we had the Channel Tunnel, it was only a matter of management to get it through to London.

The military correspondent of *The Times*, who was presumably Colonel Repington, had an article next day deriding the scheme, and making light of my picture of submarines in the Channel. Well, we have lived to see them, and I wish my argument had proved less sound. Colonel Repington proved himself so clear-sighted an observer and commentator in the last war that he can be forgiven if, for once, he was on the wrong side; but if the Channel Tunnel had been put in hand at once after that meeting and rushed to completion, I wonder if it would be an exaggeration to say that a hundred million pounds would have been saved, while what it would have meant in evacuating wounded and in communications in stormy weather could not be represented in words. Imagine the convenience and saving of time and labour when munitions could be started at Woolwich and landed at Amiens without a break.

It has been argued that if the tunnel had been built the first swoop of the Germans would have brought them to the end of it and it would have been destroyed. But this will not bear examination, for it is based on the idea that we should have left the end unprotected. It would as a matter of fact have been the most natural fortress in the world, the strongest and the strangest, for it would be the only fortress where you could increase or withdraw your garrison at will, and introduce any supplies at any time you might desire. A very few forts and trenches on those convenient chalk slopes with their wide, smooth fields of fire, would hold the tunnel. In stretching their right wing as far as Amiens the Germans were very nearly cut off, and it was by a very great effort that Von Kluck saved it. If instead of Amiens he had reached Calais with sufficient forces for a siege he would have been unable to get away. An argument based upon the supposition that we should leave the mouth of the tunnel in Picardy as unprotected as the mouth of a coal mine in Kent is surely an unsound one. Now, in 1924, they are talking of building the tunnel. I wonder what our descendants will think of the whole business – probably what we think of the men who opposed the Suez Canal.

It is a most singular thing that our navy, with so many practical and clever men in it, with a genius like Winston Churchill at the head and another genius like Lord Fisher in continual touch, did not realise, until faced with actual results, some of the most important and surely most obvious points in connection with naval warfare. It came, I suppose, from the iron bonds of tradition, and that there were so many things to supervise, but the fact remains that a perfectly overwhelming case could be made out against the higher brain department of our senior service. A war with Germany was anticipated, and, as the public imagined, was prepared for, but save for the shipbuilding programme, which left us a narrow margin of safety, and for the concentration of our distant squadrons into British waters and the elimination of many useless craft which consumed good crews, what evidence is there of foresight? It was known, for example, that Scapa Flow and Cromarty were the two possible anchorages of the fleet in a long-distance blockade, and yet no attempt had been made to mount guns or to net the entrances, so that for months there was a possibility of a shattering disaster; and Jellicoe, with the prudence which always distinguished him, had to put to sea every night lest his fleet should present a sitter to a torpedo attack. We showed intelligence in sticking always to the heavier guns, but our mines were wretchedly inefficient, our rangefinders were very inferior and our shells proved to have less penetrating and explosive force.

But the worst thing of all was the utter want of imagination shown in picturing the conditions of modern naval warfare, which must surely be done before just preparation can be made. It was clear that the effect of armour protection on one side, and of the mine and the torpedo on the other, would mean that if the ship floated there would be little loss of life, but that she was very likely to sink, in which case the whole crew would go. Therefore provision must be made for the saving of everyone on board. The authorities, however, seem to have completely under-rated the dangers of the mine and torpedo, and centred their attention upon the surface naval action, where boats, being inflammable, would be a danger and where in any case they would probably be shot to pieces before the end of the fight. The pre-war idea was to throw the boats and every other wooden object overboard before the action began.

The very first day of naval warfare showed the importance of the mine, as on August 5 the Germans laid a minefield outside the mouth of the Thames which nearly blew up their own returning ambassador, Prince Lichnowsky, and did actually cause the destruction of one of our light vessels, the *Amphion*. It was clear that one of the great dangers of the sea lay in this direction, and it soon became equally clear that nothing had been done to think out some defence. Foresight would have anticipated this situation and would have set the brains of the younger naval officers at work devising some remedy. As a matter of fact the real solution had been roughly indicated by Colonel Repington in *Blackwood's Magazine* some four years before, in which he spoke of a device called 'the otter' used by poachers for gathering up lines, and suggested that something of the sort would gather up the lines to which mines are attached. After three years of war, and very many preventable losses, including the great battleship *Audacious*, the splendid auxiliary cruiser *Laurentic* with six millions in gold on board and many other fine vessels, the cure was found in the paravane, which was an adaptation of 'the otter'. After its adoption ships could cruise over a minefield with little fear of injury, and our squadrons were no longer confined to the narrow lanes which had been swept clear.

I was from the beginning greatly impressed by this danger, and I wrote early in the war both to the papers and the Admiralty, but my device was crude and clumsy compared to what was actually done. My idea was something like a huge trident or toasting fork which could be hauled up on the bows when the waters were safe, but could be pushed forward and dip down in front when there was danger, so as to explode any mine before the ship could actually reach it. Such an apparatus would be better than nothing, but still I quite admit that it was an inadequate solution of the problem. But at least it was an attempt – and no other attempt was visible for years afterwards.

But the particular instance of mines was a small consideration beside the huge permanent incredible fact that while it was clear that a battleship could suddenly go down like a kettle with a hole in it, dragging a thousand men down with it, there was no provision by which the lives of these men could be saved. It was really unbelievable until there came the terrible example when the three cruisers, *Hogue*, *Aboukir* and *Cressy*, were all put down in a single day. A young German lieutenant with twenty men had caused us more loss than we suffered at Trafalgar. To learn how the helpless men had nowhere to turn, and how they clung on to floating petrol tins as their only safety, should have been terrible reading to those whose want of foresight had brought about such a situation. It was a dreadful object-lesson, and there seemed no reason why it should not be often repeated. I had already commented in the press upon the situation which would arise in a general action, with ships sinking all round and no boats. I suggested that it might be possible to drop the boats before battle and to have them in tow of a steam launch which could bring them up if needed. Of course I saw all the difficulties and dangers of such a course, but if one took the word of the sailors that the boats were a danger on board then I could think of no other way of working it. When I wrote about it, several naval critics, notably Commander Jane, rapped me hard over the knuckles, and deplored the intrusion of landsmen into matters of which they knew nothing. But when this great catastrophe occurred, I realised that the protection must be individual rather than collective, and that one must ventilate the thing in public with such warmth that the authorities would be compelled to do something. If wooden boats were impossible, what about india-rubber collars which would at least hold the poor fellows above the waves until some help could reach them? I opened an agitation in several papers, notably the *Daily Mail* and the *Daily Chronicle*, and within a very few days – either *post hoc* or *propter hoc* – there was a rush order for a quarter of a million collars which could be inflated by the men themselves and which were henceforth to be part of their vital equipment. The *Hampshire Telegraph*, the best informed of naval papers, said:

The Navy has to thank Sir Conan Doyle for the new life-saving apparatus the Admiralty are supplying. Some weeks ago he asked if it was not possible to manufacture a simple and easily inflatable life-belt, and, thanks to the enterprise of a rubber-manufacturing firm, a swimming collar is now being supplied to the men of the fleet in the North Sea as fast as they can be turned out. The apparatus is exceedingly simple. It is made of rubber, enclosed in a stout web casing, and weighs complete under three ounces. It can be carried in the pocket and can be inflated in position round a man's neck in about ten seconds. Its effect is to keep the man's head above water indefinitely. There is little doubt that this swimming collar will result in the saving of many lives, and the Admiralty are to be congratulated upon the promptitude with which they have adopted the suggestion of Sir Conan Doyle.

I was by no means satisfied with this, however; for, however useful in calm water on a summer day, it was clear that men would soon perish by exhaustion in a rough winter sea, and the collars would only prolong their agony. If wooden boats took up too much room and were inflammable, how about india-rubber collapsible boats? I wrote in the *Daily Mail*: 'We can spare and replace the ships. We cannot spare the men. They *must* be saved, and this is how to save them. There is nothing so urgent as this. We can view all future disasters with equanimity if only the ship's company has a fair chance for its life.' Of course one recognised that there were some situations where nothing would avail. The *Formidable* was a case in point, which was torpedoed near Plymouth on January 1, 1915. Captain Miller, of the Brixham trawler which rescued seventy men, said to the *Daily Mail* representative that I was doing a national work in my efforts to get better life-saving appliances for the men of the navy. He remarked that in calm weather collapsible boats would be of use, but they could not possibly have lived in the seas which were breaking over the *Formidable*'s whaler. The weather here was exceptional, and one cannot hope to provide for every case.

The final result of the agitation was the provision of collars, of safety waistcoats, and (as I believe) of a better supply of boats. I need hardly say that I never received a word of acknowledgment or thanks from the Admiralty. One is not likely to be thanked by a government department for supplementing its work. But it may be that some poor seaman struggling in the water sent me his good wish, and those are the thanks that I desired. There was nothing in the war which moved me more than the thought of the helpless plight of these gallant men who were sacrificed when they could so easily have been saved.

Like every man with Irish blood in his veins, I was deeply moved by the tragedy of Ireland during the war – her fine start, the want of tact with which it was met, her sad relapse, and finally her failure to rise to the great world crisis.

A letter which I value very much is one which I received from Major William Redmond just before his lamented death. What an abyss of evil Ireland would have been saved from had the spirit of this letter been the inspiration upon which she acted!

18.12.16

DEAR SIR ARTHUR CONAN DOYLE – It was very good of you to write
to me and I value very much the expression of your opinion. There
are a great many Irishmen today who feel that out of this War we
should try and build up a new Ireland. The trouble is men are so
timid about meeting each other halfway. It would be a fine memorial
to the men who have died so splendidly, if we could over their graves
build up a bridge between the North and South. I have been thinking
a lot about this lately in France – no one could help doing so when
one finds that the two sections from Ireland are actually side by side
holding the trenches! No words – not even your own – could do
justice to the splendid action of the new Irish soldiers. They never
have flinched. They never give trouble, and they are steady and sober.
Had poor Kettle lived he would have given the world a wonderful
account of things out there. I saw a good deal of Kettle, and we had
many talks of the Unity we both hoped would come out of the War. I
have been an extreme Nationalist all my life, and if others as extreme,
perhaps, on the other side will only come halfway, then I believe,
impossible as it may seem, we should be able to hit upon a plan to
satisfy the Irish sentiment and the Imperial sentiment at one and the
same time. I am sure you can do very much, as you already have done,
in this direction. I am going back for Christmas with the men I have
become attached very deeply to during the last two years.

    With many thanks for your letter,
    Yours very truly,

                              WILLIAM REDMOND, *Major*

If this letter, even now, were posted up by the Free State and Northern
governments at every crossroads of Ireland the spirit of Willie Redmond
might heal the wounds of the unhappy country.

27

A Remembrance of the Dark Years

Nightmares of the Morning – The Civilian Reserve –
The Volunteers – Domestic Life in Wartime – German Prisoners –
Cipher to our Prisoners – Sir John French – Empress Eugénie –
Miracle Town – Armour – Our Tragedy

I can never forget, and our descendants can never imagine, the strange
effect upon the mind which was produced by seeing the whole European
fabric drifting to the edge of the chasm with absolute uncertainty as to
what would happen when it toppled over. Military surprises, starvation,
revolution, bankruptcy – no one knew what so unprecedented an episode
would produce. It was all so evidently preventable, and yet it was so
madly impossible to prevent it, for the Prussians had stuck their monkey-
wrench into the machinery and it would no longer work. As a rule one
has wild dreams and wakes to sanity, but on those mornings I left sanity
when I woke and found myself in a world of nightmare dreams.

On August 4, when war seemed assured, I had a note from Mr
Goldsmith, a plumber in the village: 'There is a feeling in Crowborough that something should be done.' This made me laugh at first,
but presently I thought more seriously of it. After all, Crowborough
was one of a thousand villages, and we might be planning and acting
for all. Therefore I had notices rapidly printed. I distributed them and
put them at road corners, and the same evening (August 4) we held a
village meeting and started the Volunteers, a force which soon grew to
two hundred thousand men.

The old Volunteers had become extinct when the Territorials had
been organised some ten or twelve years before. But this new force
which I conceived was to be a universal one, where every citizen, young
and old, should be trained to arms – a great stockpot into which the
nation could dip and draw its needs. We named ourselves the Civilian
Reserve. No one, I reflected, could be the worse in such days for being
able to drill and to shoot, or for being assembled in organised units.
Government was too preoccupied to do anything, and we must show

initiative for ourselves. After I had propounded my scheme, I signed the roll myself, and a hundred and twenty men did the same. Those were the first men in the Volunteer Force. Next evening we assembled at the drill-hall, found out who could drill us, chose our non-commissioned officers and set to work to form ourselves into an efficient company. Gillette, my American actor friend, had got stranded in England, and he was an interested spectator on this occasion. For the time being I took command.

I had notified the War Office what we had done and asked for official sanction. We were careful not to stand in the way of recruiting and determined to admit none who could reasonably join up at once. When the plan began to work I wrote a description of our methods to *The Times*. As a consequence I received requests for our rules and methods from twelve hundred towns and villages. My secretary and I worked all day getting these off, and in many cases the enquiries led to the formation of similar companies.

For about a fortnight all went well. We drilled every day, though we had no weapons. At the end of that time there came a peremptory order from the War Office: 'All unauthorised bodies to be at once disbanded.' Unquestioning and cheerful obedience is the first law in time of war. The company was on parade. I read out the telegram and then said: 'Right turn! Dismiss!' With this laconic order the Civilian Reserve dissolved for ever.

But it had a speedy and glorious resurrection. There was a central body in London with some remote connection with the old Volunteer Force. Lord Desborough was chairman of this, and there could not have been a better man. The government put the formation of a volunteer force into the charge of this committee, to which I was elected. Mr Percy Harris was the secretary and showed great energy. I wrote to all the twelve hundred applicants referring them to this new centre, and we, the Crowborough body, now became the Crow-borough Company of the Sixth Royal Sussex Volunteer Regiment. That we were the first company in the country was shown by the *Volunteer Gazette* when a prize was awarded for this distinction. Under its new shape Captain St Quintin, who had been a soldier, became our leader, and Mr Gresson and Mr Druce, both of them famous cricketers, our lieutenants. Goldsmith was one of the sergeants, and I remained a full private for four years of war, and an extra half-year before we were demobilised. Our ranks fluctuated, for as the age limit of service gradually rose we passed many men into the regular army, but we filled up with new recruits, and we were always about a hundred strong. Our drill and discipline were excellent, and when we received our rifles and bayonets we soon learned to use them, nor were our marching powers contemptible when one remembers that many of the men were in their fifties and even in their sixties. It was quite usual for us to march from Crowborough to Frant, with our rifles and equipment, to drill for a long hour in a heavy marshy field, and then to march back, singing all the way. It would be a good fourteen miles, apart from the drill.

I have very pleasant recollections of that long period of service. I learned to know my neighbours who stood in the same ranks, and I hope that they also learned to know me as they could not otherwise. We had frequent camps, field days and inspections. On one occasion eight thousand of us were assembled, and I am bound to say that I have never seen a finer body of men, though they were rather of the police-constable than of the purely military type. The spirit was excellent, and I am sure that if we had had our chance we should have done well in action. But it was hard to know how to get the chance save in case of invasion. We were the remaining pivots of national life, and could only be spared for short periods or chaos would follow. But a week or two in case of invasion was well within our powers, and such a chance would have been eagerly hailed. No doubt our presence enabled the government to strip the country of regular troops far more than they would have dared otherwise to do. Twice, as Repington's *Memoirs* show, there was a question of embodying us for active service, but in each case the emergency passed.

I found the life of a private soldier a delightful one. To be led and not to lead was most restful, and so long as one's thoughts were bounded by the polishing of one's buttons and buckles, or the cleansing of one's rifle, one was quietly happy. In that long period I shared every phase of my companions' life. I have stood in the queue with my pannikin to get a welcome drink of beer, and I have slept in a bell-tent on a summer night with a Sussex yokel blissfully snoring upon each of my shoulders. Sometimes amusing situations arose. I remember a new adjutant arriving and reviewing us. When he got opposite to me in his inspection, his eyes were caught by my South African medal. 'You have seen service, my man,' said he. 'Yes, sir,' I answered. He was a little cocky fellow who might well have been my son so far as age went. When he had passed down the line, he said to our CO, St Quintin: 'Who is that big fellow on the right of the rear rank?' 'That's Sherlock Holmes,' said the CO. 'Good Lord!' said the adjutant, 'I hope he does not mind my "my manning" him!' 'He just loves it,' said St Quintin, which showed that he knew me.

The other big factor which covered the whole period of the war, and some time after it, was my writing the history of the European campaign, which I published volume by volume under the name of *The British Campaign in France and Flanders*. My information was particularly good, for I had organised a very extensive correspondence with the generals, who were by no means anxious for self-advertisement, but were, on the other hand, very keen that the deeds of their particular troops should have full justice done them. In this way I was able to be the first to describe in print the full battle line with all the divisions and even brigades in their correct places from Mons onwards to the last fight before the Armistice. When I think what a fuss was made in the old days when any correspondent got the account of a single colonial battle before his comrades, it is amazing to me that hardly a single paper ever commented, in reviewing these six successive volumes, upon the fact that I was really the only public source of supply of accurate and detailed information. I can only suppose that they could not believe it to be true. I had no help but only hindrance from the War Office, and everything I got was by means which were equally open to anyone else who took the trouble to organise them. Of course, I was bowdlerised and blue-pencilled by censors, but still the fact remains that a dozen great battle lines were first charted by me. I have since read the official account so far as it has gone, and find little to change in my own, though the German and French records are now available to broaden the picture. For the moment war literature is out of fashion, and my war history, which reflects all the passion and pain of those hard days, has never come into its own. I would reckon it the greatest and most undeserved literary disappointment of my life if I did not know that the end is not yet and that it may mirror those great times to those who are to come.

For the rest I had a great deal of literary propaganda work to do. Once it was the 'To Arms!' pamphlet, written in conjunction with Mr Smith, soon to become Lord Birkenhead. Once again it was an appeal for our ill-used prisoners. Sometimes Norway, sometimes South America, always the United States, needed treatment. As to my special missions, those I treat in separate chapters.

There are many small but very important details of domestic life during the war which have never been properly described, and could indeed best be described by a woman, for they were usually an invasion of her department. Our descendants will never realise how we were all registered and docketed and rationed, so that the state could give the least to and take the most from each of us. One had food-cards for practically everything, and the card only entitled you to get your meagre portion if it was to be had. Often it wasn't. I have been at a great lunch with half the grandees of the land, and the Prime Minister to speak. The fare was Irish stew and rice-pudding.

What could man ask for more, but it will need another war to bring it round again. There was a pleasing uncertainty about all meals. There was always a sense of adventure and a wonder whether you would really get something. It all made for appetite. Then there were the darkened windows, the sharp knocking of the police if the blind emitted any light, the vexatious summons for very small offences, the pulling down of every blind on the railway trains. At night one never knew what evil bird was flying overhead or what foul egg would be dropped. Once, as we sat in the theatre at Eastbourne, the whirr of a Zeppelin was heard above us. Half the audience slipped out, the lights were put out, and the play was finished with candles on the stage. When I was lecturing in London the same thing happened, and I finished my lecture in the dark.

Everyone found themselves doing strange things. I was not only a private in the Volunteers, but I was a signaller and I was for a time number one of a machine gun. My wife started a home for Belgian refugees in Crowborough. My son was a soldier, first, last, and all the time. My daughter Mary gave herself up altogether to public work, making shells at Vickers' and afterwards serving in a canteen. If I may quote a passage from my history:

> Grotesque combinations resulted from the eagerness of all classes to lend a hand. An observer has described how a peer and a prizefighter worked on the same bench at Woolwich, while titled ladies and young girls from cultured homes earned sixteen shillings a week at Erith and boasted in the morning of the number of shell-cases which they had turned and finished in their hours of night shift. Truly it had become a national war. Of all its memories none will be stranger than those of the peaceful middle-aged civilians who were seen eagerly reading

books of elementary drill in order to prepare themselves to meet the most famous soldiers in Europe, or of the schoolgirls and matrons who donned blue blouses and by their united work surpassed the output of the great death factories of Essen.

Every house had its vegetable garden and every poor man his allotment, that we might at the worst exist until we could win our peace. The want of sugar and the limitation of tea were the worst privations. My wife, greatly helped by a faithful servant, Jakeman, did wonders in saving food, and we always lived well within our legal rations. This did not save us once from a police raid, because some tea, sent us as a present from India, had arrived. We had already distributed a good deal of it, however, to our less fortunate neighbours, so we came well out of the matter.

I have one singular memory in having to guard German prisoners at work. The Volunteers had a turn at this work, and we spent the night at Lewes Prison. In the early morning, dark and misty, we were mustered and five prisoners handed over to each of us. Mine worked on a farm some four miles from the town, and thither I had to march them, walking behind them with my rifle on my shoulder. When I had reached the lonely country road, I thought I would get into human touch with these poor slouching wretches, who were still in their stained grey uniforms, and wearing their service caps with the bright red bands which formed a wonderful advertisement of the excellence of German dyes. I halted them, drew them up, and asked them their nationality. Three were from Württemburg and two from Prussia. I asked the Württemburgers how long they had been prisoners. They said, 'Fourteen months.' 'Then,' said I, 'you were taken by the Canadians at Ypres upon such and such a date.' They were considerably astonished, since I was simply a second-line Tommy from their point of view. Of course, I had the details of the war very clearly in my mind, and I knew that our one big haul of Württemburgers had been on that occasion. To this day they must wonder how I knew. I shall not forget that day, for I stood for eight hours leaning on a rifle, amid drizzling rain, while in a little gap of the mist I watched those men loading carts with manure. I can answer for it that they were excellent workers, and they seemed civil, tractable fellows as well.

It was in 1915 that I managed to establish a secret correspondence with the British prisoners at Magdeburg. It was not very difficult to do, and I dare say others managed it as well as I, but it had the effect of cheering them by a little authentic news, for at that time they were only permitted to see German newspapers. It came about in this way. A dear friend of my wife's, Miss Lily Loder Symonds, had a brother, Captain Willie Loder Symonds, of the Wiltshires, who had been wounded and taken in the stand of the 7th Brigade on the evening before Le Cateau. He was an ingenious fellow and had written home a letter which passed the German censor because it seemed to consist in the description of a farm, but when read carefully it was clear that it was the conditions of himself and his comrades which he was discussing. It seemed to me that if a man used such an artifice he would be prepared for a similar one in a letter from home. I took one of my books, therefore, and beginning with the third chapter – I guessed the censor would examine the first – I put little needle-pricks under the various printed letters until I had spelled out all the news. I then sent the book and also a letter. In the letter I said that the book was, I feared, rather slow in the opening, but that from Chapter 3 onwards he might find it more interesting. That was as plain as I dared to make it. Loder Symonds missed the allusion altogether, but by good luck he showed the letter to Captain the Honourable Rupert Keppel, of the Guards, who had been taken at Landrecies. He smelled a rat, borrowed the book, and found my cipher. A message came back to his father, Lord Albemarle, to the effect that he hoped Conan Doyle would send some more books. This was sent on to me, and of course showed me that it was all right. From that time onwards every month or two I pricked off my bulletin, and a long job it was. Finally, I learned that the British papers were allowed for the prisoners, so that my budget was superfluous. However, for a year or two I think it was some solace to them, for I always made it as optimistic as truth would allow – or perhaps a little more so, just to get the average right.

I had some dealings with general French, but only one interview with him. No one can help feeling a deep respect for the soldier who relieved Kimberley and headed off Cronje, or for the man who bore the first hard thrust of the German spear.

My only interview with the general was at the Horse Guards, when he talked very clearly about the military position, though most of what he said as to the changes which modern tactics and heavy guns had caused was rather self-evident. 'Your problem always is how to pass the wire and the machine guns. There is no way round. What is the good of talking of invading Austria from the south? You will find the same wire and the same machine guns. We may as well face it in Flanders as anywhere else.' This talk was shortly after Loos, when he had returned from the army and was at the head of Home Defence. 'If you want any point looked up for your history, mind you let me know and I will see that it is done.' This sounded very nice to me, who was in a perpetual state of wanting to know; but as a matter of fact I took it as a mere empty phrase, and so it proved when a week or two later I put it to the test. It was a simple question, but I never got any clear answer.

One pleasing incident occurred in 1917, when a Hull steam trawler which had been named after me, under the able handling of Skipper Addy and Lieutenant McCabe of the Naval Reserve, had an action with a heavily armed modern submarine, the fight lasting for some hours. The *Conan Doyle* was acting as flagship of a little group of trawlers, and though their guns were popguns compared with that of the German, they so peppered him that he was either sunk or took flight – anyhow, he vanished under the water. The little boat sent me its ship's bell as a souvenir of the exploit, and I sent some small remembrances in exchange. It was a fine exploit, and I was proud to be connected with it, even in so remote a way.

I have in my war chapters expressed my admiration for General Haig. On one occasion I called upon Lady Haig, when she was administering some private hospital at Farnborough. It was, so far as I could understand, one wing of the Empress Eugénie's house, and the empress invited me to lunch. There were present also Prince Victor Napoleon and his wife, who was, I think, a daughter of my old aversion, Leopold, King of the Belgians and Overlord of the Congo. The empress interested me deeply – a historical relic whom one would expect to study in old pictures and memoirs, yet there she was moving and talking before me. If Helen launched a thousand ships, Eugénie, by all accounts, did far more. Indeed, if the first German War was really from her inspiration, as Zola insists, she was at the root of all modern history. In spite of her great age, her face and figure preserved the lines of elegance and breed, the features clearly cut, the head set proudly upon the long neck. I glanced into her sitting-room as I passed the open door and noticed that she was engaged upon an enormous jigsaw puzzle, a thousand pieces if there were one. Children's toys engaged the mind which once played with empires. There is surely something fatal in that Spanish blood with its narrow fanatical religion and its masterful intolerance, magnificent but mediaeval like the Church which inspires it.

She talked very freely with me and in the most interesting manner.

It was surprising to see how fresh her mind was, and what curious information she had at her command. She told me, for example, that tetanus in France depended very much upon what soil had got into the wound, while that in turn depended upon what manures had been used for the soil – thus the percentage of tetanus cases would be quite different in a vine-growing district from in one where ordinary crops were cultivated. She spoke seriously about the war, but was confident as to the ultimate result. This graceful, withered flower in its strange setting was one of the outstanding memories of those days.

All sorts of queer odd jobs came to me as to many others in the war. I was, of course, prepared always to do absolutely anything which was suggested, though the suggestions were sometimes not very reasonable. One must not argue, but simply put one's whole weight, for what it is worth, into the scrum. Once I was directed to go up to Scotland and write up the great new munition works at Gretna, as the public needed reassurance upon the point. Pearson, the younger brother of Lord Cowdray, had built them, and they certainly deserved the name of 'Miracle Town', which I gave them in my article. The great difficulty always was to give our own people what they wanted and yet not to give the Germans that which they wanted also. Winston Churchill's remarkable memoirs – the best, in my opinion, of all the war books – have shown how heavily this pressed in high quarters. His volume is certainly a wonderful vindication of his term of office, and it was a loss to the country when he left it.

Churchill was very open to ideas and sympathetic to those who were trying for some ideal. I had pondered much over armour for the troops, and he commented on it in an inspiring letter, in which he said that the bullet-proof man and the torpedo-proof ship were our two great objects. I worked a good deal upon the question of shields, and wrote several articles about it in *The Times* and other papers, but the forces against us were strong. When I saw Mr Montague on the subject at the Ministry of Munitions, he said: 'Sir Arthur, there is no use your arguing here, for there is no one in the building who does not know that you are right. The whole difficulty lies in making the soldiers accept your views.'

One has, of course, to be reasonable on the point, and to admit that there is a limit to what a man can carry, and that greater weight means slower movement and therefore longer exposure. That is fully granted. But when the helmet in actual practice was found so useful, why should it not be supplemented by steel shoulder-guards, since the helmet might actually guide the bullets down on to the shoulders? And why not a plastron over the heart? The vital points in a man's anatomy are not really so numerous. If many a life was saved by a buckle or a cigarette-case, why should such protection not be systematised? And why in trench warfare should not strong breastplates be kept for the temporary use of any troops in the front line? I experimented with my own service rifle upon steel plates, and I was surprised to find how easy it was at twenty paces to turn a bullet. I am convinced that very many lives would have been saved had my views been adopted, and that the men in the hour of danger would have been only too glad to carry that part of their equipment.

The tank, however, was a device which carried the armour and the men also, so that it was an extension of these ideas. We can never be grateful enough to the men who thought out the tank, for I have no doubt at all that this product of British brains and British labour won the war, which would otherwise have ended in a peace of mutual exhaustion. Churchill, D'Eyncourt, Tritton, Swinton and Bertie Stern – these were in sober fact, divide the credit as you may, the men who played a very essential part in bringing down the giant.

Our household suffered terribly in the war. The first to fall was my wife's brother Malcolm Leckie, of the Army Medical Service, whose gallantry was so conspicuous that he was awarded a posthumous DSO. While he was actually dying himself, with shrapnel in his chest, he had the wounded to his bedside and bandaged them. Then came the turn of Miss Loder Symonds, who lived with us and was a beloved member of the family. Three of her brothers were killed and the fourth wounded. Finally, on an evil day for us, she also passed on. Then two brave nephews, Alec Forbes and Oscar Hornung, went down with bullets through the brain. My gallant brother-in-law, Major Oldham, was killed by a sniper during his first days in the trenches. And then finally, just as all seemed over, I had a double blow. First it was my Kingsley, my only son by my first marriage, one of the grandest boys in body and soul that ever a father was blessed with. He had started the war as a private, worked up to an acting captaincy in the 1st Hampshires and been very badly wounded on the Somme. It was pneumonia which slew him in London, and the same cursed plague carried off my soldier brother Innes, he who had shared my humble strivings at Southsea so many years ago. A career lay before him, for he was only forty and already adjutant-general of a corps, with the Legion of Honour and a great record of service. But he was called and he went like the hero he was. 'You do not complain at all, sir,' said the orderly. 'I am a soldier,' said the dying general. Thank God that I have since found that the gates are not shut, but only ajar, if one does show earnestness in the quest. Of all these that I have mentioned, there is but one from whom I have been unable to obtain clear proof of posthumous existence.

28

Experiences on the British Front

Lord Newton – How I Got Out – Sir W. Robertson – The Destroyer –
First Experience of Trenches – Ceremony at Bethune –
The Ypres Salient – Ypres – The Hull Territorial – General
Sir Douglas Haig – Artillery Duel – Kingsley – Major Wood – Paris

I had naturally wished to get out to the British front and to see things for myself. And yet I had scruples also, for when soldiers are doing a difficult job mere spectators and joy-riders are out of place. I felt what a perfect nuisance they must be, and hesitated to join them. On the other hand, I had surely more claims than most, since I was not only compiling a history of the campaign, but was continually writing in the press upon military subjects. I made up my mind, therefore, that I was justified in going, but I had as yet no opportunity.

However, it came along in a very strange way. It was in the early summer of 1916 that I had a note from Lord Newton, saying that he wished to see me at the Foreign Office. I could not conceive what he wanted to see me about, but of course I went. Lord Newton seemed to be doing general utility work which involved the interests of our prisoners in Germany, as well as press arrangements, missions, etc. The former alone would be enough for anyone, and he was exposed to severe criticism for not being sufficiently zealous in the cause. 'Newton, the Teuton,' sang the prisoners, a parody on 'Gilbert, the Filbert', one of the idiotic popular songs of pre-war days. However, I am convinced that he really did his very best, and that his policy was wise, for if it came to an interchange of revenge and barbarity between Germany and us, there was no contest. There is no use starting a game in which you are bound to be beaten. Winston Churchill had tried it in the case of the submarine officers, with the result that thirty of our own picked officers had endured much in their prisons and the policy had to be reconsidered.

Lord Newton is a wit and has a humorous face which covers a good deal of solid capacity. He plunged instantly into the business on hand.

'It is the Italian army,' said he. 'They want a bit of limelight. We propose to send several fellows on short missions to write them up. Your name has been mentioned and approved. Will you go?'

I never thought more quickly in my life than on that occasion. I had no plan when I entered the room, since I was ignorant of the proposition, but I saw my opening in a flash.

'No,' said I.

Lord Newton looked surprised.

'Why not?' he asked.

'Because I should be in a false position,' I answered. 'I have nothing to compare them with. I have not even seen the British front yet. How absurd it would be for me to approve or to condemn when they could reasonably ask me what I knew about the matter!'

'Would you go if that were set right?'

'Yes, certainly.'

'Then I don't think there will be an insuperable difficulty.'

'Well, if you can arrange that, I am entirely at your disposal.'

'By the way,' said he, 'if you go to the front, and especially to the Italian front, a uniform will be essential. What have you a right to wear?'

'I am a private in the Volunteers.'

He laughed.

'I think you would be shot at sight by both armies,' said he. 'You would be looked upon as a rare specimen. I don't think that would do.'

I had a happy thought.

'I am a deputy-lieutenant of Surrey,' said I. 'I have the right to wear a uniform when with troops.'

'Excellent!' he cried. 'Nothing could be better. Well, you will hear from me presently.'

I went straight off to my tailor, who rigged me up in a wondrous khaki garb which was something between that of a colonel and a brigadier, with silver roses instead of stars or crowns upon the shoulder-straps. As I had the right to wear several medals, including the South African, the general effect was all right, but I always felt a mighty impostor, though it was certainly very comfortable and convenient. I was still a rare specimen, and quite a number of officers of three nations made enquiry about my silver roses. A deputy-lieutenant may not be much in England, but when translated into French – my French anyhow – it has an awe-inspiring effect, and I was looked upon by them as an inscrutable but very big person with a uniform all of his own.

It was in May when I had my meeting with Lord Newton, and towards the end of the month I received a pass which would take me to the British lines. I remember the solicitude of my family, who seemed to think that I was going on active service. To quiet their kindly anxieties I said: 'My dears, I shall be held in the extreme rear, and I shall be lucky if ever I see a shell burst on the far horizon.' The sequel showed that my estimate was nearly as mistaken as theirs.

I had had some correspondence with General Robertson, and had dedicated my history of the war to him, so much was I impressed with the splendid work he had done behind the line in the early days, when Cowans and he had as much strain and anxiety from their position in the wings as any of those who were in the limelight of the stage. He was, as it happened, going over to France, and he sent me a note to ask whether I would like to share his private compartment on the train and then use his destroyer instead of the ordinary steamer. Of course I was delighted. General Robertson is a sturdy, soldierly, compact man, with a bulldog face, and looks as if he might be obstinate and even sullen if crossed. Such men are splendid if they keep their qualities for the enemy, but possibly dangerous if they use them on their associates. Certainly Robertson had a great deal of fighting to do at home as well as abroad, and was in the latter days of the war in constant conflict with the authorities, and with an open feud against the Prime Minister, but it is hard to say who was right. Perhaps, if it were not for the pressure which Robertson, Repington and others exercised, it would have been more difficult to raise those last few hundred thousand men who saved us in 1918. Like so many big men, his appearance was most deceptive, and though he looked every inch the soldier, there was nothing to show that great capacity for handling a large business which would surely have put him at the head of any commercial concern in the country. There was a Cromwellian touch in him which peeped out in occasional religious allusions. He was very engrossed in papers and figures, and I hardly had a word with him between London and Newhaven.

We went straight on to the destroyer and she cast off her moorings within a few minutes. The Channel crossing was a great experience for me, and I stood on the bridge all the time looking about for traces of war – which were not numerous. Just under the bridge stood a sturdy seaman in pea jacket and flapped cap, an intent, crouching, formidable figure, with his hand on the crank of a quick-firing gun. He never relaxed, and for the whole hour, as we tore across, his head, and occasionally his gun, was slowly traversing from right to left. The captain, a young lieutenant whose name I have forgotten, told me what hellish work it was in the winter, though perhaps 'hellish' is not the *mot juste* for that bitterly cold vigil. His ship was called the *Zulu*. Shortly afterwards it was blown up, as was its consort the *Nubian*, but as two of the halves were still serviceable, they stuck them together and made one very good ship, the *Zubian*. You can't beat the British dockyard any more than you can the British navy which it mothers. That evening we ran through some twenty miles of Northern France, and wound up at the usual guest-house, where I met several travelling Russians. Colonel Wilson, a dark, quiet, affable man, who had the thorny job of looking after the press, and Brigadier-General Charteris, a pleasant, breezy, fresh-complexioned soldier, head of the British Intelligence Department, joined us at dinner. Everything was quite comfortable, but at the same time properly plain and simple. There is nothing more hateful than luxury behind a battle line. Next day I had a wonderful twelve hours in contact with the soldiers all the time, and I will take some account of it from the notes I made at the time, but now I can expand them and give names more freely.

The crowning impression which I carried away from that wonderful day was the enormous imperturbable confidence of the army and its extraordinary efficiency in organisation, administration, material and personnel. I met in one day a sample of many types, an army commander, a corps commander, two divisional commanders, staff officers of many grades, and, above all, I met repeatedly the two very great men whom Britain has produced, the private soldier and the regimental officer. Everywhere and on every face one read the same spirit of cheerful bravery. Even the half-mad cranks whose absurd consciences prevented them from barring the way to the devil seemed to me to be turning into men under the prevailing influence. I saw a batch of them, neurotic and largely bespectacled, but working with a will by the roadside. There was no foolish bravado, no underrating of a dour opponent, but a quick, alert, confident attention to the job in hand which was an inspiration to the observer.

'Get out of the car. Don't let it stay here. It may be hit.' These words from a staff officer gave you the first idea that things were going to happen. Up to then you might have been driving through the black country in the Walsall district with the population of Aldershot let loose upon its dingy roads. 'Put on this shrapnel helmet. That hat of yours would infuriate the Boche' – this was an unkind allusion to my uniform. 'Take this gas mask. You won't need it, but it is a standing order. Now come on!'

We crossed a meadow and entered a trench. Here and there it came to the surface again where there was dead ground. At one such point an old church stood, with an unexploded shell sticking out of the wall. A century hence folk may journey to see that shell. Then on again through an endless cutting. It was slippery clay below. I had no nails in my boots, an iron pot on my head and the sun above me. I remember that walk. The telephone wires ran down the side. Here and there large thistles and other plants grew from the clay walls, so immobile had been our lines. Occasionally there were patches of untidiness. 'Shells,' said the officer laconically. There was a racket of guns before us and behind, especially behind, but danger seemed remote with all these Bairnsfather groups of cheerful Tommies at work around us. I passed one group of grimy, tattered boys. A glance at their shoulders showed me that they were of a public-school battalion, the 20th Royal Fusiliers. 'I thought you fellows were all officers now,' I remarked. 'No, sir, we like it better so.' 'Well, it will be a great memory for you. We are all in your debt.'

They saluted, and we squeezed past them. They had the fresh brown faces of boy cricketers. But their comrades were men of a different type, with hard, strong, rugged features, and the eyes of men who have seen strange sights. These were veterans, men of Mons, and their young pals of the public schools had something to live up to.

Up to this we only had two clay walls to look at. But now our interminable and tropical walk was lightened by the sight of a British aeroplane sailing overhead. Numerous shrapnel bursts were all around it, but she floated on serenely, a thing of delicate beauty against the blue background. Now another passed – and yet another. All the morning we saw them circling and swooping, and never a sign of a Boche. They told me it was nearly always so – that we held the air, and that the Boche intruder, save at early morning, was a rare bird. 'We have never met a British aeroplane which was not ready to fight,' said a captured German aviator. There was a fine, stern courtesy between the airmen on either side, each dropping notes into the other's aerodromes to tell the fate of missing officers. Had the whole war been fought by the Germans as their airmen conducted it (I do not speak, of course, of the Zeppelin murderers), a peace would eventually have been more easily arranged.

And now we were there – in what was surely the most wonderful spot in the world – the front firing trench, the outer breakwater which held back the German tide. How strange that this monstrous oscillation of giant forces, setting in from east to west, should find their equilibrium across this particular meadow of Flanders. 'How far?' I asked. 'One hundred and eighty yards,' said my guide. 'Pop!' remarked a third person just in front. 'A sniper,' said my guide; 'take a look through the periscope.' I did so. There was some rusty wire before me, then a field sloping slightly upwards with knee-deep grass, and ragged dock and fennel and nettles, then rusty wire again and a red line of broken earth. There was not a sign of movement, but sharp eyes were always watching us, even as these crouching soldiers around me were watching them. There were dead Germans in the grass before us. You need not see them to know that they were there. A wounded soldier sat in a corner nursing his leg. Here and there men popped out like rabbits from dugouts and mineshafts. Others sat on the fire-step or leaned smoking against the clay wall. Who would dream, who looked at their bold, careless faces, that this was a front line, and that at any moment it was possible that a grey wave might submerge them? With all their careless bearing, I noticed that every man had his gas mask and his rifle within easy reach.

A mile of front trenches and then we were on our way back down that weary walk. Then I was whisked off upon a ten-mile drive. There was a pause for lunch at corps headquarters, and after it we were taken to a medal presentation in the market square of Bethune. Generals Munro, Haking and Landon, famous fighting soldiers all three, were the British representatives. Munro, with a ruddy face, all brain above, all bulldog below; Haking, pale, distinguished, intellectual; Landon, a pleasant genial country squire. An elderly French general stood beside them. British infantry kept the ground. In front were about fifty Frenchmen in civil dress of every grade of life, workmen and gentlemen, in a double rank. They were all so wounded that they were back in civil life, but today they were to have some solace for their wounds. They leaned heavily on sticks, their bodies twisted and maimed, but their faces were shining with pride and joy. The French general drew his sword and addressed them. One caught words like 'honneur' and 'patrie'. They leaned forward on their crutches, hanging on every syllable which came hissing and rasping from under that heavy white moustache. Then the medals were pinned on. One poor lad was terribly wounded and needed two sticks. A little girl ran out with some flowers. He leaned forward and tried to kiss her, but the crutches slipped and he nearly fell upon her. It was a pitiful but beautiful little scene.

Next the British candidates marched up one by one for their medals, hale, hearty men, brown and fit. There was a smart young officer of Scottish Rifles; and then a selection of Worcesters, Welsh Fusiliers and Scots Fusiliers, with one funny little Highlander, a tiny figure with a soup-bowl helmet, a grinning boy's face beneath it, and a bedraggled uniform. 'Many acts of great bravery' – such was the record for which he was decorated. Even the French wounded smiled at his quaint appearance, as they did at another Briton who had acquired the chewing-gum habit, and came up for his medal as if he had been called suddenly in the middle of his dinner, which he was still endeavouring to bolt. Then came the end, with the National Anthem. The British battalion formed fours and went past. To me that was the most impressive sight of any. They were the Queen's West Surreys, a veteran battalion of the great Ypres battle. What grand fellows! As the order came, 'Eyes right,' and all those fierce, dark faces flashed round at us I felt the might of the British infantry, the intense individuality which is not incompatible with the highest discipline. Much they had endured, but a great spirit shone from their faces. I confess that as I looked at those brave English lads, and thought of what we owed to them and to their like who have passed on, I felt more emotional than befits a Briton in foreign parts. How many of them are left alive today!

Now the ceremony was ended, and once again we set out for the front. It was to an artillery observation post just opposite the Loos Salient that we were bound. In an hour I found myself, together with a razor-keen young artillery observer and an excellent old sportsman of a Russian prince, jammed into a very small space and staring through a slit at the German lines. In front of us lay a vast plain, scarred and slashed with bare places at intervals, such as you see where gravel pits break a green common. Not a sign of life or movement, save some wheeling crows. And yet down there, within a mile or so, was the population of a city. Far away a single train was puffing at the back of the German lines. We were here on a definite errand. Away to the right, nearly three miles off, was a small red house, dim to the eye but clear in the glasses, suspected as a German post. It was to go up this afternoon. The gun was some distance away, but I heard the telephone directions. ' "Mother" will soon do her in,' remarked the gunner boy cheerfully. 'Mother' was the name of the gun. 'Give her five six three four,' he cried through the phone. 'Mother' uttered a horrible bellow from somewhere on our right. An enormous spout of smoke rose ten seconds later from near the house. 'A little short,' said our gunner. 'Two and a half minutes left,' added a little small voice, which represented another observer at a different angle. 'Raise her seven five,' said our boy encouragingly. 'Mother' roared more angrily than ever. 'How will that do?' she seemed to say. 'One and a half right,' said our invisible gossip. I wondered how the folk in the house were feeling as the shells crept ever nearer. 'Gun laid, sir,' said the telephone. 'Fire!' I was looking through my glass. A flash of fire on the house, a huge pillar of dust and smoke – then it settled, and an unbroken field was there. The German post had gone up. 'It's a dear little gun,' said the officer boy. 'And her shells are reliable,' remarked a senior behind us. 'They vary with different calibres, but "Mother" never goes wrong.' The German line was very quiet. 'Pourquoi ne repondent-ils pas?' asked the Russian prince. 'Yes, they are quiet today,' answered the senior. 'But we get it in the neck sometimes.' We were all led off to be introduced to 'Mother', who sat, squat and black, amid twenty of her grimy children who waited upon her and fed her. A dainty eater was 'Mother', and nothing served her but the best and plenty of it. But she was an important parent and as the war progressed it became more and more evident that in spite of that upstart family of quick-firers it was really only the big, heavy, well-established gun which could flatten out a road to the Rhine.

I had the great joy that night of seeing my brother Innes, who had been promoted to colonel, and was acting as Assistant Adjutant-General of the 24th Division, the headquarters of which were at Bailleul, where I dined at mess and occupied a small lodging in the town, which was about six miles from the front. One more experience wound up that wonderful day. That night we took a car after dark and drove north, and ever north, until at a late hour we halted and climbed a hill in the darkness. Below was a wonderful sight. Down on the flats, in a huge semicircle, lights were rising and falling. They were very brilliant, going up for a few seconds and then dying down. Sometimes a dozen were in the air at one time. There were the dull thuds of explosions and an occasional rat-tat-tat. I have seen nothing like it, but the nearest comparison would be an enormous ten-mile railway station in full swing at night, with signals winking, lamps waving, engines hissing and carriages bumping. It was a terrible place, a place which will live as long as military history is written, for it was the Ypres Salient. What a salient too! A huge curve, as outlined by the lights, needing only a little more to be an encirclement. Something caught the rope as it closed, and that something was the British soldier. But it was a perilous place by day and by night. Never shall I forget the impression of ceaseless, malignant activity which was borne in upon me by the white, winking lights, the red sudden flares, and the horrible thudding noises in that place of death beneath me.

*   *   *

In old days we had a great name as organisers. Then came a long period when we deliberately adopted a policy of individuality and 'go as you please'. Now once again in our sore need we had called on all our power of administration and direction. And it had not deserted us. We still had it in a supreme degree. Even in peacetime we have shown it in that vast, well-oiled, swift-running noiseless machine called the British navy. But our powers had risen with the need of them. The expansion of the navy was a miracle, the management of the transport a greater one, the formation of the new army the greatest of all time. To get the men was the least of the difficulties. To put them in the field, with everything down to the lid of the last field saucepan in its place, that was the marvel. The tools of the gunners and of the sappers, to say nothing of the knowledge of how to use them, were in themselves a huge problem. But it had all been met and mastered. So don't let us talk too much about the muddling of the War Office. It has become just a little ridiculous.

I was the guest at headquarters of a divisional general, Capper, brother of the heroic leader of the 7th Division, who might truly be called one of the two fathers of the British flying force, for it was he, with Templer, who laid the first foundations from which so great an organisation has arisen. My morning was spent in visiting two fighting brigadiers, Mitford and Jelf, cheery weather-beaten soldiers, respectful, as all our soldiers are, of the prowess of the Hun, but serenely confident that we could beat him. In company with one of them I ascended a hill, the reverse slope of which was swarming with cheerful infantry in every stage of *déshabille*, for they were cleaning up after the trenches. Once over the slope we advanced with some care, and finally reached a certain spot from which we looked down upon the German line. It was an observation post, about a thousand yards from the German trenches, with our own trenches between us. We could see the two lines, sometimes only a few yards, as it seemed, apart, extending for miles on either side. The sinister silence and solitude were strangely dramatic. Such vast crowds of men, such intensity of feeling, and yet only that open rolling countryside, with never a movement in its whole expanse.

In the afternoon my brother drove me to the square at Ypres. It was the city of a dream, this modern Pompeii, destroyed, deserted and desecrated, but with a sad, proud dignity which made you involuntarily lower your voice as you passed through the ruined streets. It was a more considerable place than I had imagined, with many traces of ancient grandeur. No words can describe the absolute splintered wreck that the Huns had made of it. The effect of some of the shells had been grotesque. One boiler-plated water tower, a thing forty or fifty feet high, was actually standing on its head like a great metal top. There was not a living soul in the place save a few pickets of soldiers, and a number of cats which had become fierce and dangerous. Now and then a shell still fell, but the Huns probably knew that the devastation was already complete.

We stood in the lonely grass-grown square, once the busy centre of the town, and we marvelled at the beauty of the smashed cathedral and the tottering Cloth Hall beside it. Surely at their best they could not have looked more wonderful. If they were preserved even so, and if a heaven-inspired artist were to model a statue of Belgium in front, Belgium with one hand pointing to the treaty by which Prussia guaranteed her safety and the other to the sacrilege behind her, it would make the most impressive group in the world. It was an evil day for Belgium when her frontier was violated, but it was a worse one for Germany. I venture to prophesy that it will be regarded by history as the greatest military as well as political error that has ever been made. Had the great guns that destroyed Liège made their first breach at Verdun, what chance was there for Paris? Those few weeks of warning and preparation saved France, and left Germany like a weary and furious bull, tethered fast in the place of trespass and waiting for the inevitable poleaxe.

We were glad to get out of the place, for the gloom of it lay as heavy upon our hearts as the shrapnel helmets did upon our heads. Both were lightened as we sped back past empty and shattered villas to where, just behind the danger line, the normal life of rural Flanders was carrying on as usual. A merry sight helped to cheer us, for scudding downwind above our heads came a Boche aeroplane, with two British at her tail barking away with their machine guns, like two swift terriers after a cat. They shot rat-tat-tatting across the sky until we lost sight of them in the heat haze over the German line.

The afternoon saw us on the Sharpenburg, from which many a million will gaze in days to come, for from no other point can so much be seen. It was a spot forbid, but a special permit took us up, and the sentry on duty, having satisfied himself of our bona-fides, proceeded to tell us tales of the war in a pure Hull dialect which might have been Chinese for all that I could understand. That he was a 'Terrier' and had nine children were the only facts I could lay hold of. But I wished to be silent and to think – even, perhaps, to pray. Here, just below my feet, were the spots which our dear lads, three of them my own kith, had sanctified with their blood. Here, fighting for the freedom of the world, they cheerily gave their all. On that sloping meadow to the left of the row of houses on the opposite ridge the London Scottish fought to the death on that grim November morning when the Bavarians reeled back from their shot-torn line. That plain away on the other side of Ypres was the place where the three grand Canadian brigades, first of all men, stood up to the damnable gases of the Hun. Down yonder was Hill 60, that blood-soaked kopje. The ridge over the fields was held by the cavalry against two army corps, and there where the sun struck the red roof among the trees I could just see Gheluvelt, a name for ever to be associated with Haig and the most vital battle of the war. As I turned away I was faced by my Hull Territorial, who still said incomprehensible things. I looked at him with other eyes. He had fought on yonder plain. He had slain Huns, and he had nine children. Could anyone better epitomise the duties of a good citizen in days like these? I could have found it in my heart to salute him had I not known that it would have shocked him and made him unhappy.

Next day, it was June 1, I left my brother's kindly care. I had fears for him, for he was much overworked and worried as adjutant-generals of busy divisions are likely to be. However, he was never one to admit it or to pity himself, and he begged me to carry the cheeriest report back to his wife. It was a great pleasure to me that so many officers took me aside to say how efficient he was, and how popular. He would not have wished me to say it were he alive, but I can leave it on record now.

Yesterday had been full, but the next day was not less so, for I had been asked (or ordered) to lunch at the General Headquarters at Montreuil, the funny old town on a hill which I had learned to know well in days of peace. As we drove down a winding drive I saw two officers walking towards us. The younger of them stooped and beat the ground with his stick, from which we gathered that we were to go slow and raise no dust. We rightly conjectured that so curt an order could only come from the Chief's own aide. We saluted as we passed and carried away an impression of a heavy moustache and of abstracted blue eyes.

I had a very much more definite impression when he came back presently, and we were all shown into the dining-room. I should certainly put Douglas Haig, as I saw him that day, among the handsomest men I have ever known. He was not tall, but he was upright and well proportioned with every sign of strength and activity. But his face was remarkable for beauty and power. His eyes were very full and expressive, devoid of the fierceness of Kitchener and yet with quite as much determination. But the long powerful jaw was the feature which spoke particularly of that never-to-be-beaten quality which saved the army when the line was broken in the first Ypres battle and was destined to save it again in April 1918, when he gave out his 'back to the wall' order of the day.

He was courteous but not talkative at lunch. After lunch he took me into a side room where he showed me the line of the divisions on the map, saying that I could remember but should not take notes, which was rather maddening. Then we had a long talk over the coffee, but there were several present and nothing intimate was said. He must be worried to death with casual visitors, but still I suppose he need not invite all of them to Headquarters. He had, I thought, a truly British distrust of foreigners. 'He is the worst foreigner I have met yet,' he said, speaking of some Italian general. His kind heart was shown when I said that my son was in the line. He gave a curt order, and then nodded and smiled. 'You'll see him tomorrow,' said he.

I naturally heard a good deal about our generalissimo, besides what I actually saw. I think that he had some of the traits of Wellington, though since the war he has concerned himself with the fortunes of his comrades-in-arms a great deal more than the Iron Duke seems ever to have troubled himself to do. But in other things the parallel is close. Haig is not a game-playing man, though fond of horse exercise. Neither was the Duke. Both were abstemious with wine and tobacco. Both were reserved, reticent and had no magnetic connection with those under them. Neither Haig nor the Duke were human figures to the soldiers, nor were they often if ever seen by them, and yet in each case there was the same confidence in their judgement. Haig was a very serious man, he seldom joked and did not meet a joke halfway, so that his mess was the dullest in France. I have known a staff officer apply for an exchange so weary was he of this oppressive atmosphere. All this could equally have been said of the Duke. But these are trivialities compared to the great main fact that each brought rare qualities to the service of their country at critical moments of the world's history. There was only one other man who might have filled Haig's place, and that man was the conqueror of Palestine.

Extraordinary are the contrasts of war. Within three hours of leaving the quiet atmosphere of the headquarters château I was present at what in any other war would have been looked upon as a brisk engagement. As it was it would certainly figure in one of our desiccated reports as an activity of the artillery. The noise as we struck the line at this new point showed that the matter was serious, and indeed we had chosen the spot because it had been the storm centre of the last week. The method of approach chosen by our experienced guide was in itself a tribute to the gravity of the affair. As one comes from the settled order of Flanders into the actual scene of war, the first sign of it is one of the stationary, sausage-shaped balloons, a chain of which marks the ring in which the great wrestlers are locked. We passed under this, ascended a hill, and found ourselves in a garden where for a year no feet save those of wanderers like ourselves had stood. There was a wild, confused luxuriance of growth more beautiful to my eye than anything which the care of man can produce. One old shell-hole of vast diameter had filled itself with forget-me-nots, and appeared as a graceful basin of light blue flowers, held up as an atonement to heaven for the brutalities of man. Through the tangled bushes we crept, then across a yard – 'Please stoop and run as you pass this point' – and finally to a small opening in a wall, whence the battle lay not so much before as beside us. For a moment we had a front seat at the great world-drama, God's own problem play, working surely to its magnificent end. One felt a sort of shame to crouch here in comfort, a useless spectator, while brave men down yonder were facing that pelting shower of iron.

There was a large field on our left rear, and the German gunners had the idea that there was a concealed battery therein. They were systematically searching for it. A great shell exploded in the top corner, but got nothing more solid than a few tons of clay. You could read the mind of Gunner Fritz. 'Try the lower corner!' said he, and up went the earth-cloud once again. 'Perhaps it's hid about the middle. I'll try.' Earth again, and nothing more. 'I believe I was right the first time after all,' said hopeful Fritz. So another shell came into the top corner. The field was full of pits as a Gruyère cheese, but Fritz got nothing by his perseverance. Perhaps there never was a battery there at all. One effect he obviously did attain. He made several other British batteries exceedingly angry. 'Stop that tickling, Fritz!' was the burden of their cry. Where they were we could no more see than Fritz could, but their constant work was very clear along the German line. We appeared to be using more shrapnel and the Germans more high explosives, but that may have been just the chance of the day. The Vimy Ridge was on our right, and before us was the old French position, with the Labyrinth of terrible memories and the long hill of Lorette. When, the year before last, the French, in a three weeks' battle, fought their way up that hill, it was an exhibition of sustained courage which even their military annals can seldom have beaten.

Next day we travelled through Acheux and hit the British line once more to the east of that place. Our official chauffeur had had his instructions, and so had other people, with the result that as we swung into the broad main street of a village – Mailly, I think, was the name – there was a tall young officer standing with his back turned. He swung round at the noise of the car, and it was my boy Kingsley with his usual jolly grin upon his weather-stained features. The long arm of GHQ had stretched out and plucked him from a trench, and there he was. We had an hour's talk in a field, for there was nowhere else to go. He was hard and well and told me that all was nearly ready for a big push at the very part of the line where his battalion, the 1st Hampshires, was stationed. This was the first intimation of the great Somme battle, on the first day of which every officer of the Hampshires without exception was killed or wounded. I learned afterwards that before the battle for ten nights running Kingsley crept out to the German wire and stuck up crosses where he found the wire uncut, which were brown towards the enemy and white towards the British, as a guide to the gunners. He lay on his face sometimes with the machine guns firing just above him. For this service Colonel Palk thanked him warmly and said he should certainly have a decoration, but Palk and both majors were killed and no recommendations went forward. Two shrapnel bullets in the neck were all Kingsley got out of the battle, and two months on his back in a hospital. However, he was not a medal hunter and I never heard him complain, nor would he wear his wound badges until he was compelled.

An hour later I met another member of my household, for my secretary, Major Wood of the 5th Sussex Territorials, was Town Major of Beauquesne, where I found him at the convenient hour of lunch. He had done nearly two years of hard active service, which was pretty good for a civilian of fifty, and had led his company at Festubert and other engagements. He was now using his excellent powers of organisation and administration in making Beauquesne a well-ordered village, as later he made Doullens a well-ordered town. I expect that the British administration will remain as a wonderful legend of sanitation and cleanliness in many of these French towns of the north-east.

After inspecting Major Wood's work I went on to Amiens with him and he packed me into the train to Paris, the first part of my task thoroughly done so far as time would permit. I came away with a deep sense of the difficult task which lay before the army, but with an equally deep one of the ability of those men to do all that soldiers can be called upon to perform. But I saw no end to the war.

I had two days in Paris – a very dead-and-alive Paris, such a Paris as has seldom or never been seen before, with darkened streets and the shops nearly all closed. I stayed at the Hôtel Crillon, where were a few Russian and British officers. It was extraordinary the difference which the public made between the two. A British officer was disregarded, while a Russian general – I took a walk with one – was looked upon with an adulation which was quite comic. Men came up and made a low obeisance before him. And yet it was our army, our purse, our factories, above all our navy, which were saving the situation both for France and Russia, to whom we were bound by no alliance. There was certainly not much sign of appreciation or gratitude. It is a very singular thing how the whole world alternately leans upon and depreciates the British Empire.

29

Experiences on the Italian Front

The Polite Front – Udine – Under Fire – Carnic Alps – *Italia*
Irredenta – Trentino – The Voice of the Holy Roman Empire

Two days later I found myself, after an uneventful journey, at Padua on
my way to the Italian front. The Italian front seemed to have politely
come back to meet me, for I was awakened in the night by a
tremendous dropping of bombs and the rattle of anti-aircraft guns. I
thought I was as safe in bed as anywhere, and so it proved. Little
damage was done, but Padua and the other Italian cities were having a
bad time, and it was a one-sided arrangement, since the Italians can do
nothing without injuring their own kith and kin across the border. This
dropping of explosives on the chance of hitting one soldier among fifty
victims was surely the most monstrous development of the whole war,
and was altogether German in its origin. If international law cannot
now stamp it out, the next war will send the people flying to the caves
and calling upon the mountains to cover them, even as was foretold.

I arrived at last at Udine, the capital of the Friulian Province, where
were the Italian Headquarters – a funny little town with a huge mound
in the centre, which looked too big to be artificial, but was said to have
been thrown up by Attila. My recommendation was to the British
Mission, which was headed by Brigadier-General Delme-Radcliffe,
who received me with hospitality, a bluff, short-spoken and masterful
British soldier. The mission owned a white house on the edge of the
town. On the second floor under a window which proved to be that of
my bedroom there was a long dark smear upon the whitewashed wall.
'That's the stomach of a baker,' said the soldier-servant with a grin. I
thought it was a joke on his part, but it was literally true, for a bomb a
few days before had blown the man to bits as he passed the house, and
had plastered bits of him on the stonework. The ceiling of my bedroom
was full of holes from that or some other explosion.

There was some tendency at this time to cavil at the Italians and to
wonder why they did not make more impression upon the Austrians. As

a matter of fact they were faced by the same barbed wire and machine-gun problem which had held up everyone else. I soon saw, when I was allowed next morning to get to the front, that the conditions were very like those of Flanders in a more genial climate and in all ways less aggravated. I had been handed over to the Italian Intelligence people, who were represented by a charmingly affable nobleman, Colonel the Marquis Barbariche, and Colonel Claricetti. These two introduced me at once to General Porro, Chief of the Staff, a brown, wrinkled, walnut-faced warrior, who showed me some plans and did what he could to be helpful.

It was about a seven miles drive from Udine before we reached the nearest point of the trenches. From a mound an extraordinary view could be got of the Austrian position, the general curve of both lines being marked, as in Flanders, by the sausage balloons which float behind them. The Isonzo, which had been so bravely carried by the Italians, lay in front of me, a clear blue river, as broad as the Thames at Hampton Court. In a hollow to my left were the roofs of Gorizia, the town which the Italians were endeavouring to take. A long desolate ridge, the Carso, extended to the south of the town, and stretched down nearly to the sea. The crest was held by the Austrians, and the Italian trenches had been pushed within fifty yards of them. A lively bombardment was going on from either side, but so far as the infantry went there was none of that constant malignant petty warfare with which we were familiar in Flanders. I was anxious to see the Italian trenches, in order to compare them with our British methods, but save for the support and communication trenches I was courteously but firmly warned off.

Having got this general view of the position, I was anxious in the afternoon to visit Monfalcone, which is the small dockyard captured from the Austrians on the Adriatic. My kind Italian officer guides did not recommend the trip, as it was part of their great hospitality to shield their guest from any part of that danger which they were always ready to incur themselves. The only road to Monfalcone ran close to the Austrian position at the village of Ronchi, and afterwards kept parallel to it for some miles. I was told that it was only on odd days that the Austrian guns were active in this particular section, so I determined to trust to luck that this might not be one of them. It proved, however, to be one of the worst on record, and we were not destined to see the dockyard for which we started.

The civilian cuts a ridiculous figure when he enlarges upon small adventures which may come his way – adventures which the soldier endures in silence as part of his everyday life. On this occasion, however, the episode was all our own, and had a sporting flavour in it which made it dramatic. I know now the feeling of tense expectation with which the driven grouse whirrs onwards towards the butt. I have been behind the butt before now, and it is only poetic justice that I should see the matter from the other point of view. As we approached Ronchi we could see shrapnel breaking over the road in front of us, but we had not yet realised that it was precisely for vehicles that the Austrians were waiting, and that they had the range marked down to a yard. We went down the road all out at a steady fifty miles an hour. The village was near, and it seemed that we had got past the place of danger. We had, in fact, just reached it. At this moment there was a noise as if the whole four tyres had gone simultaneously, a most terrific bang in our very ears, merging into a second sound like a reverberating blow upon an enormous gong. As I glanced up I saw three clouds immediately above my head, two of them white and the other of a rusty red. The air was full of flying metal, and the road, as we were told afterwards by an observer, was all churned up by it. The metal base of one of the shells was found plumb in the middle of the road just where our motor had been. It was our pace that saved us. The motor was an open one, and the three shells burst, according to one of my Italian companions, who was himself an artillery officer, about ten metres above our heads. They threw forward, however, and we, travelling at so great a pace, shot from under. Before they could get in another we had swung round the curve and under the lee of a house. The good colonel wrung my hand in silence. They were both distressed, these good soldiers, under the impression that they had led me into danger. As a matter of fact it was I who owed them an apology, since they had enough risks in the way of business without taking others in order to gratify the whim of a visitor.

Our difficulties were by no means over. We found an ambulance lorry and a little group of infantry huddled under the same shelter, with the expression of people who had been caught in the rain. The road beyond was under heavy fire, as well as that by which we had come. Had the Ostro-Boches dropped a high explosive upon us they would have had a good mixed bag. But apparently they were only out for fancy shooting and disdained a sitter. Presently there came a lull and the lorry moved on, but we soon heard a burst of firing which showed that they were after it. My companions had decided that it was out of the question for us to finish our excursion. We waited for some time, therefore, and were able finally to make our retreat on foot, being joined later by the car. So ended my visit to Monfalcone, the place I did not reach. I hear that two 10,000-ton steamers were left on the stocks there by the Austrians, but were disabled before they retired. Their cabin basins and other fittings were adorning the Italian dugouts.

My second day was devoted to a view of the Italian mountain warfare in the Carnic Alps. Besides the two great fronts, one of defence (Trentino) and one of offence (Isonzo), there were very many smaller valleys which had to be guarded. The total frontier line is over four hundred miles, and it had all to be held against raids if not invasions. It was a most picturesque business. Far up in the Roccolana Valley I found the Alpini outposts, backed by artillery which had been brought into the most wonderful positions. They had taken eight-inch guns where a tourist could hardly take his knapsack. Neither side could ever make serious progress, but there were continual duels, gun against gun, or Alpini against jaeger. In a little wayside house was the brigade headquarters, and here I was entertained to lunch. It was a scene that I shall remember. They drank to England. I raised my glass to *Italia irredenta* – might it soon be *redenta*. They all sprang to their feet and the circle of dark faces flashed into flame. They keep their souls and emotions, these people. I trust that ours may not become atrophied by self-suppression.

The last day spent on the Italian front was in the Trentino. From Verona a motor drive of about twenty-five miles takes one up the valley of the Adige, and past a place of evil augury for the Austrians, the field of Rivoli. Finally, after a long drive of winding gradients, always beside the Adige, we reached Ala, where we interviewed the commander of the sector, a man who has done splendid work during the recent fighting. 'By all means you can see my front. But no motor car, please. It draws fire, and others may be hit besides you.' We proceeded on foot, therefore, along a valley which branched at the end into two passes. In both very active fighting had been going on, and as we came up the guns were baying merrily, waking up most extraordinary echoes in the hills. It was difficult to believe that it was not thunder. There was one terrible voice that broke out from time to time in the mountains – the angry voice of the Holy Roman Empire. When it came all other sounds died down into nothing. It was – so I was told – the master gun, the vast forty-two-centimetre giant which brought down the pride of Liège and Namur. The Austrians had brought one or more from Innsbruck. The Italians assure me, however, as we have ourselves discovered, that in trench work beyond a certain point the size of the guns makes little matter.

We passed a burst dugout by the roadside where a tragedy had occurred recently, for eight medical officers were killed in it by a single shell. There was no particular danger in the valley, however, and the aimed fire was all going across us to the fighting lines in the two passes above us. That to the right, the Valley of Buello, has seen some of the worst of the fighting. These two passes form the Italian left wing which has held firm all through. So has the right wing. It is only the centre which has been pushed in by the concentrated fire.

When we arrived at the spot where the two valleys forked we were halted, and were not permitted to advance to the front trenches which lay upon the crests above us. There were about a thousand yards between the adversaries. I have seen types of some of the Bosnian and Croatian prisoners, men of poor physique and intelligence, but the Italians speak with chivalrous praise of the bravery of the Hungarians and of the Austrian jaeger. Some of their proceedings disgusted them, however, and especially the fact that they used Russian prisoners to dig trenches under fire. There is no doubt of this, as some of the men were recaptured and were sent on to join their comrades in France. On the whole, however, it may be said that in the Austro-Italian war there was nothing which corresponded with the extreme bitterness of our Western conflict. The presence or absence of the Hun makes all the difference.

It was a moment of depression at the Trentino front, as there had been a setback. I may flatter myself when I think that even one solitary figure in a British uniform striding about among them was good at that particular time to their eyes. They read of allies, but they never saw any. If they had, we might have been spared the subsequent disaster at Caporetto. Certainly I was heartily welcomed there, and surrounded all the time by great mobs of soldiers, who imagined, I suppose, that I was someone of importance.

That night found me back at Verona, and next morning I was on my way to Paris with sheaves of notes about the Italian soldiers which would, I hoped, make the British public more sympathetic towards them. I was told afterwards by the Foreign Office that my mission had been an unmixed success.

I have one other association with the Italian front which I may include here. It is embalmed in the *Annals of the Psychic Research Society*. I have several times in my life awakened from sleep with some strong impressions of knowledge gained still lingering in my brain. In one case, for example, I got the strange name Nalderu so vividly that I wrote it down between two stretches of insensibility and found it on the outside of my cheque book next morning. A month later I started for Australia in the SS *Naldera* of which I had then never heard. In this particular Italian instance I got the word Piave, absolutely ringing in my head. I knew it as a river some seventy miles to the rear of the Italian front and quite unconnected with the war. None the less the impression was so strong that I wrote the incident down and had it signed by two witnesses. Months passed and the Italian battle line was rolled back to the Piave, which became a familiar word. Some said it would go back further. I was sure it would not. I argued that if the abnormal forces, whatever they may be, had taken such pains to impress the matter upon me, it must needs be good news which they were conveying, since I had needed cheering at the time. Therefore I felt sure that some great victory and the turning point of the war would come on the Piave. So sure was I that I wrote to my friend Mr Lacon Watson, who was on the Italian front, and the incident got into the Italian press. It could have nothing but a good effect upon their morale. Finally it is a matter of history how completely my impression was justified, and how the most shattering victory of the whole war was gained at that very spot.

There is the fact, amply proved by documents and beyond all possible coincidence. As to the explanation some may say that our own sub-conscious self has power of foresight. If so it is a singularly dead instinct, seldom or never used. Others may say that our 'dead' can see further than we, and try when we are asleep and in spiritual touch with us, to give us knowledge and consolation. The latter is my own solution of the mystery.

30

Experiences on the French Front

A Dreadful Reception – Robert Donald – Clemenceau –
Soissons Cathedral – The Commandant's Cane – The Extreme
Outpost – Adonis – General Henneque – Cyrano in the Argonne –
Tir Rapide – French-Canadian – Wound Stripes

When I got back to Paris I had a dreadful reception, for as I dismounted from the railway car a British military policeman in his flat red cap stepped up to me and saluted.

'This is bad news, sir,' said he.

'What is it?' I gasped.

'Lord Kitchener, sir. Drowned!'

'Good God!' I cried.

'Yes, sir.' Suddenly the machine turned for a moment into a human being. 'Too much talking in this war,' he said, and then in a moment was his stiff formal self again, and bustled off in search of deserters.

Kitchener dead! The words were like clods falling on my heart. One could not imagine him dead, that centre of energy and vitality. With a heavy spirit I drove back to my old quarters at the Hôtel Crillon, fuller than ever of red-epauletted, sword-clanking Russians. I could have cursed them, for it was in visiting their rotten, crumbling country that our hero had met his end.

At the hotel I met by appointment Mr Robert Donald, editor of the *Daily Chronicle*, which paper had been publishing my articles. Donald, a fine, solid Scot, had the advantage of talking good French and being in thorough touch with French conditions. With him I called upon M. Clemenceau, who had not at that time played any conspicuous part in the war, save as a violent critic. He lived modestly in a small house which showed that he had not used his power in the state and in journalism to any unfair personal advantage. He entered, a swarthy, wrinkled, white-haired man, with the face of a crabbed bulldog, and a cloth cap upon his head. He reminded me of old Jim Mace the bruiser, as I remember him in his final phase. His eyes looked angry, and he had a truculent, mischievous smile. I was not impressed by the judgement he showed in our conversation, if a squirt on one side and Niagara on the other can be called conversation. He was railing loudly at the English rate of exchange between the franc and the pound, which seemed to me very like kicking against the barometer. Mr Donald, who is a real authority upon finance, asked him whether France was taking the rouble at its face value; but the roaring voice, like a strong gramophone with a blunt needle, submerged all argument. Against Joffre he roared his reproaches, and intimated that he had someone else up his sleeve who could very soon bring the war to an end. A volcano of a man, dangerous sometimes to his friends, and sometimes to his foes. Let me acknowledge that I did not at the time recognise that he would ever be the opposite number to Lloyd George, and that the pair would lead us to victory.

Donald had arranged that he and I should visit the French lines in the Argonne, which was as near as we could get to Verdun, where the battle was at its height. There were a few days to spare, however, and in the meantime I got a chance of going to the Soissons front, along with Leo Maxse, editor of the *National Review*, and a M. Chevillon, who had written an excellent book on British cooperation in the war. Maxse, a dark little man, all nerves and ginger, might well plume himself that he was one of those who had foreseen the war and most loudly demanded preparation. Chevillon was a grey-bearded, father-of-a-family type, and could speak English, which promoted our closer acquaintance, as my French is adventurous but not always successful. A captain of French Intelligence, a small, silent man, took the fourth place in the car.

When our posterity hear that it was easy to run out from Paris to the line, to spend a full day on the line, and to be back again in Paris for dinner, it will make them appreciate how close a thing was the war. We passed in the first instance the woods of Villars Cotteret, where the Guards had turned upon the German van on September 1, 1914. Eighty Guardsmen were buried in the village cemetery, among them a nephew of Maxse's, to whose tomb we now made pious pilgrimage. Among the trees on either side of the road I noticed other graves of soldiers, buried where they had fallen.

Soissons proved to be a considerable wreck, though it was far from being an Ypres. But the cathedral would, and will, make many a patriotic Frenchman weep. These savages cannot keep their hands off a beautiful church. Here, absolutely unchanged through the ages, was the spot where St Louis had dedicated himself to the Crusade. Every stone of it was holy. And now the lovely old stained-glass strewed the floor, and the roof lay in a huge heap across the central aisle. A dog was climbing over it as we entered. No wonder the French fought well. Such sights would drive the mildest man to desperation. The abbé, a good priest, with a large humorous face, took us over his shattered domain. When I pointed out the desecration of the dog he shrugged his shoulders and said: 'What matter? It will have to be reconsecrated, anyhow.' He connived at my gathering up some splinters of the rich old stained-glass as souvenirs for my wife. He was full of reminiscences of the German occupation of the place. One of his personal anecdotes was indeed marvellous. It was that a lady in the local ambulance had vowed to kiss the first French soldier who re-entered the town. She did so, and it proved to be her husband. The abbé was a good, kind, truthful man – but he had a humorous face.

A walk down a ruined street brought one to the opening of the trenches. There were marks upon the walls of the German occupation, 'Berlin to Paris' with an arrow of direction adorning one corner. At another the 76th Regiment had commemorated the fact that they were there in 1870 and again in 1914. If the Soissons folk are wise, they will keep these inscriptions as reminders to the rising generation. I could imagine, however, that their inclination will be to whitewash, fumigate, and forget.

A sudden turn among some broken walls took one into the communication trench. Our guide was a commandant of the staff, a tall, thin man with hard, grey eyes and a severe face. It was the more severe towards us, as I gathered that he had been deluded into the belief that only about one out of six of our soldiers went to the trenches. For the moment he was not friends with the English. As we went along, however, we gradually got on better terms, we discovered a twinkle in the hard, grey eyes, and the day ended with an exchange of walking-sticks between him and me and a renewal of the *entente*. May my cane grow into a marshal's baton!

A charming young artillery subaltern was our guide in that maze of trenches, and we walked and walked and walked, with a brisk exchange of compliments between the '75's' of the French and the '77's' of the Germans going on high over our heads. The trenches were boarded at the sides, and had a more permanent look than those of Flanders. Presently we met a fine, brown-faced, upstanding boy, as keen as a razor, who commanded this particular section. A little farther on a helmeted captain of infantry, who was an expert sniper, joined our little party. Now we were at the very front trench. I had expected to see primeval men, bearded and shaggy. But the *poilus* have disappeared. The men around me were clean and dapper to a remarkable degree. I gathered, however, that they had their internal difficulties. On one board I read an old inscription: 'He is a Boche, but he is the inseparable companion of a French soldier.' Above was a rude drawing of a louse.

I was led to a cunning loophole, and had a glimpse through it of a little framed picture of French countryside. There were fields, a road, a sloping hill beyond with trees. Quite close, about thirty or forty yards away, was a low, red-tiled house. 'They are there,' said our guide. 'That is their outpost. We can hear them cough.' Only the guns were coughing that morning, so we heard nothing; but it was certainly wonderful to be so near to the enemy and yet in such peace. I suppose wondering visitors from Berlin were brought up also to hear the French cough. Modern warfare has certainly some extraordinary sides.

Then we were shown all the devices which a year of experience had suggested to the quick brains of our Allies. Every form of bomb, catapult and trench mortar was ready to hand. Every method of crossfire had been thought out to an exact degree. There was something, however, about the disposition of a machine gun which disturbed the commandant. He called for the officer of the gun. His thin lips got thinner and his grey eyes more austere as we waited. Presently there emerged an extraordinarily handsome youth, dark as a Spaniard, from some rabbit hole. He faced the commandant bravely, and answered back with respect but firmness. 'Pourquoi?' asked the commandant, and yet again 'Pourquoi?' Adonis had an answer for everything. Both sides appealed to the big captain of snipers, who was clearly embarrassed. He stood on one leg and scratched his chin. Finally the commandant turned away angrily in the midst of one of Adonis's voluble sentences. His face showed that the matter was not ended. War is taken very seriously in the French army, and any sort of professional mistake is very quickly punished. Many officers of high rank had been broken by the French during the war. There was no more forgiveness for the beaten general than there was in the days of the Republic when the delegate of the National Convention, with a patent portable guillotine, used to drop in at headquarters to support a more vigorous offensive.

It had come on to rain heavily, and we were forced to take refuge in the dugout of the sniper. Eight of us sat in the deep gloom huddled closely together. The commandant was still harping upon that ill-placed machine gun. He could not get over it. My imperfect ear for French could not follow all his complaints, but some defence of the offender brought forth a 'Jamais! Jamais! Jamais!' which was rapped out as if it came from the gun itself. There were eight of us in an underground burrow, and some were smoking. Better a deluge than such an atmosphere as that. But if there was a thing upon earth which the French officer shied at it was rain and mud. The reason is that he was extraordinarily natty in his person. His charming blue uniform, his facings, his brown gaiters, boots and belt were always just as smart as paint. He was the dandy of the European War. I noticed officers in the trenches with their trousers carefully pressed.

The rain had now stopped, and we climbed from our burrow. Again we were led down that endless line of communication trench, again we stumbled through the ruins, again we emerged into the street where our cars were awaiting us. Above our heads the sharp artillery duel was going merrily forward. The French were firing three or four to one, which had been my experience at every point I had touched upon the Allied front. Thanks to the extraordinary zeal of the French workers, especially of the French women, and to the clever adoption of machinery by their engineers, their supplies were abundant.

Our next expedition carried us to Chalons, where the Huns of old met disaster. From Chalons we drove some twenty miles to St Mene-hould, and learned that the trenches were about ten miles north. On this expedition there were Donald and I with an extraordinary Spaniard, half Don Quixote, half gypsy troubadour, flat hatted and clad in brown corduroy, with a single arm, having, as we heard, lost the other in some broil. As he spoke no tongue but his own we were never on terms with him.

The front at the sector which we struck was under the control of General Henneque of the 10th Division. A fine soldier this, and heaven help Germany if he and his division had invaded it, for he was, as one could see at a glance, a man of iron who had been goaded to fierceness by all that his beloved country had endured. He was a man of middle size, swarthy, hawklike, very abrupt in his movements, with two steel-grey eyes, which were the most searching that mine have ever met. His hospitality and courtesy to us were beyond all bounds, but there is another side to him, and it is one which it were wiser not to provoke. In person he took us to his lines, passing through the usual shot-torn villages behind them. Where the road dipped down into the great forest there was one particular spot which was visible to the German artillery observers. The general mentioned it at the time, but his remark seemed to have no personal interest. We understood it better on our return in the evening.

We then found ourselves in the depths of the woods – primeval woods of oak and beech – in the deep clay soil that the great oak loves. There had been rain, and the forest paths were ankle deep in mire. Everywhere, to right and left, soldiers' faces, hard and rough from a year of open air, gazed up at us from their burrows in the ground. Presently an alert, blue-clad figure stood in the path to greet us. It was the colonel of the sector. He was ridiculously like Cyrano de Bergerac as depicted by the late M. Coquelin, save that his nose was of more moderate proportion. The ruddy colouring, the bristling, feline, full-ended moustache, the solidity of pose, the backward tilt of the head, the general suggestion of the bantam cock, were all there facing us as he stood amid the leaves in the sunlight. Gauntlets and a long rapier – nothing else was wanting. Something had amused Cyrano. His moustache quivered with suppressed mirth and his blue eyes were demurely gleaming. Then the joke came out. He had spotted a German working-party, his guns had concentrated on it, and afterwards he had seen the stretchers go forward. A grim joke, it may seem. But the French saw this war from a different angle from us. If we had had the Boche sitting on our heads for two years, and were not quite sure whether we could ever get him off again, we should get Cyrano's point of view.

We passed in a little procession among the French soldiers, and viewed their multifarious arrangements. For them we were a little break in a monotonous life, and they formed up in lines as we passed. My own British uniform and the civilian dresses of my two companions interested them. As the general passed these groups, who formed themselves up in perhaps a more familiar manner than would have been usual in the British service, he glanced kindly at them with those singular eyes of his, and once or twice addressed them as 'Mes enfants'. One might conceive that all was 'go as you please' among the French. So it was as long as you went in the right way. When you strayed from it you knew it. As we passed a group of men standing on a low ridge which overlooked us there was a sudden stop. I gazed round. The general's face was steel and cement. The eyes were cold and yet fiery, sunlight upon icicles. Something had happened. Cyrano had sprung to his side. His reddish moustache had shot forward beyond his nose, and it bristled out like that of an angry cat. Both were looking up at the group above us. One wretched man detached himself from his comrades and sidled down the slope. No skipper and mate of a Yankee blood boat could have looked more ferociously at a mutineer. And yet it was all over some minor breach of discipline which was summarily disposed of by two days of confinement. Then in an instant the faces relaxed, there was a general buzz of relief, and we were back at 'Mes enfants' again.

Trenches are trenches, and the main speciality of those in the Argonne were that they were nearer to the enemy. In fact, there were places where they interlocked, and where the advanced posts lay cheek by jowl with a good steel plate to cover both cheek and jowl. We were brought to a sap-head where the Germans were at the other side of a narrow forest road. Had I leaned forward with extended hand and a Boche done the same we could have touched. I looked across, but saw only a tangle of wire and sticks. Even whispering was not permitted in those forward posts.

When we emerged from these hushed places of danger Cyrano took us all to his dugout, which was a tasty little cottage carved from the side of a hill and faced with logs. He did the honours of the humble cabin with the air of a seigneur in his château. There was little furniture, but from some broken mansion he had extracted an iron fire-back, which adorned his grate. It was a fine, mediaeval bit of work, with Venus, in her traditional costume, in the centre of it. It seemed the last touch in the picture of the gallant virile Cyrano. I only met him this once, nor shall I ever see him again, yet he stands a thing complete within my memory. Always in the cinema of memory he will walk the leafy paths of the Argonne, his fierce eyes searching for the Boche workers, his red moustache bristling over their annihilation. He seems a figure out of the past of France.

That night we dined with yet another type of the French soldier, General Antoine, who commanded the corps of which my friend had one division. Each of these French generals had a striking individuality of his own which I wish I could fix upon paper. Their only common point was that each seemed to be a rare good soldier. The corps general was Athos with a touch of d'Artagnan. He was well over six feet high, bluff, jovial, with huge, up-curling moustache and a voice that would rally a regiment. It was a grand figure, which should have been done by Van Dyck, with lace collar, hand on sword and arm akimbo. Jovial and laughing was he, but a stern and hard soldier was lurking behind the smiles. His name has appeared in history, and so has Humbert's, who ruled all the army of which the other corps is a unit. Humbert was a Lord Roberts figure, small, wiry, quick-stepping, all steel and elastic, with a short, upturned moustache, which one could imagine as crackling with electricity in moments of excitement like a cat's fur. What he does or says is quick, abrupt and to the point. He fires his remarks like pistol shots at this man or that. Once to my horror he fixed me with his hard little eyes and demanded: 'Sherlock Holmes, est-ce qu'il est un soldat dans l'armée Anglaise?' The whole table waited in an awful hush. 'Mais, mon general,' I stammered, 'il est trop vieux pour service.' There was general laughter, and I felt that I had scrambled out of an awkward place.

And talking of awkward places, I had forgotten about that spot upon the road whence the Boche observer could see our motor cars. He had actually laid a gun upon it, the rascal, and waited all the long day for our return. No sooner did we appear upon the slope than a shrapnel shell burst above us, but somewhat behind me, as well as to the left. Had it been straight the second car would have got it, and there might have been a vacancy in one of the chief editorial chairs in London. The general shouted to the driver to speed up, and we were soon safe from the German gunners. One got perfectly immune to noises in these scenes, for the guns which surrounded you made louder crashes than any shell which burst about you. It is only when you actually saw the cloud over you that your thoughts came back to yourself, and that you realised that in this wonderful drama you might be a useless super, but none the less you were on the stage and not in the stalls.

Next morning we were down in the front trenches again at another portion of the line. Far away on our right, from a spot named the Observatory, we could see the extreme left of the Verdun position and shells bursting on the Fille Morte. To the north of us was a broad expanse of sunny France, nestling villages, scattered châteaux, rustic churches, and all as inaccessible as if it were the moon. It was a terrible thing this German bar – a thing unthinkable to Britons. To stand on the edge of Yorkshire and look into Lancashire feeling that it was in other hands, that our fellow-countrymen were suffering there and waiting, waiting for help, and that we could not, after two years, come a yard nearer to them – would it not break our hearts? Could I wonder that there was no smile upon the grim faces of those Frenchmen! But when the bar was broken, when the line swept forward, when French bayonets gleamed on those uplands and French flags broke from those village spires – ah, what a day that was! Men died that day from the pure delirious joy of it.

Yet another type of French general took us round this morning! He, too, was a man apart, an unforgettable man. Conceive a man with a large, broad, good-humoured face, and two placid, dark, seal's eyes which gazed gently into yours. He was young, and had pink cheeks and a soft voice. Such was one of the most redoubtable fighters of France, this General of Division Dupont. His former staff officers told me something of the man. He was a philosopher, a fatalist, impervious to fear, a dreamer of distant dreams amid the most furious bombardment. The weight of the French assault upon the terrible Labyrinth fell at one time upon the brigade which he then commanded. He led them day after day gathering up Germans with the detached air of the man of science who is hunting for specimens. In whatever shell-hole he might chance to lunch he had his cloth spread and decorated with wild flowers plucked from the edge. I wrote of him at the time: 'If fate be kind to him, he will go far.' As a matter of fact, before the end of the war he was one of the most influential members of the General Staff, so my prophetic power was amply vindicated.

From the Observatory we saw the destruction of a German trench. There had been signs of work upon it, so it was decided to close it down. It was a very visible brown streak a thousand yards away. The word was passed back to the '75's' in the rear. There was a *tir rapide* over our heads. My word, the man who stands fast under a *tir rapide*, be he Boche, French or British, is a man of mettle! The mere passage of the shells was awe-inspiring, at first like the screaming of a wintry wind, and then thickening into the howling of a pack of wolves. The trench was a line of terrific explosions. Then the dust settled down and all was still. Where were the ants who had made the nest? Were they buried beneath it? Or had they got from under? No one could say.

There was one little gun which fascinated me, and I stood for some time watching it. Its three gunners, enormous helmeted men, evidently loved it, and touched it with a swift but tender touch in every move-ment. When it was fired it ran up an inclined plane to take off the recoil, rushing up and then turning and rattling down again upon the gunners who were used to its ways. The first time it did it, I was standing behind it, and I don't know which jumped quickest – the gun or I.

French officers above a certain rank develop and show their own individuality. In the lower grades the conditions of service enforce a certain uniformity. The British officer is a British gentleman first, and an officer afterwards. The Frenchman is an officer first, though none the less the gentleman stands behind it. One very strange type we met, however, in these Argonne woods. He was a French-Canadian who had been a French soldier, had founded a homestead in far Alberta, and had now come back of his own will, though a naturalised Briton, to the old flag. He spoke English of a kind, the quality and quantity being equally extraordinary. It poured from him and was, so far as it was intelligible, of the woolly Western variety. His views on the Germans were the most emphatic we had met. 'These Goddamn sons of' – well, let us say, 'canines!' he would shriek, shaking his fist at the woods to the north of him. A good man was our compatriot, for he had a very recent Legion of Honour pinned upon his breast. He had been put with a few men on Hill 285, a sort of volcano stuffed with mines, and was told to telephone when he needed relief. He refused to telephone, and remained there for three weeks. 'We sit like one rabbit in his hall,' he explained. He had only one grievance – there were many wild boars in the forest, but the infantry were too busy to get them. 'The Goddamn artillaree he get the wild pig!' Out of his pocket he pulled a picture of a frame house with snow round it, and a lady with two children on the stoep. It was his homestead at Trochu, seventy miles north of Calgary.

It was the evening of the third day that we turned our faces towards Paris once more. It was my last view of the French. The roar of their guns went far with me upon my way. I wrote at the time: 'Soldiers of France, farewell! In your own phrase, I salute you! Many have seen you who had more knowledge by which to judge your manifold virtues, many also who had more skill to draw you as you are, but never one, I am sure, who admired you more than I. Great was the French soldier, under Louis the Sun-King, great too under Napoleon, but never was he greater than today.'

But in spite of all their bravery only two things saved France, her field guns and the intervention of England. Surely she should have a reckoning with her pre-war military authorities. Imagine unwarlike Britain, protected by the sea, and yet having a high standard of musketry, heavy guns with every division, and khaki uniforms, while warlike France, under the very shadow of Germany, had poor musketry, primeval uniforms and no heavy guns. As to her early views of strategy they were lamentable. Every British critic, above all Lord Kitchener, knew that the attack would swing round through Belgium. France concentrated all her preparation upon the eastern frontier. It was clear also that the weaker power should be on the defensive and so bring her enemy by heavier losses down to her own weight. France attacked and broke herself in an impossible venture. There should have been a heavy reckoning against someone. The fate of England as well as of France was imperilled by the false estimates of the French General Staff.

One small visible result of my journey was the establishment of wound stripes upon the uniforms of the British. I had been struck by this very human touch among the French, which gave a man some credit and therefore some consolation for his sufferings. I represented the matter when I came back. Lest I seem to claim more than is true, I append General Robertson's letter. The second sentence refers to that campaign for the use of armour which I had prosecuted so long, and with some success as regards helmets, though there the credit was mostly due to Dr Saleeby among civilians. The letter runs thus:

War Office
August 14, 1916

Many thanks for sending me a copy of your little book. I will certainly see what can be done in regard to armour. You will remember that I took your previous tip as regards badges for wounded men.

Yours very truly,

W. R. ROBERTSON

Breaking the Hindenburg Line

I find in my diary that the Prime Minister, Mr Lloyd George, invited
me to breakfast in April 1917. Some third person was, I understand, to
have been present, but he did not arrive, so that I found myself alone in
the classic dining-room of No. 10 Downing Street, while my host was
finishing his toilet. Presently he appeared, clad in a grey suit, smart
and smiling, with no sign at all that he bore the weight of the great
European War upon his shoulders. Nothing could have been more
affable or democratic, for there was no servant present, and he poured
out the tea, while I, from a side table, brought the bacon and eggs for
both. He had certainly the Celtic power of making one absolutely at
one's ease, for there was no trace at all of pomp or ceremony – just a
pleasant, smiling, grey-haired but very virile gentleman, with twinkling
eyes and a roguish smile. No doubt there are other aspects, but that is
how he presented himself that morning.

He began by talking about the great loss which the country had
sustained in Lord Kitchener's death, speaking of him in a very kindly
and human way. At the same time he was of opinion that long tropical
service and the habit of always talking down to subordinates had had
some effect upon his mind and character. He was a strange mixture
of rather morose inactivity and sudden flashes of prevision which
amounted to genius. He was the only man who had clearly foreseen
the length of the war, and but for Turkey, Bulgaria and other complications he probably overstated it at three years. There were times
when he became so dictatorial as to be almost unbearable, and he had to
be reminded at a Cabinet Council by Lloyd George himself that he was
in the presence of twenty men who were his peers, and that he could
not refuse them information or act above their heads. I confess that it

struck me as very natural that a big man with vital knowledge in his brain should hesitate in a world crisis to confide it to twenty men, and probably twenty wives, each of whom was a possible leak. In spite of his genius Kitchener was not accessible to new ideas. He could not see clearly why such enormous munitions were necessary. He opposed tanks. He was against the Irish and Welsh separate divisions. He refused the special flags which the ladies had worked for these divisions. He was as remote from sentiment as a steam hammer, and yet he was dealing with humans who can be influenced by sentiment. He obstructed in many things, particularly in the Dardanelles. On the other hand, his steps in organising the new armies were splendid, though he had attempted – vainly – to do away with the Territorials, another example of his blindness to the practical force of sentiment. Miss Asquith had said of him, 'If he is not a great man he is a great poster,' and certainly no one else could have moved the nation to such a degree, though the long series of provocations from the Germans had made us very receptive and combative.

Lloyd George was justly proud of the splendid work of the Welsh Division at the front. He had been to Mametz Wood, the taking of which had been such a bloody, and also such a glorious, business. He listened with interest to an account which I was able to give him of some incidents in that fight, and said that it was a beautiful story. He had arranged for a Welsh painter to do the scene of the battle.

He was interested to hear how I had worked upon my history, and remarked that it was probably better done from direct human documents than from filed papers. He asked me whether I had met many of the divisional generals, and on my saying that I had, he asked me if any had struck me as outstanding among their fellows. I said I thought they were a fine level lot, but that in soldiering it was impossible to say by mere talk or appearance who was the big man at a pinch. He agreed. He seemed to have a particular feeling towards General Tom Bridges, of the 19th Division, and shortly afterwards I noticed that he was chosen for the American mission.

I talked to him about my views as to the use of armour, and found him very keen upon it. He is an excellent listener, and seems honestly interested in what you say. He said he had no doubt that in the problem of armour lay the future of warfare, but how to carry it was the crux. He said that the soldiers always obstructed the idea – which was my experience also – with a few notable exceptions. I mentioned General

Watts of the 7th Division as being interested in armour, and he agreed and seemed to know all about Watts who, though a 'dugout', was one of the finds of the war.

He was much excited about the revolution in Russia, news of which had only just come through. The Guards had turned, and that meant that all had turned. The Tsar was good but weak. The general character and probable fate of the Tsarina were not unlike those of Marie Antoinette – in fact, the whole course of events was very analogous to the French Revolution. 'Then it will last some years and end in a Napoleon,' said I. He agreed. The revolt, he said, was in no sense pro-German. The whole affair had been Byzantine, and reminded one of the old histories.

As I left he came back to armour, and said that he was about to see someone on that very subject. When I was in the hall it struck me that a few definite facts which I had in my head would be useful in such an interview, so, to the surprise of the butler, I sat down on the hall chair and wrote out on a scrap of paper a few headings which I asked him to give the Prime Minister. I don't know if they were of any use. I came away reassured, and feeling that a vigorous virile hand was at the helm.

I had not expected to see any more actual operations of the war, but early in September 1918 I had an intimation from the Australian government that I might visit their section of the line. Little did I think that this would lead to my seeing the crowning battle of the war. It was on September 26 that we actually started, the party consisting of Sir Joseph Cook, Naval Minister of the Australian Commonwealth, Commander Latham, his aide-de-camp, who in civil life is a rising barrister of Melbourne, and Mr Berry, soon to be Sir William Berry, proprietor of the *Sunday Times*. We crossed in a gale of wind, with a destroyer sheeted in foam on either side of the leave boat, each of us being obliged to wear life-belts. Several American newspaper men were on board, one of them an old friend, Bok, of the *Ladies' Home Journal*. It was too late to continue our journey when we got across, so we stayed at an inn that night, and were off to the Australian line at an early hour in the morning, our way lying through Abbeville and Amiens. The latter place was nearly deserted and very badly knocked about, far more so than I had expected.

The enemy had, as we knew, been within seven miles of Amiens – it was the Australian line which held the town safe and kept the Allied cause from desperate peril if not ruin. It did not surprise us, therefore, that we soon came upon signs of fighting. A little grove was shown us as the absolute farthest ripple of the advanced German wave. A little farther on was the sheltered town of Villers Brettoneux, with piles of empty cartridge cases at every corner to show where snipers or machine guns had lurked. A little farther on a truly monstrous gun – the largest I have ever seen – lay near the road, broken into three pieces. It was bigger to my eyes than the largest on our battleships, and had been brought up and mounted by the Germans just before the tide had turned, which was on July 5. In their retreat they had been compelled to blow it up. A party of British Guardsmen were standing round it examining it, and I exchanged a few words with them. Then we ran on through ground which was intensely interesting to me, as it was the scene of Gough's retreat, and I had just been carefully studying it at home. There was the Somme on our left, a very placid, slow-moving stream, and across it the higher ground where our III Corps had been held up on the historical August 8, the day which made Ludendorff realise, as he himself states, that the war was lost. On the plain over which we were moving the Australian and Canadian Divisions had swept, with the tanks leading the British line, as Boadicea's chariots did of old. Though I had not been over the ground before, I had visualised it so clearly in making notes about the battle that I could name every hamlet and locate every shattered church tower. Presently a hill rose on the left, which I knew to be Mount St Quentin, the taking of which by the Australians was one of the feats of the war. It had been defended by picked troops, including some of the Prussian Guards, but they were mostly taken or killed, though a flanking attack by the British Yeomanry Division had something to do with the result.

The old walled town of Peronne, sacred for ever to Sir Walter, Quentin Durward and the archers of the Scots Guards, lay before us, almost if not quite surrounded by the river, the canal and broad moats. It seemed an impossible place to take, which is of course the greatest possible trap in modern warfare, since something occurring fifty miles away may place troops behind you and cut you off. Here our long drive finished, and we were handed over to the care of Colonel Bennett, commanding the camp, a tall, bluff warrior who, if he had doffed his khaki and got into a velvet tunic, would have been the exact image of the veteran warrior in Scott's novel. He was indeed a veteran, having fought, if I remember right, not only in South Africa, but even in the Australian Suakim contingent.

A little wooden hut was put at our disposal, and there we slept, Sir Joseph Cook and I, with a small partition between us. I was bitterly cold, and so I can tell was he, for I could hear him tossing about just as I did for warmth. We had neither of us made the discovery that you may pile all the clothes you like on the top of you, but so long as there is only one layer of canvas beneath you, you are likely to be cold. We don't usually realise that the mattress is also part of the bedclothes. We both got little sleep that night.

Next morning, September 28, we were off betimes, for we had much to see, the old town for one thing, which I vowed I would visit again in time of peace. We descended Mount St Quentin and saw ample evidence of the grim struggle that had occurred there. There were many rude graves, some of them with strange inscriptions. One of them, I was told, read: 'Here lies a German who met two diggers.' The Australian Tommy was of course universally known as a digger. They make a rough, valiant, sporting but rude-handed crew. They went through the prisoners for loot, and even the officers were ransacked. Colonel Bennett told me that a colonel of the Germans was impudent when he came into his presence, so Bennett said: 'Mend your manners, or I will hand you over to the diggers!' They were waiting outside the tent for just such a chance. One German had an iron cross which was snatched from him by an Australian. The German shaped up to the man in excellent form and knocked him down. The other Australians were delighted, gave him back his cross, and made him quite a hero. I expect the looter had been an unpopular man.

The younger Australian officers were all promoted from the ranks, and many of them had their own ideas about English grammar. Bennett told me that he tried to get the reports better written. One subaltern had reported: 'As I came round the traverse I met a Bosch and we both reached for our guns, but he lost his block and I got him.' Bennett returned this for emendation. It came back: 'As I came round the traverse I met a German, and we both drew our automatic pistols, but he lost his presence of mind and I shot him.' I think I like the first style best.

I lunched that day at the headquarters of Sir John Monash, an excellent soldier who had done really splendid work, especially since the advance began. Indeed, it was his own action on July 5 which turned the tide of retreat. He showed that the long line of fighting Jews which began with Joshua still carries on. One of the Australian divisional generals, Rosenthal, was also a Jew, and the headquarters staff was full of eagle-nosed, black-haired warriors. It spoke well for them and well also for the perfect equality of the Australian system, which would have the best man at the top, be he who he might. My brother was acting as Assistant Adjutant-General to General Butler with the III British Corps on the left of the Australians, and they had kindly wired for him, so that I had the joy of having him next me at lunch, and he invited me to join the headquarters mess of his corps for dinner.

It was a wonderful experience that dinner. The great advance was to be next morning, when it was hoped that the Hindenburg Line, which was practically the frontier of Germany, would be carried. There were only six who dined in that little farmhouse messroom: Butler himself, with hard composed face, his head of sappers, head of gunners, my brother and the first and second staff officers, a little group of harassed and weary men. Yet there was no word of the huge drama upon the edge of which we were standing. Every now and then a telephone tinkled in the next room, a Staff officer rose, there were a few short words, a nod, and the incident was closed. It was a wonderful example of quiet self-control. I said to my brother, when we were alone: 'Don't you think I am out of the picture at such a moment talking about such frivolous things?' 'For God's sake keep on at it,' he said. 'It is just what they need. Give their brains something new.' So I tried to do so and we had a memorable evening.

I shall never forget the drive back of ten miles in a pitch-dark night, with not a gleam anywhere save that far aloft two little gold points glimmered now and again, like the far-off headlights of a motor transferred suddenly to the heavens. These were British aeroplanes, so lit to distinguish them from the German marauders. The whole eastern horizon was yellow-red with gunfire, and the distant roar of the artillery preparation was like the Atlantic surge upon a rock-bound coast. Along the road no lights were permitted, and several times out of the black a still blacker gloom framed itself into some motor-lorry with which only our cries saved a collision. It was wonderful and awesome, the eve of the day of judgement when Germany's last solid defence was to be smashed, and she was to be left open to that vengeance which she had so long provoked.

We were awakened early, part of our party getting away to some point which they imagined would be more adventurous than that to which we seniors should be invited, though in the sequel it hardly proved so. They saw much, however, and one of them described to me how one of the first and saddest sights was that of eighteen splendid young Americans lying dead and lonely by the roadside, caught in some unlucky shell burst. Mr Cook, Commander Latham and I had been placed under the charge of Captain Plunket, a twice-wounded Australian officer, who helped us much during the varied adventures of our exciting day.

The general programme of attack was already in our minds. Two American divisions, the 27th and 30th, one from New York the other from the South, were to rush the front line. The Australian divisions were then to pass over or through them and carry the battlefront forward. Already, as we arrived on the battlefield, the glad news came back that the Americans had done their part, and that the Australians had just been unleashed. Also that the Germans were standing to it like men.

As our car threaded the crowded street between the ruins of Templeux we met the wounded coming back, covered cars with nothing visible save protruding boots, and a constant stream of pedestrians, some limping, some with bandaged arms and faces, some supported by Red Cross men, a few in pain, most of them smiling grimly behind their cigarettes. Amid them came the first clump of prisoners, fifty or more, pitiable enough, and yet I could not pity them, the weary, shuffling, hang-dog creatures, with no touch of nobility in their features or their bearing.

The village was full of Americans and Australians, extraordinarily like each other in type. One could well have lingered, for it was all of great interest, but there were even greater interests ahead, so we turned up a hill, left our car, which had reached its limit, and proceeded on foot. The road took us through a farm, where a British anti-aircraft battery stood ready for action. Then we found open plain, and went forward, amid old trenches and rusty wire, in the direction of the battle.

We had now passed the heavy-gun positions, and were among the field guns, so that the noise was deafening. A British howitzer battery was hard at work, and we stopped to chat with the major. His crews had been at it for six hours, but were in great good humour, and chuckled mightily when the blast of one of their guns nearly drove in our ear-drums, we having got rather too far forward. The effect was that of a ringing box on the exposed ear – with which valediction we left our grinning British gunners and pushed on to the east, under a screaming canopy of our own shells. The wild, empty waste of moor was broken by a single shallow quarry or gravel-pit, in which we could see some movement. In it we found an advanced dressing station, with about a hundred American and Australian gunners and orderlies. There were dugouts in the sides of this flat excavation, and it had been an American battalion headquarters up to a few hours before. We were now about a thousand yards from the Hindenburg Line, and I learned with emotion that this spot was the Egg Redoubt, one of those advanced outposts of General Gough's army which suffered so tragic and glorious a fate in that great military epic of March 21 – one of the grandest in the whole war. The fact that we were now actually standing in the Egg Redoubt showed me, as nothing else could have done, how completely the ground had been recovered, and how the day of retribution was at hand.

We were standing near the eastward lip of the excavation, and looking over it, when it was first brought to our attention that it took two to make a battle. Up to now we had seen only one. Now two shells burst in quick succession forty yards in front of us, and a spray of earth went into the air. 'Whizz-bangs,' remarked our soldier-guide casually. Personally, I felt less keenly interested in their name than in the fact that they were there at all.

We thought we had done pretty well to get within a thousand yards of the famous line, but now came a crowning bit of good fortune, for an Australian gunner captain, a mere lad, but a soldier from his hawk's eyes to his active feet, volunteered to rush us forward to some coign of vantage known to himself. So it was Eastward Ho! once more, still over a dull, barren plain sloping gently upwards, with little sign of life. Here and there was the quick fluff of a bursting shell, but at a comfortable distance. Suddenly ahead of us a definite object broke the skyline. It was a tank, upon which the crew were working with spanners and levers, for its comrades were now far ahead, and it would fain follow. This, it seems, was the grandstand which our young gunner had selected. On to the top of it we clambered – and there, at our very feet, and less than five hundred yards away, was the rift which had been torn a few hours before in the Hindenburg Line. On the dun slope beyond it, under our very eyes, was even now being fought a part of that great fight where at last the children of light were beating down into the earth the forces of darkness. It was there. We could see it. And yet how little there was to see!

The ridge was passed, and the ground sloped down, as dark and heathy as Hindhead. In front of us lay a village. It was Bellicourt. The Hindenburg position ran through it. It lay quiet enough, and with the unaided eye one could see rusty red fields of wire in front of it. But the wire had availed nothing, nor had the trench that lurked behind it, for beyond it, beside the village of Nauroy, there was a long white line, clouds of pale steam-like vapour spouting up against a dark, rain-sodden sky. 'The Boche smoke barrage,' said our guide. 'They are going to counterattack.' Only this, the long, white, swirling cloud upon the dark plain told of the strife in front of us. With my glasses I saw what looked like tanks, but whether wrecked or in action I could not say. There was the battle – the greatest of battles – but nowhere could I see a moving figure. It is true that all the noises of the pit seemed to rise from that lonely landscape, but noise was always with us, go where we would.

The Australians were ahead where that line of smoke marked their progress. In the sloping fields, which at that point emerged out of the moor, the victorious Americans, who had done their part, were crouching. It was an assured victory upon which we gazed, achieved so rapidly that we were ourselves standing far forward in ground which had been won that day. The wounded had been brought in, and I saw no corpses. On the left the fight was very severe, and the Germans, who had been hidden in their huge dugouts, were doing their usual trick of emerging and cutting off the attack. So much we gathered afterwards, but for the moment it was the panorama before us which was engrossing all our thoughts.

Suddenly the German guns woke up. I can but pray that it was not our group which drew their fire upon the half-mended tank. Shell after shell fell in its direction, all of them short, but creeping forward with each salvo. It was time for us to go. If any man says that without a call of duty he likes being under aimed shellfire, he is not a man whose word I would trust. Some of the shells burst with a rusty-red out-flame, and we were told that they were gas shells. I may say that before we were admitted on to the battlefield at all, we were ushered one by one into a room where some devil's pipkin was bubbling in the corner, and were taught to use our gas-masks by the simple expedient of telling us that if we failed to acquire the art then and there a very painful alternative was awaiting us.

We made our way back, with no indecent haste, but certainly without loitering, across the plain, the shells always getting rather nearer, until we came to the excavation. Here we had a welcome rest, for our good gunner took us into his cubbyhole of a dugout, which would at least stop shrapnel, and we shared his tea and dried beef, a true Australian soldier's meal.

The German fire was now rather heavy, and our expert host explained that this meant that he had recovered from the shock of the attack, had reorganised his guns, and was generally his merry self once more. From where we sat we could see heavy shells bursting far to our rear, and there was an atmosphere of explosion all round us, which might have seemed alarming had it not been for the general chatty afternoon-tea appearance of all these veteran soldiers with whom it was our privilege to find ourselves. A group of sulky-looking German prisoners sat in a corner, while a lank and freckled Australian soldier, with his knee sticking out of a rent in his trousers, was walking about with four watches dangling from his hand, endeavouring vainly to sell them. Far be it from me to assert that he did not bring the watches from Sydney and choose this moment for doing a deal in them, but they were heavy old Teutonic timepieces, and the prisoners seemed to take a rather personal interest in them.

As we started on our homeward track we came, first, upon the British battery, which seemed to be limbering up with some idea of advancing and so lost its chance of administering a box on our other ear. Farther still we met our friends of the air guns, and stopped again to exchange a few impressions. They had nothing to fire at, and seemed bored to tears, for the red, white and blue machines were in full command of the sky. Soon we found our motor waiting in the lee of a ruined house, and began to thread our way back through the wonderfully picturesque streams of men – American, Australian, British and German – who were strung along the road.

And then occurred a very horrible incident. One knew, of course, that one could not wander about a battlefield and not find oneself sooner or later involved in some tragedy, but we were now out of range of any but heavy guns, and their shots were spasmodic. We had halted the car for an instant, to gather up two German helmets which Commander Latham had seen on the roadside, when there was a very heavy burst close ahead round a curve in the village street. A geyser of red brick-dust flew up into the air. An instant later our car rounded the corner. None of us will forget what we saw. There was a tangle of mutilated horses, their necks rising and sinking. Beside them a man with his hand blown off was staggering away, the blood gushing from his upturned sleeve. He was moving round and holding the arm raised and hanging, as a dog holds an injured foot. Beside the horses lay a shattered man, drenched crimson from head to foot, with two great glazed eyes looking upwards through a mask of blood. Two comrades were at hand to help, and we could only go upon our way with the ghastly picture stamped for ever upon our memory. The image of that dead driver might well haunt one in one's dreams.

Once through Templeux and on the main road for Peronne things became less exciting, and we drew up to see a column of nine hundred prisoners pass us. Each side of the causeway was lined by Australians, with their keen, clear-cut, falcon faces, and between lurched these heavy-jawed, beetle-browed, uncouth louts, new caught and staring round with bewildered eyes at their debonair captors. I saw none of that relief at getting out of it which I have read of; nor did I see any signs of fear, but the prevailing impression was an ox-like stolidity and dullness. It was a herd of beasts, not a procession of men. It was indeed farcical to think that these uniformed bumpkins represented the great military nation, while the gallant figures who lined the road belonged to the race which they had despised as being unwarlike. Time and fate between them have a pretty sense of humour. One of them caught my eye as he passed and roared out in guttural English, 'The old Jairman is out!' It was the only words I heard them speak. French cavalry troopers, stern, dignified and martial, rode at either end of the bedraggled procession.

They were great soldiers, these Australians. I think they would admit it themselves, but a spectator is bound to confirm it. There was a reckless dare-devilry, combined with a spice of cunning, which gave them a place of their own in the imperial ranks. They had a great advantage too in having a permanent organisation, the same five divisions always in the same corps under the same chief. It doubled their military value – and the same applied equally, of course, to the Canadians. None the less, they should not undervalue their British comrades or lose their sense of proportion. I had a chance of addressing some twelve hundred of them on our return that evening, and while telling them all what I thought of their splendid deeds, I ventured to remind them that seventy-two per cent of the men engaged and seventy-six per cent of the casualties were Englishmen of England.

I think that now, in these after-war days, the whole world needs to be reminded of this fact as well as the Australians did. There has been, it seems to me, a systematic depreciation of what the glorious English, apart from the British, soldiers did. England is too big to be provincial, and smaller minds sometimes take advantage of it. At the time some of the Australian papers slanged me for having given this speech to their soldiers, but I felt that it needed saying, and several of their officers thanked me warmly, saying that as they never saw anything save their own front, they were all of them losing their sense of proportion. I shall not easily forget that speech, I standing on a mound in the rain, the Australian soldiers with cloaks swathed round them like brigands, and half a dozen aeroplanes, returning from the battle, circling overhead, evidently curious as to what was going on. It seems to me now like some extraordinary dream.

Such was my scamper to the Australian front. It was as if some huge hand had lifted me from my study table, placed me where I could see what I was writing about, and then within four days laid me down once more before the familiar table, with one more wonderful experience added to my record.

And then at last came the blessed day of Armistice. I was in a staid London hotel at eleven o'clock in the morning, most prim of all the hours of the day, when a lady, well dressed and conventional, came through the turning doors, waltzed slowly round the hall with a flag in either hand, and departed without saying a word. It was the first sign that things were happening. I rushed out into the streets, and of course the news was everywhere at once. I walked down to Buckingham Palace and saw the crowds assembling there, singing and cheering. A slim, young girl had got elevated on to some high vehicle, and was leading and conducting the singing as if she was some angel in tweeds just dropped from a cloud. In the dense crowd I saw an open motor stop with four middle-aged men, one of them a hard-faced civilian, the others officers. I saw this civilian hack at the neck of a whisky bottle and drink it raw. I wish the crowd had lynched him. It was the moment for prayer, and this beast was a blot on the landscape. On the whole the people were very good and orderly. Later more exuberant elements got loose. They say that it was when the Australian wounded met the War Office flappers that the foundations of solid old London got loosened. But we have little to be ashamed of, and if ever folk rejoiced we surely had the right to do so. We did not see the new troubles ahead of us, but at least these old ones were behind. And we had gained an immense reassurance. Britain had not weakened. She was still the Britain of old.

32

The Psychic Quest

I have not obtruded the psychic question upon the reader, though it has grown in importance with the years, and has now come to absorb the whole energy of my life. I cannot, however, close these scattered memories of my adventures in thought and action without some reference, however incomplete, to that which has been far the most important thing in my life. It is the thing for which every preceding phase – my gradual religious development, my books, which gave me an introduction to the public, my modest fortune, which enables me to devote myself to unlucrative work, my platform work, which helps me to convey the message, and my physical strength, which is still sufficient to stand arduous tours and to fill the largest halls for an hour and a half with my voice – have each and all been an unconscious preparation. For thirty years I have trained myself exactly for the role without the least inward suspicion of whither I was tending.

I cannot in the limited space of a chapter go into very lengthy detail or complete argument upon the subject. It is the more unnecessary since I have already in my psychic volumes outlined very clearly how I arrived at my present knowledge. Of these volumes the first and second, called respectively *The New Revelation* and *The Vital Message*, show how gradual evidence was given me of the continuation of life, and how thorough and long were my studies before I was at last beaten out of my material agnostic position and forced to admit the validity of the proofs.

In the days of universal sorrow and loss, when the voice of Rachel was heard throughout the land, it was borne in upon me that the knowledge which had come to me thus was not for my own consolation alone, but that God had placed me in a very special position for conveying it to that world which needed it so badly.

I found in the movement many men who saw the truth as clearly as I did; but such was the clamour of the 'religious', who were opposing that which is the very essence of living religion, of the 'scientific', who broke the first laws of science by pronouncing upon a thing which they had not examined, and of the press, who held up every real or imaginary rascality as being typical of a movement which they had never understood, that the true men were abashed and shrank from the public exposition of their views. It was to combat this that I began a campaign in 1916 which can only finish when all is finished.

One grand help I had. My wife had always been averse to my psychic studies, deeming the subject to be uncanny and dangerous. Her own experiences soon convinced her to the contrary, for her brother, who was killed at Mons, came back to us in a very convincing way. From that instant she threw herself with all the whole-hearted energy of her generous nature into the work which lay before us.

A devoted mother, she was forced often to leave her children; a lover of home, she was compelled to quit it for many months at a time; distrustful of the sea, she joyfully shared my voyages. We have now travelled a good fifty thousand miles upon our quest. We have spoken face to face with a quarter of a million of people. Her social qualities, her clear sanity, her ardent charity and her gracious presence upon the platforms, all united with her private counsel and sympathy, have been such an aid to me that they have turned my work into a joy. The presence of our dear children upon our journeys has also lightened them for both of us.

I began our public expositions of the subject by three years of intermittent lecturing in this country, during which period I visited nearly every town of importance, many of them twice or thrice. Everywhere I found attentive audiences, critical, as they should be, but open to conviction. I roused antagonism only in those who had not heard me, and there were demonstrations outside the doors, but never in the halls. I cannot remember a single interruption during that long series of addresses. It was interesting to notice how I was upheld, for though I was frequently very weary before the address, and though my war lectures had often been attended by palpitation of the heart, I was never once conscious of any fatigue during or after a lecture upon psychic subjects.

On August 13, 1920, we started for Australia. In proportion to her population she had lost almost as heavily as we during the war, and I felt that my seed would fall upon fruitful ground. I have written all details of this episode in my *Wanderings of a Spiritualist*, in which the reader will find among other things some evidences of that preternatural help which went with us in our journeys. I addressed large audiences in all the big towns of Australia and New Zealand. An unfortunate shipping strike prevented me from reaching Tasmania, but otherwise the venture was an unalloyed success. Contrary to expectation I was able to pay all the expenses of our large party (we were seven) and to leave a balance behind me to help the successor whom I might choose.

At the end of March 1921, we were back in Paris again, where, greatly daring, I lectured in French upon psychic subjects. Our stay at home was not a very long one, for urgent invitations had come from America, where the Spiritualist movement had fallen into a somewhat languishing state. On April 1, 1922 our whole party started for the States. What happened to us I have recorded in *Our American Adventure*. Suffice it to say that the trip was very successful, and that from Boston to Washington, and from New York to Chicago, I spoke in all the larger cities and brought about a great revival of interest in the subject. We were back in England at the beginning of July 1922.

I was by no means satisfied about America, however, as we had not touched the great West, the land of the future. Therefore we set forth again in March 1923, getting back in August. Our adventures, which were remarkable upon the psychic side, are recorded in *Our Second American Adventure*. When I returned from that journey I had travelled fifty-five thousand miles in three years, and spoken to a quarter of a million of people. I am still unsatisfied, however, for the Southern States of the Union have not been touched, and it is possible that we may yet make a journey in that direction.

I have placed on record our experiences, and no doubt they have little interest at the moment for the general public, but the day will come, and that speedily, when people will understand that this proposition for which we are now fighting is far the most important thing for two thousand years in the history of the world and when the efforts of the pioneers will have a very real interest to all who have sufficient intelligence to follow the progress of human thought.

I am only one of many working for the cause, but I hope that I may claim that I brought into it a combative and aggressive spirit which it lacked before, and which has now so forced it upon public attention that one can hardly pick up a paper without reading some comment upon it. If some of these papers are hopelessly ignorant and prejudiced, it is not a bad thing for the cause. If you have a bad case, constant publicity is a misfortune, but if you have a good one, its goodness will always assert itself, however much it may be misrepresented.

Many Spiritualists have taken the view that since we know these comforting and wonderful things, and since the world chooses not to examine the evidence, we may be content with our own happy assurance. This seems to me an immoral view.

If God has sent a great new message of exceeding joy down to earth, then it is for, us, to whom it has been clearly revealed, to pass it on at any cost of time, money and labour. It is not given to us for selfish enjoyment, but for general consolation. If the sick man turns from the physician, then it cannot be helped, but at least the healing draught should be offered.

The greater the difficulty in breaking down the wall of apathy, ignorance and materialism, the more is it a challenge to our manhood to attack and ever attack in the same bulldog spirit with which Foch faced the German lines.

I trust that the record of my previous life will assure the reader that I have within my limitations preserved a sane and balanced judgement, since I have never hitherto been extreme in my views and since what I have said has so often been endorsed by the actual course of events. But never have I said anything with the same certainty of conviction with which I now say that this new knowledge is going to sweep the earth and to revolutionise human views upon every topic save only on fundamental morality, which is a fixed thing.

All modern inventions and discoveries will sink into insignificance beside those psychic facts which will force themselves within a few years upon the universal human mind.

The subject has been obscured by the introduction of all sorts of side issues, some of interest but not vital, others quite irrelevant. There is a class of investigator who loves to wander round in a circle, and to drag you with him if you are weak enough to accept such guidance. He trips continually over his own brains, and can never persuade himself that the simple and obvious explanation is also the true one. His intellect becomes a positive curse to him, for he uses it to avoid the straight road and to fashion out some strange devious path which lands him at last in a quagmire, whilst the direct and honest mind has kept firmly to the highway of knowledge. When I meet men of this type, and then come in contact with the lowly congregations of religious Spiritualists, I think always of Christ's words when He thanked God that He had revealed these things to babes and withheld them from the wise and the prudent. I think also of a dictum of Baron Reichenbach: 'There is a scientific incredulity which exceeds in stupidity the obtuseness of the clodhopper.'

But what I say in no way applies to the reasonable researcher whose experiences are real stepping-stones leading to his fixed conclusion. There must to every man be this novitiate in knowledge. The matter is too serious to be taken without due intellectual conviction.

It must not be imagined that I entirely deny the existence of fraud. But it is far less common than is supposed, and as for its being universal, which is the theory of the conjurers and some other critics, such an opinion is beyond reason or argument. In an experience with mediums which has been excelled by very few living men, and which has embraced three continents, I have not encountered fraud more than three or four times.

There is conscious and unconscious fraud, and it is the existence of the latter which complicates the question so badly. Conscious fraud usually arises from a temporary failure of real psychic power, and a consequent attempt to replace it by an imitation. Unconscious fraud comes in that curious halfway state which I have called the 'half-trance condition' when the medium seems normal, and yet is actually hardly responsible for his actions.

At such a time the process by which his personality leaves his body seems to have set in, and his higher qualities have already passed, so that he can apparently no longer inhibit the promptings received from the suggestion of those around him, or from his own unchecked desires. Thus one will find mediums doing stupid and obvious things which expose them to the charge of cheating. Then if the observer disregards these and waits, the true psychic phenomena of unmistakable character will follow as he sinks more deeply into trance.

This was, I gather, noticeable in the case of Eusapia Paladino, but I have seen it with several others. In those cases where a medium has left the cabinet and is found wandering about among the sitters, as has happened with Mrs Corner, with Madame d'Esperance and with Craddock – all of them mediums who have given many proofs of their real powers – I am convinced that the very natural supposition that they are fraudulent is really quite a mistaken one.

When, on the other hand, it is found that the medium has introduced false drapery or accessories, which has sometimes occurred, we are in the presence of the most odious and blasphemous crime which a human being can commit.

People ask me, not unnaturally, what is it which makes me so perfectly certain that this thing is true. That I am perfectly certain is surely demonstrated by the mere fact that I have abandoned my congenial and lucrative work, left my home for long periods at a time, and subjected myself to all sorts of inconveniences, losses and even insults, in order to get the facts home to the people.

To give all my reasons would be to write a book rather than a chapter, but I may say briefly that there is no physical sense which I possess which has not been separately assured, and that there is no conceivable method by which a spirit could show its presence which I have not on many occasions experienced. In the presence of Miss Besinnet as medium and of several witnesses I have seen my mother and my nephew, young Oscar Hornung, as plainly as ever I saw them in life – so plainly that I could almost have counted the wrinkles of the one and the freckles of the other.

In the darkness the face of my mother shone up, peaceful, happy, slightly inclined to one side, the eyes closed. My wife upon my right and the lady upon my left both saw it as clearly as I did. The lady had not known my mother in life but she said, 'How wonderfully like she is to her son,' which will show how clear was the detail of the features.

On another occasion my son came back to me. Six persons heard his conversation with me, and signed a paper afterwards to that effect. It was in his voice and concerned itself with what was unknown to the medium, who was bound and breathing deeply in his chair. If the evidence of six persons of standing and honour may not be taken, then how can any human fact be established?

My brother, General Doyle, came back with the same medium, but on another occasion. He discussed the health of his widow. She was a Danish lady, and he wanted her to use a masseur in Copenhagen. He gave the name. I made enquiries and found that such a man did exist. Whence came this knowledge? Who was it who took so close an interest in the health of this lady? If it was not her dead husband then who was it?

All fine-drawn theories of the subconscious go to pieces before the plain statement of the intelligence, 'I am a spirit. I am Innes. I am your brother.'

I have clasped materialised hands.

I have held long conversations with the direct voice.

I have smelt the peculiar ozone-like smell of ectoplasm.

I have listened to prophecies which were quickly fulfilled.

I have seen the 'dead' glimmer up upon a photographic plate which no hand but mine had touched.

I have received through the hand of my own wife notebooks full of information which was utterly beyond her ken.

I have seen heavy articles swimming in the air, untouched by human hand, and obeying directions given to unseen operators.

I have seen spirits walk round the room in fair light and join in the talk of the company.

I have known an untrained woman possessed by an artist spirit and rapidly produce a picture now hanging in my drawing-room which few living painters could have bettered.

I have read books which might have come from great thinkers and scholars and which were actually written by unlettered men who acted as the medium of the unseen intelligence so superior to their own. I have recognised the style of a dead writer which no parodist could have copied and which was written in his own handwriting.

I have heard singing beyond earthly power and whistling done with no pause for the intake of breath.

I have seen objects from a distance projected into a room with closed doors and windows.

If a man could see, hear and feel all this, and yet remain unconvinced of unseen intelligent forces around him, he would have good cause to doubt his own sanity. Why should he heed the chatter of irresponsible journalists or the head-shaking of inexperienced men of science when he has himself had so many proofs? They are babies in this matter and should be sitting at his feet.

It is not, however, a question to be argued in a detached and impersonal way, as if one were talking of the Baconian theory or the existence of Atlantis. It is intimate, personal and vital to the last degree.

A closed mind means an earthbound soul, and that in turn means future darkness and misery. If you know what is coming, you can avoid it. If you do not, you run grave risk. Some Jeremiah or Savonarola is needed who will shriek this into the ears of the world. A new conception of sin is needed. The mere carnal frailties of humanity, the weaknesses of the body, are not to be lightly condoned, but are not the serious part of the human reckoning. It is the fixed condition of mind, narrowness, bigotry, materialism – in a word, the sins not of the body, but of the spirit – which are the real permanent things and condemn the individual to the lower spheres until he has learnt his lesson.

We know this from our rescue circles when these poor souls come back to bewail their errors and to learn those truths which they might have learnt here, had their minds not been closed by apathy or prejudice.

The radical mistake which science has made in investigating the subject is that it has never troubled to grasp the fact that it is not the medium who is producing the phenomena. It has always treated him as if he were a conjurer, and said, 'Do this or do that,' failing to understand that little or nothing comes *from* him, but all or nearly all comes *through* him. I say 'nearly' all, for I believe that some simple phenomena, such as the rap, can within limits be produced by the medium's own will.

It is this false view of science which has prevented sceptics from realising that a gentle and receptive state of mind on the part of sitters and an easy natural atmosphere for the medium are absolutely essential in order to produce harmony with the outside forces.

If in the greatest of all séances, that of the upper room on the day of Pentecost, an aggressive sceptic had insisted upon test conditions of his own foolish devising, where would the rushing wind and the tongues of fire have been? 'All with one accord,' says the writer of the Acts of the Apostles, and that is the essential condition. I have sat with saintly people, and I too have felt the rushing wind, seen the flickering tongues and heard the great voice, but how could such results come where harmony did not reign?

That is the radical mistake which science has made. Men know well that even in their own coarse, material work the presence of a scrap of metal may upset the whole balance of a great magnetic installation, and yet they will not take the word of those who are in a position to speak from experience that a psychic condition may upset a psychic experiment.

But indeed when we speak of science in this connection it is a confusion of thought. The fact that a man is a great zoologist like Lankester, or a great physicist like Tyndall or Faraday, does not give his opinion any weight in a subject which is outside his own speciality. There is many an unknown Smith and Jones whose twenty years of practical work have put him in a far stronger position than that of these intolerant scientists; while as to the real Spiritualist leaders, men of many experiences and much reading and thought, it is they who are the real scientific experts who are in a position to teach the world. One does not lose one's judgement when one becomes a Spiritualist. One is as much a researcher as ever, but one understands better what it is that one is studying and how to study it.

This controversy with bumptious and ignorant people is a mere passing thing which matters nothing. The real controversy, which does matter very much, is with the Continental school who study ectoplasm and other semi-material manifestations, but who have not gone to the length of seeing independent spirit behind them. Richet, Schrenck-Notzing and other great investigators are still in this midway position, and Flammarion is little more advanced. Richet goes to the length of admitting that he has assured himself by personal observation of the materialised form that it can walk and talk and leave moulds of its hands. So far he has gone. And yet even now he clings to the idea that these phenomena may be the externalisation of some latent powers of the human body and mind.

Such an explanation seems to me to be the desperate defence of the last trench by one of those old-time materialists who say with Brewster: 'Spirit is the last thing which we will concede;' adding as their reason, 'it upsets the work of fifty years.' It is hard when a man has taught all his life that the brain governs spirit to have to learn after all that it may be spirit which acts independently of the human brain. But it is their super-materialism which is the real difficulty with which we now have to contend.

And what is the end of it all?

I have no idea. How could those who first noted the electric twitching of muscles foresee the Atlantic cable or the arc lamp? Our information is that some great shock is coming shortly to the human race which will finally break down its apathy, and which will be accompanied by such psychic signs that the survivors will be unable any longer to deny the truths which we preach.

The real meaning of our movement will then be seen, for it will become apparent that we have accustomed the public mind to such ideas, and provided a body of definite teaching, both scientific and religious, to which they can turn for guidance.

As to the prophecy of disaster, I admit that we have to be on our guard. Even the Christ circle was woefully deceived, and declared confidently that the world would not survive their own generation. Various creeds, too, have made vain predictions of the end of the world.

I am keenly aware of all this, and also of the difficulty in reckoning time when seen from the other side. But, making every allowance for this, the information upon the point has been so detailed, and has reached me from so many entirely independent sources, that I have been forced to take it seriously, and to think that some great watershed of human experience may be passed within a few years – the greatest, we are told, that our long-suffering race has yet encountered.

People who have not gone into the subject may well ask, 'But what do you get out of it? How are you the better?' We can only answer that all life has changed to us since this definite knowledge has come. No longer are we shut in by death. We are out of the valley and up on the ridge, with vast clear vistas before us.

Why should we fear a death which we know for certain is the doorway to unutterable happiness?

Why should we fear our dear ones' death if we can be so near to them afterwards?

Am I not far nearer to my son than if he were alive and serving in that Army Medical Service which would have taken him to the ends of the earth? There is never a month, often never a week, that I do not commune with him. Is it not evident that such facts as these change the whole aspect of life, and turn the grey mist of dissolution into a rosy dawn?

You may say that we have already all these assurances in the Christian revelation. It is true, and that is why we are not anti-Christian so long as Christianity is the teaching of humble Christ and not of his arrogant representatives.

Every form of Christianity is represented in our ranks, often by clergymen of the various denominations. But there is nothing precise in the definitions of the other world as given in the holy writings. The information we have depicts a heaven of congenial work and of congenial play, with every mental and physical activity of life carried on to a higher plane – a heaven of art, of science, of intellect, of organisation, of combat with evil, of home circles, of flowers, of wide travel, of sports, of the mating of souls, of complete harmony. This is what our 'dead' friends describe.

On the other hand, we hear from them, and sometimes directly, of the hells, which are temporary spheres of purification. We hear of the mists, the darkness, the aimless wanderings, the mental confusion, the remorse.

'Our condition is horrible,' wrote one of them to me recently at a séance. These things are real and vivid and provable to us. That is why we are an enormous force for the resuscitation of true religion, and why the clergy take a heavy responsibility when they oppose us.

The final result upon scientific thought is unthinkable, save that the sources of all force would be traced rather to spiritual than to material causes.

In religion one can perhaps see a little more clearly. Theology and dogma would disappear.

People would realise that such questions as the number of persons in God, or the process of Christ's birth, have no bearing at all upon the development of man's spirit, which is the sole object of life.

All religions would be equal, for all alike produce gentle, unselfish souls who are God's elect. Christian, Jew, Buddhist and Mohammedan would shed their distinctive doctrines, follow their own high teachers on a common path of morality and forget all that antagonism which has made religion a curse rather than a blessing to the world.

We shall be in close touch with other-world forces, and knowledge will supersede that faith which has in the past planted a dozen different signposts to point in as many different directions.

Such will be the future, so far as I can dimly see it, and all this will spring from the seed which now we tend and water amid the cold blasts of a hostile world.

Do not let it be thought that I claim any special leadership in this movement. I do what I can, but many others have done what they could – many humble workers who have endured loss and insult, but who will come to be recognised as the modern Apostles. For my part, I can only claim that I have been an instrument so fashioned that I have had some particular advantages in getting this teaching across to the people.

That is the work which will occupy, either by voice or pen, the remainder of my life. What immediate shape it will take I cannot say. Human plans are vain things and it is better for the tool to lie passive until the great hand moves it once more.